Bargaining and Learning in Recurring Crises

Bargaining and Learning in Recurring Crises

The Soviet-American, Egyptian-Israeli, and Indo-Pakistani Rivalries

Russell J. Leng

Ann Arbor

THE UNIVERSITY OF MICHIGAN PRESS

To Cilla

Copyright © by the University of Michigan 2000
All rights reserved
Published in the United States of America by
The University of Michigan Press
Manufactured in the United States of America
⊗ Printed on acid-free paper

2003   2002   2001   2000   4   3   2   1

*A CIP catalog record for this book is available
from the British Library.*

Library of Congress Cataloging-in-Publication Data

Leng, Russell J.
    Bargaining and learning in recurring crises : the Soviet-American,
Egyptian-Israeli, and Indo-Pakistani rivalries / Russell J. Leng.
        p.   cm.
    Includes bibliographical references and index.
    ISBN 0-472-09703-2 (cloth : acid-free paper) — ISBN 0-472-06703-6
(paper : acid-free paper)
    1. Diplomatic negotiations in international disputes—Case studies.
I. Title.

JZ6045 .L46   2000
327.1'7—dc21   00-023332

Contents

Figures

Maps

Tables

Preface

War remains the ultimate puzzle for students of international politics. My own preoccupation with war's immediate causes has led me to focus most of my research on the behavior of states in militarized crises—that is, those interstate disputes where there is a serious threat of war. Most militarized crises do not end in war, but almost all wars are preceded by militarized crises. Thus, the overarching question behind all of my research on crisis behavior has been why some crises end in war and others do not.

My interest in the crisis behavior and learning of states engaged in long-term rivalries began with an article published several years ago (Leng 1983). That article undertook a quantitative examination of the behavior of six pairs of states that found themselves in three recurring crises within a relatively short period of time. The study was designed to provide a crude test of several hypotheses on learning that were based on realpolitik assumptions. The findings indicated that states' behaviors were remarkably consistent with the hypotheses, and I speculated that they resulted from realpolitik learning. But, given the limitations of the study, there was no way of knowing whether the observed behavior resulted from learning or from other coincidental causes. The desire to obtain a more complete understanding of what was happening in at least some of the most prominent rivalries, along with a personal fascination with the rivalries and the crises that they produced, led to the research described in this book.

The research design reflects a conviction that the most significant research on international conflict and cooperation is that combining quantitative methods with well-structured qualitative case studies. My own research has been almost exclusively quantitative, although it has used hypotheses and findings from the qualitative work of others. This book is my first serious attempt to combine the two approaches.

The Soviet-American, Egyptian-Israeli, and Indo-Pakistani rivalries were obvious candidates for the case studies. They were recent, contemporaneous, and highly prominent, and the superpower rivalry interacted with each of the others. I expected it to be a fairly short project. But the complexity of each of the twelve crises, coupled with my own fascination with them, extended the project over three summers and a year's leave of absence from teaching.

I have tried to write the book so that educated readers who share my fascination with the behavior of states in extremis but who are less comfortable with statistical methods can follow the descriptions and analyses with little difficulty. The quantitative information, which is intended to complement the qualitative discussions and to facilitate comparisons across crises, consists of tables, figures, and simple summary statistics. Although I have focused attention on issues related to crisis behavior and learning, chapters 3–5 provide detailed narrative accounts of the evolution of each of the three rivalries. I also have used explanatory footnotes fairly extensively to include useful information that would otherwise divert attention from the main discussion. The appendix includes a "Note on Sources" for readers interested in more complete examinations of particular crises.

Chapter 6 integrates the findings from each of the three rivalries and illustrates some striking similarities in crisis bargaining and learning across crises and rivalries. The chapter also illustrates the pervasive influence of a shared culture of political realism on crisis diplomacy and learning.

Research support from the National Science Foundation (Grant SBR-9422561) allowed me to employ Middlebury undergraduates to assist in collecting data and information on the 12 crises over three summers. Without their assistance, I doubt that the project would have been possible. Betsy Heckman assisted with the research on the Soviet-American crises; Damjan de Krnjevic-Miskovic and Heather Thompson assisted with the Egyptian-Israeli crises; and Senake Gajameragedara, Bijay Rout, and Brandon Baldwin assisted with the Indo-Pakistani crises. Chris Leatham drew the maps.

The U.S. Institute of Peace provided financial assistance that allowed me to extend a half-year leave of absence to a full year to complete the manuscript. The quality of the finished product has benefited considerably from the suggestions of several colleague-friends: Jack Levy, Zeev Maoz, Robert Pack, J. David Singer, and Allison Stanger read and commented on sections of earlier drafts. George Bellerose offered valuable editorial assistance. Middlebury College not only provided the leave to complete this project but has enthusiastically supported my research over the past three decades.

None of those listed above are responsible for any errors, omissions, or good suggestions ignored. The opinions, findings, and conclusions or recommendations expressed in this book are those of the author and do not necessarily reflect the views of the U.S. Institute of Peace or the National Science Foundation.

CHAPTER 1

Learning and Crisis Bargaining

A disproportionately high percentage of interstate crises and wars have involved the same pairs of states in repeated confrontations (see Goertz and Diehl 1993, 1995). The three most prominent interstate rivalries since World War II—those between the United States and the Soviet Union, Egypt and Israel, and India and Pakistan—accounted for 12 militarized crises and seven of the 12 interstate wars that occurred between 1946 and 1973 (Small and Singer 1982:59).[1] This book concerns the crisis behavior of those three pairs of rival states and what they learned from their crisis experiences.

The Soviet-American, Egyptian-Israeli, and Indo-Pakistani rivalries have been chosen partly because of their historical importance but also because they offer diversity with regard to the types of states involved, the issues at stake, and the levels of hostility. The Soviet-American rivalry, which dominated international politics in the post–World War II era, pitted two nuclear superpowers against each other in a series of ideological and strategic confrontations that threatened global war. The superpower rivalry also is the only enduring rivalry since 1816 in which the parties avoided hostilities despite finding themselves in four militarized crises. Two developing states became embroiled in an ongoing territorial dispute inflamed by religious conflict in the Indo-Pakistani rivalry, with all four crises escalating to military hostilities. The Egyptian-Israeli rivalry pitted a small, Western-style democracy against an authoritarian Middle Eastern regime in four territorial disputes, all of which ended in war.

The three rivalries were historically unique in that they each produced four militarized crises within the same 25-year period. That phenomenon

---

1. Small and Singer include the hostilities between Israel and Egypt in 1969–70 as an interstate war. The conflict is not included among the Egyptian-Israeli crises in this study because the hostilities began with no militarized crisis preceding the war. The first Kashmir crisis escalated to an extrasystemic war—that is, a war in which a member of the interstate system participated on only one side (Small and Singer 1982:99). Indian forces became engaged in combat with Pathen tribesmen from Pakistan, but Indian and Pakistani troops avoided direct hostilities. Thus there are seven interstate wars, including five between Egypt and Israel and two between India and Pakistan.

provides an advantage to the researcher interested in drawing comparisons across cases and takes on added significance because the crisis behavior and learning of the rival states in the Egyptian-Israeli and Indo-Pakistani rivalries were influenced by the Cold War rivalry between the United States and the Soviet Union. A list of the 12 militarized crises appears in table 1.1.

There have been a number of recent quantitative (Leng 1993; Brecher 1993) and comparative qualitative studies (Lebow 1981; George 1991a; Snyder and Diesing 1977) focusing on the behavior and bargaining of states in militarized crises. None of those studies, however, has closely examined the crisis behavior of the participants over the entire course of their rivalries. By the same token, those quantitative studies that have focused on the evolution of enduring rivalries (Hensel 1994; Goertz and Diehl 1998) have not examined the behavior and bargaining of the rival states within the recurring disputes. Thus, this study is unique in providing detailed examinations of the crisis behavior and learning of three pairs of states over the course of their enduring rivalries. It also differs from the extant research in combining quantitative descriptions with qualitative case studies of each of the 12 crises.

The study focuses on the lessons that key policymakers in the six states drew from their recurring crises and how those lessons affected their states' behavior in subsequent crises. The analysis will show that learning by policymakers in the rival states was constrained by their realpolitik

TABLE 1.1. Soviet-American, Egyptian-Israeli, and Indo-Pakistani Crises

Soviet Union and United States	
Berlin Blockade	March 20, 1948–May 12, 1949
Berlin Wall	June 4, 1961–November 20, 1961
Cuban Missile	September 4, 1962–November 20, 1962
Middle East Alert	October 8, 1973–October 31, 1973
Egypt and Israel	
Palestine	August 31, 1947–May 15, 1948
Suez	July 26, 1956–October 31, 1956
Six Day War	November 6, 1966–June 5, 1967
October War	January 31, 1973–October 6, 1973
India and Pakistan	
First Kashmir	October 22, 1947–January 1, 1949
Rann of Kutch	March 20, 1965–June 30, 1965
Second Kashmir	December 21, 1964–August 5, 1965
Bangladesh	March 15, 1971–December 3, 1971

beliefs. Because policymakers were predisposed to draw lessons from their crisis experiences that were consistent with those beliefs, they were inclined to pursue coercive bargaining strategies that increased the likelihood of war.

A related question is why the states in the three rivalries continued to find themselves in recurring crises. After all, the best learning is that which leads to the avoidance of militarized crises. But the realpolitik beliefs that encouraged the policymakers in the rival states to adopt crisis bargaining strategies with a high risk of war also encouraged them to employ influence tactics that led to recurring crises. In fact, some of those crises were deliberately initiated by one of the rival states.

The research described in the following chapters employs detailed quantitative descriptions of the behavior of the three pairs of rival states and complements these quantitative descriptions with qualitative case studies of each of the 12 crises. The quantitative mappings of patterns of escalation and de-escalation and summary statistical measures of escalation, reciprocity, and negotiation provide the most reliable means of drawing comparisons between crises within each rivalry as well as across the three rivalries (see chap. 2). But it is necessary to go beyond the descriptions of state behavior to obtain information on policymakers' perceptions, judgments, and decisions. That information is essential to drawing connections between state behavior and learning. Therefore, I have complemented the behavioral data with qualitative descriptions of the relationships between rival states; rival policymakers' perceptions of each other's intentions, capabilities, and motivations; and, most important, the lessons that key policymakers drew from their crisis experiences. Combining the two approaches offers the most effective means of identifying linkages between the lessons drawn by policymakers from their crisis experiences and the subsequent behavior of their states.

Research Questions

The recurring crises in the Soviet-American, Egyptian-Israeli, and Indo-Pakistani rivalries raise the question of what, if anything, policymakers learned from their crisis experiences to guide their states in future militarized crises. The issue of learning raises a number of more specific research questions:

1. *Do we find essentially the same interactions and influence strategies from one crisis to the next?* When states repeat the same influence strategies from crisis to crisis it suggests either that there has been no learning or that learning has reinforced existing beliefs. The question becomes partic-

ularly pertinent to the Egyptian-Israeli and Indo-Pakistani rivalries, where all eight crises escalated to hostilities.

2. *Did the rival states manage their crises more or less effectively over the course of the rivalry?* The answer turns on the definition of *effective crisis management.* If the definition means terminating a crisis peacefully with a low level of escalation in hostile behavior, then the changes had mixed consequences in the Soviet-American crises and decidedly dysfunctional consequences in the Egyptian-Israeli and Indo-Pakistani crises. If *effective crisis management* is defined according to a state's success in achieving its objectives at what it considers a reasonable cost, the answer is more complicated.

3. *Is it possible to ascribe any behavioral changes to experiential learning?* The most difficult judgment—and it must be a matter of judgment—in this study is distinguishing experiential learning from behavioral changes caused by other variables. Chapter 2 describes how that judgment is reached. In essence, I have used a process of elimination by considering all other plausible competing explanations before deciding that learning influenced the behavioral change.

4. *Did rival states draw the same lessons from their recurring crises? Did the states in different rivalries draw similar lessons from their crisis experiences?* The answer to both questions, in several instances, is yes, which suggests that rival states' policymakers held similar beliefs regarding crisis bargaining.

5. *When learning occurred, did it lead to more or less effective crisis management?* This study will show that, with one or two exceptions, the policymakers in the six states drew lessons from their crisis experiences that led to more coercive bargaining and more violent outcomes in subsequent crises. The study concludes that a combination of self-reinforcing hostility generated by recurring crises, misapplied analogies to past crises, and the realpolitik belief systems of key policymakers resulted in learning that, with few exceptions, was dysfunctional.

The research techniques employed in answering these questions are described in chapter 2. The remainder of this chapter defines some key concepts and then discusses theoretical issues related to the identification of learning and its influence on state behavior.

Crisis Bargaining and Learning

The term *crisis,* as I will use it, refers to a militarized interstate crisis—that is, a dispute that has escalated to the point where each side has threatened, displayed, or used military force (Leng and Singer 1988:159). The 12 cases in this study are all militarized crises. By the same token, when I refer to actions taken by states, such as Israel or Egypt, the reference is to the actions ordered by key policymakers who have the power to make foreign policy decisions on the state's behalf.

Crisis bargaining is defined broadly to include any actions taken by a state to influence the behavior of another state over the course of a dispute. The overall mix of tactics used by one state to influence the behavior of another during a crisis represents the state's influence strategy. Influence strategies are described in detail in chapter 2.

Experiential learning is defined as a change in beliefs resulting from the observation and interpretation of experience.[2] As the discussion below will show, the beliefs of greatest interest in this study are those relating to the attributes of interstate crises, the intentions and motivation of the rival state, and what constitutes the most effective strategies and tactics in a militarized crisis.

Although this is a study of the relationship between learning and crisis behavior, it is important to emphasize that learning is neither a necessary nor a sufficient cause of changes in state behavior. Governments may change their policies for many reasons unrelated to learning, such as changes in the their relationship with the rival state or in the issues at stake (see chap. 2). By the same token, when learning occurs, it may not be reflected in state behavior. Policymakers who draw lessons from experience may be unable to apply them because of other constraints, such as governmental or domestic political considerations. Those behavior changes that do result from learning may lead either to more or to less effective crisis management. Learning, as it is defined here, has no normative connotations.

The investigation is concerned with the actions taken by states, but states, as large organizations, do not learn per se. Experiential learning occurs at the individual level; however, crisis decision making is likely to be performed by a group of high-level policymakers. Lessons learned by individuals affect policy only when they are communicated to and accepted by officials responsible for foreign-policy decisions, including the chief executive, who act in the name of the state (see Levy 1994a:287–88).

Experiential learning may result from personal participation in crises or indirectly from the observation and interpretation of earlier crises. Policymakers also may draw lessons that lead to adjustments in their bargaining during the course of an evolving crisis. As a crisis evolves, policy-

---

2. This definition is a shortened version of Levy's (1994a:283) lengthier definition of experiential learning as "a change of beliefs (or the degree of confidence in one's beliefs) or the development of new beliefs, skills, or procedures as result of the observation and interpretation of experience."

makers within each state are engaged in a process that combines attempts to influence the other state's behavior with signals of their own state's intentions and desires. One might also say that each state is engaged in "teaching" as it signals its intentions and resolve through its influence attempts and responses to the influence attempts of an adversary state. Learning occurs as policymakers attempt to discern the intentions and degree of resolve of the adversary state based on *its* influence attempts and responses to influence attempts. Those interpretations may or may not be accurate. During the Alert Crisis of 1973, for example, Soviet Premier Leonid Brezhnev changed his view of American intentions on the basis of what he wrongly interpreted as an American deception when Israeli forces violated a superpower-brokered cease-fire. That interpretation prompted his threat to intervene unilaterally.

Instances of applied learning in the three rivalries most often grew out of the states' experiences in preceding crises. But policymakers also may draw on lessons obtained from events occurring between crises. Brezhnev's initial strategy of attempting to collaborate with the United States to achieve a cease-fire in the 1973 Middle East war was encouraged by the success of Soviet-American negotiations that led to the SALT I accord and other agreements during the early 1970s.

In sum, the application of experiential learning can occur in three ways: (1) lessons drawn during the course of one crisis may be applied in a subsequent crisis; (2) lessons drawn from events occurring during the interval between two crises may be applied in the later crisis; and (3) lessons drawn during the course of a crisis may be applied in that crisis.

Levy (1994a:285) makes a useful distinction between causal learning and diagnostic learning. *Causal learning* refers to changes in beliefs regarding the consequences of actions and optimal strategies or tactics. *Diagnostic learning* refers to changes in one's interpretation of situations and of the rival state's intentions, capabilities, and resolve. Each type of learning can affect future state behavior, and diagnostic learning can change or reinforce causal beliefs. For example, Pakistani President Ayub Khan drew diagnostic lessons regarding the resolve of the Indian government from his experience with India during the Rann of Kutch crisis in the spring of 1965. Those diagnostic lessons affected his causal beliefs regarding the best strategy for dealing with India in the second Kashmir Crisis a few months later.

A second useful distinction is with regard to the level of learning. Several scholars (Tetlock 1991:27–31; Nye 1989; Levy 1994a:286) distinguish between learning that leads to changes in means and that which leads to changes in goals and/or in policymakers' perceptions of the relationship with the rival state. *Learning about means* refers to changes in policymakers' influence strategies and tactics without affecting goals or objectives. *Learning about ends* includes a modification of goals as well as means.[3] Tetlock (1991:27–31) argues that beliefs about goals are considerably more resistant to change than are beliefs about strategies or tactics. Nye (1989) refers to learning about means as "simple" learning and learning that leads to changed views of a state's ends as "complex learning." The distinction is important to an investigation of the issue of whether states can draw lessons from experience that lead to the changes in beliefs that are necessary to terminate enduring rivalries.

The beliefs held by individual policymakers play such an important role in predisposing them to draw certain types of lessons from their crisis experiences that it is worth a brief digression to consider that role.

Political Belief Systems

Policymakers' political belief systems frame their understandings of a given foreign-policy problem. The belief system predisposes them to give greater saliency to certain types of events and to evaluate them in particular ways. The perceived saliency of events influences whether they will be remembered; how they are evaluated determines what lessons are drawn from them (see Bandura 1971, 1973). At the center of the political belief system is the individual's worldview or perspective on the fundamental relationship among states (see George 1969, 1979; Holsti 1979). That perspective influences policymakers' views of the nature of interstate conflict, of relations with the adversary state, and of the adversary state's intentions and motivation in the current dispute. Policymakers' political belief systems exert a strong influence over what events are perceived as most salient, how they are evaluated, the intensity with which they are remembered, and how they will affect the future crisis behavior of a particular state.

The belief system exerts a particularly strong influence in militarized crises, when decisions must be made with greater urgency and the incoming information is likely to be incomplete and ambiguous. As they draw lessons from their crisis experiences, policymakers also are likely to be predisposed to draw analogies to past disputes with the adversary, whether experienced directly or vicariously, that yield lessons consistent with their beliefs. A phenomenon created by the stress of an escalating conflict that is

---

3. Breslauer and Tetlock (1991:8–10) describe the distinction as one between "learning how," that is, how to pursue one's goals more effectively, and "learning that," which refers to obtaining a new understanding of its relationship with the adversary, which leads to a shift in goals.

particularly relevant to this study is "attributional distortion" (Hayden and Mischel 1976). *Attributional distortion* is the tendency of individuals to attribute actions by the other party that are consistent with existing beliefs to dispositional causes and to attribute actions that are inconsistent with those beliefs to environmental causes. For example, Pakistani President Ayub Khan interpreted India's military caution when hostilities broke out in the Rann of Kutch crisis in 1965 as a consequence of what he viewed as the pacifistic character of Hindus while ignoring how the battlefield conditions uniquely favored Pakistan. Ayub misinterpreted the situation and drew a lesson that led him to miscalculate Pakistan's relative military capabilities in the second Kashmir Crisis a few months later. He did so because the Indian behavior during the preceding crisis was consistent with his existing beliefs regarding the character of his adversary.

Realism, Realpolitik, and the Psychological Perspective

I have argued elsewhere (Leng 1993:1–10) that state leaders' belief systems are formed within a culture of political realism that pervades the interstate system. Culture, as it is intended here, refers to a shared understanding of the nature of international politics and the behavior of states.

Realism and Realpolitik

The classical realist tradition views relations among states as driven by considerations of power and interest. Realists assume that states, like individuals, act according to their interests and that the dominant interest of any state in an anarchic and insecure world is to protect or extend its power. Competition among insecure, power-seeking states defines the nexus of interstate relations. It is a zero-sum competition, where one state's gain in power and security is a rival state's loss. At their best, state relations are based on reciprocal cooperation that serves the interests of both sides; at their worst they are based on deterrence and war. The realist tradition is most often contrasted with political idealism, which views state behavior as constrained by the same ethical and legal considerations as interpersonal relations. But realism, not idealism, has dominated the culture of the modern interstate system.

The realist culture encourages realpolitik foreign policies. A policy of realpolitik is based on considerations of power and interest and on influence strategies that demonstrate the state's power and its willingness to use it. Realpolitik does not rule out collaborative policies when they serve the interests of both states, but the more common condition among insecure states is that of unrestrained competition, especially in the case of a rivalry that has escalated to a militarized crisis. The application of realpolitik to crisis behavior appears in the work of conflict strategists, or "deterrence theorists," who view crisis bargaining, in Kahn's (1965:16) words, as a "competition in risk-taking," where the risk is war. Bargaining power in an escalating crisis becomes a function of perceived comparative resolve as the two sides compete at demonstrating their willingness to accept the risk of war (Snyder and Diesing 1977: chap. 3).

A realpolitik foreign policy, particularly in its extension to crisis bargaining, relies on the rationality of the key policymakers in the rival states. Classical realists, such as Morgenthau (1946, 1978), do not deny the role played by emotion and misperception in conflicts among nations, yet their policy prescriptions are based on the assumption of competition with a calculating, rational adversary. Realists argue not that states always behave rationally but that the expectation of rational behavior leads to the most effective bargaining strategies. The difference between the expected behavior of states and the actual effects of cognitive errors and emotional arousal on state policymakers in militarized crises is viewed as analogous to that between the carefully calculated military strategies mapped out by generals and the chaotic fighting that takes place on the battlefield. In neither instance is fully rational behavior expected, but its assumption, realists argue, offers the best basis on which to design an effective course of action. In fact, the manipulative bargaining strategies of conflict strategists, such as Kahn and Schelling (1960, 1966), who worked within the realist tradition, can be seen as an extension of the theory of war to militarized crises. Just as strategies of war are concerned with the application of force, conflict strategists are concerned with the "exploitation of potential force" (Schelling 1960:5)—that is, the successful use of coercion.

The Psychological Perspective
Criticism of the realist tradition has come from two sources. One has been the idealist tradition mentioned earlier. The other, which I have described as a psychological perspective because it is so often associated with the work of social and cognitive psychologists, views the onset of a crisis as a pathology, a problem that has arisen in the relationship between states (see Leng 1993:10–18; Rubin, Pruitt, and Kim 1994; Holsti 1989).

For realists, the goal of crisis bargaining is to win; for those viewing crises from a psychological perspective, the goal is to find a means of moderating and ultimately resolving the dispute. Those taking a psychological perspective on crisis behavior would argue that a realpolitik approach to crisis bargaining creates two risks. The first risk is one of omission. In their intense competition, the parties may overlook opportunities to find common ground that would lead to integrative solutions that would serve the interests of both sides.

The second risk, according to the psychological perspective, is that the influence strategies and tactics prescribed by conflict strategists will lead to uncontrollable escalation and war. There are two putative sources of this danger. The first is that the escalating coercive actions and reactions of the two states can lead to an uncontrollable conflict spiral. With both sides determined to demonstrate their resolve, the escalation becomes self-generating as the parties become locked into tit-for-tat exchanges of increasingly coercive behavior. Either what began as limited military hostilities escalates to war, or one side, recognizing the strategic advantage of striking first, launches a preemptive attack on the other (Rapoport 1960: chap.1; North, Holsti, and Brody 1964). The second putative source of the problem results from the realpolitik presumption of rationality. The counterview is that the escalating hostility exacerbates national leaders' emotional reactions—notably fear and anger (Baron 1977; Berkowitz 1993, 1994)—to the coercive actions of the other side, while their cognitive performance is likely to be weakened by the stresses produced by the increasing risk of war (Holsti 1972, 1989). As the crisis escalates, the relationship between the adversary states worsens—coercion begets coercion—and the danger of misperception, miscalculation, or emotionally driven behavior increases.

Hawks and Doves

Elements of the realist and psychological perspectives on crisis behavior can be seen in the beliefs of different policymakers in the states in this study. I will use the terms *hawk* and *dove* to categorize those beliefs to maintain a distinction between the views held by policymakers and the theorizing of social scientists represented by the realist and psychological perspectives.

The distinction between hawks and doves was coined during the Cuban Missile Crisis to describe the contending influence strategies advocated by different members of President John F. Kennedy's policy-making team. The dichotomy was a bit too crude even for its original application, but it is useful for distinguishing between two ends of a continuum on which to position policymakers' beliefs.[4]

Hawks' views are consistent with a realpolitik perspective. Hawks take a strictly competitive approach to crisis bargaining, distrust the adversary's intentions, and place more faith in coercive bargaining than in negotiation. The term *dove* has come to represent individuals whose views

---

4. Snyder and Diesing (1977:309–10) added "middle-liner" to describe those halfway between the two types.

are closer the psychological perspective. Doves view the crisis as a resolvable problem in the relationship with the other party and see the coercive bargaining advocated by hawks as potentially pathological. Consequently, doves are more likely to seek problem-solving approaches to crisis management. Because I will describe individual policymakers according to the two types, it may be helpful to provide a more complete breakdown of the differences between hawks and doves.

Interstate Conflict

Hawks' perspective is consistent with the realist view that interstate relations are essentially competitive and dominated by concerns for power and security. Only firmly demonstrating resolve in the face of potential aggression or, if necessary, striking first provides security in a militarized crisis.

Doves stress the dangers of mutual miscalculation and uncontrollable escalation associated with a conflict spiral (North, Holsti, and Brody 1964; Jervis 1976: chap. 3). Doves do not disagree with hawks regarding the insecurities of the interstate system, but doves believe that policies based solely on deterrence exacerbate the situation. For doves, a state's major problem in a crisis is not being bullied but becoming trapped in a conflict spiral. Doves view militarized crises as problems in the relations between mutually insecure states that possess complementary as well as conflicting interests. For doves the immediate objective is to manage the crisis so that it does not escalate to war; the ultimate goal is to work with the other party to find a solution that serves mutual interests—that is, to find common ground.

Judging the Adversary's Intentions and Resolve

Hawks' and doves' different worldviews can lead to divergent interpretations of adversary states' intentions. Hawks are likely to view the adversary state as a power-seeking entity with expansionist goals. Doves are more likely to view the adversary as motivated by concerns for its own security, so that hostile actions are interpreted as expressions of insecurity and conciliatory actions are interpreted as attempts to find common ground.

Estimates of the adversary's resolve, coupled with policymakers' estimates of their state's comparative war-fighting capabilities, influence perceptions of the consequences of escalating conflict and of the balance to be struck between exercising caution and demonstrating resolve. Hawks are inclined to link estimates of the adversary's willingness to risk war to its perception of the balance in usable military capabilities, thus assuming that the adversary will retreat in the face of a demonstration of superior strength and resolve. Because doves are more likely to view the adversary's motivation as linked to a perceived threat to its security, they are more likely to assume that the adversary will react aggressively to attempts at coercion, regardless of the military balance.

Perspectives on Escalation and Risk

Policymakers' judgments regarding the proper balance between prudence and resolve in an escalating crisis are likely to turn on two questions: What is the likelihood that the escalation will lead to war? And if the dispute does escalate to war, what are the consequent costs and risks?

The answer to the first question turns on the policymaker's view of the nature of the escalatory process as well as of the intentions and motivation of the adversary. Hawks view crisis bargaining as a process in which each side employs coercive tactics to uncover the other side's resistance point while demonstrating resolve. As the crisis evolves, each side gains an increasingly better understanding of the other's intentions, motivation, and capabilities through influence attempts and the responses to them. This perspective assumes that the escalation is not likely to spiral out of control and that the threshold between coercive bargaining and war is clear to both sides. The risk from being misperceived as weak is presumed to be greater than the risk of war from either side's misperception of the other's intentions or motivation.

Doves, conversely, are more likely to focus on the risks of the escalation spiraling out of control through mutual misperceptions of the other side's intentions and through the emotions associated with an escalating crisis. Doves are concerned less with the danger of appearing weak than with appearing aggressive, of pushing the other side into overreacting and assuming prematurely that the threshold between coercive bargaining and war has been crossed.

How policymakers view the costs and risks associated with war turns partly on their perceptions of the two sides' comparative war-fighting capabilities, including assistance from third parties, and partly on estimates of the costs of war in human suffering and property damage. The latter becomes particularly salient in the face of the threat of nuclear war. In fact, how the special character of nuclear war might affect perspectives on escalation and risk raises some interesting questions.

Nuclear Crises

In a conventional militarized crisis, war may be preferred to surrendering to the demands of the other side; in a nuclear crisis, war is a catastrophe for both sides. But the potentially catastrophic consequences of a nuclear war also could raise each side's tolerance level—its willingness to accept coercion before responding with force. The mutual desire to avoid nuclear war can encourage hawkish policymakers on each side to perceive the other as having a greater tolerance for being bullied. Mutual fear of the consequences of nuclear war then could have the ironic effect of encouraging higher escalation.

The unacceptability of war also has the effect of making the crisis the ultima ratio; therefore, it becomes more important to policymakers concerned with their state's reputation for resolve to demonstrate a willingness to run risks and to hold their ground in the face of bullying (Snyder and Diesing 1977:453–57). Geller (1990) has found some empirical evidence that nuclear crises are more likely to escalate to a higher magnitude of hostility.

Doves would counter that the stress generated by an escalating nuclear crisis and its potentially catastrophic consequences increase the other side's insecurity and the likelihood that it would misperceive demonstrations of resolve as preparations for war. The size of the stakes could add to the risk of the crisis escalating out of control. As chapter 3 will demonstrate, the fear of events running out of control ultimately brought Kennedy and Khrushchev back from the brink of war in the Cuban Missile Crisis.

Attitudes toward Bargaining and Negotiation
Hawks advocate the use of coercive influence strategies to demonstrate greater resolve and risk acceptance. In the competition that characterizes a militarized crisis, unilateral offers of accommodation, hawks argue, are likely to be interpreted as evidence of weakness. By the same token, expressing a willingness to negotiate prior to demonstrating superior resolve tempts the other side into aggressive action to take advantage of perceived weakness.

Doves, conversely, believe that heavy coercive tactics run the risk of unintentionally signaling aggressive intentions and escalating the crisis. Therefore, doves view early negotiation—and open communication more generally—as essential to avoid misperceptions. Doves argue that the failure to communicate effectively is likely to lead to miscalculations of intentions, which will encourage escalation or even a misguided preemptive attack.

Summary

The study starts from the assumption that the belief systems of foreign policymakers influence their understanding of interstate conflict and its consequences, their perceptions of the intentions and motivations of adversary states, and their predictions with regard to the adversary's behavior. Those beliefs are formed within a culture of political realism that encourages foreign policies based on realpolitik. Realpolitik has been extended to prescriptive theorizing on crisis bargaining by conflict strategists advocating bargaining designed to demonstrate a state's willingness to risk war to achieve its objectives. Critics of those views, who take a more psychological perspective, argue that a realpolitik approach is likely to obscure opportunities to find integrative solutions and that competitive risk-taking is likely to escalate to a self-generating conflict spiral, which can be exacerbated by stress-induced cognitive limitations and emotional arousal.

The terms *hawk* and *dove* are used to describe the views of real-world policymakers that are analogous to the realist and psychological perspectives. The beliefs of individual policymakers, as well as the balance of views within the decision-making body, can be classified along a hawk-dove continuum. Where policymakers' political belief systems fall on the continuum between these two perspectives influences attitudes regarding the other side's intentions and the risks of escalation, the choice of influence strategies, and views regarding the efficacy of negotiation. In the course of the discussions of individual policymakers in chapters 3–5, beliefs will be described as more or less hawkish or dovish with regard to the foreign-policy issues mentioned previously.

The belief systems of makers of foreign policy are particularly important to this study because they affect learning by predisposing policymakers to draw certain lessons rather than others from their state's crisis experiences.

Political Beliefs and Learning

The discussion to this point has viewed policymakers as active problem solvers who attempt to predict how an adversary state will react to different influence tactics. Those predictions are influenced by the inferences that policymakers draw regarding significant attributes of the adversary, specifically its leaders' intentions, motivation, and approach to bargaining. Attribution theorists have found that in making these inferences, individuals behave like "naive scientists"—that is, they are likely to draw causal connections and lessons from salient past events, especially those that they have experienced or directly observed (Nisbett and Ross 1980:43–51). Crises are highly salient events, so one would expect the views of participants or close observers to be influenced by those experiences.

Historical Analogies

Political scientists as well as cognitive psychologists have become interested in the role played by "cognitive schemata," generic concepts that enable individuals to classify and categorize individuals, events, and situations according to familiar types (Larson 1985:50–57; Tetlock 1991; Jarosz and Nye 1993:144–47). Viewed from this perspective, the individual is less a problem solver, seeking to find causal connections and judge probabilities, than a categorizer, classifying individuals and situations according to generic types. When in 1947 Harry S. Truman compared the Soviet regime to those of Napoleon and Hitler, the president was classifying it according to a particular type: an expansionist authoritarian regime out to conquer all of Europe. Individuals as well as situations are often pigeonholed according to past experiences.

Direct analogies to specific individuals or events can perform the same role as schemata. In the crisis preceding the October War of 1973, for example, Israeli policymakers misinterpreted Anwar Sadat's intentions partly because they saw him as another Gamal Abdel Nasser (see chap. 4). Policymakers are likely to turn to historical analogies to diagnose foreign-policy problems like militarized crises (see May 1973).

When individuals draw historical analogies to fit new situations, all other things being equal, their choices depend on the ease with which the analogies can be recalled. Ease of recall is affected by the salience of the analogy. It favors situations where the recaller had firsthand experience, which were particularly significant or dramatic, and which were similar in type to the current situation (Kahneman and Tversky 1982:163–78).

A policymaker who participated in, or closely observed a militarized crisis is likely to be predisposed to draw an analogy to that crisis in choosing an influence strategy in a succeeding crisis with the same adversary. The most prominent influences from a preceding crisis experience are the perceived effects of the crisis bargaining of the state on the behavior of the adversary, the evolution of the crisis, and the crisis outcome. A tendency to see their own state's behavior as decisive encourages policymakers to consider successful or unsuccessful crisis outcomes as consequences of the influence strategies they employed (see Jervis 1976:299–330).

Some notes of caution are in order, however, before drawing causal links between historical analogies and learning. The lessons drawn from preceding crises vary among different participants. Jarosz and Nye (1993), for example, have shown how different members of Kennedy's foreign policy–making team drew different conclusions from the Cuban Missile Crisis experience. Their lessons were generally consistent with their belief systems before the crisis began. Advisers with hawkish views tended to focus on the application of coercive diplomacy in forcing the Soviet removal of the missiles. Advisers with more dovish views focused on the importance of avoiding uncontrollable escalation and providing the Soviets with a face-saving avenue of retreat. References to historical analogies may be chosen in policy discussions because they conveniently support existing beliefs and are rhetorically useful rather than because they have provided new lessons for the policymaker.

Resistance to Learning

Research in cognitive psychology suggests that belief systems are highly resistant to change. Earlier work in this field, which is identified with the cognitive dissonance theory of Festinger (1957), views individuals as "consistency seekers" who seek cognitive harmony among their beliefs. When one belief contradicts another, the individual is presumed to become motivated to eliminate the inconsistency. When strongly held beliefs are confronted by contradictory information, the individual is likely to reinterpret the information to fit the existing belief. In international politics, where incoming information is likely to be incomplete and ambiguous and where policymakers may have staked their political credibility on the validity of their beliefs, there is both psychological and political pressure to adjust reality to fit existing beliefs. For example, in the weeks preceding the 1973 Middle East war, Israeli and American intelligence services were so attached to a particular conception of Egyptian military intentions that intelligence agents misread evidence of Egyptian preparations for a military offensive in the Sinai (Shlaim 1976; Kissinger 1982).

Most evidence to date suggests that belief systems are highly resistant to change but that the willingness of individual policymakers to adjust their beliefs depends on how fully formed the belief is prior to receiving the new information and on the salience of the experience challenging the belief (see Jarosz and Nye 1993; Larson 1985). Despite two crushing military defeats at the hands of Israel, Egypt's Nasser found it difficult to change his image of Israel as nothing more than a creation of Western imperialism, and he remained publicly committed to eliminating the state of Israel and based his strategy almost solely on gaining the military capability to do so. When Sadat took office after Nasser's death in 1970, he was not burdened with Nasser's strong commitment to a particular set of beliefs. Sadat accepted Israel's permanence as a state and sought more limited military and diplomatic objectives.

In sum, foreign policymakers are predisposed to interpret events and situations in a manner that is consistent with the intensity of their beliefs regarding the nature of interstate conflict and of their relationship with the rival state. As they draw lessons from their crisis experiences, they also are likely to select analogies from past disputes with the adversary that yield lessons that are consistent with their beliefs. Changes in beliefs are more likely to occur when the beliefs are not fully formed, when policymakers have not made strong commitments to them, and when the experience challenging the belief is particularly salient.

Other Sources of Changes in Crisis Behavior

Experiential learning is just one of many potential influences on state behavior. In fact, what might be described as learning may be merely adaptations to environmental changes. Those changes may occur at several levels: in the rival state, in the dyadic relationship between the disputants, or in the international system or the region. Several factors within each of these categories must be considered before drawing any conclusions regarding changes in state behavior resulting from lessons drawn from previous crises.

Changes within Rival States

One or more of four categories of internal changes could significantly affect a state's influence strategies and tactics in a militarized crisis: (1) leadership turnover, (2) regime changes, (3) governmental politics, and (4) domestic politics. Given the prominence of a militarized crisis, the highest level of national leadership is likely to make decisions during a crisis. Turnover in national leadership can alter the framing of situations and events. New national leaders may hold different beliefs regarding the nature of international conflict, the attributes of rival states, and the most effective means of dealing with those states. Egypt's leadership change from Nasser to Sadat is one example. Besides changes in individual leaders, states can undergo changes in the regime types, which can strongly affect state behavior. For example, a military coup in Pakistan had a significant effect on the Indo-Pakistani rivalry.

Political changes within the foreign policy–making body can occur, however, without major regime changes. The ebb and flow of the influence of different coalitions of hawks and doves can significantly influence strategies and tactics. The Israeli decision to launch a preemptive attack on Egypt in 1967, for example, was facilitated by the formation of a "unity cabinet" that shifted the balance to favor a more hawkish coalition.

Finally, the domestic political situation—the political security of the regime, political stability more generally, and the state of the economy—can affect a state's crisis behavior. Public perception of the state's handling of previous crises also affects national leaders. For example, Indian Prime Minister Lal Shastri felt pressured to take a more resolute stand during the second Kashmir Crisis in 1965 after being severely criticized for not being more resolute during the Rann of Kutch crisis a few months earlier. Conversely, policymakers may believe that they cannot implement lessons drawn from previous crises because of their concerns about domestic reactions.

Changes in the Relationship between Rivals

Three relationship changes are likely to be particularly salient in influencing crisis behavior: (1) changes in a state's perception of the rivalry or of the rival state; (2) changes in the structure of the crisis; and (3) changes in the strategic situation—that is, which side is defending and which side is challenging the status quo. The first factor is potentially the most complex. The degree of hostility between the rivals may change because of the intensity of their last crisis or because of other events occurring between crises. For example, was it the experience of the 1962 Cuban Missile Crisis or the atmosphere of détente that had the strongest influence on Soviet bargaining in the Alert Crisis of 1973?

The key components of the crisis structure are the interests at stake for each of the parties and their perceived comparative war-fighting capabilities (Leng 1993; Snyder and Diesing 1977). Snyder and Diesing's (1977) comparative study of 13 crises suggested that there is a strong relationship between the crisis structure and crisis outcomes. My quantitative study of 40 crises (Leng 1993: chaps. 3, 5) found that changes in the comparative war-fighting capabilities of the participants as well as in the interests at stake for each of the sides were positively associated with changes in the influence strategies and tactics chosen from one crisis to the next. Brecher and James (1986:64–68) have reported similar findings. Among the crises in this study, Pakistan's acquisition of advanced weapons from the United States emboldened Ayub Khan's regime to employ a more assertive, risk-acceptant bargaining strategy in the Rann of Kutch and second Kashmir Crisis with India in 1965. India's bargaining strategy in the second Kashmir Crisis was more assertive than during the Rann of Kutch crisis not only because of the domestic pressures cited earlier but also because India enjoyed a more favorable military position in the second Kashmir Crisis and because the stakes were higher (see chap. 5).

Another potentially important structural relationship concerns the relative position of the two parties vis-à-vis the status quo. Tversky and Kahneman (1986) have found that subjects tend to be risk adverse in seeking gains and risk acceptant in avoiding losses. Extending these findings to interstate conflict, policymakers who perceive themselves as defenders of the status quo and seek to avoid losses are more likely to accept high risks than those who are challenging the status quo. Some recent case studies of interstate disputes support that proposition (Farnham 1994). However, both sides may perceive themselves as defenders of the status quo. Consider the situation when one party changes the situation through a fait accompli. Now the party that was the original challenger is defending a new status quo—that is, the status quo created by the fait accompli. But the other party still sees itself as defending the status quo ante. Thus, both parties see themselves as defenders of the status quo, and each presumably is willing to accept a high risk. That situation occurred during the early phase of the Cuban Missile Crisis, for example, after the United States discovered the missile installations in Cuba. The United States was determined to prevent the permanent placement of the missiles in Cuba; the Soviet Union was determined to prevent their forced withdrawal.

A satisfied and uncompromising defender of the status quo places an unsatisfied challenger in a difficult position. It must either accept the existing situation or resort to a high-risk coercive strategy of its own to budge the status quo defender. The strategies adopted by the challenging parties are among the more intriguing findings in the study. In some instances, states simply resorted to war. But in other instances, states either attempted fait accompli or deliberately created a crisis to encourage outside intervention by influential third parties to force negotiations that would result in a revision of the status quo. The latter approaches were adopted by Pakistan in its two crises with India in 1965 and by Egypt in 1973.

Changes in the Global System or Region

Changes that occur in the structure of the international system or in the region may affect rival states' behavior. The Egyptian-Israeli and Indo-Pakistani rivalries were affected by the global competition between the United States and the Soviet Union. The comparative military capabilities of the four minor powers were affected by the ebb and flow of military aid from each of the superpowers. The superpowers shared an interest in containing the level of hostilities growing out of crises in the Middle East and South Asia to avoid being drawn into hostilities with each other. The propensity of the superpowers to intervene diplomatically emboldened both Egypt and Pakistan to undertake high-risk challenges to the status quo. The policymakers who accepted the risks relied on superpower intervention to limit the magnitude and severity of hostilities.

Regional politics also played a significant role in the Middle East and

South Asian crises. Egypt's desire to maintain its leadership position among Arab states in the Middle East encouraged its involvement in the 1948 and 1967 crises. The triangular relationship among China, India, and Pakistan affected the policies of both India and Pakistan as well as the relationship between those two states and each of the superpowers.

Each of these potential influences on crisis behavior must be considered before claiming that policymakers based their actions on lessons drawn from preceding crises. Nevertheless, findings from my earlier studies of recurrent crises (Leng 1983, 1993) suggest that learning from a previous crisis with the same adversary is likely to exert a strong influence on subsequent crisis behavior. Moreover, the prominence of a militarized crisis as the final crossroads between war and peace is likely to make management of the crisis override other domestic and international considerations. To cite a prominent example, during the Cuban Missile Crisis President Kennedy pursued the strategy of a partial blockade despite pressure from congressional leaders, who favored removing the offensive missiles by force (May and Zelikow 1997:245–75).

Conclusion

The role of learning in interstate conflicts poses difficult issues for both policymakers and researchers. For policymakers the issue is whether the lessons will lead to more or to less effective crisis management. The predisposition of policymakers to draw lessons consistent with their existing political beliefs does not favor radical changes. In fact, a key factor in perpetuating the three rivalries in this study was the failure of the leaders of the six states to draw lessons beyond the boundaries of their realpolitik belief systems.

If effective crisis management is defined in terms of serving the national interest without going to war, the prevalence of realpolitik beliefs, which encourage hawkish influence strategies, is not encouraging. Conversely, evidence of policymakers' propensity to draw analogies from salient events in the past to interpret current situations suggests that preceding crisis experiences, particularly those that are traumatic, can lead to significant changes in behavior.

Chapter 2 describes the research design for the quantitative descriptions of the crisis behavior and the qualitative case studies of the 12 crises. It also discusses some methodological issues related to the search for answers to the five questions posed at the beginning of this chapter.

CHAPTER 2

Research Design

As noted in chapter 1, the search for evidence of learning among the states in the three rivalries employs a hybrid approach that combines quantitative descriptions of state behavior with information gleaned from qualitative case studies. The following sections describe the procedures for generating the quantitative data, collecting the qualitative information, and the approach to integrating the two research methods.

The quantitative data provide the most reliable means of comparing the behavior of the rival states from one crisis to the next as well as across rivalries. Visual displays of the escalation/de-escalation of each of the crises along with statistical measures of escalation, reciprocity, and negotiation allow for a degree of comparability across crises that would not be possible with strictly qualitative descriptions. Moreover, the operational procedures for determining the participant states' predominant influence strategies offer the most reliable means of categorizing and comparing the bargaining of states from one crisis to the next. Each of the quantitative descriptors has been tested and employed in my previous studies of crisis behavior (see Leng 1993, 1983; Leng and Singer 1988).

Quantitative Descriptors

Quantitative descriptions of behavior provide the primary source of information to answer the first two research questions, which focus on changes in the behavior of the participant states and on whether any observed changes led to more effective crisis management.

Militarized Interstate Crises

The primary unit of observation for the quantitative research is the militarized interstate crisis (MIC). As noted in chapter 1, MICs are disputes between members of the interstate system that have escalated to the point where there is a high probability of war. An MIC is defined operationally as a dispute between two members of the interstate system that has escalated to the point where each side has threatened, displayed, or employed military force against the other. If one side challenges the other with a threat of force, the other must resist for the dispute to qualify as an MIC (Leng and Singer 1988:159).

Crisis Behavior

The behavioral descriptors consist of coded descriptions of the actions that the rival states direct at each other during the course of the MIC. The data on crisis behavior have been drawn from the Behavioral Correlates of War (BCOW) data set. The BCOW data consist of descriptions of state actions drawn from narrative accounts in the press, diplomatic histories, memoirs, and documents. These accounts are consolidated to form a complete chronology of each state's actions during a crisis. Then the actions by the participant states are coded in accordance with a typology of events designed for the analysis of interstate bargaining.[1] The BCOW coding scheme describes each action, whether verbal or physical, that a state directs at another during the course of a crisis according to the following components: the actor and target states, the date, the place where the action occurred, the duration of the action, any increases or decreases in the intensity of physical actions over time, and the classification of the action according to one of 107 action types. The American blockade of Cuba during the Cuban Missile Crisis, for example, is described as an action taken by the United States and directed at both the Soviet Union and Cuba beginning on October 23, 1962. The action is identified as continuing on each day until the blockade was lifted on November 20. The action itself is classified as a military blockade, which is one of the categories in the coding scheme. If the blockade was strengthened or reduced during the crisis, those changes in the intensity of the action also would be coded.

Verbal actions are grouped into three general categories: comments, requests, and intended actions (threats and promises). Along with a description of the conditions attached to verbal actions, such as the conditions for carrying out a threat or fulfilling a promise, there is a full description of the action commented on, requested, or intended. Combinations of requested and intended actions, such as Kennedy's demand (request) that the missiles be removed from Cuba and his accompanying threats

---

1. The theoretical foundation for the BCOW project and its relationship to other event data projects are described in Leng and Singer 1988. That article also includes an overview of the BCOW data set, including the action typology, data sources, coding rules, and intercoder reliability tests as well as operational procedures and findings from earlier studies.

(intended actions), represent the specific influence attempts employed by states in the course of bargaining with their rivals.

Although each crisis is treated as a dyadic dispute between the rival states, the actions of allies and, in some instances, actions directed against allies of the adversary state are included in the quantitative descriptions of patterns of escalation/de-escalation to obtain more complete descriptions. In the Berlin crises, Soviet actions directed at the Western states as a group or at West Germany are included along with those directed solely at the United States. During the Cuban Missile Crisis, U.S. actions that ostensibly have Cuba as their direct target but directly affect the Soviet Union are included along with those actions directed to the Soviet Union. The Egyptian-Israeli crises, which were effectively Arab-Israeli crises, include collective Arab actions in which Egypt participated.

Describing Crisis Behavior

The search for an answer to the first research question, which asks whether there are significant changes in the behavior of individual rival states from one crisis to the next, focuses on three components of each state's crisis behavior: (1) its influence strategies, (2) the mix of its cooperative and conflictual actions as measured by the magnitude, intensity, and rate of escalation/de-escalation, and (3) its willingness to seek a negotiated settlement as indicated by the timing of the beginning of negotiations with the other party.

The second research question asks whether the parties within a given rivalry have managed their recurring crises more or less effectively with each succeeding crisis. Five indicators are used to obtain cross-crisis comparisons: (1) the aggregate pattern of escalation/de-escalation over the course of the crisis; (2) the degree of reciprocity exhibited in the exchanges of cooperative and conflictual actions by the two sides; (3) the timing and intensity of negotiation; (4) the duration of the crisis; and (5) the crisis outcome. The following section describes the purpose of each indicator and how it was constructed.[2]

Escalation

The pattern of escalation/de-escalation during a crisis indicates the extent to which the crisis was effectively managed or threatened to spiral out of

---

2. Interested readers can find a more complete description of the construction of each of the indicators in Leng 1993: chap. 4.

control. This pattern also provides one of the most direct approaches to observing changes in the behavior of the participants from one crisis to the next.

The descriptions of patterns of escalation/de-escalation are obtained from the BCOW data described previously. Each coded action is classified as having a positive, negative, or neutral impact on the target. Weights are then assigned to the positive and negative actions. The blockade of Cuba, for example, would be assigned a negative weight of two on a hostility scale of one to three. Kennedy's verbal negative comments on the Soviet action would be assigned a negative action score of one. The scores for the positive and negative actions are aggregated on each day of the crisis, with the aggregate positive action score subtracted from the aggregate score for the negative actions to obtain daily hostility scores for each crisis participant.

Besides the visual picture obtained by a frequency distribution of the level of hostility over the course of the crisis, there are three summary statistical measures: (1) the magnitude of the escalation—that is, the maximum level of hostility achieved at the peak of the crisis, (2) the intensity of the escalation, as indicated by the mean magnitude of hostility over the course of the crisis, and (3) the rate of escalation—that is, how rapidly the crisis escalates. To obtain a composite escalation score, the state's scores on each of the three escalation measures are standardized and summed. The standard scores are obtained by comparing the individual escalation scores for that state from each of the four recurring crises between the two rival states. The crisis escalation score is simply the summed aggregate of the individual state scores.

Reciprocity

Reciprocity is the basic norm for cooperation in politically decentralized systems like the international system, and reciprocity has provided a working norm for diplomacy. A measure of reciprocity indicates the extent to which the two parties responded in kind to each other's actions—either through tit-for-tat responses to coercive actions or by reciprocating cooperative moves to resolve the crisis, or both. A high degree of reciprocity in coercive actions can indicate that the two sides have become locked-in to mutually reinforcing coercive actions, whereas a high degree of reciprocity in cooperative actions indicates the presence of mutually reinforcing accommodative moves.

There are two dimensions to reciprocity: (1) the distance between the escalation/de-escalation patterns of the two sides and (2) the degree of congruity in the direction in which each party is moving from one observation point to the next—that is, toward more conflictual or more cooperative behavior. The distance score indicates whether one side exhibited considerably more conflictual behavior than the other during the crisis or whether the two sides generally responded to each other's actions in kind and magnitude. The direction score measures the extent to which the rival states each were moving toward more cooperative or conflictual behavior at the same time or whether as one side was increasing its hostility, the other was becoming more accommodative.[3] A high degree of reciprocity would indicate that the hostility exhibited by the two parties was of roughly the same magnitude at each time interval and that the parties moved toward greater or lesser hostility at the same time. As with the escalation measure, a composite reciprocity score is computed by standardizing each of the indicators within the sample of crises between the two participants and then summing the standardized scores.

Comparisons across Crises

The standardized scores of escalation and reciprocity provide a means of comparing the crises within a particular rivalry along those two dimensions. They make it possible, for example, to observe that the Cuban Missile Crisis has the highest rate of escalation of any of the Soviet-American crises, but that the Berlin Blockade Crisis reached a higher magnitude of hostility. Comparisons across the three rivalries can be obtained by standardizing the scores within the larger sample of 12 crises.

There also is the question of how the scores of the crises in the three rivalries compare to those for interstate crises more generally. To obtain a rough comparison, I employ a larger stratified sample of 34 militarized crises.[4] The behavioral data and the escalation and reciprocity measures for each of those crises were generated in the same manner as the crises in this study (see Leng 1993). The scores for the crisis of interest from the current study is added to the larger sample, standardized within that sample, and then ranked in the sample. The crises in the larger sample occurred over a longer time interval (1816–1980) and often under very different circumstances from those in this study, so it would be a mistake to carry the comparisons too far. Nevertheless, the rankings within the larger sample provide some substance to judgments as to whether, for example, the rate of escalation of the Cuban Missile Crisis was unusually rapid. A list of the crises in the larger sample appears in the appendix.

---

3. Fuller descriptions of the construction of the operational indicators and the summary measure of reciprocity appear in Leng 1993:70–72.

4. The sample has been stratified to include a representative number of cases that ended in war and cases that were resolved peacefully within different diplomatic eras.

Crisis Types

The comparisons of escalation and reciprocity scores with those in the larger sample provide a rough means of identifying the scores as relatively high or low in comparison to other militarized crises. By combining the composite escalation and reciprocity scores it is possible to type crises according to their overall behavioral attributes. A crisis with high scores on both escalation and reciprocity, for example, would appear to fit the model of a conflict spiral, or what Rapoport (1960: chap. 1) described as a Fight. My previous studies (Leng 1993: chap. 4; Leng 1987), have used a simple four-category typology with crises classified as Fights (high escalation, high reciprocity), Resistance (high escalation, low reciprocity), Standoffs (low escalation, high reciprocity), and Put-Downs (low escalation, low reciprocity). I will use the four types in this study to obtain simple broad behavioral comparisons across the crises in the study. A brief description of the characteristics of each of the types follows.

Fight. A Fight is characterized by symmetrical rapidly escalating hostility in which the two sides become locked-in to tit-for-tat coercive exchanges.

Resistance. These asymmetrical crises typically are disputes in which one antagonist pursues an escalating coercive influence strategy while the other stands firm and responds in kind to the coercive behavior. The level of reciprocity generally is low because one party leads in escalating the coercive behavior throughout the crisis. Resistance is a high-escalation version of what Rubin, Pruitt, and Kim (1994:73–76) describe as an "aggressor-defender" model of escalation.

Standoff. A Standoff exhibits the high reciprocity of a Fight, but the escalation is controlled: neither party is willing to allow the risk of war to exceed a certain level. Consequently, the type exhibits low escalation but high reciprocity. The high reciprocity score usually is associated with relatively intensive negotiation.

Put-Down. The low escalation and low reciprocity of a Put-Down generally occurs in crises in which one party effectively bullies another into yielding quickly. One antagonist employs escalating coercive tactics, but the other responds only at a moderate level of hostility before yielding. Put-Downs typically are disputes between adversaries that are unevenly matched in capabilities.

An examination of the association of each of the types with crisis outcomes found that Fights are highly associated with escalation to war, that

Resistance crises tend to end either in war or in a diplomatic victory for the challenger, that Standoffs most often end in compromise settlements, and that Put-Downs most often end in a diplomatic victory for the challenger or, not infrequently, in war (see Leng 1993:85–89). The types most frequently found in the current study—Fight and Resistance—do not depart from those patterns.

The operational procedure for typing the crises in this study will be based on the rankings of the composite escalation and reciprocity scores for individual crises within the larger sample of 34 crises described earlier. Those crises with standardized escalation or reciprocity scores above the median for that sample are described as having high escalation or reciprocity, and those below the median are described as low. This is a crude measure, and, given the differences among the cases in this study, which all occur within intense rivalries, and the larger sample of crises, the placement of particular crises in one category or another can be problematic. Therefore, the typing of crises in this study is used only to provide consistent descriptions of the overall behavioral patterns of crises, not for predictive purposes.

Negotiation

The willingness of rival states to meet together to attempt to resolve the crisis through negotiations should illustrate something about their influence strategies as well as their perceptions of each other's intentions and flexibility. One also would expect to find a positive association between direct negotiations to resolve the crisis and the effective management of crises.

There are two negotiation indicators of interest: (1) the timing of the start of negotiations and (2) the intensity of negotiation. The timing of negotiation is calculated by counting the number of days elapsed between the onset of the crisis and the first day of direct negotiations between the rival states. The intensity of negotiation is the percentage of crisis days on which negotiations took place.

Hawkish policymakers are inclined to advocate demonstrating firmness prior to opening negotiations to negotiate from strength; dovish policymakers are more likely to urge early negotiations to reduce the risk of the crisis escalating out of control. How quickly negotiations begin offers an indicator of whether the parties are bent on demonstrating their resolve or on placing a brake on the escalation of the crisis.

The measure of the intensity of negotiations also provides an indicator of the quality of communication. All interactions, whether words or deeds, are forms of communication, but insofar as the management of the crisis is concerned, there is a qualitative difference between other forms of communication and that which occurs when the two sides engage in direct talks to reach an agreement on de-escalating or settling the crisis.

Influence Strategies

A search for significant changes in the behavior of the participants from crisis to crisis ultimately must focus on their influence strategies. A party's influence strategy is the predominant mix of tactics that it employs during the crisis to influence its rival's behavior.

Crisis bargaining can be viewed as a series of influence attempts (demands that may or may not be accompanied by inducements) by one side and responses by the other. Each influence attempt–response sequence consists of three moves: (1) state A attempts to influence the behavior of state B through a demand that may be accompanied by positive and/or negative inducements; (2) state B responds to the influence attempt; (3) state A observes state B's response and uses that information to select the inducement(s) to accompany its next demand. Inducements employed by state A may include promises, rewards, threats, or punishments of varying types and degrees as well as varieties of carrot-and-stick inducements combining positive and negative elements. Responses by state B can include complying with A's demand, placating A with a positive action short of outright compliance, ignoring the demand, or responding with a defiant counterthreat or punishment. The response can also be mixed: it can include both positive and negative actions. These influence attempt–response sequences represent the tactical moves that comprise each side's influence strategy.

To achieve consistency in comparisons across crises, influence strategies are categorized according to five basic types: Bullying, Cautious Bullying, Reciprocating, Trial and Error, and Stonewalling.[5] A brief description of each of the types follows.

> *Bullying.* A Bullying strategy consists of escalating coercive tactics. It is designed to raise the costs of noncompliance for the other party while raising estimates of the bullying party's resolve and risk acceptance. Threats that are ignored or met with defiance are followed by more coercive threats and punishments until either the

---

5. The typology of influence strategies used in earlier studies has included a sixth type: Appeasing (Leng 1993; Leng 1983; Leng and Wheeler 1979). Negative responses by the other side are met with increasingly accommodative promises and rewards by the appeaser. There are no instances of Appeasing strategies in the any of the crises included in this study, so I have not included it in the present typology.

other party complies with the bullying party's demands or the crisis escalates to war.

Cautious Bullying. A Cautious Bullying influence strategy differs from a Bullying strategy in that the party avoids pushing the other party into a choice of war or surrender. Bargaining still consists primarily of escalating coercive inducements, but the Cautious Bullying party avoids initiating military hostilities and is likely to mix threats of force with promises or rewards. Cautious Bullying influence strategies are most often employed by states that have vital interests at stake but prefer some compromise to war.

Reciprocating. A Reciprocating influence strategy consists of a firm but flexible mix of tit-for-tat responses to both cooperative and coercive inducements by the other party with occasional accommodative initiatives. The strategy normally begins with a demonstration of firmness in the face of coercive moves by the other party before moving to accommodative initiatives.[6] The objective is to demonstrate firmness in the face of attempts at coercion without giving the impression of aggressive intentions and while indicating a willingness to move to a mutually accommodative settlement if the other party is willing to respond in kind.

Trial and Error. A party adopting a Trial and Error approach adjusts its influence tactics according to the other party's response to the preceding influence attempt. Inducements that produce positive responses are repeated; inducements that produce negative responses are changed. The policymakers proceed inductively, by trying one tactic after another until the desired result is achieved. What appears as a Trial and Error approach, however, may not be a conscious strategy but the result of uncertainty or may reflect changes in the relative influence of coalitions of hawks and doves as the crisis evolves.

Stonewalling. A state employing a Stonewalling influence strategy ignores the influence attempts of the other party without initiating any coercive or accommodative moves of its own. The strategy is most commonly employed by states that have an advantage in military capabilities and are satisfied with the status quo.

---

6. A Reciprocating strategy, which begins with a demonstration of firmness and allows for occasional departures from strict tit for tat in the form of cooperative initiatives, should be distinguished from Axelrod's (1984) Tit for Tat (TFT), which starts with a cooperative move and then strictly follows tit for tat for the reminder of the dispute (see Leng 1993: chap. 8).

Stonewalling may indicate that a government is immobilized by indecision but it can also result from a decision that bargaining with the other side is fruitless or unnecessary.[7]

Determining the category that best describes the actions of a particular state in a given crisis is based on three operational indicators and, in ambiguous cases, the descriptions of diplomatic historians. The three operational indicators are: (1) the pattern of escalation/de-escalation exhibited by the actions of the actor over the course of the crisis, (2) the influence attempts employed by the actor, and (3) the actor's responses to influence attempts by the other party. I have previously provided descriptions of the rules for determining each categorization (Leng 1993: appendixes 4–6).

A complication in the identification of influence strategies arises in those cases in which states switch influence strategies during a crisis. Because these changes can represent responses to learning, it is important that they be identified. Therefore, I have departed from a previous approach, which focused solely on the state's predominant influence strategy, to identify the state's initial influence strategy and any subsequent shift to another type of influence strategy. Identifying such shifts requires a heavier reliance on qualitative information than the strictly operational procedures that I have employed in the past, but I have confidence in the accuracy of the judgments reached in those few cases in which there were within-crisis changes in influence strategies.

My previous research has supported the effectiveness of Reciprocating strategies in attaining diplomatic victories or compromise outcomes. It also has found that Bullying strategies are positively associated with war outcomes (Leng 1993; Leng and Wheeler 1979).

Duration

A simple measure of the quality of crisis management is the time required to terminate the crisis. Crisis duration is defined operationally as the number of days from the initial precipitant to the crisis outcome.[8] A shorter crisis, of course, is not necessarily a more effectively managed crisis. Crises that quickly escalate to war are not effectively managed, and quick settle-

---

7. More detailed discussions of the five types, with analysis of the relative effectiveness of each in a sample of 40 crises, appear in Leng 1993: chap. 7.

8. The precipitant action is defined operationally as having at least one of the following attributes: (1) an explicit threat, display, or use of force; (2) a challenge to the vital interests of the target—that is, its territorial integrity or political independence; or (3) a serious affront to the dignity or prestige of the target state (Leng and Singer 1988:160).

ments in others may result from alarm over unusually high escalation early in the crisis. Nevertheless, a pattern of increasingly shorter crises ending in settlements, particularly when coupled with lower escalation and intensive negotiation, suggests more effective crisis management.

Crisis Outcomes

The crisis outcome provides the most straightforward measure of the effectiveness of crisis management. A crisis may end in a diplomatic victory for one side (and a diplomatic defeat for the other), a tie, or war. Ties represent either compromises or stalemates with no settlement (Leng and Singer 1988:160–61).

If one assumes that the effective management of a crisis refers to the ability of the contending parties to terminate the crisis and reduce the conflict between them with a minimum of hostility, then it is possible to draw an initial judgment from the crisis outcome. A crisis that ended in a negotiated settlement would be more effectively managed than a crisis that ended in a stalemate, and a crisis that ended peacefully would be more effectively managed than one that ended in war. It is important, however, to make a distinction between the criteria for effective management that might be applied by a student of conflict resolution and those applied by the crisis participants. If the criteria for effective management are defined in terms of the interests of the state and its success in serving those interests, then there may be cases where a state prefers a stalemate or even war to a negotiated settlement. As chapters 4 and 5 will show, those situations were not uncommon in the Egyptian-Israeli and Indo-Pakistani rivalries.

Answering Questions 1 and 2

The first research question asks whether there were significant changes in the behavior of the rival states from one crisis to the next. The criterion for a significant change in a state's bargaining behavior is a switch in its influence strategy at the beginning of the next crisis. In addition to being the primary descriptor of a state's overall approach to bargaining, the typology of influence strategies requires that there be a substantial shift in a state's bargaining behavior to move from one category to another. The escalation and negotiation indicators provide more complete descriptions of the observed changes.

Question 2 asks whether the rival states' management of their crises improved with experience—that is, over the course of successive crises. If one assumes that effective crisis management refers to the ability of the rival states to resolve their crises peacefully with a low level of escalation, then the unit of observation is the crisis. The indicators of interest are duration of the crisis, measures of escalation and reciprocity, the timing and intensity of negotiation, and the crisis outcome. Crises that are shorter, with lower levels of escalation, greater reciprocity in cooperative behavior, earlier and more intensive negotiations, and peaceful settlements presumably have been more successfully managed. If one judges effective crisis management in terms of the ability of particular states to serve their interests, the analysis becomes more subjective. It must rely on qualitative information regarding the ability of the state to successfully carry out its strategy and achieve its objectives at what its leaders considered acceptable costs.

Qualitative Analysis

Question 3 asks if there is a systematic relationship between observed changes in crisis behavior and experiential learning by policymakers or whether the changes may be more plausibly attributed to other variables. This question requires both the observation of overt behavior and inferences regarding the policymakers' thinking. Drawing such an inference, given the ratio between the large number of putative predictor variables listed in chapter 1 and the relatively small number of observations, rules out a purely quantitative approach. Therefore, in seeking an answer to question 3, the quantitative descriptors of crisis behavior are augmented with qualitative information drawn from the accounts of diplomatic historians and political scientists, the memoirs of crisis participants, and the public record.

Data Collection and Comparability

The completeness and reliability of sources vary across cases. No other source matches the completeness of the taped White House meetings of President Kennedy's policy-making team during the Cuban Missile Crisis (May and Zelikow 1997). At the other end of the continuum, a half century after the event there is "nothing even remotely resembling a consensus" regarding Pakistan's role in the invasion of Kashmir by Pathen tribesmen that set off the First Kashmir War of 1947 (Wirsing 1994:39). On balance, the available information on the making of American and Israeli foreign policy is the most complete. Available information on Soviet perceptions and policy-making during the Cold War crises has grown dramatically with the opening of Soviet archives since the early 1990s. New information on Egyptian and Pakistani policy-making also has become available with the recent publication of the memoirs of some key participants. The sources that were most useful are cited in the "Note on Sources" in the appendix. Those instances for which there is insufficient information or contradictory accounts are noted in the text or notes.

The qualitative information has been collected in a manner that is systematic and consistent across cases to come as close as possible to matching the degree of reliability achieved in the generation of the quantitative data. The qualitative descriptions and analyses focus on the same variables and research questions in all 12 cases. This information has been coupled with quantitative descriptions and summary statistics to provide comparability across crises and crisis participants.

Answering Question 3

To establish that states have applied lessons drawn from previous crises, one must find changes in behavior from one crisis to the next that cannot be explained plausibly by other variables. Chapter 1 presented a listing of potential sources of changes in crisis behavior other than learning. Those changes can result from internal and external events occurring between crises, changes in the relationship between the rival states, and differences in crisis structure (interests at stake, comparative capabilities, perceived intentions). The influence of these variables on crisis behavior depends on policymakers' perceptions and beliefs.

The discussion of learning in chapter 1 emphasized the intervening influence of political belief systems on the lessons that policymakers draw from crises. Belief systems predispose policymakers to select particular events as salient and to draw certain lessons from them. Thus, an important component of the collection of qualitative information is the identification of where key policymakers, particularly the state leader, stand on the continuum between hawkish and dovish views of crisis diplomacy. Particularly important are their beliefs regarding (1) the effects of crisis escalation, (2) the costs and risks of war, (3) the efficacy of negotiation, and (4) the intentions and motivation, or resolve, of the rival state's leadership.

When policymakers use historical analogies from previous crises to justify influence strategies in subsequent crises, it would appear to provide strong evidence of learning. But policymakers may simply use convenient historical analogies to provide convincing arguments to support their existing beliefs. This issue underlines the importance of obtaining information on key policymakers' belief systems and counsels caution in drawing inferences about lessons drawn from experience.

Inferring Learning

Figure 2.1 illustrates the paths of the potential causes of changes in crisis behavior discussed previously. There are three steps to determining whether changes in crisis behavior have been influenced by learning from previous crises or learning from experience in the current crisis and in estimating the strength of that influence. In the following discussion, crisis C represents the current crisis, crisis C-1 represents a previous crisis.

1. The determination that the behavior of state A in crisis C is significantly different from its behavior in crisis C-1 or from its earlier behavior in crisis C is obtained from the quantitative indicators described earlier.
2. The case is then analyzed qualitatively to determine whether there is evidence indicating that policymakers in state A drew lessons, either from direct experience or vicariously, from crisis C-1, or from preceding events in crisis C that are consistent with state A's subsequent behavior in crisis C. If a consistent relationship does not exist, state A's behavior in crisis C is assumed not to have been influenced significantly by lessons drawn from its experience in crisis C-1 or from its experience in crisis C. That determination does not mean that learning did not take place, only that it did not result in significant changes in subsequent crisis behavior. State A's policymakers may have drawn certain lessons from state A's experience in crisis C-1 or from earlier in crisis C, but those lessons may have been confounded by any one of the other factors listed in chapter 1.
3. When there is a positive association between the lessons drawn by policymakers from crisis C-1, or from crisis C, and the state's subsequent behavior in crisis C, it is necessary to ascertain whether those lessons represented necessary or sufficient conditions for changes in state behavior.

First, what appears to be the application of learning may be merely an adaptation to fit a new situation, such as a change in the crisis structure. Thus, determining whether learning was a necessary condition for behavioral changes requires a careful examination of other potential causes of changes. Each variable other than learning in figure 2.1 must be examined qualitatively to determine whether its variance could cause the observed changes in the behavior of state A. When the answer is yes, I attempt to estimate the influence of those variables relative to learning by examining the available qualitative information.

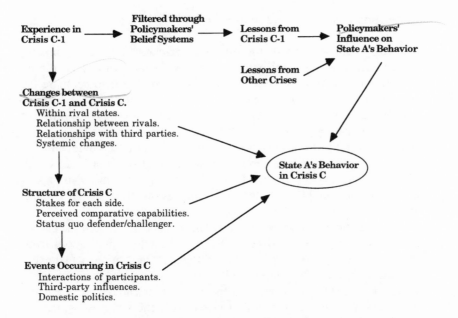

Fig. 2.1.   Potential influences on crisis behavior

The second part of the question asks whether the lessons drawn from crisis C-1 or from crisis C represent a sufficient condition for subsequent behavioral changes observed in crisis C or whether other conditions also were necessary. For example, was an improved relationship with the adversary state a necessary condition for experiential learning to influence state A's subsequent behavior?

A related question is whether policymakers' belief systems limit their learning. Do only those lessons consistent with a policymaker's belief system influence subsequent crisis behavior? That was the implication of the findings from my earlier quantitative study of learning in recurring crises (Leng 1983). Thus, it is important to ask whether any changes in state behavior varied from the views held by key policymakers prior to the crisis or whether their adjustments in behavior remained consistent with those beliefs.

Steps 2 and 3 obviously require subjective judgments. But by systematically posing the same questions for each observation, every effort has been made to make those judgments as informed and unbiased as possible.

Comparing Crisis Learning across Rivalries

The search for answers to the first three research questions compares events and situations confronted by the rival states before and during recurring crises within a given rivalry. The next step is to compare the behavioral patterns observed across rivalries in an attempt to answer the fourth question: Is there any consistency in the lessons drawn by different states from their crisis experiences? This step entails a return to the quantitative descriptors for an analysis of variations in the effects of learning on subsequent crisis behavior. Do leaders in different states or leaders with different belief systems draw different lessons from similar crisis experiences? Or are they likely to draw the same lessons from similar circumstances?

Two comparisons are of interest. The first is that between the pair of states within a particular rivalry. Did they draw the same lessons from their shared crisis experiences? Or did differences in their particular experiences, perceptions, situations, and/or belief systems lead to significantly different lessons? The answers to these questions should provide some information about the potency of crisis experiences and the extent to which rival policymakers share the same belief systems.

The second comparison is that among states embroiled in different rivalries. Is there any consistency in the types of lessons that they drew from their different crisis experiences? If so, it suggests that there is a shared set of beliefs regarding the nature of interstate conflict, such as realpolitik, that retains its potency across a wide variety of states and circumstances.

The quantitative descriptors of particular interest in seeking answers to both parts of question 4 are (1) the predominant influence strategies of the two sides and (2) the degree of reciprocity in their interactions. Crisis adversaries that employ the same influence strategies and reciprocate each other's actions are likely to have drawn similar lessons from previous crisis experiences.

Question 5 asks whether changes in crisis behavior resulting from learning led to more or less effective management. The answer depends on the answers to the three preceding questions.

Organization

Chapters 3–5 are devoted to the Soviet-American, Egyptian-Israeli, and Indo-Pakistani rivalries, respectively. Within each chapter, the descriptions and analyses proceed chronologically through each of the crises between the two adversary states.

The analysis of each case begins with a narrative discussion of salient events occurring between that crisis and the preceding crisis between the participants and then considers the likely effects of those events on the relationship between the two states. The discussion of the crisis begins with an analysis of the key policymakers' perceptions of the intentions and motivation of the other party, the interests at stake, and the comparative capabilities of the two sides. A chronological narrative account describes the key events in the evolution of the crisis. The narrative account is followed by a quantitative description of the crisis, including patterns of escalation/de-escalation, reciprocity, and negotiation. This macroscopic analysis of the crisis is followed by an examination of the influence strategies of each of the rival states. Narrative descriptions complement the operational classifications of the influence strategies.

The description and analysis of each crisis concludes with a discussion of evidence of learning. The discussion of each crisis is followed by a narrative description of events between that crisis and the following crisis between the rival states. After all four crises have been described and analyzed, the chapter concludes with a discussion of behavior and learning over the course of the rivalry.

Chapter 6 integrates the findings from all three rivalries and attempts to answer the five research questions.

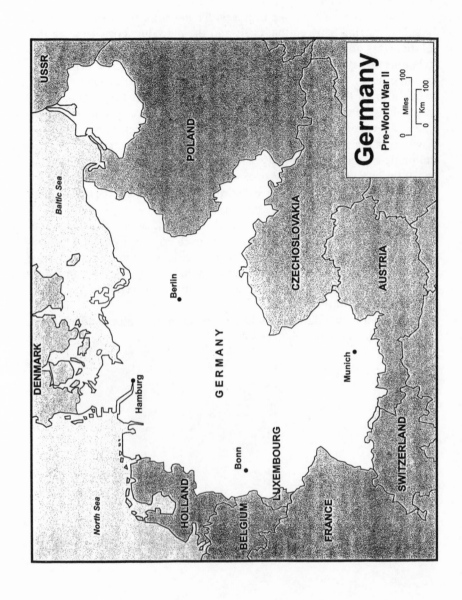

Germany
Pre-World War II

USSR

Baltic Sea

POLAND

DENMARK

North Sea

Hamburg

Berlin

GERMANY

CZECHOSLOVAKIA

AUSTRIA

Munich

HOLLAND

Bonn

LUXEMBOURG

BELGIUM

FRANCE

SWITZERLAND

0   Miles   100
0   Km   100

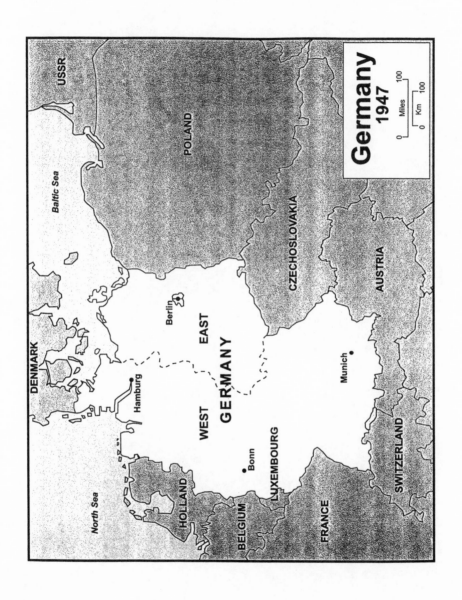

Germany
1947

CHAPTER 3

The Soviet-American Rivalry

The coalition of necessity that joined the United States and Britain with the Soviet Union to defeat Germany in World War II became the first victim of its success. When Germany's defeat in 1945 removed the necessity for united action, a cold war between the Western powers, led by the United States, and the Soviet Union began over the future of Europe.

The three members of the victorious coalition—the United States, the Soviet Union, and Britain—agreed that Germany should be denazified, demilitarized, and decentralized. But the Western powers and the Soviet Union remained divided on other issues regarding Germany's future. The division of Germany between western and eastern halves, which had been created by the advancing allied forces, remained in place. Negotiations on a peace treaty to determine Germany's long-term future were left in the hands of a council of ministers, composed of the foreign ministers of the three allied powers plus France and China. Those negotiations never got off the ground.

The city of Berlin, which was located within the Soviet-occupied eastern half of Germany, was partitioned among the four allied powers (the United States, Britain, the Soviet Union, and France). The Western powers soon consolidated the three sectors of what became known as West Berlin, with the Soviet Union remaining in control in the eastern sector. As the Cold War intensified, the differences between the superpowers over the status of Berlin took on increasing importance. For the United States, the Western sector of Berlin within the Soviet-controlled half of Germany was a symbolic island of freedom, but it also presented a major security problem. For the Soviet Union, Western control of half of Berlin was a geopolitical abnormality that threatened Soviet political control over eastern Germany.

Berlin was the focus of the first two superpower crises—the Berlin Blockade Crisis of 1948–49 and the Berlin Wall Crisis of 1961. But shortly after the Berlin Blockade Crisis, the Cold War competition had become global, with the victory of communist forces in China in 1949 and the outbreak of the Korean War in 1950. The Cuban Missile Crisis took place in the Western hemisphere. The last superpower crisis, the

Alert Crisis of 1973, was over influence in the Middle East. The super-power competition also exerted a significant influence over the course of the Egyptian-Israeli and Indo-Pakistani rivalries, which are examined in chapters 4 and 5.

This chapter examines each of the four superpower crises and asks what lessons key Soviet and American policymakers drew from those experiences. The examination of each crisis is divided into three sections: a description of the crisis structure, a description of the behavior of the participants, and a discussion of the crisis outcome and the lessons drawn from the crisis. The description of the crisis structure includes each party's perceptions of the other's intentions and motivations and the comparative capabilities of the two sides. There are three parts to the examination of the behavior of the rival states: (1) a narrative description of the evolution of the crisis; (2) a quantitative analysis of escalation, reciprocity, and the intensity of negotiation; and (3) a description of each participant's influence strategies. The final section describes the crisis outcome and then discusses what lessons, if any, the leaders of the superpowers drew from the crisis. The chapter concludes with a summary discussion of learning in the Soviet-American rivalry.

Berlin Blockade Crisis, 1948–49

By 1948 Stalin had consolidated his hold on Eastern Europe, and the United States had announced the Truman Doctrine and the Marshall Plan. Europe had become divided between the two contending ideological camps, with the dividing line running through Germany. Given the unsettled and ambiguous status of Berlin, with its Western zones perched precariously in the center of East Germany, it is not surprising that the city became the focal point for the first major Cold War confrontation.

Crisis Structure

Soviet Union
Perceptions of American Intentions. Following the erratic and tense collaboration of the Big Three during World War II, Stalin remained deeply distrustful of Western intentions. By the fall of 1947, Soviet rhetoric shifted from the immediate postwar doctrine of pragmatic collaboration to a militant and defensive foreign policy. The immediate precipitant appears to have been the Marshall Plan for the reconstruction of Western Europe. The Soviets viewed the plan as the opening salvo in an American campaign to extend its influence over all of Europe, thereby threatening the Soviet

sphere of influence in Eastern Europe (see Zubok and Pleshakov 1996:50–51, 104–8; Taubman 1982:175–76; Ulam 1983, 15–16).

Soviet fears were exacerbated by Western plans to reconstruct western Germany as a strong independent state and a 1948 decision to introduce Western currency into Berlin. These moves appeared to Stalin to be part of a coordinated strategy to reunite and rearm Germany and ally it with the capitalist West. To make matters worse, members of the Soviet-installed Socialist German Unity Party warned Stalin that they were likely to suffer a humiliating defeat in Berlin-wide elections scheduled for October 1948 (Zubok and Pleshakov 1996:51–52).

Soviet Interests.   As World War II drew near a close, Soviet policy-makers believed that the USSR's future security depended on a Europe divided into spheres of influence among America, Britain, and the Soviet Union, with "friendly governments" along the Soviet border and, above all, a permanently weakened Germany (see Pechatnov 1995:16). Stalin had made it clear at Yalta that his first concern regarding Germany was that it remain too weak to challenge Soviet security. Soviet policymakers sought to achieve that goal through heavy reparations, extended occupation, and reeducation. After being blocked by the West from exacting permanently crippling reparations throughout all of Germany, Stalin had decided by 1948 to support the permanent division of Germany and to solidify his hold on the eastern zone, including Berlin (Zubok and Pleshakov 1996:130–31; Djilas 1962:153). Stalin preferred Western control over half of Germany to an independent and rearmed West German state. Berlin, however, could not be allowed to remain as a Western outpost in eastern Germany, and the Soviets feared that the introduction of Western currency would block efforts to gradually incorporate Berlin into the economy of the Soviet zone.

Soviet Capabilities.   Stalin was aware of the weakness of the Soviet military in the years immediately following World War II and of the overwhelming industrial advantages of the United States in a protracted war (Shulman 1963:20). On the other hand, Britain's and France's war-fighting capabilities had been seriously weakened by the war, and the United States had rushed to demobilize. Some analysts (Adomeit 1982:138; Davison 1958:156) have argued that the Soviets' manpower advantage in Germany made them confident that they could prevail over the Western forces should the crisis escalate to war. Others (Ulam 1983:8–11; Shulman 1963:20) argue that Stalin was well aware of the gap between American and Soviet industrial capabilities as well as the implications of the vast losses of Russian manpower in World War II and of a war-weary populace desperate for peace. Stalin, they argue, had to realize that the advantages he enjoyed in a short, localized conflict would dissipate quickly in a protracted and expanded war. Moreover, the United States enjoyed a nuclear-weapons monopoly in 1948.

United States
Perceptions of Soviet Intentions.   After the 1947 fall of Czechoslovakia to a Soviet-supported communist coup and threats of communist victories in Greece and Turkey, the dominant American view was that Soviet intentions in Europe and in Germany in particular were imperialistic (Shlaim 1983:21; Adomeit 1982:70; Ulam 1983:5). "They understand one language [power] and that is the language they are going to get from me from this point on," Truman vowed (quoted in Larson 1985:319). Truman began referring to the Soviet regime as a "Frankenstein dictatorship" out to overturn the status quo in Europe in the same manner as Napoleon or Hitler (M. Truman 1973:359–60).

The Truman administration's view of Soviet motivation would have pleased prospect theorists. The administration believed that, whatever territorial gains the Soviets achieved, they would be willing to accept high risks, including the risk of war, to defend those gains (W. B. Smith 1950:47; Ulam 1983:11). Conversely, Soviet offensive moves were designed to be low-risk efforts "to probe for soft spots," in the Western perimeter (H. S. Truman 1956:139; Kennan 1947:575). The blockade of Berlin, like the Soviet actions in Iran, Turkey, and Greece, was seen as a Soviet test of the West's resolve rather than a Soviet response to a perceived threat to its security. The administration assumed that, once faced with Western opposition, the Soviets would accept the situation philosophically, retreat, and wait patiently for another opportunity. But there was always the danger that, in the course of a confrontation like that over Berlin, a low-level military incident might cause the dispute to suddenly escalate to all-out war (H. S. Truman 1956:30).

American Interests.   By 1948, the Western powers had committed themselves to a strong West German state as a bulwark against the spread of Soviet communism. The Truman administration viewed the West's position in Berlin as vital to Germany's future and, ultimately, the future of Europe (H. S. Truman 1956:130; Shlaim 1983:196). Beyond the perception that Berlin was strategically vital to Western interests, there were reputational interests at stake, specifically America's reputation for resolve in the face of Soviet expansion, or, as Truman put it, "our capacity and will to resist" (H. S. Truman 1956:139). In what would become a familiar historical analogy during the Cold War, American leaders asserted that they did not want Berlin to become the "Munich of 1948" (Shlaim 1983:212).

American policymakers, however, were well aware of the psychological war-weariness of their citizenry just three years after the end of World

War II; consequently, these leaders were loath to become engaged in a war with the Soviets over Germany. The need to avoid war was all the more important given the American leaders' perception that the West was at a military disadvantage in Germany.

American Capabilities. Berlin was militarily indefensible. Western troops were outnumbered by almost three to one in Berlin, and the city was surrounded by an additional 300,000 Soviet troops in East Germany. But, as I noted earlier, the United States held two trump cards in any protracted or expanded war. The most significant was its superior industrial strength. America's strong industrial economy emerged even stronger at the conclusion of World War II, whereas the Soviet economy was devastated by the war. The second trump card was the American monopoly on atomic weapons. Some American policymakers believed that the bomb would deter the Soviets from allowing the crisis to escalate to war. American policymakers believed that the West would be at a decided immediate military disadvantage but would prevail in a protracted war.

Crisis Behavior

The precipitant to the crisis occurred on March 20, 1948, when the head of the Soviet delegation, Marshal Sokolovsky, walked out of an Allied Control Council meeting after accusing the Western powers of planning for a separate West German state.[1] On March 31, when American military passenger trains moving through a Soviet checkpoint refused to allow Soviet inspectors to board the trains, Soviet authorities stopped the trains and forced them to turn back. Over the next two months the Soviets intensified the dispute by gradually instituting a partial blockade of highway, rail, and river traffic because of alleged "technical difficulties."

With Allied Control Council talks broken off, the Western powers decided to introduce their own currency, the B mark, into western Germany and the western zones of Berlin. On June 7, the Western powers also published their plans for a separate West German state. Four days later, on the night of June 11–12, the Soviets halted rail traffic between western Germany and Berlin. Then the autobahn bridge over the Elbe was closed for "repairs," seriously hindering travel into and out of Berlin by road. A last-ditch meeting of the four powers on June 22 got nowhere. Separate currencies were introduced into the Western and Soviet zones of Berlin on June 23. On the next day, the Soviets stopped all highway, rail, and river

---

1. Snyder and Diesing (1977:560) identify the specific precipitant to the crisis as the publication of Western plans for a separate West Germany on June 7, 1948, but most scholars treat the March 20 diplomatic blowup as the start of the crisis. By June, the Soviets already had taken a number of steps to restrict travel to and from Berlin.

traffic to and from the West; cut electrical power from East Berlin to West Berlin; and ordered an embargo on the shipment of food through eastern Germany to West Berlin. The blockade had begun. Three days later, on June 26, the Western powers began to airlift food and other necessities to West Berlin.

The three Western military governors met with Marshal Sokolovsky on July 3, only to be told that the blockade would remain until the West abandoned plans for a West German state. The United States declared its resolve to maintain the Western position in Berlin. By mid-July, General Lucius Clay, the military governor of Berlin, urged Truman to send an armed convoy to Berlin to "help" the Soviets remove the "technical difficulties" allegedly causing the blockade. Truman instead opted for increasing the airlift and attempting additional negotiation with the Soviets. A meeting of the American, British, and French ambassadors with Stalin and Molotov on August 2 appeared to reach an agreement on a formula to resolve the dispute: the Soviets would end the blockade in return for a Western agreement that the Soviet-introduced marks would be Berlin's sole currency. But in subsequent meetings during August the formula collapsed in attempts to hammer out the details. After meetings in early September met a similar fate, the Soviets increased their "air maneuvers" over the Berlin corridor.

Under American initiative, on September 9 the Western powers brought the matter before the United Nations Security Council, where the nonpermanent members attempted to mediate, without success. By this time the Western airlift, which had been begun as a stopgap measure, was carrying a daily average of 5,500 tons of supplies into Berlin. On December 24, the three Western powers officially rejected the formula of early August and announced that they were proceeding immediately with the introduction of the new B mark as the sole legal tender in the Western sectors of Berlin. On January 18, 1949, the West began a counterblockade to curtail the movement of critical goods to the Soviet sector.

As the Western position hardened, the Soviet stand began to soften. On January 30, Stalin indicated that he might lift the blockade if the Western powers would postpone the establishment of a West German state until after a meeting of the Council of Ministers had considered the German problem as a whole. No reference was made to the currency issue.[2] The American representative to the United Nations, Philip Jessup, asked his Soviet counterpart, Jacob Malik, if the currency omission was acciden-

2. The Council of Ministers was the group of five foreign ministers that had been established at Potsdam to continue the negotiations for a peace treaty formally ending World War II.

tal. A month passed before Malik was authorized to reply that it was not. The Soviets would agree to lift the blockade in return for an end to the Western blockade and a meeting of the Council of Ministers. The tone of Soviet statements became more threatening as Western negotiations on the formation of the North Atlantic Treaty Organization (NATO) neared agreement. The NATO treaty was signed on April 4, and four days later the Western powers announced that they had completed plans for the establishment of a West German state. Nevertheless, with the airlift setting new records and the counterblockade having an increasingly severe effect on the eastern zone, the Soviets were committed to reaching an agreement to end the crisis. An agreement was reached between the American and Soviet negotiators on May 4, and the Soviet blockade was lifted on May 12, 1949. It had lasted 323 days.

Patterns of Behavior

The quantitative analysis of the behavior of the two sides in the Berlin Blockade Crisis begins with a description of two key crisis attributes: the observed pattern of escalation/de-escalation and the degree of reciprocity in the behavior of the two sides. As the first of the Soviet-American crises, the patterns of escalation and reciprocity in the Berlin Blockade provide a benchmark for judging whether the superpowers became more or less effective at managing their recurring crises over the course of rivalry.

The time series in figure 3.1 provides a visual image of the evolution of the crisis, depicting the magnitude of hostility for each side, measured at weekly intervals, over the course of the crisis. The solid line represents the aggregated hostility scores for those actions taken by the United States, Great Britain, and the Western allies acting jointly that are directed toward the Soviet Union or toward German authorities in the Soviet zone. The broken line depicts the aggregated weekly hostility scores for Soviet actions directed toward the United States, Great Britain, or the German authorities in the western zones. The hostility scores for each side represent the mix of cooperative and conflictive actions undertaken by that side during seven-day intervals beginning with the onset of the crisis on March 20, 1948. The weekly intervals are identified by the hash marks on the horizontal axis, with the dates specified for every other week. Key events in the evolution of the crisis are depicted by the numbered arrows and are identified in the notes below the figure.

Figure 3.1 exhibits the one-sidedness of the crisis in its early phase, when the Soviet Union broke off negotiations and began impeding Western travel to Berlin. The hostility scores escalate dramatically as the Soviets intensified travel restrictions during June. The magnitude of hostile

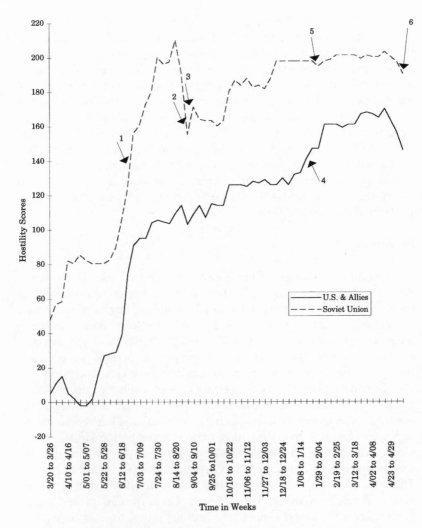

Fig. 3.1. Berlin Blockade, 1948–49
Key dates are indicated with arrows: (1) 6/23: blockade begins; (2) 8/31: four-power negotiation; (3) 9/4: Soviets harass air corridors; (4) 1/18: counterblockade begins; (5) 1/30: Stalin softens position; (6) 5/12: blockade ends.

Soviet actions declined during the ongoing negotiations in August and rose again when talks broke down in September. The overall magnitude of hostility in Western actions lagged behind that of the Soviets as the Western powers attempted to combine efforts at negotiation with the airlift in the summer and early fall of 1948. In fact, the magnitude of contentious action on the part of the West did not approximate that of the Soviets until the end of the crisis.

An interesting phase began in late December, when the Western powers moved to a tougher negotiating stand, and extended through January 1949, when the West began its counterblockade (point 4 in figure 3.1). During this period, the magnitude of Western hostility rose, while that of the Soviets remained relatively constant. The turning point in the crisis occurred on January 30 (point 5), when Stalin hinted at a willingness to make concessions.

The pattern of behavior in figure 3.1 is consistent with the Resistance crisis type described in chapter 2—that is, an asymmetrical crisis with high escalation and low reciprocity in the interactions of the two sides. One side leads in escalating coercive behavior, while the other side demonstrates its resolve by matching that behavior, although at a lower magnitude of hostility. As the label implies, the Resistance type is identified not only by the escalating coercive behavior of the more aggressive side but also by the firmness of the responses of the other side.

The visual impression from figure 3.1 is supported by the statistical indicators described in chapter 2. Table 3.1 lists the scores for the three

TABLE 3.1. United States–Soviet Union: Escalation Scores

Crisis	Magnitude Score (Rank)	Intensity Score (Rank)	Rate Score (Rank)	Rank U.S.-USSR Crises	Rank in Larger Sample	Combined Escalation Score
Berlin Blockade	380.5 (4)	268.51 (1)	3.53 (13)	1	3	2.92
U.S. West	170.00	105.66	2.20	1		2.55
USSR	210.25	162.85	1.33	1		3.24
Berlin Wall	137.5 (13)	66.94 (13)	3.76 (13)	3	14	−1.21
U.S. West	70.00	32.40	1.43	3		−1.78
USSR	67.50	34.52	2.33	3		0.11
Cuban Missile	192.5 (9)	87.57 (10)	11.77 (5)	2	7	1.40
U.S.	130.50	59.67	8.86	2		2.41
USSR and Cuba	69.00	27.92	2.91	2		0.59
Alert Crisis	45 (31)	31.83 (21)	0.6 (27)	4	28	−3.11
U.S.	28.00	22.33	0.40	4		−3.18
USSR	17.00	9.50	0.20	4		−3.07
Mean (U.S.–USSR)	118.75	59.70	6.19			

escalation indicators for each of the participants in the Berlin Blockade and the other three superpower crises. The table also includes the rankings for the composite escalation scores of each of the superpower crises as well as for where each crisis would rank if it were compared to the other crises in the larger sample of 34 militarized crises in appendix 2.

As table 3.1 illustrates, when the Berlin Blockade Crisis is added to the larger sample for comparative purposes, it ranks thirteenth out of 35 crises in rate of escalation, fourth in magnitude, and first in intensity of escalation. The intensity measure captures the sustained high level of pre-dominantly conflictual actions over the course of the crisis, and the magnitude indicator represents the peak magnitude of hostility. The rate of escalation (the increase in the magnitude of escalation over time) is reduced by the extended period of stalemate from October to April. But the combined escalation score for the Berlin Blockade Crisis would rank third among all the cases in the larger sample of 35 crises, behind only the pre–World War I and Italo-Ethiopian war crises, and higher than that in 12 of the 13 crises in the larger sample that escalated to war. The Berlin Blockade was extraordinarily severe for a dispute that did not end in war.

Table 3.2 presents the reciprocity scores and rankings for each of the four superpower crises.

The reciprocity scores for the Berlin Blockade Crisis would rank near the bottom in the larger sample, which indicates that this crisis was particularly one sided, with the Soviet Union leading in escalating the hostility. The Berlin Blockade Crisis ranks thirty-third on the distance indicator, which measures the extent to which the two sides are consistently matching each other's level of hostility over the evolution of the crisis. On the direction indicator, which measures the extent to which the two sides are converging toward greater cooperation or conflict at the same time, as opposed to moving in opposite directions, it ranks twenty-fourth. Thus, not only are the Soviet actions considerably more conflictual than those of

TABLE 3.2. United States–Soviet Union: Reciprocity Scores

Crisis	Reciprocity Indicators		Combined Reciprocity Score	Rank U.S.–USSR Crises	Rank in Larger Sample
	Direction Score (Rank)	Distance Score (Rank)			
Berlin Blockade	7.52 (24)	52.71 (33)	0.39	3	31
Berlin Wall	7.67 (27)	2.10 (5)	−1.86	1	17
Cuban Missile	11.59 (33)	35.33 (33)	1.36	4	32
Middle East Alert	12.00 (34)	.50	0.12	2	28
Mean	9.70	21.77			

the West, but when one side is moving toward greater cooperation, the other is likely to be becoming more contentious. On the combined reciprocity measure, the Berlin Blockade ranks thirty-first out of the 35 crises in the sample.

One finding from my earlier study of interstate crisis behavior across a variety of militarized cases was that crises with escalation patterns classified as Resistance tended to end in a diplomatic victory for one side or to escalate to war. There were very few compromise outcomes (see Leng 1993: chap. 4). One reason for this phenomenon may be the lack of what Zartman (1986:206) has called a "mutually hurting stalemate," which would provide the necessary "ripeness" for a compromise settlement. In the early stages of the Berlin Blockade, extending from June through early September, only the Western side was "hurting." With the successful expansion of the airlift and the institution of the counterblockade in January, the tables were gradually turned. There never was a time when the stalemate was severely hurting both sides; thus, the deadlock continued until the political balance tilted decisively in favor of the West and Stalin yielded. A better sense of just why the crisis evolved as it did and ended with Stalin yielding can be obtained by examining the influence strategies of the two sides.

Influence Strategies

The Soviet influence strategy is classified as Cautious Bullying, and the U.S. strategy is classified as Reciprocating (chap. 2).

Soviet Union

When an actor employs a Bullying influence strategy, its demands are accompanied by escalating coercive inducements. Any response short of compliance is met with a more severe threat and/or punishment. A Cautious Bullying strategy is distinguished from a Bullying strategy per se by the avoidance of the initiation of military hostilities and, in most instances, a willingness to negotiate. Stalin pursued an escalating coercive strategy, but he refrained from the use of ultimatums or explicit threats of force, avoided hostilities, and was receptive to negotiations to resolve the crisis.[3]

The centerpiece of Stalin's Cautious Bullying strategy was the blockade. Stalin began with moves that were relatively low risk and deliberately ambiguous. The "technical problems," which were the initial justification for closing bridges into Berlin, could be fixed overnight if the Soviets

---

3. The operational classification of the Soviet strategy is consistent with Adomeit's characterization (1982:315–16) in his case study of the crisis.

decided that the Western reaction required a quick retreat. But if the escalation of the coercion was cautious, it also was unrelenting. Stalin's methodical tightening of his stranglehold on Berlin can be seen in the chronological list of Soviet border restrictions and threats appearing in table 3.3.

The blockade was a good example of what Schelling has labeled the "diplomacy of violence" (1966: chap. 1): inflicting increasing pain and suffering until the other side yields to one's demands. The suffering and the threat of more to come were designed to reduce the morale of the West Berliners to the point where their Western allies would feel compelled to negotiate an agreement that would establish a Soviet-zone currency for all of Berlin and scrap plans for an independent West Germany. But as Fish (1991:208) has pointed out, a serious drawback to the Soviet strategy was that it left the West with a peaceful way out of the crisis without sacrificing what it considered a vital interest.

Once it became clear that the West would not mount a military challenge to the blockade, Stalin responded in a positive way to an American proposal for negotiations while tightening the blockade (see Adomeit 1982:99, 168; Taubman 1982:188–91). But when the negotiations collapsed in early September, the Soviet strategy became more bellicose, with open harassment of the air corridors. By late winter, Stalin realized that he had underestimated the Western airlift's ability to sustain West Berliners' health and morale. The success of the airlift in the face of Soviet attempts to strangle West Berlin had become increasingly costly to Soviet prestige, as the West's counterblockade was creating more tangible economic costs to the Soviets. Faced with no alternative other than initiating actions that would create a high risk of war, Stalin prudently moved to a more accommodating bargaining strategy.

United States

The influence attempts and responses to Soviet influence attempts by the United States and by the Western allies acting jointly are consistent with a Reciprocating strategy. The objective of a Reciprocating strategy is to demonstrate resolve in a nonaggressive manner while exhibiting a willingness to move to a negotiated settlement of the dispute. Initially, this strategy consists primarily of responding in a firm but nonprovocative manner to coercive influence attempts and responding in kind to cooperative initiatives. When confronted with a Bullying opponent, the actor employing a Reciprocating strategy demonstrates its firmness before offering any cooperative initiatives (Leng 1993: chap. 7).

The airlift demonstrated the Western resolve to maintain the status of West Berlin without escalating the conflict. When Stalin indicated a will-

TABLE 3.3.   Tightening the Blockade of Berlin

Date	Actions
March 21, 1948	Guards added at Berlin border.
March 31, 1948	Military rail traffic stopped for two days.
April 1, 1948	Roads to Berlin blocked for one day.
April 5, 1948	Soviet fighters harass British passenger planes.
April 9, 1948	Parcel post restricted.
April 11, 1948	Traffic through Vienna curbed.
April 12, 1948	Military trains to and from Vienna stopped.
April 20, 1948	British barge traffic restricted.
April 22, 1948	Passenger train service from West Berlin curtailed.
June 9, 1948	More border restrictions imposed on shipping.
June 11, 1948	Rail traffic interrupted for two days.
June 12, 1948	The autobahn to Berlin closed.
June 15, 1948	Coal shipments halted; transit posts closed; new restrictions imposed on travel by Germans; highway bridges closed. (Ferry remains open.)
June 17, 1948	All but one land entry point closed. Germans required to obtain special passes.
June 24, 1948	Complete blockade of city. Electricity cut.
June 25, 1948	All food shipments banned.
July 6, 1948	Soviet warplanes buzz Berlin air lanes.
July 8, 1948	Soviets increase buzzing of planes.
July 9, 1948	Restrictions placed on traffic leaving West Berlin. Soviets halt payments to Allies of occupation costs.
July 13, 1948	Soviets increase travel restrictions.
July 15, 1948	Fighter activity in Berlin air corridors increased.
July 22, 1948	Step up of harassment of air corridors.
August 20, 1948	The West not permitted to deliver goods to Berlin as part of reparations debt.
September 22, 1948	Trading between East and West Berlin stopped.
September 29, 1948	Soviets buzz several freight planes.
October 11, 1948	Soviet plane buzzes a British transport.
October 18, 1948	Soviets arm new police as defiance and unrest spread.
October 19, 1948	Soviets tighten travel restrictions.
December 9, 1948	Further tightening of blockade.
February 17, 1949	Barricades erected to stop black-market traffic.
May 18, 1949	New restrictions imposed on trucking.
May 19, 1949	The autobahn opened to trucking for five hours.
May 20, 1949	The autobahn reopened. The blockade lifted.

ingness to negotiate in late July, the Western powers immediately agreed. When the Soviets followed the collapse of the summer talks with an increase in the harassment of Western flights into Berlin, the West responded with its counterblockade. When Stalin finally offered to yield in return for face-saving talks among the Council of Ministers, the West accepted the offer.

At the outset of the crisis, however, the American strategy was not yet focused. Truman's advisers were divided: hawks favored a military escort through the Soviet zone of eastern Germany to reopen land access to West Berlin; doves were ready to abandon the city; still others sought a middle ground.

Clay, a leading hawk, thought that "the chances of such a convoy being met with force, with a subsequent development of hostilities, were small" (Clay 1950:374). Truman's State Department advisers as well as the British and French were less sanguine and feared the uncertainties of escalation. Truman rejected both extremes. But he had no real strategy beyond standing firm and seeking a negotiated solution to the crisis. By offering to negotiate early in the crisis, Truman's approach diverged from the more common tactic of first demonstrating resolve and then moving to cooperative initiatives. That is the period when Soviet coercion escalated most rapidly.

Truman initially saw the airlift, which ultimately proved to be a brilliant means of circumventing Stalin's attempted fait accompli, simply as a necessary stopgap measure while he tried to think of what to do next. "We will have to deal with the situation as it develops," was all that Truman could tell his aides (McCullough 1992:630). By mid-July consideration of the military option was abandoned in favor of combining an expanded airlift with negotiation. With the success of the airlift confirmed by the end of winter, the U.S. negotiating position hardened. By that time Stalin was ready to drop his other substantive demands in return for an end to the counterblockade.

The success of the American strategy was tied to the success of the airlift. It was America's finest hour in the Cold War.

Outcome and Lessons

Soviet Union
In the aftermath of the Berlin Blockade Crisis, the Soviets turned their attention away from Berlin and toward the larger issue of relations with the West. The ideological militancy that began in the fall of 1947 and the confrontation with the West over Germany had failed. The Western alliance had been solidified in NATO, the West remained well entrenched in Berlin, and West Germany was on its way to becoming an independent state. After Stalin's death, Soviet leaders criticized his policy of ideological confrontation during this period and the aggressive strategy that led to the Berlin Blockade and its outcome. Khrushchev in particular argued that Stalin "failed to take into account the realities facing him" and consequently was forced to capitulate (Khrushchev 1974:191–92). But Stalin

would remain in command in the Soviet Union until 1953. Some Western analysts have argued that the Soviets moved to a more peaceful or flexible agenda in their dealings with the West following the blockade crisis (see Adomeit 1982:177; Shulman 1963: chap. 2). Others see an even more rigid policy, with an abandonment of efforts at serious negotiation to resolve differences while avoiding direct confrontations (Taubman 1982: chap. 8). It would be, as Taubman put it (1982:197), "a kind of hunkering down for the long haul" of the Cold War.

United States

American policymakers had cited the Munich precedent as a reason for standing firm in Berlin, and the outcome of the Berlin Blockade Crisis appeared to confirm their judgment. The crisis outcome also reinforced the belief that the way to deal with the Soviets was by leading from strength. Western efforts at negotiation early in the crisis had led only to additional Soviet demands. The airlift, the counterblockade, and Western resolve led to the lifting of the blockade. The Berlin Blockade Crisis reinforced the views that Truman had acquired in response to Soviet actions in Eastern Europe and the Balkans during the two years proceeding the crisis. One must deal with the Soviets "in a manner they could never interpret as weakness" (H. S. Truman 1956:171).

Among Truman's advisers, Secretary of State Dean Acheson would remain most influential in dealing with the Soviets in future crises.[4] The hawkish Acheson returned to serve as the head of Kennedy's task force on strategy during the 1961 Berlin crisis and served as one of Kennedy's advisers during the Cuban Missile Crisis. Acheson (1969:362–63) wrote that the blockade crisis provided a lesson about Soviet diplomacy that was reinforced by Soviet behavior during the 1950s:

> What one may learn from these experiences is that the Soviet authorities are not moved to agreement by negotiation—that is, by a series of mutual concessions calculated to move parties seeking agreement closer to an acceptable one. Theirs is a more primitive form of political method. They cling stubbornly to a position hoping to force an opponent to accept it. When and if action by the opponent demonstrates the Soviet position to be untenable, they hastily abandon it—after asking and having been refused an unwarranted price.

Acheson concluded that the best response to such an approach is to

---

4. Acheson began the crisis as undersecretary of state. When Truman began his first elected term in January 1949, Acheson replaced George Marshall as secretary of state.

stonewall: to stand firm until the Soviets retreat from their attempt at coercion. Acheson's beliefs are consistent with the view of Soviet strategy as a series of probes to discover soft spots in the Western defense, a perspective that Acheson developed at the time he was drafting the Truman Doctrine. Nevertheless, it should be emphasized that prior to the Berlin crisis, the United States had never been engaged in a direct confrontation with the Soviet Union, and neither Truman nor his advisers had any clearly formed views of how to manage a militarized Soviet-American crisis. The blockade crisis experience—the failure of the summer attempts at negotiation and the ultimate success of standing firm in the face of Soviet demands—provided the basis for the Stonewalling influence strategy advocated by Acheson in the next Berlin crisis.

Following two unsettling events that occurred later that year—the communist victory in China and the explosion of the first Soviet atomic bomb—the State Department published National Security Council document 68 (NSC 68) in April 1950. NSC 68 was an American blueprint for the Cold War that asserted that the Soviet Union, an immoral regime driven by Marxist ideology, was out to seek domination of the world through whatever means possible, including a sudden surprise attack on the United States. The American coping strategy was to continue the policy of containment: to "confront the Russians with unalterable counterforce at every point where they show signs of encroaching upon the interests of a peaceful and stable world" (Kennan 1947:581).

Berlin Wall Crisis, 1961

The Intercrisis Period, 1949–61

A dozen years elapsed between the first and second Berlin crises. During that time, important changes occurred in the relationship between the superpowers. The U.S. nuclear monopoly ended; communist regimes became solidly established in Eastern Europe and China; the Western and Eastern blocs were formalized into two competing alliances; the Korean War was fought to a virtual stalemate; and in 1953 Stalin died.

In mid-June 1953, Russian troops were called on to restore order when demonstrations and riots occurred throughout East German cities in the wake of severe food shortages following Sovietization of East German agriculture. The Soviet military intervention on East German leader Walter Ulbricht's behalf effectively tightened the Kremlin's commitment to the East German regime (Ostermann 1994). For its part, the West moved ahead with its plans to rearm West Germany as an independent state and to admit it to NATO in May 1955. Soviet concerns now focused on the potential nuclear armament of Germany and the political and military union of Western Europe. Consequently, Soviet diplomatic initiatives in the late 1950s were directed at obtaining a peace treaty recognizing the territorial status quo for Germany and prohibiting West German access to nuclear weapons. These diplomatic initiatives, however, were received coolly by the West.

Soviet Union

Major shifts in foreign policy frequently follow turnovers in leadership. After Stalin's death, the Soviet leadership's approach to the United States shifted from Stalin's defensive, confrontational stance to the more self-confident and open diplomacy of "peaceful coexistence" enunciated by Malenkov and continued by Khrushchev.

The long-term Soviet goals in Europe had not changed from those sought by Stalin. What had changed in the years between the two Berlin crises was the Soviet regime's view of how it might pursue those goals. Khrushchev did not share Stalin's fear of an American invasion of the USSR; consequently, Khrushchev was willing to undertake bolder initiatives—peaceful as well as coercive—to resolve the German question.

Khrushchev began a diplomatic offensive. The Soviets applied for membership in NATO, and, in an attempt to block the rearming of West Germany, Khrushchev proposed a neutralized and unarmed Germany to act as a buffer between East and West. The West rejected both proposals. Then, during the Twentieth Party Congress, in 1956, Khrushchev surprised his audience by denouncing Stalin's confrontational foreign policy. But when demonstrations against a Soviet puppet government in Hungary turned into a full-scale revolt and the Suez Crisis erupted into war in the Middle East in the fall of 1956, Khrushchev put down the Hungarian revolt with an iron fist and engaged in "rocket-rattling" against British and French intervention in Suez. Then, in the fall of 1957, the Soviets stunned the West by launching a rocket into outer space.

On November 27, 1958, Khrushchev sent his first ultimatum to the Western powers. If an agreement regarding the long-term status of Berlin was not reached within six months, the Soviet Union would sign a separate peace treaty with the German Democratic Republic (GDR). A separate peace treaty with the GDR would end any Soviet responsibility to maintain Western access through the GDR to West Berlin. The Western powers rejected the deadline but did agree to negotiations. The diplomatic time bomb was defused when Khrushchev accepted the Western offer to negotiate and indefinitely extended the ultimatum deadline.

Negotiations among the foreign ministers of the Western powers and the Soviet Union in the spring and summer of 1959 did not yield any significant results, nor did a summit meeting between Eisenhower and Khrushchev that September. Although Eisenhower was willing to admit that the status of West Berlin was "abnormal," the talks produced no substantive progress, and another summit was scheduled to be held in Paris on May 14, 1960.[5] But in early February, Eisenhower stunned the Soviets by publicly indicating a willingness to share American nuclear secrets with the West Germans. By the spring of 1960, it had become clear to the Soviets that the Western powers were not ready to budge on the Berlin question (see Zubok 1993:12–13). When, on May 1, an American U-2 spy plane was shot down over Soviet territory, Khrushchev aborted the Paris summit.

An underlying pattern to Khrushchev's diplomacy was to lead with a strong coercive initiative to demonstrate his resolve, which would be followed by an expressed willingness to negotiate. If negotiations failed, he would return to coercion. Just a month after he issued his 1958 ultimatum on Berlin, the Kremlin informed the United States that Khrushchev would welcome a visit from Vice President Nixon as the prelude to renewed negotiations on Berlin (Zubok 1993:9). When the United States called his bluff on the 1958 ultimatum, Khrushchev retreated in the name of prudence. "We are realists and we will never pursue a gambling policy," Khrushchev said in 1960 (quoted in Adomeit 1982:199). But after watching America's inexperienced young president fail to follow through with the Bay of Pigs invasion, Khrushchev returned to the use of the ultimatum at his Vienna meeting with Kennedy in the spring of 1961.

In sum, leadership changes led to Soviet strategy changes that were observable before the Berlin Wall Crisis. The ideological offensive that preceded the first Berlin crisis was replaced by the policy of peaceful coexistence. Khrushchev's diplomacy was both more forthcoming and more assertive than Stalin's as well as less consistent in its application. Khrushchev also attempted to avoid what he perceived to be the twin weaknesses in Stalin's diplomacy: an excessive reliance on military coercion and an unreasonable fear of a military response from the West.

United States

American leadership changed with the election of Dwight Eisenhower in 1952, but the policy of containment remained in place. Conciliatory moves by the Soviet regime, such as those during the transition after Stalin's

---

5. See Kissinger (1994:580–82) for a discussion of the American position on the issue of the "abnormality" of West Berlin. Kissinger argues that after Camp David, Eisenhower's fallback position of a "guaranteed" free city differed from Khrushchev's only in labeling.

death, were interpreted as signs of Soviet weakness that should be exploited with additional pressure from the West.

Despite the Eisenhower administration's rhetoric about "rolling back" communism in Eastern Europe, the United States reacted passively when Soviet tanks were sent to put down an anti-Soviet revolution in Hungary in the fall of 1956. The failed Hungarian uprising was followed almost immediately by a diplomatic crisis in Western relations, when the United States found itself standing alongside the Soviet Union in condemning Britain and France for their intervention in Suez (see chap. 4). Fearing additional Soviet gains in the Middle East, Eisenhower pledged in 1957 to send American troops to assist any Middle Eastern country requesting help against communist aggression. The next year, American forces were sent to Lebanon as a show of force.

John F. Kennedy replaced Eisenhower as president in 1961. Kennedy's first major foreign policy action was a disaster—the Bay of Pigs invasion of Cuba in April of that year. The invasion was attempted by Cuban émigrés with the clandestine training and support of the United States. When the invasion turned into a fiasco, Kennedy aborted the planned American air support and assumed full responsibility for the failure. Six weeks later he held his first summit with Khrushchev in Vienna.

When one compares the 1961 bargaining strategy of the Kennedy administration with that of the Truman administration in 1948, the most notable difference is the higher degree of flexibility in Kennedy's approach to the Soviets. Kennedy was ready to seek diplomatic means to attempt to resolve Soviet-American differences in Europe, even if doing so meant some changes in the status of West Berlin and greater recognition to the GDR. One of his first foreign policy moves was to send Khrushchev a personal note suggesting a summit meeting to discuss the Berlin issue.

Kennedy's belief in pursuing diplomatic solutions to East-West problems paralleled Khrushchev's move away from Stalin's purely military approach. Kennedy sought to place less emphasis on the essentially military approach identified with containment in favor of direct negotiations with the Soviets (Kissinger 1994:585). But, like Khrushchev, Kennedy firmly believed in negotiating from strength. Ten days before the Vienna summit meeting with Khrushchev, he asked the Congress for a major increase in American defense spending.

Kennedy saw the Vienna summit as an opportunity to open a dialogue with Khrushchev on Soviet-American relations more generally and on German issues in particular. In a press conference on the eve of the Vienna meeting, Kennedy remarked on how, in studying the origins of World War I, he was impressed by the "serious miscalculations which were made by the leaders on both sides" (*New York Times,* June 3, 1961:1). But when Kennedy brought up the subject during the Vienna summit, Khrushchev snapped back, "We don't make mistakes. . . . We will not make war by mistake" (Chang and Kornbluh 1992:10–13). The exchange was typical of the ill-fated summit.

Crisis Structure

Soviet Union

Perceptions of American Intentions.   The major change between 1948 and 1961 in the official Soviet view of its relationship with the United States was the Soviet belief in the idea of peaceful coexistence, the possibility of continuing the socialist-capitalist competition without war between the superpowers (Khrushchev 1959). Khrushchev did not assume that U.S. hostility toward the Soviet Union had abated but rather that the "correlation of forces" now made the costs of an all-out war virtually unthinkable for sober-minded policymakers on both sides. More specifically, Khrushchev did not believe that the West would risk war to defend its access to West Berlin (Khrushchev 1970:458; Zubok 1993:18). As he prepared the groundwork for his 1961 ultimatum, Khrushchev assured the East German leader, Walter Ulbricht, that the West would not start a war over a separate Soviet peace treaty with the GDR. Therefore, the Soviet Union was ready to work with the GDR to use coercive means of "gradually crowding out the Western powers from West Berlin, but without war" (Zubok 1993:14–15).

Khrushchev's belief regarding the West's desire to avoid war was strengthened by what he perceived to be prior successes in using threats against the West, particularly his rocket-rattling during the Suez crisis in 1956 and his veiled threat to retaliate with a move against West Berlin if the United States had attacked Cuba during the Bay of Pigs operation in 1961 (Khrushchev 1970:436).[6] Khrushchev also was convinced that the West could be persuaded to compromise on the Berlin issue rather than have to contend with the consequences of a Soviet–East German peace treaty. Zubok (1993:7) suggests that Khrushchev may have concluded from the Taiwan Straits Crisis of 1958 that since the United States, when under pressure, resorted to a "two Chinas" policy, it might be willing under similar circumstances to accept a "two Germanys" policy as well.

---

6. Soviet threats were not the major reasons for the Western decisions to abort planned interventions in either instance. The British and French found themselves alone diplomatically in 1956, with even the United States opposing their intervention. The Bay of Pigs invasion was such a complete failure from the start that the planned American air support would have been useless.

Soviet Interests. The conclusion of a German peace settlement was
Khrushchev's first priority (see Zubok 1993). The Soviets feared the
nuclear armament of a revanchist West Germany, and by the late-1950s
the Soviet leadership was becoming alarmed by the GDR's economic
decline. As an island of Western freedom and prosperity in the heart of
East Germany, West Berlin was a continuing ideological embarrassment
to the GDR and the Soviet Union. As a lure to skilled workers and technicians to migrate to the West, it was draining the lifeblood of the already
anemic GDR economy. Increasing West German economic influence
could lead to the complete collapse of the GDR economy. These problems
could be eliminated by forcing the Western powers from Berlin. It was not
necessary for Berlin to fall under Soviet control; it would be enough that it
be declared a neutral "free city" without a direct link to the West. Ending
the "abnormal" situation in West Berlin would open the door for a peace
treaty that would lead to Western recognition of East Germany and guarantee the postwar boundaries dividing Europe into Soviet and Western
spheres of influence.]A related objective was to secure a negotiated agreement that would make it impossible for the West German Bundeswehr to
acquire nuclear weapons.

Another factor that may have influenced Khrushchev was the deterioration of the Soviet-Chinese relationship. Fear of appearing soft in the
eyes of his increasingly critical Chinese comrades may have provided
added encouragement to his decision to issue the ultimatum to Kennedy in
the spring of 1961.

Soviet Capabilities. In 1961 as in 1948, the Soviets enjoyed local conventional military superiority. Western defense forces relied heavily on a
nuclear response, but now the Soviets also had nuclear arms. The United
States enjoyed strategic superiority, but the Soviets had made dramatic
gains, particularly in their delivery capabilities since the successful launching of their Sputnik rocket into space in 1957. Moreover, Khrushchev was
aware of the existential deterrent effect of the costs of nuclear war, regardless of which side emerged as the ultimate military victor. Those costs
would be particularly high for America's European allies. Khrushchev was
delighted when West Germany's prime minister, Konrad Adenauer, noted
that in the event of nuclear war, his country would be the first to perish
(Khrushchev 1970:569). One potential consequence of the mutual awareness of the catastrophic consequences of a nuclear war is that it could raise
the "provocation threshold," thereby allowing more room for coercive tactics short of war. The change in the nuclear correlation of forces led
Khrushchev to believe that he had a greater range of coercive options than
Stalin had in the 1948 crisis.

United States

Perceptions of Soviet Intentions.   Following the Vienna summit, Kennedy formed a task force to determine Khrushchev's intentions and to devise a strategy for dealing with the ultimatum. Acheson headed the task force. Acheson, along with other blockade veterans, established a direct link to the American experience during the Berlin Blockade Crisis. The Kennedy foreign-policy team was divided between hawkish cold warriors, such as Acheson, Paul Nitze, and Clay, and the more dovish views of Ambassador Llewellyn Thompson, Averill Harriman, and Charles Bohlen. Newcomers in the administration, such as Secretary of State Dean Rusk, Undersecretary for European Affairs George Ball, and United Nations Ambassador Adlai Stevenson, were more dovish.

Acheson interpreted Khrushchev's latest ultimatum as an attempt to test American resolve and, by forcing the West to retreat from its commitment to Berlin, to shift the global balance of power (Schlesinger 1965:381). The difference between the two crises, according to Acheson, lay in the changed Soviet view of the capabilities of the two sides. Khrushchev, Acheson's task force concluded, had dared to precipitate the crisis at the Vienna meeting only because the Soviet fear of nuclear war had declined (Schlesinger 1965:381–82).

American Interests.   Kennedy agreed with Acheson's interpretation of the American interests at stake. "If we don't meet our commitments in Berlin, it will mean the destruction of NATO and a dangerous situation for the whole world. All Europe is at stake in West Berlin" (Kennedy, quoted in Schlesinger 1965:379–80). Put in those terms, there was no doubt that the fate of West Berlin was viewed as a vital security interest.

American Capabilities.   Despite campaigning for president on an alleged nuclear "missile gap" favoring the Soviet Union, Kennedy discovered on assuming office that the United States enjoyed a substantial strategic advantage over the Soviets. Nevertheless, the Soviets held a significant advantage in local conventional forces. Kennedy realized, as had Truman before him, that Berlin was militarily indefensible in the face of a direct Soviet attack. American troops in Berlin were nothing more than hostages to guarantee the American commitment to respond forcefully to any attack.

The presence of nuclear arms on both sides was the difference between 1961 and 1948. The stakes would have to be as high as Kennedy had described them for the United States to risk the consequences of a nuclear war. The other substantive element that had changed was the status of Germany itself. West and East Germany were now both independent states. Western Berlin's "abnormal" status in East Germany already had been the subject of a possible compromise by Eisenhower. As he took office,

Kennedy was ready to attempt a more flexible diplomatic strategy to resolve the Berlin and Germany questions once and for all. Khrushchev's ultimatum at the Vienna meeting in June, however, created a new situation.

Crisis Behavior

The precipitant to the Berlin Wall crisis occurred on June 4, 1961, during the Vienna summit. Khrushchev demanded a German peace treaty that would declare Berlin a free city. If the outstanding German issues were not settled by the end of the year, the Soviet Union would sign a separate peace treaty with East Germany. To drive home the seriousness of his intent, Khrushchev made the ultimatum public on June 15. On June 21 he announced that the Soviets would begin new nuclear tests. Kennedy stated at a June 28 press conference that he viewed the Soviet moves as an attempt to drive the West out of Berlin, but he gave no indication of the U.S. intended response. On the same day, the Kremlin held an air show to demonstrate the Soviets' newest military advances, and four days later Khrushchev approved additional defense appropriations.

The official American response to the ultimatum did not come until July 25, when Kennedy declared that the United States was determined to defend West Berlin against any unilateral Soviet action. To back up his warning, he asked Congress to approve new defense appropriations. Khrushchev reacted defiantly: "We will respond to your war in kind," he told U.S. representative John McCloy (Zubok 1993:21). Then, at a meeting of Warsaw Pact leaders at the beginning of August, Khrushchev appeared to have second thoughts. He warned his allies of a dangerous new situation in the United States. Kennedy was losing control; the government was unstable: "Hence everything is possible in the United States. War is also possible. . . . When our 'friend' Dulles was alive, there was more stability. . . . Dulles would reach the brink, as he put it himself, but he would never leap over the brink, and he still retained his credibility" (Zubok 1993:21–22). Khrushchev worried aloud that hawkish elements in the United States might push the inexperienced president into war. Shortly after the conference, however, Khrushchev received a KGB report indicating that the Western powers were not willing to risk war over Berlin (Zubok 1993:24).

On August 9, Khrushchev responded more moderately to Kennedy's speech by welcoming a peaceful solution to the crisis, provided that it included a German peace treaty. But at the same time, Khrushchev announced that a resumption of nuclear tests would take place at the end of the month.

Throughout the spring and early summer of 1961, the GDR moved to increase its control over access between the western and eastern sectors of Berlin. Following a meeting of socialist bloc leaders in August, the participants declared that the flow of refugees from the GDR to West Berlin would have to be stopped to halt the accelerating deterioration of the GDR economy. On the same day, August 13, construction began on the wall separating East and West Berlin. On the next day the GDR closed the Brandenburg Gate and severed telephone and telegraph communication between the east and west sectors of Berlin. The immediate U.S. response was muted, but four days later Kennedy ordered an increase in the size of the U.S. garrison in West Berlin and dispatched Vice President Lyndon Baines Johnson and General Clay to West Berlin to underline the American determination to defend the city.

On August 23, the GDR further tightened access between the two sectors of Berlin. That same day a Soviet threat to interrupt air access to the city was met by a show of force by the United States. A GDR decree prohibiting movement to within 100 meters of the wall on either side was met by the movement of Western forces to the edge of the wall. Khrushchev continued publicly to push for negotiations on his terms. Then, on September 5, Khrushchev sent a private message to Kennedy indicating the Soviet leader's desire to conclude a peace treaty that would not damage U.S. prestige and would guarantee a free Berlin. Meetings between the two sides began on September 21 and continued through early October. No real substantive progress was made, but, on October 17, Khrushchev withdrew the ultimatum.

The crisis appeared to be over; instead, it flared up briefly a few days later over a minor incident that led to a Soviet misperception of American intentions. On October 22, when the GDR attempted to block passage of a U.S. official through Checkpoint Charlie, the United States sent a tank escort to the wall. The procedure was repeated over the next few days. Then, on October 27, in response to an erroneous intelligence report indicating that the United States was preparing to storm the wall, the Soviets sent their own tanks rumbling to the other side of the border, within 100 yards of the Americans (see Zubok 1993:24). The confrontation lasted 16 hours, with the Soviets tanks withdrawing on the morning of October 28, after Kennedy assured Khrushchev that the United States did not intend to storm the wall. On November 9, 1961, a vague agreement was reached for a formula for future negotiations to ultimately settle the German question. It would be another 14 years before a German peace treaty was signed. The wall remained in place for 28 years.

Patterns of Behavior

The time series of the mix of weighted Western and Soviet actions over the course of the crisis, which appears in figure 3.2, provides a useful graphical description of the evolution of the crisis.[7]

The modest upward trend in Soviet hostility during the month following Khrushchev's ultimatum reflects the Soviet shows of force and Khrushchev's public statements. During the same period the United States was relatively inactive. The hostile actions by both sides rapidly increased in the weeks immediately following Kennedy's July 25 speech. The pattern reflects the U.S. determination to back up Kennedy's verbal threats with physical shows of force as well as the Soviet Union's defiant reaction to Kennedy's threat. The crisis continued to escalate following the beginning of the construction of the wall on August 13. Khrushchev moved to more accommodative diplomacy when he agreed to negotiations in early September, as the United States and its allies continued their shows of force. The escalation subsided by early October and then flared up briefly with the confrontation at the wall in late October.

In the narrative summary above, and in the extant qualitative analyses of the 1961 crisis, the construction of the wall is seen as the key turning point. After Kennedy's July 25 speech, Khrushchev recognized that Kennedy could not be coerced into yielding, so Khrushchev turned to the wall as a relatively low risk means of resolving the immediate crisis in East Germany. The pattern in figure 3.2, however, illustrates the lasting escalatory effects of U.S. decisions to back up its July 25 threat as well as the escalation immediately following the wall's construction. Khrushchev responded to Kennedy's July 25 address by announcing a number of Soviet initiatives, including nuclear tests that would take place later in the month. The pattern illustrates a problem in the use of coercive influence tactics—that is, the ripple effect of one coercive action that sets off a tit-for-tat sequence of escalatory moves on both sides as each side attempts to demonstrate its resolve.

But the 1961 Berlin crisis did not escalate out of control. When the larger sample of crises in the appendix is used as a benchmark, the Berlin Wall Crisis ranks slightly above the median (fourteenth out of 35) on all three escalation measures, but the scores are well below those for the Berlin Blockade Crisis (table 3.1).

---

7. Actions taken by the NATO allies together are included in the calculation of U.S. actions, and actions taken by East Germany are included along with Soviet actions. Each of the two parties on either side also serve as targets of actions by each the two parties on the other side.

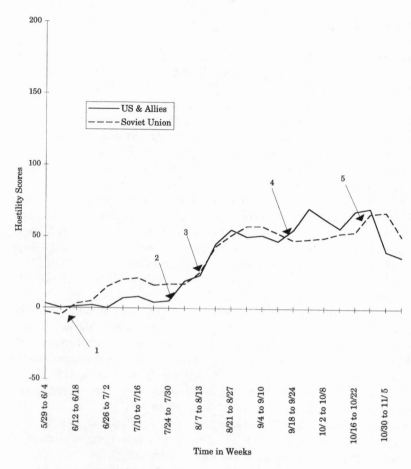

Fig. 3.2. Berlin Wall, 1961
Key dates are indicated with arrows: (1) 6/4: Soviet ultimatum; (2) 7/25: United States expresses determination to defend Berlin; (3) 8/13: construction of wall begins; (4) 9/21: United States and Soviet Union begin negotiations; (5) 10/27: border confrontation.

The reciprocity scores for the Berlin Wall Crisis, which appear in table 3.2, are intriguing. When the Berlin Wall crisis is added to the larger sample of 34 crises, it ranks fifth on the distance measure, indicating that the two sides matched each other in the magnitude of hostility over the course of the crisis. But, the direction measure, which indicates the degree to which the parties are moving toward more accommodative or more coercive bargaining at the same time, ranks twenty-seventh—that is, near the bottom of the sample. As one side was moving toward more cooperative behavior, the other was becoming more conflictual. In fact, while the distance score for the Berlin Wall Crisis (2.10) is much lower than that for the Berlin Blockade Crisis (57.43), the direction score (7.67) for the wall crisis is higher than that for the blockade crisis (6.80). The pattern does not change appreciably if cooperative and conflictive actions are treated separately, with individual distance and direction scores calculated for each.

Figure 3.2 contains several crossover points, which indicate when the magnitude of hostility for one side passes that of the other. In some instances these points occur when one party is moving toward more accommodative behavior as the mix of behavior for the other is becoming more conflictual. The two most intriguing crossover points in the Berlin Wall Crisis occur at the end of August, when an escalation in coercive actions by the Soviet side occurred in conjunction with a modest decline in hostility by the West, and in mid-September, when the two positions were reversed.

The pattern in late August may be explained partly by the implementation of decisions made earlier in the month, particularly the Soviet nuclear tests and military maneuvers that were planned earlier but were conducted during that period. But the pattern also reflects actions by the GDR, which called up more troops and increased the harassment of Western officials crossing the border. Perhaps most significant, Khrushchev restated his determination to sign a peace treaty with East Germany without offering any room for compromise with the West. These actions appear to be Khrushchev's last concerted efforts at coercing the West into negotiations on his terms. The timing is significant because the escalation in coercive actions came at a time when it was clear that the West did not intend to challenge the wall. Khrushchev may have interpreted the U.S. failure to challenge his fait accompli as an indication of weak resolve that could be exploited through added coercion. The wall, after all, was a fallback position; Khrushchev still held out hope of gaining a peace treaty recognizing the current division of Europe.

The crossover resulting from the increase in coercive actions by the West, conversely, came in late September, as serious negotiations finally were underway. On September 24, the United States increased autobahn patrols across East Germany, and Kennedy asserted that he would not hesitate to use nuclear weapons to defend West Berlin. The demonstrated firmness is consistent with Kennedy's expressed belief in negotiating from strength. That view could only be reinforced by the events that had occurred in the months since Kennedy's conciliatory overtures on Berlin at the June summit meeting in Vienna.

A comparison of the patterns of behavior in the two Berlin crises yields some interesting similarities. The Soviet Union challenged the status quo and took the lead in escalating both crises, which quickly became deadlocked. But the differences are more striking. The Berlin Blockade escalated to a much higher magnitude of hostility and remained deadlocked at that level far longer than the Berlin Wall Crisis. The 1961 crisis was less intense, less severe, and lasted only half as long as the Berlin Blockade Crisis.

Both Kennedy and Khrushchev placed greater stock in negotiation than did their predecessors, and their bargaining during the course of the Berlin Wall Crisis reflects those beliefs. During the Berlin Blockade Crisis, there were 42 days of negotiations during the 427 days of the crisis; the parties were engaged in negotiations roughly 10 percent of the time. During the 1961 crisis, there were 39 days of negotiation in a crisis that lasted 165 days; the two sides were negotiating 24 percent of the time. The negotiations that took place during the 1961 crisis also took place at a higher diplomatic level, including direct communications between Kennedy and Khrushchev.

Influence Strategies

The operational categorization of influence strategies classifies the overall Soviet influence strategy as Cautious Bullying, and the U.S. influence strategy as Reciprocating. These are the same influence strategies identified for the two sides in the Berlin Blockade Crisis. There are, however, some interesting differences between the two cases.

Soviet Union

In the late 1950s, the sudden swings from accommodation to attempts at coercion and back again in Soviet policy over Berlin and Germany gave the appearance of a Trial and Error influence strategy. Khrushchev would announce a deadline for a German settlement only to retreat and move to negotiation when confronted with stiffened Western resolve. Then, when negotiations became stalemated, he would turn to another attempt at coercion. Khrushchev openly criticized Stalin for being too inflexible and distrustful of the West. But Khrushchev's two-handed approach to the United States probably combined greater optimism regarding the possibilities of achieving a negotiated settlement on Berlin with a fear that too much reasonableness might be interpreted as a sign of weakness, as Taubman (1982:234) has argued.

Despite the urgings of some of his advisers to attempt to pursue a dialogue with Kennedy, Khrushchev was convinced that he could pressure the American president into yielding concessions on Berlin (Zubok and

Pleshakov 1996:242–43). The openness of the threat, which the Soviets published, coupled with a new ultimatum placed the Soviet reputation for resolve on the line in a way that Stalin avoided when he announced that "technical difficulties" necessitated the blockade in 1948.

Following the ultimatum, the Soviets pursued an escalating coercive strategy. Like Stalin, Khrushchev's objective was to coerce the West into accepting his terms. When Khrushchev attempted his own fait accompli in Berlin, he proceeded with caution comparable to that of Stalin. The construction of the wall, as the early phases of Stalin's blockade, began slowly, as the Soviets tested the Western response.

Khrushchev avoided pushing the West into a situation where its reputation for resolve would be tested directly. His comments on the Soviet decision to back away from the tank confrontation at the wall in late October are revealing:

> They had taken the initiative in moving up to the border in the first place and therefore they would, so to say, have been in a difficult moral position if we forced them to turn their backs on the barrels of our cannons. Therefore we decided that at this point we should take the initiative ourselves and give the Americans an opportunity to pull back from the border once the threat of our tanks had been removed. (Khrushchev 1970:460)

What Khrushchev refers to as a "difficult moral position" is the threat to Kennedy's reputation for resolve. The statement becomes particularly interesting in light of Khrushchev's strategy in the Cuban Missile Crisis.

United States

Khrushchev's bullying at Vienna reinforced the hawkish side of Kennedy's concern with avoiding miscalculation. It would be necessary to clearly demonstrate American resolve before attempting any future negotiations with Khrushchev (see Schick 1971:144; Slusser 1973:24).

The influence strategy recommended by Acheson's task force was a replay of the first Berlin crisis: Stonewall all Soviet demands and, if necessary, mount an airlift (Schlesinger 1965:381–82). Others in the Kennedy administration, such as Rusk and Stevenson, favored negotiations. Kennedy chose a middle ground. He would seek a negotiated settlement but would do so only after the United States and its Western allies had demonstrated their resolve through a military show of strength. Kennedy's bargaining is consistent with that of a Reciprocating influence strategy: after demonstrating firmness, the actor responds in a tit-for-tat manner to both coercive and accommodative actions by the other party while indicating flexibility by offering to negotiate.

The wall created a dilemma for this strategy because it shifted the initiative back to the United States. From a legal perspective the wall challenged the status quo, as it violated the right of free movement throughout Berlin, but it did not affect Western access to West Berlin through East Germany. The White House's reaction to the wall was partly relief, because it ended the refugee problem that threatened to propel the crisis to war (Beschloss 1991:310–12; Schick 1971:167). But by not challenging the wall's construction, the United States weakened its reputation for resolve. The United States used shows of force to demonstrate its firmness with regard to any additional Soviet moves that might threaten Western access to Berlin but acquiesced in accepting the restriction of movement by German civilians between the two sectors of Berlin.

Outcome and Lessons

The Berlin Wall Crisis ended in a stalemate. Although Kennedy agreed to seek a settlement of the German issues in future negotiations, the parties still had not agreed on a formula. From the Soviet perspective, the wall ended the immediate threat to the GDR's health, but Khrushchev failed to achieve his major objectives: the end of the Western presence in Berlin and a German settlement that would legitimize the status quo in Europe and prevent the nuclear armament of West Germany. The construction of the wall to keep Germans from fleeing the socialist regime in East Germany also became a long-term ideological embarrassment to the Soviet Union. Khrushchev later described the outcome of the crisis as a "material" but not a "moral" victory (Khrushchev 1970:507–8).

The United States was able to maintain the status of West Berlin in the face of another Soviet attempt at coercion. But American acquiescence in the construction of the wall hurt Kennedy's reputation for resolve, and the presence of the wall weakened morale in West Germany.

I have argued elsewhere (Leng 1983) that national leaders are likely to draw superficial lessons from their experiences in crises and that they are predisposed to view the crisis outcome as a consequence of the influence strategies and tactics that they employed. That tendency is demonstrated by the two sides in the early phase of the Cuban Missile Crisis, which occurred less than a year after the Berlin Wall Crisis.

Soviet Union
There is no evidence that Khrushchev changed his basic beliefs about the Soviet-American relationship as a result of the Berlin Wall Crisis, but

there are indications of changes in his views regarding tactics. During the course of the crisis and in his remarks shortly thereafter, Khrushchev displayed a new sensitivity to Kennedy's concern with his reputation for resolve and the consequent risks associated with pushing the American president too far. The tone of Khrushchev's remarks following Kennedy's July 25 threat and after the late October confrontation contradicts the Soviet leader's earlier view that Stalin was guilty of overestimating the risks of war in a confrontation with the United States. Khrushchev's remarks were couched in terms of Kennedy's ability to withstand the pressures of hawkish elements, most notably the Pentagon and the CIA, but they show an awareness of the dangers associated with the loss of control in an escalating crisis.

Two American administrations now had stood firm in the face of Khrushchev's ultimatums and, in the Berlin Wall Crisis, displays of military force. What the Soviets did manage to achieve in the Berlin Wall crisis came through unilateral action in the form of a fait accompli. It has been argued that the success of the fait accompli was the principal lesson that Khrushchev drew from the 1961 crisis, a lesson that he attempted to apply in Cuba less than a year later (see Adomeit 1982: 303).

United States

Kennedy's early hopes of resolving Soviet-American issues through bilateral negotiations were dampened by his experience with Khrushchev in Vienna and the subsequent crisis. As for dealing with the Soviet leader in a crisis, Khrushchev's behavior during the crisis reinforced each side of Kennedy's dual perspective on crisis bargaining: the importance of demonstrating firmness to avoid being bullied, and the importance of avoiding actions that might cause misperceptions of aggressive intentions. Both imperatives required open communication between the two sides. Khrushchev's withdrawal of the ultimatum deadline in September confirmed the wisdom of the first imperative; the removal of Soviet tanks from the Wall in October, following personal reassurances from Kennedy, confirmed the second imperative.

Shortly after the 1961 crisis, Kennedy confided to an adviser that the time might come when it would be necessary to run "the supreme risk to convince Khrushchev that conciliation did not mean humiliation" (Schlesinger 1965:391). Conversely, Khrushchev's attempts at verbal bullying and his unpredictability reinforced the view among Kennedy and his advisers that the Soviet leader was a loose cannon with whom communications would have to be handled with care (Blight and Welch 1989:34).

Cuban Missile Crisis, 1962

Intercrisis Period, 1961–62

The tension that existed during the Berlin Wall Crisis subsided, but the mutual hostility and distrust did not. Each government warily eyed the other as it looked for ways to gain a strategic advantage. During the 11 months between the two crises, there was no change in the relationship between the two sides, only in the arena in which the conflict would be resumed.

Berlin remained at the top of the foreign-policy agenda for both superpowers in the winter and spring of 1962. The negotiations that had been agreed on in November began in early January, stalemated, and ended in early March with military demonstrations by both sides. The Soviets resumed their harassment of Western flights in and out of Berlin. In late July, Khrushchev issued another threat to sign a separate Soviet–East German peace treaty.

The United States also had been working to increase the diplomatic and economic isolation of the socialist Castro regime in Cuba. In January, under the prodding of the United States, the Organization of American States expelled Cuba, instituted an arms embargo, and agreed to take collective action should Cuba threaten any state in the hemisphere. An American trade embargo followed. Under the direction of the president's brother, Attorney General Robert Kennedy, planning also continued for a clandestine attempt to assassinate Castro.

Since the Bay of Pigs invasion in 1961, the Soviet Union had stepped up its military assistance to Cuba. In early August the CIA warned Kennedy that the Soviets might be placing medium-range missiles in Cuba, and by the end of the month it became clear that Soviet technicians were building coastal and air defense systems in Cuba. The CIA did not know that in late May 1962 the Soviet politburo had approved Operation Anadyr, a plan to secretly install ground-to-ground medium-range ballistic missiles (MRBM) and intermediate-range ballistic missiles (IRBM) in Cuba. Both weapons carried nuclear warheads.[8]

When Robert Kennedy met with Soviet Ambassador Anatoly Dobrynin on September 4, Dobrynin assured Kennedy that no ground-to-ground or offensive missiles would be placed in Cuba. President Kennedy nevertheless publicly warned the Soviets of the consequences of doing so. The Soviets responded, a week later, by warning the United States that any

---

8. When Kennedy issued his September 4 warning, there already were 36 SS-4 MRBMs and 24 SS-5 IRBMs in Cuba, along with their nuclear warheads. MRBMs have a range of approximately 1,110 miles; IRBMs have a range of more than 2,000 miles.

attempt to interfere with Soviet ships bound for Cuba or a United States attack on Cuba itself could lead to nuclear war. Kennedy warned the Soviets on September 13 that the United States would do "whatever must be done to protect its own security and that of its allies" if the Soviets were to attempt to place offensive missiles in Cuba (U.S. Department of State 1962:482). One month later, on October 14, an American U-2 flight over Cuba yielded photos of the Soviet offensive missile installations.

Crisis Structure

Soviet Union
Perceptions of American Intentions. Khrushchev publicly ridiculed the Monroe Doctrine as irrelevant to contemporary international politics, but he recognized that the United States was not likely to reconcile itself to the long-term presence of a socialist Cuba with revolutionary hemispheric ambitions. "Everyone agreed that America would not leave Cuba alone unless we did something" (Khrushchev 1970:492). But if Kennedy was unwilling to risk attacking Cuba in support of the Bay of Pigs operation in 1961, why would he risk a nuclear war over the placement of missiles in Cuba in 1962? Khrushchev's optimism regarding the American reaction was not shared by some of his most senior advisers, including his first deputy, Anastas Mikoyan, and his foreign minister, Andrei Gromyko (Zubok and Pleshakov 1996:261). But Khrushchev was firmly in command in the Kremlin in the spring of 1962 and confident of his own judgments.

Khrushchev probably underestimated the degree of threat that the missiles would pose in the minds of the Americans, who were accustomed to enjoying unchallenged hegemony within the Western Hemisphere. European nations, like the Soviet Union, had become accustomed to living in close proximity to hostile adversaries over centuries. The Soviets had acquiesced when the United States placed missiles in Turkey; Khrushchev could not understand why the United States would risk nuclear war over missiles in Cuba. Failure to perceive this difference also may have contributed to Khrushchev's failure to perceive the harm to Kennedy's reputation, both at home and among American allies, that would come from the unchallenged installation of the missiles.

Soviet Interests. A number of reasons have been put forward to explain the Soviet desire to place missiles in Cuba: to defend the Castro regime, to reduce the missile gap with the United States, to barter for the removal of American missiles from Turkey, to pressure the United States to reach a Berlin settlement, to increase Soviet prestige, to improve the Soviet image of power vis-à-vis the United States, and to strengthen

Khrushchev's position in the face of challenges from hard-liners within the Kremlin (Blight and Welch 1989:117). But, according to Soviet analysts and Khrushchev's own account, the first two reasons were the most important: to defend Cuba and to improve the strategic military balance (Khrushchev 1970:493–96; Zubok and Pleshakov 1996:260–61). These more tangible interests were tied to a reputational interest in the continuing ideological and strategic rivalry with the United States. It was not a question just of the defense of the Cuban revolution but also of the credibility of the Soviet Union's ability to protect its Cuban ally. The nuclear missile defenses in Cuba would deter another American invasion, preserve the Cuban revolution, and strengthen the credibility of Soviet power.

Capabilities. American officials publicly stated in October 1961 that there was a significant strategic missile gap that favored the United States. The numerical balance was roughly 5,000 to 300 in favor of the United States, or about 17 to 1. Placing the missiles in Cuba would not close the gap but would increase the number of Soviet warheads that could reach American targets.[9] The presence of Soviet missiles in Cuba would change the U.S. perception of its vulnerability, which would reduce the likelihood of an American preemptive nuclear attack.

With regard to the Cuban crisis itself, the Soviets had to be well aware of the local advantage that the United States enjoyed with its conventional naval forces in the Caribbean as well as that afforded by ground and air forces within easy striking distance. The Soviets could retaliate with military action in Berlin, where they enjoyed a significant advantage in conventional forces, but to do so would risk all-out war. Unless and until the missiles were operational, the Soviet Union would be at a significant military disadvantage in the event of a superpower crisis.

United States
Perceptions of Soviet Intentions.   Prior to the discovery of the missile sites on October 14, President Kennedy and his advisers assumed that the Soviets, well aware of the strategic and local balance of forces, would not attempt to install offensive missiles in Cuba. Moreover, the administration assumed that the Soviets fully understood Kennedy's September warnings against placing offensive ground-to-ground weapons in Cuba (Blight and Welch 1989:302–3). When Republican congressmen attacked the administration in September for ignoring alleged evidence of Soviet missile emplacements in Cuba, the Kennedy administration dismissed the charges as campaign rhetoric. As late as October 14, the day the CIA discovered

---

9. The Kennedy administration estimated that the planned 64 medium- and intermediate-range missiles would double the Soviet nuclear striking capacity against the United States (Schlesinger 1965:796).

the missile sites, National Security Adviser McGeorge Bundy publicly stated that he doubted that the Soviets would try to place offensive nuclear weapons in Cuba.

When the missiles were discovered, President Kennedy formed an ad hoc advisory group consisting of key members of the cabinet, presidential advisers, and foreign policy advisers from previous administrations. When the group, which became known as ExComm, for the Executive Committee of the National Security Council, first met on October 16, Kennedy expressed his stunned bewilderment: "why is it—can any Russian expert tell us—why they . . . ? After all, Khrushchev demonstrated a sense of caution over Berlin" (May and Zelikow 1997:99). The president's principal speechwriter, Theodore Sorensen, later acknowledged, "None of us knew. We could only speculate about what Khrushchev was up to" (Blight and Welch 1989:118). Within a few days Kennedy became convinced that the missile installations were designed to increase Soviet prestige and to place pressure on Berlin (May and Zelikow 1997:177).

American Interests. Kennedy and his advisers did not consider the missile emplacements a significant threat to the American strategic advantage (May and Zelikow 1997:90–99). The more serious threat was to the Kennedy administration's reputation for resolve, particularly after the president's explicit September warnings that he would not permit the installation of offensive missiles in Cuba. Kennedy summed up that view on October 16: "Last month I said we weren't going to [allow it]. Last month I should have said I don't care. But when we said we're *not* going to, and then they go ahead and do it, and then we do nothing, then I would think that our risks increase" (May and Zelikow 1997:92).

There was no doubt that the first priority for the United States was the removal of the missile installations and the MRBMs and IRBMs. The second priority was to do so without allowing the crisis to escalate to a nuclear war. If there were some hawks who did not fear the possibility of nuclear war, either through an accident or miscalculation leading to a preemptive strike, Kennedy was not among them (see May and Zelikow 1997:165–66, 195). The third priority was to achieve the removal of the missiles without yielding concessions that would weaken President Kennedy's reputation for resolve in dealing with the Soviet Union.

Capabilities. As noted earlier, the United States enjoyed a significant advantage in strategic nuclear weapons; however, members of the ExComm have subsequently stated that the American nuclear advantage never entered into their thinking. Rather, American policymakers considered the advantage in conventional forces, particularly the immediately deployable naval forces, the decisive element should hostilities occur (Rusk et al. 1982:85).

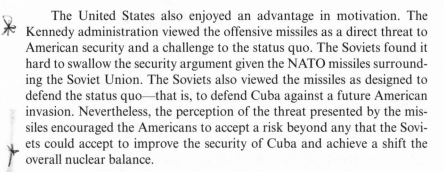

The United States also enjoyed an advantage in motivation. The Kennedy administration viewed the offensive missiles as a direct threat to American security and a challenge to the status quo. The Soviets found it hard to swallow the security argument given the NATO missiles surrounding the Soviet Union. The Soviets also viewed the missiles as designed to defend the status quo—that is, to defend Cuba against a future American invasion. Nevertheless, the perception of the threat presented by the missiles encouraged the Americans to accept a risk beyond any that the Soviets could accept to improve the security of Cuba and achieve a shift the overall nuclear balance.

Crisis Behavior

Unaware that the missile sites had been discovered, the Soviets continued to deny any intention of placing offensive missiles in Cuba. In meetings with Kennedy and later with Secretary of State Rusk on October 18, Soviet Foreign Minister Gromyko continued to insist that the Soviet actions in Cuba were purely defensive. Despite allusions by Rusk to changes in Cuba "since July" that had seriously complicated the situation, Gromyko assumed that the United States was unaware of the Soviet designs for the ground-to-ground missiles (Gromyko 1995:67).

On October 22, Kennedy addressed the nation on television. He reported the discovery of the missiles and announced plans to institute the blockade, which was labeled a "quarantine" to avoid direct comparisons to Stalin's 1948 blockade of Berlin (May and Zelikow 1997:209). "All ships of any kind bound for Cuba from whatever nation or port will if found to contain cargoes of offensive weapons, be turned back. . . . We are not at this time denying the necessities of life as the Soviets attempted to do in their Berlin blockade of 1948" (Chang and Kornbluh 1992:152). Kennedy also announced plans to take the matter to the Organization of American States and the United Nations Security Council, to reinforce the American base at Guantanamo, and to place all American forces on alert.

Khrushchev's initial reaction to Kennedy's speech mirrored Kennedy's reaction to the discovery of the missiles: surprise and outrage. Khrushchev accused the United States of violating international law and undertaking a "path of aggressive actions both against Cuba and against the Soviet Union." He insisted that the weapons were solely for defensive purposes, and he warned that the American actions could "lead to catastrophic consequences for world peace" (Chang and Kornbluh 1992:156). Khrushchev ordered that work on the missile sites be speeded up to make them operational as soon as possible and that Soviet ships bound for Cuban ports stay on course (Medvedev 1985:52; Blight and Welch 1989:

306). On the evening of October 23, Robert Kennedy met with Soviet Ambassador Dobrynin. The president's brother asked Dobrynin what orders had been given the captains of Soviet ships bound for Cuba. Dobrynin responded that current orders were "not to obey any unlawful demands to stop or be searched on the open sea" (Dobrynin 1995b:73).

On October 24, United Nations Secretary-General U Thant proposed a voluntary suspension of Soviet arms shipments to Cuba and of the United States blockade for two to three weeks. The Soviet Union accepted the proposal, but the United States rejected it. On the same day, the United States placed its Strategic Air Command forces on defense condition (DEFCON) II alert status.[10] The Soviets followed suit by placing Warsaw Pact forces on alert, but Soviet ships approaching the blockade, with the exception of one oil tanker, either slowed down or reversed course.[11] In a meeting with American businessman William Knox, however, Khrushchev threatened to sink any quarantine vessels that attempted to stop Soviet ships; Khrushchev asserted that the United States would have to learn to live with the missiles in Cuba, just as the Soviets had learned to live with the American missiles in Turkey.

The United States increased the diplomatic pressure on the Soviets on October 25. Kennedy sent a letter to Khrushchev reminding him of precrisis American warnings against the placement of offensive missiles in Cuba, while U.S. Ambassador Stevenson publicly confronted Soviet Ambassador Zorin at the United Nations Security Council with photos of the missile installations. By the end of the day, at least a dozen Soviet ships had turned back from Cuba to avoid the blockade.

On October 26, Khrushchev initiated the first concessionary move in a rambling and emotional letter to Kennedy. After noting that an outbreak of war would be a catastrophe for both sides, Khrushchev implied that a U.S. promise not to invade Cuba would eliminate any need for nuclear missiles to defend the island (Chang and Kornbluh 1992:185–88). A similar deal was discussed in greater detail that same day in an unofficial meeting between a Soviet intelligence officer and an American reporter.[12] But, on the next day, Khrushchev sent a second message, which, unlike his first letter, was read on Moscow radio. The second letter added a new condition for the removal of the missiles—a reciprocal American dismantling of its Jupiter missile installations in Turkey. Then, on the same morning,

---

10. DEFCON II is the highest state of alert of U.S. forces short of going to war.

11. The order to do so, which countermanded Khrushchev's earlier order, apparently came from Khrushchev's most influential adviser, First Deputy Prime Minister Anastas Mikoyan (see Medvedev 1985:52).

12. The Scali-Fomin meetings were less significant, at least in Soviet eyes, than was initially believed (Fursenko and Naftali 1995:58, 60–62).

an American pilot was killed when his U-2 flight over Cuba was shot down by a Soviet surface-to-air missile. The Soviet bargaining position appeared to have hardened, and the missile sites were on the verge of becoming operational.

President Kennedy and other members of the ExComm decided on a two-pronged approach. On the evening of October 27, Kennedy sent a letter to Khrushchev accepting the implied terms of Khrushchev's first letter: an end to the blockade and a U.S. pledge not to invade Cuba in return for United Nations–verified removal of the Soviet nuclear missiles. That same evening, Robert Kennedy met with Soviet Ambassador Dobrynin and offered assurances that the United States would remove the Jupiter missiles in Turkey in four to five months provided that the concession was kept secret. According to Dobrynin's account, Robert Kennedy warned that the United States was determined to remove the Cuban missile installations, with bombing if necessary, and that he feared that could lead to a "chain reaction" escalating to nuclear war. Kennedy requested an answer from the Soviets the next day; however, according to Dobrynin's telegram to Moscow, Kennedy emphasized that the request was "just that—a request, and not an ultimatum." Dobrynin ended his telegram by noting that Kennedy "persistently returned to one topic: time is of the essence and we shouldn't miss the chance" (Dobrynin 1995b:79–80).

On the next day Khrushchev responded positively to President Kennedy's carrot-and-stick initiative in a communiqué to Washington and a public radio address to the Soviet Union. Kennedy welcomed Khrushchev's acceptance of the American proposal and commented that it came just in time, as "developments were approaching a point where events could become unmanageable" (Chang and Kornbluh 1992:230). Although problems remained in obtaining the Cuban government's agreement, the crisis was effectively over. The quarantine was lifted on November 20.

Patterns of Behavior

The most striking element of the pattern that appears in the time series in figure 3.3 is the high rate of escalation, particularly in the period from October 16, when the discovery of missile sites was reported to Kennedy, to October 28, when the Soviets agreed to remove the missiles.

The overall rate of escalation for the Cuban Missile Crisis is the highest of the four Soviet-American crises, by a considerable margin (see table 3.1). In fact, this rate is higher than that of any of the other nonwar crises in the larger sample in the appendix. The other two escalation indicators—intensity and magnitude—are second only to the Berlin Blockade Crisis

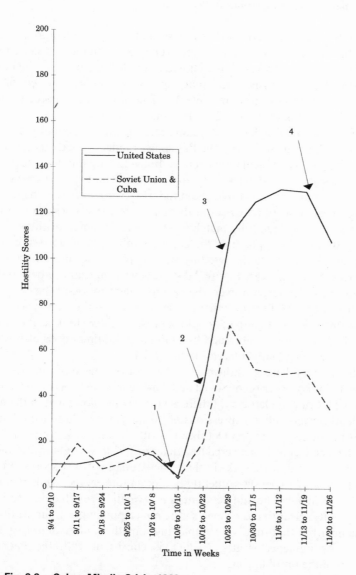

Fig. 3.3. Cuban Missile Crisis, 1962
Key dates are indicated with arrows: (1) 10/14: United States discovers
missile sites; (2) 10/22: Kennedy's quarantine speech; (3) 10/27: U.S. ultimatum; (4) 11/20: United States and Soviet Union reach agreement.

among the Soviet-American crises. A second interesting feature in figure 3.3 is the seemingly low degree of reciprocity between the two sides. Once the missiles were discovered, the United States led in escalating the hostility throughout the crisis. The visual impression in figure 3.3 is confirmed by the statistical indicators in table 3.2. The composite reciprocity score for the Cuban Missile Crisis ranks last among the four superpower crises.

The pattern of high escalation and relatively low reciprocity depicted in figure 3.3 is consistent with the Resistance model of escalation, wherein one party adopts an escalating coercive Bullying bargaining strategy, and the other side responds in a tit-for-tat manner. The U.S. coercive moves led the escalatory process throughout the crisis, with the Soviets reacting at a lower level of hostility. Crises of this type tend either to escalate to war, with the resisting side fully matching the coercive moves of the bullying side so that the later phase of the crisis resembles the reciprocal conflict spiral of a Fight, or to the resisting side's capitulation in the face of the increasing threat of war. Figure 3.3 depicts what appears to be a typical example of the latter; however, the narrative description of the events on October 27 and 28 illustrates that the denouement of the Cuban crisis was not as one sided as figure 3.3 would suggest. A closer look at the crisis's critical 13 days can be obtained by examining the time series of hostility scores observed at daily intervals in figure 3.4.

Soviet confidence that the missiles had not yet been discovered is manifested in the comparison of Soviet and American actions between October 16 and 22. Prior to October 22 there is virtually no movement in the magnitude of Soviet-Cuban expressions of hostility, while that of the United States begins to escalate on October 16, with the dramatic jump on October 22, when Kennedy delivered his "quarantine" speech. On the following day, there is an upward spike in the Soviet-Cuban hostility scores, but the Soviet-Cuban pattern subsequently becomes more erratic, while the magnitude of American hostility continues to escalate. From the time series in figure 3.4 it is clear that the Soviets were not responding in a simple tit-for-tat manner but that they were employing something more akin to a Trial and Error influence strategy, which is consistent with the narrative account of the unfolding crisis.

The erratic pattern demonstrates the inconsistent behavior of the Soviets and the Cubans. On October 24, for example, Khrushchev placed Soviet forces on alert and threatened to sink any American ships that attempted to enforce the blockade. However, his first deputy, Mikoyan, ordered Soviet ships approaching the blockade to slow down or reverse course, and by the afternoon of October 25, more than a dozen had done so. As expected, the U.S. hostility scores peak on October 27; those for the Soviets and Cuba remain constant with the downing of the American U-2

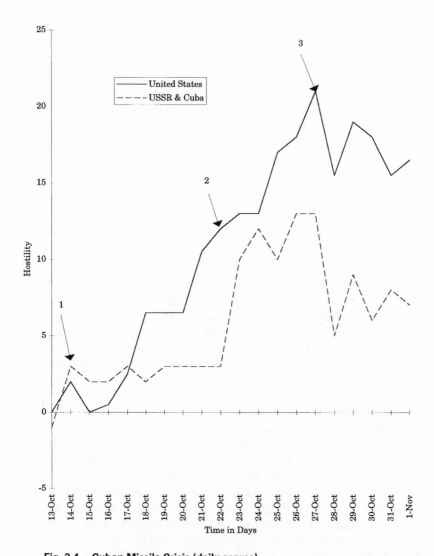

Fig. 3.4. Cuban Missile Crisis (daily scores)
Key dates are indicated with arrows: (1) 10/14: United States discovers
missile sites; (2) 10/22: Kennedy's quarantine speech; (3) 10/27: U.S. ultimatum.

balanced by the positive tone of Khrushchev's message (despite the added demand) and Dobrynin's meeting with Kennedy. The Kremlin did not order the firing of the missile at the U-2, but it should also be noted that, despite the added demand, Khrushchev's October 27 message was devoid of the rocket-rattling that accompanied his conciliatory remarks in the October 26 message. On October 26 a distressed Khrushchev reiterated his determination, while expressing his worries and offering to give the United States assurances of his good intentions; on October 27 he was ready to do business, albeit with tougher conditions.

Influence Strategies

The Soviet Union

The Soviet Union began the Cuban Missile Crisis with a Cautious Bullying influence strategy but then switched to Trial and Error following the institution of the American blockade. Actors employing Trial and Error influence strategies adjust their positive and/or negative inducements to the other party's responses. If the other side reacts with defiance to a threat, for example, the actor accompanies its next demand with a carrot-and-stick inducement or even a simple promise. Conversely, if the threat succeeds, another threat is likely to follow. The actor moves from one tactic to another, repeating those that produce accommodative responses and modifying or abandoning those that do not succeed (see Leng 1993: 142–43).

Khrushchev decided on his own to secretly install the missiles in Cuba and consulted his advisers only after he had made up his mind. Key advisers, including First Deputy Secretary Mikoyan and Foreign Minister Gromyko, then warned him of the enormous risk he would be taking (Zubok and Pleshakov 1996:260–61). Khrushchev himself did not underestimate U.S. resolve to defend its strategic position, but the Berlin Wall Crisis had shown him that the Soviets could prevail if they could move to a defensive position and demonstrate their determination to stand firm. The fait accompli would shift the status quo in the Soviets' favor and allow them to take a firm defensive stand against any subsequent U.S. challenges. Khrushchev's previous observation and experiences with Kennedy convinced the Soviet leader that the American president was too cautious to risk nuclear war over Cuba (Zubok and Pleshakov 1996:265; Dobrynin 1995a:72).

The initial Cautious Bullying strategy was not unlike those employed in the two Berlin crises. Just as the tightening of the blockade in the spring 1948 proceeded in gradual and cautious steps and a temporary fence preceded work on the Berlin Wall in 1961, the Soviet operation in Cuba began cautiously. The Soviets began sending military personnel to the island in the late spring of 1962 and gradually increased their numbers. When these moves went unopposed, the Soviets moved ahead with the shipments of weapons. Once the Soviets began shipping equipment for the installation of the missiles, the operation was shrouded in secrecy, and with the secrecy came greater risks. In the summer of 1948, Stalin's blockade could have been canceled overnight with an announcement that the "technical problems" had been fixed. But when the missile installations were discovered before they were operational, there was no avenue of retreat without a significant cost to the Soviet reputation for resolve. Everything depended on making the missiles operational before they were discovered by the United States. Recent information from Khrushchev's former advisers suggests that Soviet pressure on Berlin during the summer of 1962, including warnings of signing a separate peace treaty with East Germany after the American midterm elections, was a diplomatic diversionary tactic intended to draw the White House's attention away from Cuba (Hershberg 1996–97:272–73).

Once the missiles were operational, Khrushchev planned to make a dramatic announcement at the opening of the United Nations General Assembly in November 1962. Kennedy would be forced to accommodate himself to the shift in the strategic balance (Khrushchev 1970:493–94). There is no evidence that the Soviets had planned for the possibility that the Americans would discover the missiles before they were operational and militarily challenge the would-be fait accompli.

The strategy began to unravel when the United States discovered the missile sites before they became operational. Khrushchev's erratic behavior following Kennedy's quarantine speech is not inconsistent with the oscillations in earlier bargaining with the West: a coercive initiative followed by an offer to negotiate when the West resisted, and then another attempt at coercion when negotiations became stalemated. But Khrushchev's behavior during the missile crisis was unusually emotional and erratic, even by his standards.

According to his former advisers, Khrushchev reacted to Kennedy's October 22 speech with shock, outrage, and fear (Zubok and Pleshakov 1996:266). Khrushchev's initial response was a reflection of his anger as well as a show of bravado. But in a rambling private message to Kennedy just a few days later, Khrushchev expressed his fear that events were running out of control. As in the Berlin Wall Crisis, Khrushchev feared that Kennedy would not be able to resist pressure from hawks to take military action. Khrushchev's October 26 message, in fact, was prompted by an erroneous intelligence report of an imminent American invasion of Cuba (Zubok and Peshakov 1996:266–67). When he learned on the next day that the report was inaccurate and possibly had been planted by the Americans, Khrushchev changed course and sent his second message, which added the demand for a withdrawal of the American missiles in Turkey to balance the Soviet withdrawal of missiles from Cuba. Then, when the downing of the American U-2 occurred later in the day, Khrushchev was again seized by fear that the escalation was running out of control. After ordering that no nuclear weapons be used in the event of an American invasion of Cuba, he called together members of the presidium and secretariat for a marathon meeting to discuss what to do if an invasion occurred (Zubok and Pleshakov 1996:267).

The United States

The predominant American influence strategy is classified as Cautious Bullying. To place the American use of a Cautious Bullying strategy in perspective, it must be considered within the context of the preceding Soviet-American crises over Berlin. The Berlin Wall Crisis had left the larger issue of the ultimate fate of Berlin unresolved, with the Soviets frustrated over the continued Western presence and the Americans uneasy regarding Soviet intentions. Much of the Kennedy team's discussion regarding different strategic options in the Cuban crisis turned on the issue of how each would affect Soviet policy toward Berlin. Kennedy initially interpreted Khrushchev's attempt to put the missile bases in Cuba as a prelude to putting a "squeeze" on Berlin; therefore, it was especially important for the United States to respond forcefully (May and Zelikow 1997:90, 230, 235). Kennedy was concerned that failing to respond forcefully would encourage Khrushchev to build up the missile bases in Cuba and then apply pressure on Berlin, but the president also worried that any direct U.S. action against Cuba would cause Khrushchev to retaliate with military action against Berlin (May and Zelikow 1996:90, 176, 546). That view was reinforced during Kennedy's October 18 meeting with Gromyko, when the Soviet foreign minister warned that if the United States was not more forthcoming after the November U.S. elections, the Soviets would be "compelled" to take steps to end the Western presence in West Berlin (168).

As the ExComm's first meeting, on October 16, came to a close, Kennedy noted the pressure of time and concluded that at the very least, "We're going to take out those missiles" (May and Zelikow 1997:71). Later that evening, however, Secretary of Defense Robert McNamara suggested a naval blockade of Cuba, which would include the search and seizure of offensive weapons bound for the island (May and Zelikow 1997:113), and the ExComm became divided into three groups. The terms *hawks* and *doves* were coined during the missile crisis to differentiate between those favoring quick military action—an air strike or an invasion of the island—and those opting for a negotiated settlement through an exchange of the American missiles in Turkey for the Soviet missiles in Cuba. President Kennedy ultimately chose a middle-ground approach, instituting the blockade, backed by military shows of force, and signaling a willingness to negotiate.

The blockade offered the advantage of demonstrating American resolve to block delivery of any additional missiles without initiating military action against Cuba or Soviet forces. The initiative for beginning hostilities was shifted back to the Soviets, who would have to decide whether to challenge the blockade. The one weakness in the strategy was that it did not provide a means for removing the missiles and dismantling the missile sites in Cuba. To pursue that effort, Kennedy turned to verbal threats and promises coupled with shows of force.

After his October 22 address denouncing Khrushchev's actions and announcing the blockade measures, Kennedy took pains to keep communication open and to indicate to Khrushchev the president's own concern with being forced to take action that could cause the crisis to escalate out of control. Nevertheless, as the high rate of escalation illustrates, the crisis came dangerously close to spiraling out of control.

Influence Strategies and Escalation
Kennedy's realpolitik concern with his reputation for resolve does not sufficiently explain the bellicosity of his October 22 speech, which marked the beginning of the rapid escalation of the crisis depicted by figure 3.3. The "quarantine" speech was designed partly to demonstrate his toughness to a domestic audience in a midterm election year, but it also reflected Kennedy's anger at being deliberately deceived by Khrushchev. As the address was being prepared, the president instructed Sorensen to emphasize Khrushchev's personal responsibility for the scheme (May and Zelikow 1997:209–10). When Kennedy publicly addressed the nation—and the world—he denounced Khrushchev's stratagem as a "clandestine, reckless, and provocative threat to world peace" comparable to Hitler's actions in the 1930s and called on the Cubans to rise against the "puppets and agents of an international conspiracy" (Chang and Kornbluh 1992:150–54). The rhetoric did not match the restrained American military actions.

Caught in the act, challenged militarily, compared to Hitler, and accused of lying, it is not surprising that Khrushchev reacted defiantly. Kennedy expressed his outrage at the discovery of the missile sites in his

October 22 speech; Khrushchev reacted in kind to the substantive and rhetorical content of the speech. The two events set in motion the rapid escalation that immediately followed.

Two days after the speech, Robert Kennedy met with Soviet Ambassador Dobrynin and, according to Dobrynin's summary of the meeting, told him,

> The president felt himself deceived, and deceived intentionally. It was ... a heavy blow to everything in which he had believed and which he had striven to preserve in personal relations with the head of the Soviet government: mutual trust in each other's assurances. As a result, the reaction which found its reflection in the president's declaration and the extremely serious current events which are connected with it and can lead no one knows where. (Dobrynin 1995b:72)[13]

Prior to Kennedy's October 22 speech, each of the superpower leaders had underestimated the risk acceptance of the other. Khrushchev expected Kennedy to be too cautious to challenge the missile installations, and Kennedy was surprised by the audacity of Khrushchev's risky attempted fait accompli. Both leaders based their impressions on their previous experience with the other, particularly the Berlin Wall Crisis; neither considered the realpolitik lessons that the other might have drawn from that experience.

Just as the two leaders reacted with outrage to the other's actions at the outset of the crisis, each expressed a growing fear of the risk of nuclear war as the crisis rapidly escalated. On October 19, President Kennedy remarked to the Joint Chiefs of Staff that if he took military action, "there's bound to be a reprisal from the Soviet Union, there always is—[of] their just going in and taking Berlin by force. Which leaves me with only one alternative, which is to fire nuclear weapons—which is a hell of an alternative" (May and Zelikow 1997:176). Some of Khrushchev's former advisers have described the Soviet leader as increasingly "gripped with fear" as the crisis escalated (Zubok and Pleshakov 1996:266). The fears of an American invasion of Cuba were not allayed by Dobrynin's description of the American president as a "hot-headed gambler" and erroneous KGB reports of an imminent American invasion of Cuba (Dobrynin 1996–97:288; Zubok and Pleshakov 1996:267).

Khrushchev's emotional message to Kennedy on October 26 emphasized the risk of events running out of control, and the Soviet leader

---

13. Dobrynin's summary of the substantive content is consistent with that reported by Robert Kennedy (see May and Zelikow 1997:607–9).

appealed to the American president not to "give way to passions" and to work to untie the "knot of war" to avoid a nuclear catastrophe (May and Zelikow 1997:488, 490). When a Soviet missile downed an American U-2 reconnaissance plane over Cuba on October 27, both leaders began to fear that they were losing control of the escalation. Members of Kennedy's ExComm speculated that the downing of the U-2 was a deliberate escalation designed to coincide with a second Soviet message, which had arrived that morning and which raised the ante for a negotiated agreement to include the trade of the American missiles in Turkey for those in Cuba (May and Zelikow 1997:572, 597).[14] In fact, the downing of the U-2, which was ordered by a Soviet officer who apparently mistook it for an incoming missile attack, was a breakdown in the Soviet chain of command that alarmed the Kremlin as well (Blight and Welch 1989:310–11). The action provided both leaders with a glimpse of the kind of event that could push the crisis past the threshold to war.

It is significant that when the crisis reached its peak on October 27, both leaders took immediate action to reduce the risk of war. Khrushchev ordered that in the event of an American invasion of Cuba, under no circumstances should nuclear weapons be fired. Kennedy, recognizing the possibility of a Soviet counterstrike against the Jupiter missiles in Turkey, ordered that those missiles be defused, lest a lower-ranking commander fire them in retaliation.

Soviet Ambassador Dobrynin's report of his meeting with Robert Kennedy on the evening of October 27 described the president's brother as "very upset; in any case I've never seen him like this before. True, twice he tried to return to the topic of 'deception,' (that he talked about so persistently during our previous meeting) [but he] persistently returned to one topic: time is of the essence and we shouldn't miss the chance" (Dobrynin 1995b:80). Dobrynin's remarks about Kennedy's emotional state may or may not be accurate, and, in either case, they refer to Robert Kennedy, not to the president. But Robert Kennedy's expressed concerns reflected those of his brother, who, as the crisis escalated, worried about the possibility of a misperception or miscalculation by Khrushchev or of events escalating out of control. Given the quality of intelligence the Soviet leader was receiving as well as the breakdown in the chain of command that led to the U-2 incident, Kennedy's concern was justified. However, the Americans had their own difficulties in interpreting Khrushchev's intentions.

---

14. According to Zubok and Pleshakov (1996:267), when Khrushchev learned that the intelligence reports of an imminent American invasion were incorrect, his confidence returned and he decided it would be safe to reintroduce the demand for the missile trade. The second message was sent before the U-2 incident.

The behavior of the two leaders is more consistent with the spiral model of conflict behavior—as well as awareness on the part of both leaders of its risks—than with the calculated application of escalating coercion that is prescribed by the deterrence model of crisis bargaining. There were serious misperceptions of the adversary's intentions by both sides, and both leaders possessed a growing sense that events were escalating out of control.

The turning point in the crisis came with the American carrot-and-stick ultimatum, which Robert Kennedy delivered to Dobrynin on the evening of October 27 with the disclaimer that it was not intended as an ultimatum.[15] How the United States would respond if the Soviets rejected its demands had not been decided at the time; however, Kennedy did have a diplomatic backup plan. Secretary of State Dean Rusk would ask United Nations Secretary-General U Thant to propose publicly that the American missiles in Turkey be traded for those in Cuba (see Rusk 1990:240–41). But at the time the ultimatum was presented to Dobrynin, Kennedy and his advisers had not yet decided whether they would adopt this approach or opt for a military strike against the missile sites if the Soviets rejected the ultimatum (see McNamara, in Blight and Welch 1989:262).

Outcome and Lessons

Both sides claimed diplomatic victories in Cuba. Khrushchev later wrote that the crisis was a "triumph of Soviet policy. . . . We won a socialist Cuba" (Khrushchev 1970:504). But the consensus of less partial observers was that the Soviet retreat represented a diplomatic triumph for the United States. Despite the eventual removal of the Jupiter missiles from Turkey and the American pledge to refrain from invading Cuba, the most significant component of the outcome was the Soviet abandonment of the attempted fait accompli. The Soviets were forced to remove the missiles and dismantle the installations. Khrushchev's attempt to achieve strategic parity had been blocked, and the Soviet reputation for resolve suffered irreparably. Khrushchev did achieve his most immediate objective: assurance that the United States would not invade Cuba, but it came at a high price.

The lessons that the two leaders drew from the Cuban Missile Crisis experience were not new. Instead, these lessons reinforced the appreciation

---

15. It still is not clear whether Khrushchev understood the influence attempt as an ultimatum. Fyodor Burlatsky notes that it "looked like" an ultimatum because of the time limit and that Khrushchev was "in a hurry to reply" (Blight and Welch 1989:261–62).

of the risks associated with a conflict spiral and of the importance that national leaders attach to reputational interests.

Kennedy had expressed his concern about the risks of miscalculation leading to escalation during the Vienna summit in June 1961. Although Khrushchev responded contemptuously at the time, once the Berlin Wall Crisis began to escalate, Khrushchev worried aloud about a miscalculation on Kennedy's part. Thus, both leaders were aware of the risk of spiraling conflict before the Cuban Missile Crisis, but its frightening escalation led to a fuller appreciation of those risks. In that respect, learning occurred during the missile crisis. The evidence can be seen in Khrushchev's October 26 letter to Kennedy, which referred to the two leaders working together to loosen the "knot of war," in Robert Kennedy's urgent expression of events running out of control in his conversation with Dobrynin on the evening of the next day, and in President Kennedy's October 28 message to Khrushchev, which referred to "events becoming unmanageable" (May and Zelikow 1997:636).

The period after the crisis led to efforts to reduce Cold War tensions, with the partial Test Ban Treaty of 1963 the most notable accomplishment. The recognition of the importance of open communication at the highest levels of government led to the 1963 agreement to establish a "Hot Line" electronically linking the Kremlin and the White House. Each side also recognized the importance of avoiding unnecessary threats to the other's prestige. Kennedy warned his advisers against gloating over the American victory (Schlesinger 1965:831), and Khrushchev went out of his way to praise Kennedy's diplomacy.

Missing from the lessons drawn by the two leaders, however, is a mutual recognition that their actions were driven by a sense of insecurity based on the perception of threat from the other. In that sense, the beliefs of the leaders of each of the superpowers remained more consistent with realpolitik than with the conflict-spiral model of interstate conflict.

There also were lessons that were specific to the experience of each of the states—that is, those lessons drawn from the Soviet Union's diplomatic defeat and the U.S. success.

Soviet Union
Having failed in his effort to bully the Americans, Khrushchev turned to more accommodative negotiation. But his realpolitik belief in bargaining from strength had not changed. A program to increase Soviet naval capabilities was launched to avoid a repetition of their marked disadvantage in naval strength in the Cuban crisis.

Khrushchev's handling of the missile crisis weakened his stature among Kremlin foreign-policy elites as well as Warsaw Pact allies (Zubok and Pleshakov 1996:268–69). When he was removed from office on October 14, 1964, two years to the day from when the United States discovered the missile sites in Cuba, the action had more to do with internal Communist Party politics, Soviet-Chinese relations, and economic problems than with lingering resentment over his handling of the Cuban crisis. Nevertheless, the personal criticisms of Khrushchev most frequently leveled by his former associates have focused on those traits that led to his audacious but inconsistent diplomacy during the Cuban crisis. The missile crisis, according to one Soviet participant, was the result of Khrushchev's misguided "adventurism" (S. Mikoyan, quoted in Blight and Welch 1989:284). The high level of risk distinguished Khrushchev's attempted fait accompli in the Cuban crisis from Stalin's cautiously implemented fait accompli in the Berlin Blockade Crisis. The Soviets, it would seem, preferred Stalin's stolid caution to Khrushchev's self-confident audacity.

United States

A quarter of a century after the Cuban Missile Crisis, President Kennedy's advisers remained wedded to the views that they held when American options were being discussed at the beginning of the crisis (see Blight and Welch 1989). After studying the views of hawks and doves on President Kennedy's ExComm, Jarosz and Nye (1993:164) concluded that the crisis experience reinforced the views of participants in both groups. Administration doves, such as McNamara, Bundy, Sorensen, and Ball, found that the rapid escalation of the crisis confirmed their fears about the danger of events running out of control and of a Soviet miscalculation of America's defensive actions as preparation for war. Hawks, most notably Nitze, Douglas Dillon, John McCone, and Acheson, found that the Soviet decision to back down in the face of American threats confirmed their view that the graduated use of coercion can be effectively managed and that the main threat from Soviet miscalculation was that of perceiving the United States as irresolute.

Kennedy came to the crisis with an appreciation for the merits of both sides. On the one hand, his experiences in dealings with the Soviets, particularly the Vienna meeting and the Berlin Wall Crisis, had impressed him with the importance of demonstrating resolve in the face of Soviet challenges and having the military superiority to back it up. On the other hand, Kennedy was concerned from the start of the crisis with the danger of events escalating out of control. The Cautious Bullying influence strategy that he chose attempted to reconcile the two approaches: the outcome of the crisis most likely reinforced both views. Official statements by American policymakers, however, reflected the more hawkish perspective (see Jarosz and Nye 1993:171–73).

Alert Crisis, 1973

The Intercrisis Period, 1963–73

The 11 years between the Cuban Missile Crisis and the Middle East Alert
Crisis of 1973 included the most significant changes in superpower relations since the beginning of the Cold War. Within two years President
Kennedy was assassinated, the United States had committed itself to
active military intervention in the conflict in Vietnam, Khrushchev was
removed from office in the Soviet Union, and increasingly hostile relations
between the Soviet Union and China were punctuated by China's first successful test of an atomic bomb.

After China and India fought a brief war in the fall of 1962, the Soviet
Union increased its military aid to India, which the USSR saw as a counterbalance not only to American military support of Pakistan but also to
China's rising influence. Although American support of Pakistan waned
somewhat as that country moved toward a closer relationship with China,
the two superpowers found themselves on opposite sides in the three Indo-
Pakistani crises between 1965 and 1971 (see chap. 5).

The other major arena in which the superpowers found themselves in
intense competition was the Middle East. When war broke out in the Middle East in 1967, the Soviet Union accepted the defeat of its Egyptian and
Syrian allies by Israel rather than risk a direct confrontation with the
United States, which had emerged as Israel's chief defender (see chap. 4).
But after the Arab defeat, the Soviets strengthened their military commitment to assist the Arab states, particularly Egypt and Syria. During
Nasser's "war of attrition" with Israel in 1969–70, the Soviets supplied
combat air personnel to help Nasser defend Egyptian airspace against
Israel's "deep penetration" raids. The superpowers, however, carefully
avoided any direct confrontations. When the Soviet Union and other Warsaw Pact members invaded Czechoslovakia to end the Prague Spring in
1968, the United States satisfied itself with verbal protests.

A major change in the American foreign-policy team occurred in
1969 with the election of Republican Richard Nixon and Nixon's choice of
Henry Kissinger as his national security adviser. Nixon and Kissinger were
political realists with a strong faith in the balance of power as the key to
maintaining peace between the superpowers (Kissinger 1994:705). Nixon
and Kissinger also viewed the Soviet policy as dictated by more traditional
considerations of power politics rather than by revolutionary ideological
goals. "We will regard our Communist adversaries first and foremost as
nations pursuing their own interests as they perceive those interests, just as
we follow our own interests as we see them" (*Public Papers* 1972:179). The

new leaders believed a relaxation of tensions was possible on the basis of mutual interest. Such a relaxation was also viewed as essential to enabling the United States to crawl out of the Vietnam quagmire, which virtually consumed American foreign policy in the decade following the Cuban Missile Crisis. Kissinger believed that détente with the Soviets and improved relations with China were the best diplomatic means of under-cutting the communist powers' support of North Vietnam and persuading the North Vietnamese to except a negotiated settlement of the war (Kissinger 1979:1,302).

The Nixon administration's desire to relax superpower tensions and to settle major outstanding issues was reciprocated by the Brezhnev regime in Moscow. Brezhnev was the antithesis of Khrushchev in style: a cautious, risk-adverse consensus-builder, although, like Khrushchev, Brezhnev was an emotional man with a short temper. During his tenure the Soviet Union embarked on a program to achieve strategic parity with the United States while pursuing détente. By the early 1970s the Soviet strategic arms buildup had all but erased U.S. nuclear superiority. Nixon and Kissinger accepted the new reality and stepped up talks to achieve a measure of nuclear arms control.

The United States, meanwhile, had begun edging toward more amicable relations with China. Those efforts culminated in Nixon's 1971 visit to Beijing. Nevertheless, the movement toward détente gathered momentum. A quadripartite power agreement to guarantee free access to West Berlin and freedom within the city was reached in 1971. In May 1972, the United States and Soviet Union signed the SALT I agreement limiting strategic arms. A more general statement, the Basic Principles Agreement (BPA), outlined additional steps to further détente. Both agreements represented a mutual recognition and acceptance of relative nuclear parity—a major gain for the Soviets—as well as the need to avoid future militarized crises.

Along with statements regarding future efforts at arms control and cultural, economic, and scientific exchanges, the BPA stated the superpowers' commitment to "do their utmost to avoid military confrontations and to prevent the outbreak of nuclear war." The two countries pledged to settle their differences by peaceful means "in a spirit of reciprocity, mutual accommodation, and mutual benefit," and renounced the threat or use of force in their relations with each other (BPA, art. 2). The commitment was restated in June 1973, when Brezhnev visited the United States and the Agreement on the Prevention of Nuclear War (APNW) was signed. This document included the statement that in the event of any situation, anywhere in the world, that involved the risk of nuclear war, the two superpowers would "enter into urgent consultations with each other and make every effort to avoid this risk" (APNW, art. 4). With a treaty ending the American participation in the Vietnam War the previous winter, conditions appeared to be auspicious for a new era of superpower cooperation.

By the summer of 1973, superpower relations were the best that they had been since World War II. The major outstanding differences between the two sides—Vietnam, Cuba, and Berlin—had been settled. There was relative strategic military parity between the two sides, each recognized that the other shared its desire to avoid war, the ideological tensions between the two sides had subsided considerably, and frequent and open communication occurred between the Nixon and Brezhnev administrations. Moreover, there was a marked change from the interpersonal tensions between Kennedy and Khrushchev that preceded the Berlin Wall and Cuban Missile Crises. Nixon and Brezhnev had developed a strong rapport with each other, as had Kissinger and Gromyko. Those relationships were tested when another war began in the Middle East in October.

Crisis Structure

Soviet Union

Perceptions of American Intentions. The Soviet leadership saw the recent events as marking a historic change in superpower relations that would lead to the "solution of emerging problems by negotiation, and the development of mutually advantageous cooperation in many spheres" (G. Arbatov, quoted in Lebow and Stein 1994:154). The two sides shared interests in moderating the arms race, achieving mutually beneficial trade relations, and avoiding confrontations that could lead to nuclear war.

Interests. The overarching foreign-policy aims of Brezhnev and his foreign minister, Andrei Gromyko, were the achievement of strategic parity with the United States and the pursuit of détente. By the summer of 1973, both goals had been realized.

Soviet interests in the Middle East, however, suffered a setback in July 1972 when Egyptian president Anwar el-Sadat expelled 20,000 Soviet advisers and opened back-channel negotiations with the United States in the hope of convincing the Americans to pressure Israel to return the Sinai territory to Egypt.

Ironically, the Soviets' improved relations with the United States weakened their allies' confidence in the USSR's willingness to challenge the Americans. Arab leaders worried that the Kremlin's concern with its relationship with the United States would cause the Soviets to back away from supporting the Arabs in future confrontations with Israel. Those concerns placed additional pressure on the Kremlin to demonstrate its support of the Arab cause. After Sadat expelled the Soviet military advisers, the Soviet leaders provided more military aid to Egypt to avoid losing their most important ally in the Middle East.

Capabilities. Strategic parity with the United States encouraged the Soviet belief that the USSR should play a role on the world stage equal to that of the United States, a role that the United States appeared to confirm in its acceptance of the 1972 BPA. When war broke out in the Middle East in 1973, the Soviets assumed that they would play a role equal to the United States in influencing the diplomatic course of events. As for the local balance of forces, Brezhnev, Gromyko, and other members of the politburo did not believe that the Arab forces could prevail in a war with the Israelis, despite the Soviet supply of sophisticated military weapons and materiel to Egypt in 1973 (Lebow and Stein 1994:199–200).

Over almost two decades, the Soviet Union had established a dependency relationship with Egypt by becoming Egypt's principal supplier of arms and military advice. But after the expulsion of the Soviet advisers, Sadat began edging away from dependency on the Soviet Union to seek a new relationship with the United States. The Soviets found not only that they were unable to control the actions of Egypt during the crisis but that their own policy decisions were influenced by the desire to maintain a positive relationship with their most important Middle East ally.

Brezhnev was firmly in control of Soviet foreign policy in 1973. But unlike Stalin and Khrushchev, who initiated new policies on their own and assumed authoritarian control over decision making, Brezhnev preferred to work as a consensus builder in the politburo. Not all politburo members, however, supported détente, a factor that Brezhnev had to consider during the Alert Crisis.

United States
Perceptions of Soviet Intentions. Nixon entered office with a reputation as a staunch anticommunist cold warrior. But once in office, his views came to resemble the realpolitik beliefs of his national security adviser, Henry Kissinger. Kissinger viewed the Soviet Union as a traditional great power pursuing its own interests rather than as a global revolutionary driven by ideological objectives. As Nixon gravitated toward those views, he came to believe that a "realistic accommodation of conflicting interests" could lead to a true relaxation of tensions without any changes in the Soviet system (*Public Papers* 1972:179). Like Brezhnev, Nixon was convinced that his long-term adversary shared his desire to avoid confrontations that risked escalating to nuclear war.

Nevertheless, Nixon and Kissinger took a decidedly realpolitik view of the superpower relationship in those areas where the two countries were competing for influence, such as the Middle East. The two sides might collaborate to prevent a Middle East conflict from escalating to the point where there was a high risk of a superpower confrontation, but in all other respects, the United States would do what it could to reduce Soviet influence and increase its own within the region.

Interests. The foremost American interest remained its relationship with the Soviet Union, but the strategic importance of the Middle East made superpower competition for influence in the region inevitable. Thus, the United States pursued two potentially contradictory objectives: avoiding a superpower confrontation that would threaten détente while extending American influence within the region at the expense of Soviet influence (see Kissinger 1982:586). The dual strategy was complicated further by the U.S. commitment to Israel's security.

Capabilities. American policymakers were confident that Israel's demonstrated military superiority over its Arab neighbors would discourage Egypt's President Sadat from attempting to recover the Sinai by force. Consequently, Soviet warnings of the likelihood of war were ignored. When war did break out, Kissinger reckoned that Sadat's decision to expel Soviet advisers, coupled with his back-channel communications with the White House, meant that Sadat recognized the futility of relying on the Soviet Union to achieve his diplomatic objectives. The United States was now in a position to dominate events, Kissinger reasoned (Kissinger 1982:468).

During the war, a key variable was America's ability to influence the actions of Israel. As Israel's only major power ally and primary source of military assistance, the United States possessed considerable influence over its Middle East client. Nevertheless, exerting control during the course of a war became problematic, particularly because America's interests regarding the Soviet Union and Egypt conflicted with Israel's military objectives.

American policy during the Alert Crisis was directed from the White House by President Nixon and by Kissinger, who had been appointed secretary of state shortly before the onset of the Middle East war. During the crisis, however, Nixon became incapacitated by the domestic and personal crisis created by the congressional investigation of the Watergate break-in.[16] Consequently, beginning with his trip to Moscow and during the most critical hours of the Alert Crisis, American foreign policy was

---

16. During the evening of October 24, Nixon remained in his personal chambers and did not participate in the discussions leading to the drafting of the response to Brezhnev or the alert of U.S. forces, although the president approved both actions.

directed almost single-handedly by Kissinger, in consultation with a small number of other foreign-policy officials.[17]

Crisis Behavior

The 1973 Middle East war began on October 6 with Egyptian and Syrian offensives. Egyptian forces broke through Israeli defenses on the east bank of the Suez Canal and achieved a series of early battlefield successes. The Soviets, fearing that the Arab gains were temporary, pressed for a cease-fire just two days after the war began, but the Egyptians, confident of additional military gains, rejected these proposals.

By October 10, Egyptian and Israeli forces were stalemated on the battlefield, although Israel had successfully counterattacked against Syria. When the Soviet Union began an airlift of supplies to Syria, the United States urged that the superpowers show mutual restraint in resupplying their allies, but within a few days the Americans began their own airlift to resupply Israeli forces. By October 12, the Soviets had brought several proposals for a cease-fire to the United Nations Security Council, but the United States delayed while Israeli forces were being resupplied. On the next day Egypt launched an unsuccessful tank attack in the Sinai.

The tide of the war then turned in Israel's favor. On October 16, Israeli forces crossed the Suez Canal. The Soviets, concerned about the constant drain of military equipment, an impending Arab defeat, and a possible superpower confrontation, urged Sadat to accept a cease-fire, but the Egyptian president refused. The Soviets proposed that Nixon send Kissinger to Moscow to prepare a joint Soviet-American proposal for a cease-fire coupled with an Israeli withdrawal from the Arab territories occupied by Israel after the 1967 war. The United States agreed to the meeting, but Kissinger deliberately delayed traveling to Moscow for 72 hours to enable Israel to make further advances on the battlefield before the superpowers agreed on a cease-fire (Kissinger 1982:539–40). By the time Kissinger arrived in Moscow on October 20, the Israeli advance had prompted Sadat to join in calling for a cease-fire.

Meanwhile, Arab oil ministers agreed to cut oil production and to place an embargo on the sale of oil to states aiding the Israeli war effort. As these events were occurring in the Middle East, the Nixon administration faced a growing crisis at home, which was punctuated by Nixon's dismissal of the Watergate special prosecutor, Archibald Cox. Brezhnev and Kissinger nevertheless met on October 21 and agreed to a cease-fire reso-

---

17. The others were Secretary of Defense James Schlesinger, CIA Director William Colby, Chairman of the Joint Chiefs of Staff Admiral Thomas Moorer, and Nixon's chief of staff, Alexander Haig.

lution. The resolution, which was adopted by the United Nations Security Council the next day, was not linked to a general settlement or to Israeli withdrawal from the occupied territories. Kissinger traveled to Tel Aviv to obtain Israeli agreement to the cease-fire, while Brezhnev obtained Sadat's agreement.

The cease-fire resolution had two important omissions: there were no provisions for its supervision or for its enforcement.[18] Violations began almost immediately. By the afternoon of October 23, Israeli forces had completely encircled Egypt's Third Army on the west side of the Suez Canal. Sadat, who had been maintaining day-to-day contact with the United States during the crisis, sent a message to Nixon urging that the United States send American observers to monitor the cease-fire. The United States rejected the proposal, and the cease-fire violations continued, with each side blaming the other. That evening the Security Council passed another resolution for a cease-fire to begin the next morning. All three contending Middle East parties agreed to adhere to the cease-fire.

On the afternoon of October 24, Sadat sent a second urgent message to Nixon stating that Israel was initiating new attacks; Sadat urged the United States to intervene with troops to fulfill its "promise" to guarantee the cease-fire.[19] When Sadat did not receive an acceptable reply from the United States, he sent separate messages to the United States and Soviet Union asking the two superpowers to act jointly to send observers or troops to implement the cease-fire on the Egyptian side of the Suez Canal.

The United States rejected the idea, but the Soviets indicated that they would support a Security Council resolution for the dispatch of a joint Soviet-American peacekeeping force to guarantee the cease-fire. At 9:35 P.M. on October 24, Brezhnev sent a letter to Nixon again urging the joint Soviet-American force, but this time the Soviet leader added the warning that "if you find it impossible to act jointly with us in this matter, we should be forced with the necessity urgently to consider the question of taking appropriate steps unilaterally" (Israelian 1995:169). At the time the message was received, American intelligence had information indicating preparations for the movement of four Soviet airborne divisions, amphibious vessels headed toward Egypt, and extensive military communication activity. Kissinger interpreted Brezhnev's ambiguous warning as "in effect an ultimatum" and became determined to reject the demand in a manner

---

18. Lebow and Stein (1994:213–19) point out that the details of the cease-fire, including even its starting time, received minimal attention during the Kissinger-Brezhnev talks, with unfortunate consequences.

19. Sadat believed that the Soviet-American cease-fire resolution committed each of the superpowers to guarantee that their respective allies would observe the cease-fire. The United States denied that any such guarantee had been made (see Kissinger 1982:576).

that would shock the Soviets into abandoning the threatened unilateral action (Kissinger 1982:583–84).

The United States responded by placing its forces on worldwide alert. Kissinger then sent a message to Sadat asking him to withdraw his proposal for the joint peacekeeping force. Shortly after midnight, U.S. intelligence received information of Soviet preparations for air transport planes preparing to fly from Budapest to Egypt. The United States instructed the Eighty-second Airborne Division to be ready for possible movement and ordered two aircraft carriers to the Mediterranean.

After waiting several hours for the alert to be picked up by Soviet intelligence, Kissinger responded, in Nixon's name, to Brezhnev's message: "we could in no event accept unilateral action. . . . [S]uch action would produce incalculable consequences which would be in the interest of neither of our countries and which would end all we have striven so hard to achieve" (Kissinger 1982:591). The United States now had evidence that the cease-fire was being observed by all parties, Kissinger said. Furthermore, the United States was prepared to work with the Soviets in agreeing to temporary American and Soviet noncombat participation in an expanded United Nations supervisory force to observe the cease-fire. Less than three hours later, at 8:00 A.M., the United States received a message from Egypt indicating that Sadat had withdrawn his request for joint Soviet-American intervention in favor of a United Nations peacekeeping force. The withdrawal of the Egyptian request effectively eliminated the rationale for unilateral Soviet intervention.

At noon on October 25, Kissinger gave a press conference that was conciliatory in tone. A little over two hours later, Brezhnev sent a message to Nixon that accepted Kissinger's face-saving proposal for joint noncombat observers to monitor the cease-fire as part of an expanded United Nations force. Later that afternoon, the United Nations Security Council passed Resolution 340, which ordered Egyptian and Israeli troops to return to the lines at the time of the original cease-fire on October 22 and established an international force to observe the cease-fire. The immediate Soviet-American crisis was over, although the dire situation facing Egypt's surrounded Third Army remained unresolved. Over the next few days, with considerable American pressure on Israel and a historic October 28 meeting between Israeli and Egyptian military officers to discuss the implementation of Resolution 340, an agreement was reached to resupply the Third Army with food and other necessities.

Patterns of Behavior

The time series of weekly hostility scores for the two sides appears in figure 3.5. The most striking attributes of figure 3.5 are the short duration of the crisis and the relatively low level of escalation. The Alert Crisis was by far the shortest of the four Soviet-American crises. The confrontation phase of the crisis—that is, the time between the initial Soviet threat and the resolution of the crisis—lasted less than 24 hours. The Alert Crisis ranks last among the four crises in both the magnitude and intensity of escalation (table 3.1), and although this crisis ranks second in the rate of escalation, the composite escalation score is the lowest of the four Soviet-American crises. The crisis was resolved quickly, with a relatively low danger of escalating out of control.

In fact, the two superpowers exhibited an unprecedented degree of consultation and negotiation to achieve a cease-fire and prepare the groundwork for a postwar diplomatic settlement. Besides the use of the Hot Line between Moscow and Washington on October 23, there were nearly daily communications between the two superpowers from the beginning of the war on October 6 to the resolution of the crisis on October 25. During the peak of the crisis, October 23–25, there was intensive communication between the Kremlin and the White House. The leaders of the two superpowers were not burdened by the deep mutual distrust that existed between Truman and Stalin and between Kennedy and Khrushchev before the previous three crises. Nixon and Brezhnev as well as Kissinger and Gromyko had developed cordial working relationships, and each man believed that his counterpart shared the desire to avoid a confrontation. During the height of the crisis, Brezhnev reportedly assured politburo members, "Nixon feels deep respect for all Soviet leaders and for me personally" (quoted in Lebow and Stein 1994:212).

At first glance, there also appears to be empirical evidence of cooperation between the superpowers when the composite reciprocity score for the Alert Crisis is compared to the other superpower crises (table 3.2). The composite reciprocity score for the Alert Crisis ranks second only to the Berlin Wall Crisis among the four superpower crises. That comparison, however, is deceptive. When the reciprocity score is compared to the scores for the 34 crises in the larger sample, it is close to the bottom of the third quartile. In fact, there are rather different messages from the two reciprocity indicators, distance and direction. Given the relatively low level of escalation, the hostility scores of the two sides are never far apart; consequently, the distance score for the crisis is the lowest among the Soviet-American crises. Conversely, the direction score, which indicates the extent to which the two parties are moving toward more or less cooperation or conflict at the same time, is relatively high, which indicates that the parties frequently were moving in different directions. The two scores indicate that while the two sides exercised comparable amounts of caution in avoiding the escalation of the crisis, they were not together with regard to

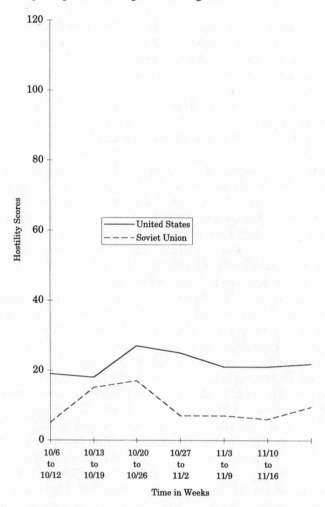

Fig. 3.5.   Alert Crisis, 1973

when they sought to collaborate or to demonstrate their resolve. They were out of sync.

The differences between these two indicators of reciprocity can be seen in figure 3.6, which is a time series of the daily hostility scores for the two sides. The daily scores for the two sides are never very far apart, but they frequently are not moving in the same direction.

The overall pattern exhibited in figure 3.6—relatively low escalation and reciprocity—is consistent with the crisis type described as a Put-Down

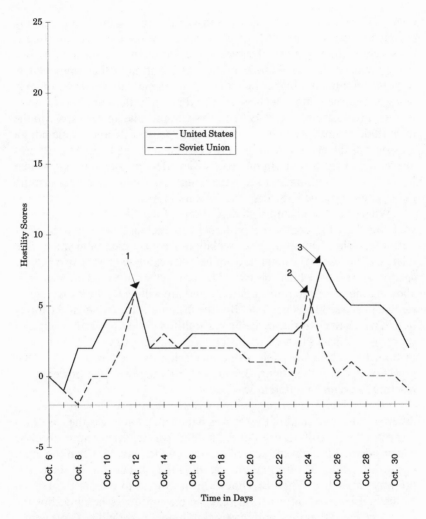

Fig. 3.6. Alert Crisis, 1973 (daily scores)
Key dates are indicated with arrows: (1) 10/12: United States begins air-lift to Israel and warns Soviet Union against intervention; (2) 10/24: Brezhnev's warning to United States; (3) 10/25: U.S. alert and response to Brezhnev.

(chap. 2). A Put-Down typically occurs when one party employs escalating coercive tactics and the other quickly yields, but there is a variant that is consistent with the pattern observed in the Alert Crisis. In those cases, one party escalates the magnitude of hostility, but the other immediately responds in kind at a higher magnitude, and the initial threatener quickly de-escalates (see Leng 1993:80–81). The time series in figure 3.6 is consistent with the pattern associated with this variant. The upward spike in the magnitude of hostility that occurs between October 24 and 25 includes a crossover as the magnitude of hostility exhibited by the United States rises above that of the Soviet Union. The Soviet effort at coercion represented by Brezhnev's warning and accompanying Soviet military moves is more than matched by the U.S. alert and military moves.

When the several empirical descriptors of the Alert Crisis are considered together, the composite pattern is intriguing. The first four crisis attributes—short duration, low escalation, frequent communication, and relative closeness in the magnitude of hostility exhibited by the two sides—suggest a crisis in which the two sides are well aware of the dangers of allowing the confrontation to escalate and are willing to work together to resolve it as quickly as possible. But the fifth indicator—that is, the direction in which the two sides are moving at different times over the course of the crisis—indicates that when one party was moving toward greater cooperation, the other was likely to be increasing its coercive actions. That aspect of the pattern in figure 3.6 suggests that the two superpowers were reacting to events in different ways.

One explanation for this anomaly is that the two sides were receiving different information about what was happening. Such was the case with regard to the state of the cease-fire. Not only was it never completely clear which side had broken the cease-fire, but, on October 24, when the crisis reached its peak, the information regarding the current state of the cease-fire was unreliable. When Brezhnev sent his threat to Nixon, the United States had received information that the cease-fire was holding, but the Soviets believed that the fighting was continuing. A second possible explanation is that the two sides misread each other's intentions. Brezhnev viewed the Israeli violations of the cease-fire as part of a deliberate strategy of deception on the part of the United States; consequently, he was reacting partly in anger when he attached the threat of unilateral intervention to the end of his October 24 appeal for joint Soviet-American intervention to monitor the cease-fire (see Lebow and Stein 1994:244). Brezhnev nevertheless intended his message primarily as a plea for joint action, but it was interpreted by Kissinger as an attempt to bully the United States with an ultimatum (Kissinger 1982:583–84). A third possibility is that despite the spirit of cooperation in crisis management promised by détente, the two sides were pursuing competing objectives, with competitive influence strategies—that is, because each side was intent on assisting its ally, the timing of its efforts to achieve a working cease-fire was related to the battlefield success of its ally. The three possibilities are not mutually exclusive.

Influence Strategies

The Soviet strategy is classified as a predominantly Trial and Error influence strategy. The United States employed a Reciprocating influence strategy. Thus the Alert Crisis is the first of the four Soviet-American crises in which neither side resorted to a Bullying or Cautious Bullying influence strategy.

Soviet Union. The Soviet strategy prior to the October War and up to the confrontation phase of the Alert crisis was consistent with the spirit of superpower détente and with the APNW, which called for superpower consultations to control conflicts that had the potential to escalate to a nuclear confrontation. Brezhnev and his advisers were caught between their commitment to détente and their growing fear that their most important Middle Eastern ally might defect to the United States if they did not assist Egypt in preparing for a war that would seriously endanger détente. They tried to have their cake and eat it, too. The Soviets decided to appease Sadat by supplying him with the sophisticated aircraft and missiles that he would need to mount a military campaign while intensifying their diplomatic efforts to dissuade him from launching that campaign. It was a contradictory strategy that, as Lebow and Stein argue (1994:172), appeared to be based on denial and wishful thinking.

When war broke out, Soviet policymakers were surprised by Egypt's initial victories but did not expect them to last. The Soviets responded by ordering a massive airlift to provide Sadat with additional military hardware while drafting plans for a cease-fire brokered by the superpowers. If all went well, the Kremlin would have demonstrated its support of Egypt, would have achieved a cease-fire that would consolidate Egypt's early military gains, and would have worked with the United States in the spirit of the APNW accord to prevent a superpower confrontation.

Soviet leaders' first efforts at convincing Sadat and Syrian President Hafiz al-Assad to accept a cease-fire came just three days after the beginning of the war, but the Soviet initiative was rejected by the Arab leaders, who expected to achieve additional military gains. As the conflict on the battlefield reached a stalemate and then turned in Israel's favor, Soviet efforts intensified, with the agreement for a cease-fire reached during Kissinger's meeting with Brezhnev on October 21.

When the cease-fire was broken and with the consequent Israeli encirclement of Egypt's Third Army, the Soviets became alarmed by the prospect of another humiliating Arab defeat. This concern led to the frantic communications with Washington, the proposal for a joint Soviet-American force to oversee the cease-fire, and finally, after the cease-fire was once again broken, Brezhnev's warning of unilateral Soviet intervention. Brezhnev's reaction to the repeated violations of the cease-fire can be likened to Kennedy's sense of betrayal when he discovered the Soviet offensive missile sites in Cuba in 1962. According to Dobrynin, Brezhnev felt that Kissinger had deliberately deceived the Soviet leader to allow a complete Israeli victory (see Lebow and Stein 1994:243). Brezhnev's proposal of the joint superpower force may have been intended as a cooperative offer, and the threat was vaguely worded to avoid "frighten[ing] the Americans too much" (Israelian 1995:169). There was no explicit Soviet commitment to act: Brezhnev warned that if the United States would not cooperate, the Soviets would be forced "to consider the question of taking appropriate steps unilaterally." But despite the careful hedging, the threat of unilateral action, coupled with Soviet activity to ready airborne and naval units for action, was a shift away from what had been an essentially cooperative bargaining strategy to what Kissinger perceived as an attempt at coercion.[20]

When the United States responded with the alert, the Soviet leaders were surprised at what they considered an overreaction. "What has this to do with the letter that I sent to Nixon?" Brezhnev reportedly asked (Israelian 1995:179). Hawks on the politburo, most notably Defense Minister Andrei Grechko and KGB chief Yuri Andropov favored a tit-for-tat response—a mobilization of Soviet forces. But Deputy Prime Minister Aleksey Kosygin is quoted as saying, "We shall send two divisions to the Near East and in response the Americans will send two divisions as well. If we send five divisions, the Americans will send their five" (Israelian 1995:27). Foreign Minister Gromyko reportedly added: "Where is the brink, the line between peace and a new nuclear war? Who can draw that line?" (Israelian 1995:181). In the end, Brezhnev and his colleagues were not willing to risk the escalation of the crisis to a direct Soviet-American military confrontation or, for that matter, to risk the future of détente for the strategic benefit of an ally that had rejected their warnings against going to war.

In sum, the Soviets began the crisis with an essentially cooperative strategy based on the assumption that the new relationship that came with

---

20. Some Soviet officials have since claimed that the military activities were unrelated to Brezhnev's threatening message and were undertaken by the military without the politburo's knowledge (see Lebow and Stein 1994:235).

achieving strategic parity would lead to a joint Soviet-American effort to intervene diplomatically to avoid a superpower confrontation. The strategy appeared to bear fruit when Kissinger and Brezhnev agreed to superpower sponsorship of the cease-fire agreement. But when it appeared that the cease-fire might collapse completely, with the war ending in a decisive Israeli victory, Brezhnev felt deceived by Kissinger and angrily reacted by attempting to coerce the Americans into cooperating. When that strategy failed to work, the Soviets returned to a cooperative strategy. The pattern is that of a Trial and Error influence strategy, but, unlike Khrushchev's strategy during the Cuban Missile Crisis, which began with an attempt at bullying, Brezhnev's strategy began with a concerted effort at cooperation that failed largely because of the difficulties that both sides faced in attempting to influence their allies' behavior.

United States

From Kissinger's realpolitik perspective, there was a side benefit to the Soviet-American détente in the Middle East. Détente raised questions among Arab leaders regarding the Soviet Union's willingness to risk its relationship with the United States to support the Arab campaign against Israel. When Sadat expelled Soviet advisers in 1972 and opened back-channel communications with the White House, Kissinger saw an opportunity to encourage the defection of the Soviet Union's principal Middle East ally by convincing Sadat that only the United States could exert the diplomatic influence to persuade Israel to agree to a settlement that would return the Sinai to Egypt (Kissinger 1982:594). Given Israel's demonstrated military superiority in previous wars with the Arabs, Kissinger thought it highly unlikely that Sadat would attempt to regain the territory by force.

When the war did occur, Nixon and Kissinger favored a stalemate on the battlefield to provide the basis for meaningful negotiations between Israel and the Arabs rather than another decisive Israeli victory (Nixon 1978:921; Kissinger 1982:468). To expand American influence in the region at the expense of the Soviets, it was important that the diplomatic initiatives come from the United States. Kissinger was determined to control the course of diplomacy in the Middle East. But, for the United States to maintain such control, it would have to be viewed as an honest broker, not simply as Israel's principal ally. For these reasons—confidence in Israel's military superiority, the desire to avoid a decisive Israeli victory, and concern with maintaining good relations with Arab states—the United States held back from an effort to resupply Israel during the first week of the war, despite Israeli battlefield losses. Although the overall American strategy during the Alert Crisis is consistent with a Reciprocating influence strategy, during the early phase of the war the strategy would be more accurately described as Stonewalling, as Kissinger deflected Soviet proposals for a cease-fire while waiting for the tide of war to turn in Israel's favor.

Once Israel managed to reverse the situation on the battlefield in its favor, Kissinger agreed to a revised version of Brezhnev's proposal for a cease-fire. But just as the Soviet Union was unable to persuade Egypt to accept a cease-fire while enjoying success on the battlefield, Kissinger had difficulty convincing the Israelis to accept the cease-fire when they were on the offensive. He also found it difficult to obtain Israeli compliance once the cease-fire was in place.

In his memoirs, Kissinger describes Brezhnev's threat of unilateral intervention as "an ultimatum" and the ensuing overnight crisis as a "game of chicken" in which the United States could not yield to bullying (1982:583, 589). The DEFCON III alert of United States forces around the world sent a strong signal, but Kissinger's verbal response to Brezhnev, which was sent in Nixon's name, was quite measured. After rejecting the joint action, the message states that unilateral action by the Soviets would "produce incalculable consequences which would be in the interest of neither of our countries and which would end all we have striven so hard to achieve." This statement was not an ultimatum but a warning of the dangers of escalation and of the threat to the future of détente. Kissinger also offered a carrot by agreeing to join the Soviet Union in providing non-combatant personnel to an expanded United Nations truce supervisory force (Kissinger 1982:591) as an alternative to Brezhnev's proposal for a joint Soviet-American peacekeeping force.

Kissinger's response is a good example of a Reciprocating influence strategy. It was firm but roughly proportionate—the alert in response to Brezhnev's threat and the observed Soviet military activity—and flexible. In that respect, it is useful to compare this reaction with Kennedy's Cautious Bullying strategy during the Cuban Missile Crisis.[21] Kennedy made a strong commitment to his compellent threats by stating them publicly and by being explicit with regard to the actions that would be taken and the conditions under which they would be carried out. Moreover,

---

21. Lebow and Stein (1994:268–69) agree with the Soviets in finding the alert an overreaction that only resulted in "anger, disappointment, and bitterness" on the part of Soviet leaders. It may be true, as Lebow and Stein argue, that the U.S. threat was irrelevant because Brezhnev's threat of unilateral action was a bluff, but why should Kissinger have been expected to know that information? There was certainly no hint in the message itself or in the way in which it was delivered. The Soviets later said that the military activities that accompanied Brezhnev's warning were unrelated, but again, why should the Americans have known that fact?

Kennedy warned Khrushchev that the stated actions might be only the beginning of American military action and that the United States would not shrink from the risk of nuclear war if necessary. Kissinger's warning was vaguely stated, it did not commit the United States to any course of action, and it offered to meet Brezhnev's demands halfway. The situations, of course, were very different. Kennedy was engaged in an effort at compellence after having discovered Khrushchev's attempted fait accompli; Kissinger was attempting to deter a Soviet overreaction to the breakdown of a cease-fire that both superpowers sought. The stakes were considerably higher in the Cuban Missile Crisis.

The comparison of the two cases nevertheless is useful in a consideration of whether the Cuban Missile Crisis experience had provided Nixon and Kissinger with any lessons about crisis management. It can be argued that there is evidence that the earlier crisis did yield such lessons, as evidenced by Kissinger's comments during his press conference on the morning of October 25, 1973, a few hours after Nixon ordered the alert.

Those remarks contained implied comparisons to the Cuban crisis: "We are not seeking an opportunity to confront the Soviet Union. We are not asking the Soviet Union to pull back from anything it has done. . . . The measures we took were precautionary in nature. They were not directed at any actions that had already been taken" (Kissinger 1982:532–41).

The comments by Soviet politburo members, which are reported by Israelian (1995), focus on two factors: the risk of spiraling escalation and the loss of the benefits of détente. There is currently no access to detailed accounts of politburo discussions during the first three Soviet-American crises, but it appears unlikely that the first consideration would have been stated so explicitly before the Cuban Missile Crisis. The concern with losing the benefits of cooperation would not have been a consideration in any of the earlier crises.

When Brezhnev responded positively to Kissinger's message later on October 25, the Soviet leader's message to Nixon conveyed no indication that there had been a serious disagreement, much less a militarized crisis between the two superpowers.

Outcome and Lessons

Soviet Union

The Kremlin treated the Alert Crisis as a victory for Soviet diplomacy, but the incident was, in fact, a major setback. From a strictly realpolitik perspective, the outcome weakened the Soviet reputation for resolve. Brezhnev reacted out of anger, and his bluff was called. Second, the United

States now would supplant Soviet influence over Egypt, the most important of the Soviet Union's Middle Eastern allies. Sadat now recognized that only the United States could exert the influence over Israel that would be necessary for Egypt to regain the Sinai territory. Soviet relations with Syria were weakened seriously by Moscow's failure to obtain an early cease-fire. Détente was another casualty. The Alert Crisis left behind a residue of anger and distrust, particularly on the Soviet side, that seriously weakened détente.

United States
Despite the moderate tones of Kissinger's October 25 press conference, the official American view of the outcome of the Alert Crisis was decidedly hawkish. Once again the United States had demonstrated its resolve in the face of a Soviet threat and emerged triumphant. Kissinger's discussion in his memoirs is hawkish as well: "Once Brezhnev's big bluff had failed, Soviet threats had lost much of their credibility," and the United States had emerged as the "pivotal factor" in the Middle Eastern diplomacy (1982:612). Kissinger, the practitioner of realpolitik, shed no tears over the costs to Soviet-American détente.

Lessons from the Alert Crisis
The trust that appeared to have developed between American and Soviet policymakers during détente evaporated during the Alert Crisis; in the second half of the 1970s a revival of tensions between the superpowers led to a renewal of the arms race.

Despite the mutually acknowledged importance of détente and the shared desire to avoid a confrontation that could lead to the risk of nuclear war, each of the superpowers continued to view their relationship as essentially competitive. As the Middle East crisis developed, the Soviet leadership feared the strategic consequences of losing an ally in its competition with the United States; the United States welcomed the opportunity to turn the fear into reality. The Soviet Union armed Egypt for a war that the USSR viewed as ill conceived—and that would almost certainly endanger the Soviet-U.S. relationship—to avoid a strategic loss that would weaken the USSR's competitive position vis-à-vis the United States. When Sadat launched his attack across the Suez Canal, the United States seized the opportunity to increase its influence within the Arab world by driving a wedge between the Soviet Union and Egypt. The Alert Crisis is emblematic of a relationship that was a mix of competition and collaboration from the start. But each side chose competition over collaboration. Collaboration demands mutual restraint, not only in eschewing opportunities for relative gains but also in avoiding overreactions to minor setbacks. Kissinger's attempt to manipulate the Middle East war to displace Soviet influence in the area violated the former; Brezhnev's reaction to the collapse of the cease-fire violated the latter. Conversely, both sides showed considerable restraint in quickly dampening the risk of escalation at the height of the crisis.

Some of the restraint shown during the peak of the crisis can be attributed to the relationship developed between the American and Soviet leaders during the course of détente, but it would not be unreasonable to attribute some of the restraint to the Cuban Missile Crisis experience as well. Lebow and Stein (1994:265–68) quote a number of Soviet participants who assert that the Soviets had no intention of sending troops into the Middle East, even before the United States reacted with the alert, because of the danger of escalation. The fear of escalation was related to the possibility of Soviet troops becoming engaged in hostilities with Israeli forces, which might then lead to a more dangerous superpower confrontation.

To be sure, Brezhnev's threat and Kissinger's response demonstrate that, despite the lessons of the Cuban Missile Crisis, the leaders of two superpowers still were capable of misinterpreting the actions of the other and, in Brezhnev's case, making rash moves based on emotional reactions. But when the United States placed its forces on alert and began troop movements, the Soviet politburo rejected responding in a tit-for-tat manner. Consequently, the Alert Crisis did not escalate to the same magnitude as the preceding crises. Moreover, the intensity of communication was higher than in any previous superpower crisis, the bargaining was devoid of inflammatory rhetoric, and each side was sensitive to the other's concern for its reputation for resolve. The tone of Kissinger's response to Brezhnev's October 24 message and especially Kissinger's press conference provided a clear path of retreat for Brezhnev, who gracefully took it.

It could be argued that the agreements and expectations that grew out of détente, at least on the Soviet side, represented a degree of complex learning—that is, a changed view of the nature of the superpower relationship and the goals to be pursued. Brezhnev and Gromyko expected to collaborate with the United States in managing the Middle East war to avoid a superpower confrontation. But the hope of superpower collaboration to attain a cease-fire—in a war the Soviets expected their Arab allies to lose if it continued for any length of time—did not stop the Kremlin from supplying military aid to both Egypt and Syria. To put it another way, it is not possible to separate the Soviet interest in attaining a quick cease-fire and consequent peace conference brokered by the two superpowers from prudential realpolitik considerations. By the same token, Kissinger's collaboration to achieve the cease-fire cannot be separated from his realpolitik goals in seeking a stalemated outcome.

There was a shift in each side's approach to the superpower competition, which was expressed in the BPA and APNW accords. The agreement to take collaborative action to manage disputes, including those between other states, to avoid superpower crises certainly represented a more dovish view of the nature of crisis behavior and escalation, but it was within the context of a realpolitik understanding of the superpower rivalry. Like the doctrine of peaceful coexistence introduced after Stalin's death in the 1950s, this new approach was designed to keep the competition within bounds, not to end it.

After the crisis, each side returned to a more hawkish view of the superpower competition. Kissinger moved quickly to parlay his gains in prying Egypt away from its long-standing alliance with the Soviet Union to impose himself as the principal mediator, without Soviet participation, in an Egyptian-Israeli disengagement accord, which was then followed by a similar initiative with Syria, another Soviet client. The Soviets viewed Kissinger's actions as a betrayal of the joint Soviet-American peacemaking effort promised in the Alert Crisis settlement. They intensified their own efforts to gain influence in the Third World, particularly Africa. The Alert Crisis strengthened the influence of hawks within both governments. In the United States, the presumed effectiveness of the alert provided another argument to support a strategy of deterrence that relied on military power and a demonstrated willingness to use it. In the Soviet Union, the outcome confirmed the views of those who distrusted American intentions and reinforced the notion that Soviet-American relations were a zero-sum game.

If the superpowers still had not learned how to reshape their essentially competitive relationship, there is evidence that they had learned how to manage their crises more effectively. The bargaining of the Alert Crisis shows the limits to what can be obtained by a prudential application of realpolitik in a situation fraught with the risks of a conflict spiral. Anything more would have required a different view of the superpower relationship—that is, complex learning. But the collaborative relationship associated with détente did not extend to the competition in the Middle East.

Conclusions

Crisis Behavior and Bargaining

The first question posed in chapter 1 asks whether there are observable changes in the patterns of behavior and influence strategies employed by the superpowers from one crisis to the next. The answer is a qualified yes.

The answer is qualified because, despite significant differences in the duration of the crises and in patterns of escalation and reciprocity, there are some striking similarities in influence strategies. Each of the first three crises began with a Soviet attempt at a fait accompli to alter the strategic status quo, and, in each instance the United States resisted the challenge. Within each of those crises, serious efforts to negotiate a settlement did not begin until the crisis reached a stalemate and each side had demonstrated its firmness. Each side's predominant influence strategy remained the same in the two Berlin crises, although the escalation was lower, and the intensity of negotiation was significantly higher in the second Berlin crisis.

As table 3.4 illustrates, the superpowers' influence strategies changed in the Cuban Missile Crisis, when the United States found itself in the position of having to compel the Soviet Union to remove the missiles from Cuba. The American influence strategy shifted from Reciprocating to Cautious Bullying. Despite beginning the crisis with another attempted fait accompli, the Soviet Union shifted from a Bullying strategy to what is best described as a Trial and Error influence strategy, as Khrushchev, in a pattern that had been observed in his earlier disputes with the United States, oscillated between coercion and accommodation. The Alert Crisis was the only superpower crisis in which neither side employed a Cautious Bullying influence strategy. The United States returned to a Reciprocating influence strategy, while the Soviets again employed a predominantly Trial and Error strategy.

In sum, the major changes in crisis behavior were the reduction in escalation and increase in communication between the two Berlin crises, the dramatic rate of escalation in the Cuban Missile Crisis, the low level of escalation and high intensity of communication in the Alert Crisis, and the changes in influence strategies that occurred in the Cuban Missile and Alert Crises. What is missing in these observed changes is any consistent pattern of increasingly hostile or accommodative behavior.

The second research question asks whether the observed changes led to more effective crisis management. The most obvious pattern of change

TABLE 3.4.   Soviet-American Crises: Influence Strategies and Outcomes

Crisis	Influence Strategy		Outcome
	Soviet Union	United States	
Berlin Blockade	Cautious Bullying	Reciprocating	U.S. victory
Berlin Wall	Cautious Bullying	Reciprocating	Stalemate
Cuban Missile	Cautious Bullying/ Trial and Error	Cautious Bullying	U.S. victory
Middle East Alert	Trial and Error	Reciprocating	U.S. victory

across the four crises is the progressively shorter duration of each crisis. Since none of the crises escalated to war, the consistently shorter duration suggests increasing alertness to the necessity of reaching a settlement and a greater willingness to do so. That impression, however, is contradicted by the patterns of behavior described previously—the significant increase in escalation from the second to the third of the four superpower crises. An intriguing pattern, however, can be seen in the negative association between the degree of escalation and the intensity of negotiation over the course of particular crises. As table 3.5 illustrates, there is an inverse relationship between negotiation and escalation in the rankings of the four superpower crises. The two crises with the lowest escalation scores—the Berlin Wall and Alert Crises—also have the highest reciprocity scores and the most intensive negotiation. In each instance there were leaders on both sides who believed in the importance of open communication and the feasibility of finding negotiated solutions to superpower differences.

Learning

Is there evidence of experiential learning in the superpower rivalry? The answer again is a qualified yes. The answer must be qualified for two reasons. First, for the reasons mentioned in chapter 1, evidence of the presence of learning, even by national leaders, is not the same as evidence that the lessons affected state behavior. Whether learning did or did not affect the behavior of the superpowers from one crisis to the next, and especially how much effect it had, given the other likely influences on behavior considered in the preceding accounts of each of the four crises, cannot be determined empirically in this study. Thus, the discussion that follows is based on what appear to be plausible judgments. Second, the evidence of learning that does surface from those accounts is sometimes vicarious—that is, it comes from crises other than those in which the individuals participated actively.

Khrushchev and Kennedy drew lessons from their experiences in the Berlin Wall Crisis that appear to have influenced their behavior in the

TABLE 3.5.   Negotiation in Soviet-American Crises

Crisis	Duration in Days	Days preceding First Negotiation	Days of Negotiation (%)	Escalation Rank
Berlin Blockade	420	105 (8/2)	10	1
Berlin Wall	166	97 (9/21)	21	3
Cuban Missile	79	10 (10/24)	16	2
Middle East Alert	33	16 (10/21)	30	4

Cuban Missile Crisis. But they also drew lessons from other disputes, including those in which they were not major participants. The lessons that Khrushchev drew from the Berlin Wall Crisis were reinforced by his observation of Kennedy's handling of the Bay of Pigs invasion as well as the Soviet leader's impression of Kennedy during the Vienna summit. Kennedy's beliefs in the importance of open communication to avoid miscalculation during the Berlin Wall and Cuban Missile Crises were drawn from his reading of Tuchman's (1962) historical account of the 1914 crisis. Conversely, the members of Kennedy's foreign-policy team who had participated in the Berlin Blockade Crisis were highly skeptical of negotiating with the Soviets during the Berlin Wall Crisis.

One lesson that both superpower leaders drew from the Berlin Wall Crisis was that they had to demonstrate greater resolve in the next superpower confrontation. Khrushchev's belief that Stalin had overestimated U.S. willingness to go to war was reinforced by the Bay of Pigs and his experience during the Berlin Wall Crisis. The successful use of a fait accompli, in the form of the wall, encouraged his more audacious attempt in the Cuban Missile Crisis. Conversely, Kennedy worried that Khrushchev's observation of the president's handling of the Bay of Pigs operation, his conciliatory efforts at the Vienna summit, and his acceptance of the Berlin Wall had left Khrushchev with the impression that Kennedy was irresolute. The discovery of Khrushchev's attempted fait accompli in Cuba must have confirmed those fears.

The Alert Crisis was the shortest of the four crises; it has the lowest escalation score on all three indicators, the second highest reciprocity score, and the highest percentage of days on which the two sides negotiated with each other. Did the quick resolution of that crisis benefit from lessons drawn from the Cuban Missile Crisis experience 12 years earlier? The Soviet interest in collaboration and the intense communication that occurred between the two sides during the Alert Crisis can be attributed largely to the atmosphere of détente that had been created in the years preceding the crisis. Whether the mutual interest in détente can be linked to lessons drawn from the Cuban Missile Crisis is a matter of speculation.

Perhaps the most important learning in the Soviet-American rivalry was diagnostic—that is, it offered a better understanding by each of the other's motivation and intentions. The key lesson that both sides drew from the Cuban Missile Crisis was that each of them not only viewed a superpower war as catastrophic but also recognized that the other shared that view. The United States recognized not only that the Soviet Union shared its aversion to war but that the Soviet Union also was aware of the American aversion to war. During the Berlin Blockade Crisis, neither superpower was confident of the other's attitude toward war. In fact,

Khrushchev later criticized Stalin for being obsessed with the fear of a Western attack. During the Berlin Wall Crisis, Khrushchev began to wonder aloud if Kennedy's hawkish advisers might push the inexperienced president into war. As the Cuban Missile Crisis rapidly escalated, particularly after the downing of the U-2, both sides worried that events might push one or the other into war. But the experience of the Cuban Missile Crisis and the communications between the two sides that occurred during and after the crisis finally led to a mutual realization of their shared concern with the risk of nuclear war. That realization, coupled with the atmosphere created by détente, made possible the BPA and APNW accords in the early 1970s and is reflected in the caution and concern with escalation by both sides during the Alert Crisis.

The answer to the question of whether the lessons that the leaders of the superpowers drew from their states' crisis experiences were functional or dysfunctional is also mixed. To the extent that the lessons that Kennedy and Khrushchev drew from their experiences in the Berlin Wall Crisis influenced their behavior in the Cuban Missile Crisis, the consequences were dysfunctional—they encouraged the rapid escalation of the crisis. But there is some evidence that the diagnostic lessons drawn after the Cuban Missile Crisis led to greater moderation during the Alert Crisis.

Is there evidence that the learning by the leadership of either of the superpowers extended beyond simple, or tactical, learning to complex learning—that is, to a new interpretation of their relationship with the adversary and/or goals to be pursued? In this instance, the answer is a qualified no. The Soviet leadership's pursuit of a collaborative effort to manage the Middle East war of 1973, consistent with the APNW accord, appears to represent a changed view of the superpower relationship and the goals to be pursued. But the Soviet concern with the new relationship and especially preserving the economic and political benefits of détente was not sufficient to prevent it from providing Egypt with the military hardware necessary for Sadat to begin the war that led to the superpower confrontation or, while calling for a cease-fire, to order a massive airlift of additional military assistance to allow Egypt to continue its offensive. When the cease-fire collapsed, and Brezhnev perceived that Kissinger had taken advantage of the Soviet collaboration to obtain an Israeli victory, the Soviet view of the superpower relationship returned to an exclusively competitive approach.

Nixon and Kissinger pursued a realpolitik approach to the superpower relationship throughout the crisis. Détente represented a recognition of the new strategic balance and, initially, a means of enlisting Soviet support in bringing the Vietnam War to an end. When the war broke out in the Middle East, Nixon and Kissinger viewed the superpower relationship in purely competitive terms. It was an opportunity to replace Soviet influence in Egypt with that of the United States. The restraint shown by Kissinger in his bargaining during the crisis was a tactical adjustment consistent with a prudential application of realpolitik. Thus, the answer to the question regarding complex learning ultimately is that it did not occur, with the qualification that the Soviet leadership temporarily underwent a shift in its view of its relationship with the United States.

The behavior and learning in the superpower crises was bounded by the policymakers' realpolitik belief systems. That the crises themselves were kept in bounds resulted primarily from a mutual fear of the catastrophic consequences of war.

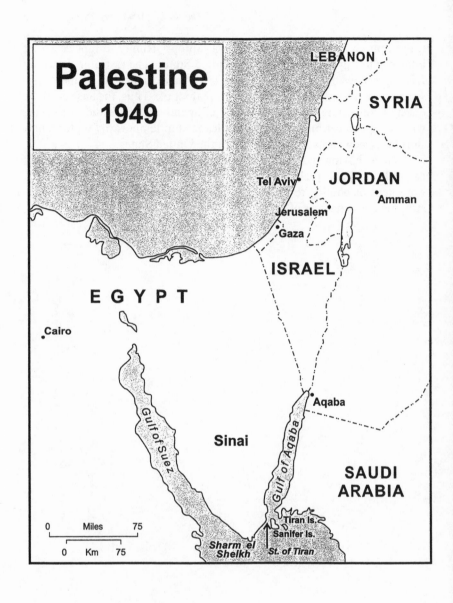

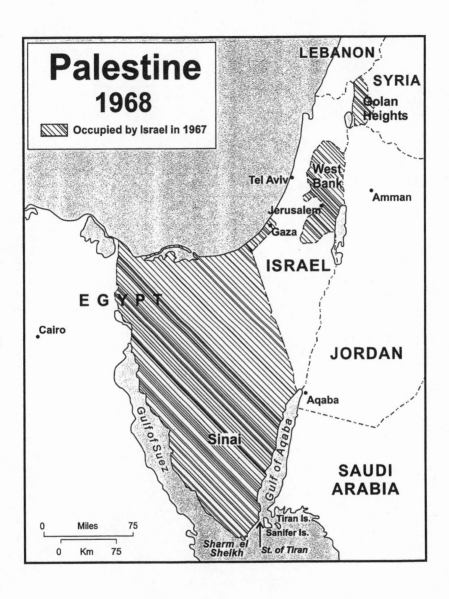

Palestine
1968

▨ Occupied by Israel in 1967

LEBANON

SYRIA

Golan
Heights

Tel Aviv

West
Bank

Amman

Jerusalem

Gaza

ISRAEL

E G Y P T

Cairo

JORDAN

Aqaba

Gulf of Suez

Sinai

Gulf of Aqaba

SAUDI
ARABIA

Tiran Is.
Sanfer Is.

Sharm el
Shelkh

St. of Tiran

0   Miles   75

0   Km   75

CHAPTER 4

The Egyptian-Israeli Rivalry

The Egyptian-Israeli rivalry lasted from the birth of Israel in 1948 until 1979, when the two states signed a peace treaty mediated by the United States. Egypt and Israel became engaged in four militarized crises between 1948 and 1973, and all four ended in war. A fifth war, the "war of attrition," occurred between the 1967 and 1973 crises. The crisis outcomes are not surprising given the interests at stake. The issue at the center of the rivalry, at least until after the 1967 Six Day War, was Israel's existence. Egypt fought the 1973 war to regain territory that Israel had seized from Egypt six years earlier.

Do the concepts of learning and effective crisis management have any meaning in such circumstances? Both sides drew lessons from their crisis experiences, but the causal lessons dealt with military issues rather than with crisis management per se. Understanding why Egypt and Israel drew those lessons can demonstrate something about why they found themselves in five wars in 25 years.

Background

The four Egyptian-Israeli crises must be viewed in light of both centuries-old and twentieth-century tensions between Arabs and Jews over rights to the Holy Land. The Zionist movement at the end of the nineteenth century, which led to the migration of thousands of Jews to a hoped-for Palestine homeland, triggered growing tensions in the twentieth century. In 1917, British Foreign Minister Arthur Balfour issued a declaration stating Great Britain's intention to support the establishment of a Jewish homeland in Palestine. The Balfour Declaration further fueled the Zionists' dream of a Jewish state while outraging Arabs, who outnumbered Jews by ten to one in Palestine. Realization of the Zionist aspirations was postponed indefinitely, however, when Britain accepted a League of Nations mandate over Palestine in 1922. The first Arab anti-Zionist riots occurred in the same year.

Tensions increased during the 1930s when Jews fleeing Hitler's Germany swelled the ranks of Jews in Palestine. To placate the Arabs and to preserve the possibility of a binational state, in 1939 the British issued the MacDonald White Paper on Palestine. The white paper placed a ceiling on Jewish immigration and placed strict regulations on Zionist land purchases. Nevertheless, tens of thousands of Jews who had managed to survive the Holocaust sought refuge in Palestine after World War II. A growing number of clashes broke out between Arabs and Jews as well as between both groups and the British authorities.

The British were caught between two nationalist movements. Besides attempting to contain the violent conflict between Palestinian Arabs and Jews, the British were pressured by Arab states, such as Egypt, which sought full independence, as well as Jewish groups fighting for an end to immigration restrictions. By the summer of 1947, the war-weary British had had enough; they turned the Palestine problem over to the United Nations. On November 29, 1947, after months of investigation and debate, the United Nations General Assembly voted to partition Palestine into two states, one Arab and one Jewish. The partition plan granted 57 percent of Palestine, including the more fertile coastal area, to the Jews, who at the time represented 33 percent of the population and owned just 7 percent of the land (Gerner 1991:45). The plan was hailed by the Zionists and unanimously rejected by the Arab states. On the next day, Arab snipers attacked a Jerusalem-bound bus, killing five Jewish passengers.

Palestine Crisis, 1948–49

The first of the four Egyptian-Israeli crises set the stage for the three crises and four wars that followed over the next 25 years. Israel's experience in 1948–49 set in place an image of Egyptian intentions that led to a strategy of deterrence and the use of force that did not change until after the 1973 Middle East war. Egypt's determination to eliminate Israel did not change until after the third Arab-Israeli crisis—that is, after its defeat in the 1967 Six Day War.

Crisis Structure

The Palestine crisis took place between the leaders of the Jewish Zionist movement in Palestine, who founded the new state of Israel on May 14, 1948, and Palestinian Arabs and the member states of the Arab League, who opposed the establishment of the Jewish state. The Arab League, which had been formed on March 22, 1945, included Syria, Transjordan, Saudi Arabia, Lebanon, Yemen, and Egypt.

Egypt
Perceptions of the Jewish leadership. Although the Secretary-General of the Arab League, Azzam Pasha, was an Egyptian, Egypt did not assume a leadership role in the anti-Zionist movement until late in the crisis. The Egyptian leadership initially viewed Zionist organizations such as the Irgun, Haganah, and Stern as little more than criminal gangs (Heikal 1988:116). In fact, the Egyptians had no particular animus toward the Jews, who were viewed with some sympathy as fellow freedom fighters against British colonial rule (Sachar 1981:42).

Egyptian interests. Egyptian Prime Minister Malmud al-Nuqrashi's first priority was to free Egypt from British domination. As the Palestine crisis intensified, the Egyptian government was preoccupied with delicate negotiations with Great Britain over the future of the Suez Canal and the Sudan. Having little interest in the United Nations debate over the partition of Palestine, the Egyptian government allowed the more radical Arab states to carry the anti-Zionist banner. But after the partition vote, large-scale popular anti-Zionist—and anti-British—demonstrations within Egypt forced the Nuqrashi government to declare a state of national emergency.

The Palestine issue also affected Egypt's leadership role in the Middle East. Nuqrashi as well as Azzam favored assisting the Palestinian Arabs by supplying them with arms for guerrilla warfare while continuing efforts to achieve a negotiated settlement. But Iraq, Transjordan, and the mufti of Jerusalem were in favor of armed intervention against the Zionists. Transjordan's King Abdullah launched a public attack on the Egyptians by claiming that only Egypt's hesitation prevented the Arab states from intervening militarily in Palestine (Heikal 1988:117). Then, in April 1948, Abdullah announced that he would send Transjordan's Arab Legion into Palestine once the British mandate ended. To prevent Abdullah from achieving leadership of the Arab effort, the Egyptian government decided to join the cause of the "liberation" of Palestine for the Palestinian Arabs (Rabinovich 1991:168). The Egyptian government accepted the costs and risks of war to maintain its positions at home and among their Arab neighbors.

Egyptian capabilities. The combined forces of the Arab states had an enormous advantage over the Israelis in both weapons and manpower. Even though Abdullah declared himself commander in chief of the intervening forces, there was no real coordination among the separate armies. Each fought on its own. The ill-prepared Egyptian expeditionary force entered Palestine in old tourist cars provided by a travel agency; they lacked maps and were led by largely incompetent officers (Heikal 1988:117).

Israel

Perceptions of Arab and Egyptian intentions.   The Zionist leaders had no illusions regarding the Arab states' intentions. War was unavoidable, and Egypt was considered the strongest of the Arab powers (Sachar 1976:348). However indifferent the Nuqrashi government may have appeared, Egypt voted in the United Nations General Assembly against partition; in fact, Egypt declared the decision outside the scope of the association's charter and, therefore, null and void (Israel Department of Information 1960:34). Moreover, the secretary-general of the Arab League, which vowed to block partition, was an Egyptian.

Israeli interests.   The Zionist leaders' first two priorities were to create a Jewish state—not a binational state—to serve as a homeland for Jews in Palestine and then to insure its long-term survival. The latter would be achieved through two means: immigration to achieve a Jewish majority and a larger population base within Israel, and the creation of a strong defense force (Moore 1975:260–62).

Israeli capabilities.   The Zionist leadership began at a decided disadvantage in money, weapons, and manpower vis-à-vis the Arabs. Only states can purchase military equipment on the international market, and Israel was not a state prior to the day when it was attacked. The Zionist leaders obtained smuggled arms through black markets, but they were markedly inferior to those belonging to the armies of the new state's seven Arab enemies. The Arabs had tanks; Israel had a few ancient cannons. The Arab states had established armies; Israel was in the process of building and training an army. Israel's military advantages lay in its motivation, the initiative given to its midlevel officers, and its unity (Peres 1995:60; Sachar 1981:51).

The Superpowers

After World War II, the Truman administration found itself caught between its close relationship with Great Britain, its strategic interest in maintaining good relations with the Arabs to retain access to Middle East oil, and American popular support for the Zionist movement. American domestic politics exerted the strongest influence on Truman, who faced reelection in 1948. Truman opposed the British restrictions on Jewish immigration, and he instructed the American United Nations delegation to support the United Nations partition plan. Following the partition vote, the Truman administration was pressured by American Jewish groups as well as others sympathetic to the cause to guarantee the security of the promised Jewish state in the face of the Arab League's pledge to crush it. These pressures, however, came at a time when the administration was becoming increasingly concerned about the course of the Cold War. Secretary of State George Marshall and his colleagues placed a high priority on the availability of Arab oil in the event of a conflict in Europe; they had no interest in intervening against Arab armies in Palestine. On March 19, 1948, the American United Nations delegation proposed a "cooling off period," during which Palestine would remain under a United Nations trusteeship, instead of implementing the partition plan that summer. The proposal created a domestic crisis for President Truman, who had not been informed of the initiative. To make matters worse, on the previous evening Truman had privately assured Jewish leader Chaim Weizmann that America would support the establishment of Israel (McCullough 1992:608–10). Truman attempted to straddle the issue until Haganah leader David Ben-Gurion announced Israel's creation on May 14. Eleven minutes after Ben-Gurion's announcement, the United States announced its de facto recognition of Israel. Throughout the war, however, the United States maintained an embargo on the shipment of arms to Israel and pushed hard for a mediated settlement of the war.

The Soviet Union granted Israel de jure recognition shortly after the American declaration of de facto recognition. The American action was prompted by domestic considerations and, in Truman's case, sympathy for the Jewish cause; the Soviet decision appears to have been motivated by ideological considerations. From the Soviet perspective, the Jews, like the Arabs, were engaged in a struggle against Western (British) imperialism. Ben-Gurion's dramatic proclamation of Israeli statehood underscored the departure of the British. Soviet support of Israeli independence may appear odd in light of subsequent Soviet efforts to court the Arab states; however, the Soviet Union did not become actively involved in Arab Middle East until after the Palestine War.

Crisis Behavior

Shortly after the United Nations vote, on December 9, 1947, leaders of the Arab League states met in Cairo, where they resolved to block the partition plan. They agreed to provide money and weapons to the Palestinian Arabs and to form an army of volunteers from Arab states. Clashes between armed elements of the local Arab population and Jewish settlers had begun almost immediately after the United Nations vote on partition. Jewish terrorist groups also struck at the Arab civilian population. On three occasions between late December and early January, the Irgun and the Stern Gang tossed bombs into Arab crowds in Jerusalem's Old City (Rabinovich 1991:76).

Arab terrorist activities became more organized with the formation of the Palestine Liberation Army in early January. Jewish forces, meanwhile, were beginning to clandestinely obtain shipments of arms. On April 9, Jewish irregulars engaged in a reprisal raid against the village of Deir Yassin, where more than 200 Arabs, including women and children, were slain following the capture of the village. The incident created a climate of fear, which encouraged the flight of Arabs from areas controlled by Jewish forces. Four days later Arab terrorists retaliated by attacking a convoy of Jewish medical personnel, killing 77 Jews. When Jewish forces captured Haifa following the departure of the British on April 22, Arab residents fled the city.

Two hours before the termination of the British mandate on May 14, 1948, Ben-Gurion announced Israel's creation. Regular armies from Egypt, Iraq, Syria, and Lebanon, with volunteers from Saudi Arabia, Libya, and Yemen, attacked the new state on the next day. Despite early Arab gains, the newly formed Israeli Defense Force (IDF) gradually gained the upper hand over its less motivated and disorganized adversaries. Truces arranged by the United Nations and its representative, Count Folke Bernadotte, came and went as the war settled into a struggle primarily between Israel and Egypt. Bernadotte was assassinated by right-wing Jewish extremists in September; two months later, a member of the radical Muslim Brotherhood assassinated Egyptian Prime Minister Nuqrashi.

After Israeli forces penetrated into Egyptian territory in late December, the two sides agreed to a United Nations–mediated cease-fire on January 7, 1949. Israel and Egypt signed an armistice agreement on February 24, 1949. Only 150,000 of the more than 900,000 Palestinian Arabs remained within the territory now controlled by Israel. Large Arab refugee settlements were created in the West Bank area (280,000), which was now controlled by Jordan, and the Gaza Strip (190,000), which was controlled by Egypt. Israeli territory had expanded to include all of the Galilee and the Negev as well as sections of central Palestine. Jerusalem was divided between Israel and Jordan.

Patterns of Behavior

Time series of the evolution of the Palestinian crisis are depicted in figures 4.1 and 4.2. Figure 4.1 includes the actions of the Palestinian Arabs, Transjordan, Syria, and Lebanon as well as those of Egypt. Figure 4.2 is limited to the actions of Egypt on one side and to the actions of Israel and Zionist groups within Palestine prior to the creation of Israel on the other side. Figure 4.1 shows the relatively intense activity, primarily from the Arab side, prior to Ben-Gurion's pronouncement of the establishment of

Israel on May 14, when the crisis escalated to war. In both figures, the Arab side leads in hostility throughout the crisis, but the magnitude of hostility remains relatively flat prior to May 14. The modest spikes in the magnitude of hostility in figure 4.1 represent clashes between Arab and Jewish Palestinian groups.

As noted earlier, Egypt was a somewhat reluctant participant in the military intervention against Israel. Its activities prior to May 14 consisted almost solely of actions taken to increase its military preparedness as a member of the Arab League. Once the war began, however, Egypt assumed a leading role. The pattern would be repeated in the 1967 Arab-Israeli crisis: a crisis with Israel is precipitated and escalated by conflict between Israel and other Arabs, with Egypt playing only a marginal role until late in the crisis, then becoming Israel's main adversary.

The interactions between the two sides in both figures 4.1 and 4.2 are almost exclusively military. The escalation scores for the crisis, which appear in table 4.1, indicate that, taken as a whole, the Palestine crisis exhibited a relatively high level of escalation. Its combined escalation score would place it in sixth place compared to the 34 crises in the appendix. But, as a dyadic crisis between Egypt and Israel, it would rank near the bottom of the sample, ranking twenty-fourth, and it ranks next to last in escalation among the four Egyptian-Israeli crises. The comparative scores, which are consistent with the visual impression in figures 4.1 and 4.2, underline Egypt's marginal role prior to the outbreak of war.

Table 4.2 contains the reciprocity scores for the four Arab-Israeli/Egyptian-Israeli crises. The comparatively high distance score (37.82) for the Palestine crisis reflects the Arab side's higher magnitude of hostility throughout the crisis. The direction score, which would rank near the median of the larger sample, reflects two crosscurrents in the evolution of the crisis. The score is as low as it is because there is no movement by either party toward more cooperative behavior at any time during the crisis; however, the two are not always moving together in escalating the magnitude of hostility.

Prior to the outbreak of war, there were no attempts to resolve the crisis through negotiations. In fact, there was no perceived common ground on which to negotiate. The Arab states were determined to block the establishment of a Jewish state; Zionist leader Moshe Sharett told the United Nations Security Council in February 1948 that "no reduction of Jewish rights either in territory or in sovereignty would be accepted by the Jewish people" (Israeli Department of Information 1960:35).

The overall picture that emerges from the behavioral data is that of a crisis consisting primarily of military clashes that do not escalate until the final week before the outbreak of war. In essence, the Palestine crisis con-

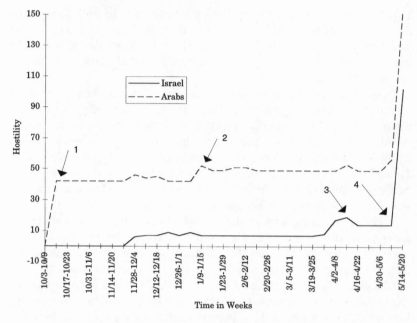

Fig. 4.1. Palestine Crisis, 1947–48 (Arabs-Jews)
Key dates are indicated with arrows: (1) 10/10: Arab League states move
troops to Palestine border; (2) 1/10: Palestine Liberation Army attacks
Jewish settlements; (3) 9/4: Deir Yassin massacre by Jewish irregulars;
(4) 5/14: Ben-Gurion declares state of Israel.

sists of two sides preparing for a war that both sides know will break out
on a set date—May 14. The United Nations decision to partition Palestine
made war virtually inevitable.

Influence Strategies

The influence strategies of both Egypt and Israel are categorized as Bullying, although the intentions of the two sides depart from the usual interpretation of a Bullying strategy as designed to coerce the other into yielding. In this instance, coercion short of war was not considered sufficient.
Both sides relied on brute force. In fact, there was little interaction
between the Egyptians and the Zionists prior to the war; the action that
did take place took the form of military preparations. There were no direct
verbal communications between the two parties.

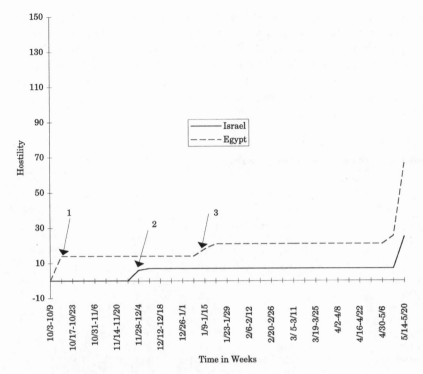

Fig. 4.2.   Palestine Crisis, 1947–48 (Egypt-Israel)
Key dates are indicated with arrows: (1) 10/10: Egypt moves forces to
Palestine border; (2) 11/29: Jews intensify arms buildup; (3) 1/12: Egypt
increases arms buildup.

Egypt

The Egyptian government's approach to the Palestine problem evolved
from relative indifference in the fall of 1947 to indecision in the late winter
of 1948 to a more active role in the month leading up to the war. Egypt
pursued a Bullying influence strategy but did so reluctantly.

Prior to the onset of war, Egypt's Nuqrashi continued to expect that
the United Nations would find a way diplomatically to resolve the crisis.
Even when the army began to move on May 15, Nuqrashi is said to have
assured the commander of Egypt's expeditionary force that the United
Nations Security Council would order a cease-fire before the fighting escalated. But such was not the case. Shortly after its ill-prepared army stum-
bled into war, Egypt found that it was carrying the main burden of the
Arab effort against Israel.

There are two themes in the Egyptian approach that would be

repeated in subsequent crises. The first, which recurs in 1967, is Egypt's late entrance into a crisis precipitated by more radical Arab states, with Egypt's participation resulting from the government's desire to secure its leadership position among Middle Eastern Arab states. The second theme, which recurs in both 1967 and 1973, is the government's expectation that it would be spared the costs of a major war by the diplomatic intervention of the major powers.

TABLE 4.1. Middle East Crises: Escalation Scores

Crises: All Participants	Magnitude Score (Rank)[a]	Intensity Score (Rank)	Rate Score (Rank)	Rank Arabs-Israel	Rank in Larger Sample
Palestine	262.5 (6)	58.79 (14)	11.96 (5)	2	7
Arabs	160.5	48.97	5.02		
Israel	102	9.82	6.94		
Suez	368 (5)	166.18 (2)	22.88 (3)	1	3
Egypt (Br. & Fr.)	67	30.41	2.56		
Israel	39	8.18	2.31		
Britain, France	262	127.58	16.38		
Six Day War	298 (6)	43.61 (18)	9.8 (10)	3	9
Arabs	167	25.52	5.47		
Israel	131	18.1	4.33		
October War	159 (13)	52.41 (15)	4.09 (12)	4	14
Arabs	109	37.97	2.74		
Israel	50	14.44	1.34		
Mean score	132.64	38.37	6.14		

Crises: Egypt-Israel Only	Magnitude Score (Rank)	Intensity Score (Rank)	Rate Score (Rank)	Rank Egypt-Israel	Rank in Larger Sample
Palestine	91.5 (21)	24.85 (28)	2.86 (23)	3	24
Egypt	66.5	19.03	2.08		
Israel	25	5.82	0.78		
Suez	65 (27)	11.41 (28)	3.94 (13)	4	24
Egypt	26	3.24	1.63		
Israel	39	8.18	2.31		
Six Day War	190 (9)	15.1 (25)	6.27 (11)	1	14
Egypt	113	9.48	3.67		
Israel	77	5.61	2.6		
October War	87 (22)	32.28 (21)	2.09 (15)	2	23
Egypt	65	26.42	1.46		
Israel	22	5.86	0.63		
Mean score	108.38	20.91	3.79		

[a]Rank in larger sample.

Israel

Following the Arab League's declaration of its determination to block the establishment of a Jewish state, the Zionists devoted their efforts to prepare for a war that they viewed as unavoidable. Weapons were acquired by every possible means. On May 30, two weeks after the Arab invasions, Israel incorporated the various Zionist forces into a single national group, the IDF. Out of necessity, the Israeli influence strategy, like that of the Egyptians, was purely military. Once Israel had achieved a military victory, Ben-Gurion would be willing to make concessions to achieve a "stable peace," but the military victory would have to come first (Zweig 1991:191; Avi-Hai 1974:176).

Outcome and Lessons

The February 24, 1949 armistice did not lead to a peace settlement. The partition plan died in the war as the Palestinian Arab territory was swallowed up by Israel, Egypt in the Gaza area, and Transjordan on the West Bank. The Arab states remained committed to the elimination of the Jewish state. Their cause was now embraced by nearly 800,000 Palestinian Arab refugees.

Egypt

The Egyptian army's battlefield failures were followed by political chaos in the country. When a gunman from the Muslim Brotherhood assassinated Prime Minister Nuqrashi on December 28, 1948, the country was on the verge of civil war. The Egyptian government blamed the military defeat on

TABLE 4.2. **Middle East Crises: Reciprocity Scores**

Crisis	Direction Score (Rank)[a]	Distance Score (Rank)[a]	Rank in Sample	Rank Arab-Israel	Reciprocity Std. Score[a]
All Participants					
Palestine	4.02 (19)	37.82 (28)	23	3	0.91
Suez	17.5 (34)	105.35 (34)	34	4	−3.37
Six Day War	6.4 (23)	7.42 (16)	17	2	1.21
October War	4.77 (20)	23.53 (22)	20	1	1.16
Egypt-Israel Only					
Palestine	2.97 (10)	13.21 (20)	14	3	−0.41
Suez	4.15 (19)	3.24 (6)	17	2	−0.36
Six Day War	1.67 (3)	3.87 (7)	3	1	2.37
October War	3.11 (11)	20.56 (21)	17	4	−1.60

[a]Rank in larger sample.

the machinations of the British, whom the Egyptians accused of providing the Israelis with intelligence, and the Americans, whom the Egyptians accused of acting in concert with the British to deny arms to the Arab states while aiding Israel (Sachar 1981:65–66).

There is no evidence that Egypt drew any lessons in crisis management from the Palestinian crisis, although the country did recognize its immediate military weakness. After the war the government turned to less risky tactics to pursue the ongoing conflict with Israel: diplomatic isolation, economic boycotts, and cross-border raids by irregular forces.

Israel
The Israelis were exhilarated by their hard-fought independence, but the Ben-Gurion government took a realpolitik view of the future of the small Jewish state, which was surrounded and vastly outnumbered by hostile Arab neighbors. Ben-Gurion considered offering some territorial concessions and technical assistance to Transjordan and Egypt in return for diplomatic recognition of Israel, but he was skeptical of the permanence of any such agreements even if they were attainable (Avi-Hai 1974:176–78). The lesson that Ben-Gurion drew from Israel's founding was that its survival depended on its military strength and, ultimately, immigration. "Immigration is the foremost factor for our security. . . . Without immigration we are destined for destruction: 700,000 Jews surrounded by a sea of Arabs will not survive," Ben-Gurion told his citizens (Avi-Hai 1974:176–77).

Suez Crisis, 1956

The Suez Crisis began as a crisis between Egypt and Britain, with France joining with Britain. Israel entered late and did so only to launch a surprise attack against Egypt. Nevertheless, the crisis led to important lessons for both Israel and Egypt that affected their behavior in the 1967 Six Day War as well as their relationships with the United States and the Soviet Union.

The Intercrisis Period, 1949–56

When Egypt and Israel signed an armistice agreement at the end of February 1949, the border generally followed the prewar boundary between Palestine and Egypt. The armistice was intended as the first step toward a peace agreement, but the United Nations Conciliation Commission was unable to bring the parties together for official negotiations, and unofficial meetings were unproductive. By November 1951, the commission abandoned the effort.

Egypt, meanwhile, occupied the islands of Tiran and Sanafir, which were located at the entrance to the Gulf of Aqaba. Egypt also established shore batteries at Sharm al-Sheikh on the southern tip of the Sinai. Egypt thereby obtained strategic control over the Strait of Tiran, effectively controlling access to the entrance to the strait. Eilat provided Israel's only direct access to the Red Sea for trade with Asia as well as access to oil from Persian Gulf states. By late 1953, the Egyptian Coast Guard was regulating—and restricting—Israeli commerce through the strait. Egypt had been harassing ships navigating the Suez Canal to do business with Israel since 1950. In addition, the Arab League enacted a boycott of companies doing business with Israel.

Border raids intensified in the early 1950s. By the spring of 1954, Israel had lodged more than 400 complaints to the Mixed Armistice Commission to protest raids coming from the Gaza Strip. Fedayeen squads composed of Palestinian commandos, unofficially trained and equipped by Egypt, began to penetrate deeply into Israel over the next two years. The raids produced increasingly severe Israeli retaliations. In February 1955, Israel carried out a raid into Gaza, where the IDF briefly seized the Egyptian army headquarters.

Changes in Egypt

Major changes occurred within Egypt and in its relations with the Western powers and the Soviet Union in the years following the Palestine crisis. With anticolonial sentiment against Britain running high, a group of Egyptian army officers, led by Gamal Abdel Nasser, staged a successful coup in July 1952. When Nasser assumed the role of prime minister in the spring of 1954, he transformed Egypt from a docile client state of Great Britain to a fiercely anti-imperial, revolutionary power. Nasser's own ambitions extended to leadership not only of the Arab Middle East but also of all of the Islamic world.

Nasser's anti-imperialism quickly strained relations with Great Britain and France. He encouraged East Africans to rebel against British rule and he supported the revolutionary forces in their revolt against French rule in Algeria. Just as Nasser's anti-imperialism alienated Britain and France, his increasingly friendly relations with the Soviet Union alienated the United States.

Israel's presence in the Middle East was viewed by Nasser as an extension of Western imperialism. He demanded restoration of the 1947 partition boundaries and resettlement of Palestinian refugees as minimal conditions for peace. There is scant evidence, however, that Nasser had any interest in peace with Israel. After the embarrassment of Israel's Gaza raid in 1955, which led refugees in the Gaza strip to riot against Egypt's failure to protect them, Nasser turned to an overtly belligerent policy. The fedayeen raids were increased, and Egypt began a more energetic effort to increase its military capabilities. In September 1955, with the assistance of the Soviet Union, Egypt agreed to a major arms purchase from Czechoslovakia.[1]

Changes in Israel

Israel's insecurity was heightened by the Arab economic boycott, Egypt's partial blockade of Israeli shipping, Nasser's hostile pan-Arabism, and the fedayeen raids. Although the Israeli government could be described as moderately dovish under Sharett's leadership in 1954, it engineered a secret arms purchase from France well before Nasser's deal with Czechoslovakia.

The return of Ben-Gurion in the wake of a 1955 government scandal led to a more overtly hawkish Israeli foreign policy.[2] Following the announcement of Nasser's arms deal with Czechoslovakia, Ben-Gurion ordered Israeli Chief of Staff Moshe Dayan to prepare a contingency plan to capture the Strait of Tiran, Sharm al-Sheikh, and the islands in the Gulf of Aqaba (Sachar 1976:482). By the end of November 1955, Israeli troops had forced the Egyptian army completely out of the DMZ. In April 1956, two Israeli retaliations to fedayeen raids resulted in the deaths of 116 Egyptians (Sachar 1976:488; Wheelock 1960:233).

The Regional and Global Context

The Egyptian-Israeli component of the Suez Crisis was imbedded in the crisis between Britain and Egypt over the Suez Canal. The British were supported by the French, who had their own differences with Nasser because of his support of the Algerian forces fighting to gain independence from France.

Stalin's death in 1953 had led to a relaxation in tensions between the Eastern and Western blocs, which was exemplified by the cordial spirit of

---

1. The agreement would supply Egypt with 500 armored vehicles, 200 fighter and transport planes, and 50 Iluyshin-28 bombers (Dupuy 1978:132).

2. The Lavon Affair originated in a clandestine Israeli operation in Cairo in the summer of 1954. Israeli agents posing as Arabs attempted to sabotage British and American property in the hope of discouraging improved relations between those governments and Egypt. The participants were caught by the Egyptian government, which released the details of the plot and then hanged two of the agents. Israeli Defense Minister Pinchas Lavon was accused of having authorized the operation and was replaced by Ben-Gurion as defense minister in February 1955.

the Geneva summit meeting of the heads of state of the Soviet Union, United States, Great Britain, and France in July 1955. The euphoria of Geneva, however, was dampened somewhat by American Secretary of State John Foster Dulles's call for rolling back Soviet control over Eastern Europe. After Khrushchev himself called for some relaxation of that control in conjunction with his attack on Stalin at the twentieth congress of Soviet Communist Party in February 1956, the Kremlin found itself faced with national liberation movements in Eastern Europe. Labor unrest led to a coup in Poland in which liberal communists temporarily seized control of the government and police forces in mid-October. Then, during the peak of the Suez Crisis, the Hungarians overthrew the Soviet puppet regime in Budapest. On October 29, the day the Israelis attacked across the Sinai, the Soviets were negotiating with the new Hungarian government. The outbreak of the Suez war afforded Khrushchev not only an opportunity to champion the cause of anti-imperialism against the Western powers but also an opportunity to crush the Hungarian revolution while the Western powers were preoccupied with their own crisis. On November 1 Soviet tanks rumbled across the Hungarian border and crushed the revolt.

In the United States, the Eisenhower administration was nearing the end of a presidential campaign when the two crises exploded. The American government, which was caught between support for its closest ally and its American ideological opposition to colonialism, had encouraged the British to seek a diplomatic settlement of the Suez dispute through the United Nations. The United States knew nothing of the planned invasion. When the war broke out, just days before the November 6 presidential election, Dulles and Eisenhower were caught off guard. Furious at being left in the dark and aware of the parallel that would be drawn to the Soviet intervention in Hungary, Eisenhower found himself in the awkward position of joining the Soviet Union in pressuring the Israelis, British, and French to bring a quick halt to the fighting (see Neustadt 1970:23–26).

Crisis Structure

Egypt
Perception of Israeli intentions.   Although Nasser viewed Israel as a creation of Western imperialism, he thought it unlikely that Britain and France would collude with Israel. Nasser assumed that the Western powers would avoid the political costs among Middle East Arabs that would follow any military collusion with Israel and that Israel, which already had a military edge over Egypt, would not want to appear dependent on the Western powers (Hewedy, in Louis and Owen 1989:169; Calvocoressi 1967:47–48). Following the February 1955 Gaza raid, Nasser became

more convinced of Israel's aggressive intentions, and he feared the possibility that the British might use an Egyptian-Israeli war as a pretext to intervene militarily in their former mandate (Nutting 1972:168). Consequently, he sought to reduce the tensions along the Egyptian-Israeli border during the Suez Crisis; still, he did not draw a connection between the dispute with Britain and France and a possible Israeli attack.

Egyptian interests. Nasser's primary goals were to secure the political independence of Egypt, to maintain his own political power within Egypt, and to expand his influence in the Arab world. Political independence required standing firm with regard to the nationalization of the canal, but it also meant avoiding any actions that would encourage the British or French to intervene militarily in their former mandates.

Egypt also continued its policy of refusing to negotiate with Israel lest it lend legitimacy to the Jewish state. Nasser rejected the idea of peace with Israel as a potential threat to his ideological and political power, Egyptian morale, and even the Egyptian economy (Wheelock 1960:234).

Egyptian capabilities. Only about a quarter of the tanks, fighters, and bombers that Egypt had received from Russia via Czechoslovakia were in service or operational in 1956. Moreover, Egyptian tank crews and pilots were still in the process of learning how to handle the new weapons and planes (Nutting 1972:170). Egyptian intelligence was aware of the arms transfers of tanks, planes, and artillery to Israel and viewed Egypt's largely untrained forces as at a significant comparative disadvantage (Louis and Owen 1989:168–69).

Israel
Perception of Egyptian intentions. By the end of the Palestine War, Israel's leaders had concluded that relations with their Arab neighbors hinged on their relationship with Egypt, the most powerful and influential Arab state (Lucas 1975:357). The ascendancy of Nasser, with his ideology of militant Arab nationalism, ended any hopes that the relationship could be improved through diplomacy.

During the early 1950s Israel became increasingly diplomatically isolated, not only by Arab states but also by nonaligned states, the Soviet bloc, and even many European countries. The frequent armed clashes, fedayeen raids, and belligerent rhetoric of Arab leaders, coupled with the continuing economic boycott and the blockade of the Gulf of Aqaba, created an atmosphere of growing insecurity (Dayan 1966:4). When Jordan joined the Joint Egypt-Syria Military Command in mid-October 1956, Israeli policymakers became convinced that the Arab states, led by Egypt, were set on annihilating Israel (Dayan 1966:5, 15). The Nasser regime's rhetoric reinforced those perceptions: "Weep O Israel because Egypt's Arabs have already found their way to Tel Aviv. . . . There will be no more peace on the borders, because we demand the death of Israel," Cairo radio crowed after a fedayeen raid (Meir 1973:92).

Ben-Gurion concluded that peace with Egypt was impossible; furthermore, Arab unity could lead ultimately to the complete encirclement and destruction of Israel (Avi-Hai 1974:188). By the fall of 1956, Israeli leaders believed that their nation's security was more threatened than at any time since 1948.

Israeli interests. Security was Israel's paramount concern, and Ben-Gurion believed that Israel's security depended "first and foremost upon its ability to defend itself by its own power and to deter its enemies until these enemies cease being its enemies" (Avi-Hai 1974:125–26). Ben-Gurion's deterrence strategy had three components: immigration to increase the size of Israel, acquisition of modern arms, and retaliatory raids. But Israel's long-term security also depended on its economic health. The Arab-led boycott, Egypt's closure of the Suez Canal to Israeli trade, and Egypt's blockade of Aqaba and Israel's access to southern waters threatened Israeli's long-term health (Dayan 1966:207).

Capabilities. Egyptian access to Soviet arms, which had the potential to lead to Arab military superiority, was a consideration in the Israeli decision to undertake the preemptive war in 1956. With most of the Egyptian weapons not yet operational in the fall of 1956, Israeli policymakers recognized that they enjoyed a short military window of opportunity. Nevertheless, the military balance was too close for Israel to have attacked Egypt alone. British and French airpower were considered necessary for a successful attack with minimal casualties (Avi-Hai 1974:134; Dayan 1966:61). When the French approached the Ben-Gurion government with a plan for a joint effort with Britain and France, which also would supply additional modern weapons to Israel, the military balance shifted decisively in Israel's favor.

Crisis Behavior

American-British agreements to finance Egypt's construction of a massive dam on the Nile at Aswan had been based on the hope that Nasser might be persuaded to join the Western side in the Cold War. When Nasser reached an agreement to acquire Soviet arms through Czechoslovakia, U.S. Secretary of State Dulles advised President Eisenhower to cancel the financial assistance. The United States and Britain agreed in May 1956 to allow the funding for Egypt's Aswan Dam to "wither on the vine," although the official American and British announcements did not come until late July.[3] Nasser responded by turning to the Soviet Union for assistance in building the dam and by nationalizing the Suez Canal on July 26. The British and French saw Nasser's nationalization of the canal as a violation of their legal rights. In addition, the British perceived a threat to the remains of their empire. Both countries also saw Nasser's aggressive nationalism as a wider threat to the stability and peace of the Middle East and Western influence in the oil-rich region.

The British and French almost immediately began preparing tentative plans for an invasion of Egypt to regain control of the canal. In early August, the French informally contacted the Israeli government to see if it would join in the military invasion. The Israelis responded positively. The United States, meanwhile, publicly rejected using force to regain control of the canal. Dulles made several efforts through the United Nations to find the means of circumventing Nasser's fait accompli without resorting to force. The United States developed a scheme, the so-called Suez Canal Users Association (SCUA). The maritime powers would pilot ships through the canal and collect passage fees, thereby denying the income to Egypt, which was not included in the plan. The plan was impractical as well as irrelevant in light of the British-French plans. On September 23, Ben-Gurion told the French that Israel was ready to join in a joint invasion if the French would provide air cover for the Israeli attack in the Sinai and would supply Israel with 100 tanks and other military materiel. The French readily agreed to Israel's conditions.

The United Nations Security Council began discussing the Suez Crisis in early October. The Security Council meetings, along with private meetings among the foreign ministers of Britain, France, and Egypt, made no progress. In fact, Britain, France, and Israel were moving ahead with plans for their joint invasion. A secret accord among the three states was signed at Sèvres on October 24. It was a complicated scheme. The action would begin with a surprise Israeli attack across the Sinai. Britain and France then would demand a cease-fire, which would include the use of British and French troops to "secure" the canal, and threaten to intervene militarily if the demand were rejected. Israel would accept the ultimatum, but with Egypt's expected rejection, British and French forces would intervene to occupy the canal and possibly move on to Cairo to depose Nasser.

Israel invaded on October 29, with thrusts directed to the canal, Gaza, and Sharm al-Sheikh, and quickly advanced across the Sinai. On

3. Nasser received word of the American-British plans and warned that if they were carried out, he would nationalize the canal and find other sources for funding. The warning, which was passed to the British embassy, apparently was not transmitted to London or Washington (see Ovendale 1984:143).

the next day the British and French delivered their ultimatum, which Nasser, as expected, rejected. Britain and France commenced bombing raids on October 31. Nasser, with his armies hopelessly unprepared, ordered a guerrilla resistance and began sinking ships to block the canal. By November 2, Israeli forces were in full control of the Sinai and Gaza. American and Soviet efforts to obtain a cease-fire resolution in the United Nations Security Council were vetoed by Britain and France, whose troops were advancing on the canal with little resistance. The superpowers asked the General Assembly for a resolution calling for a cease-fire and withdrawal of British, French, and Israeli troops. At the initiative of Canadian United Nations representative Lester Pearson, on November 4 the General Assembly approved plans for a United Nations Emergency Force (UNEF) to enter the area and monitor a cease-fire; Egypt accepted the proposal the following day.

Israel already had achieved its military objectives, but Britain now faced a financial crisis. An international loss of confidence in Britain's financial stability had led to a disastrous run on gold and silver. The United States threatened to exacerbate the monetary crisis by blocking International Monetary Fund (IMF) assistance, and the Soviet Union was threatening military intervention if Britain did not accept the cease-fire proposal. On the same day, November 5, the Soviets crushed the Hungarian rebellion in Budapest. The next day, as Eisenhower was reelected as president, Britain, France, and Israel accepted the cease-fire. A month later, UNEF troops entered the Sinai. On December 10, the IMF agreed to a loan of $561 million to rescue Britain from its monetary crisis.

Patterns of Behavior

Escalation

The larger Suez Crisis, which includes the actions of Britain and France as well as those of Egypt and Israel, ranks as one of the most severe crises within the three rivalries. The rate of escalation appearing in table 4.1 (22.9) is double that for the Cuban Missile Crisis (table 3.1), which escalates at the highest rate of the American-Soviet crises. The scores for severity and intensity are exceeded only by those for the Berlin Blockade Crisis.

Figure 4.3 depicts the pattern of escalation for the larger Suez Crisis, including Britain and France. Figure 4.4 depicts the pattern of escalation for Egypt and Israel only.

As figure 4.3 illustrates, most of the hostility is directed at, rather than from, Egypt. Once he had carried out his fait accompli, Nasser recognized that he was at a military disadvantage and avoided taking steps that might give the British or French an excuse to reoccupy the area (Nutting

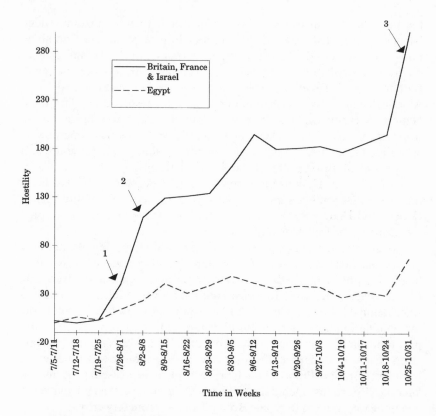

Fig. 4.3.   Suez Crisis, 1956
Key dates are indicated with arrows: (1) 7/26: Egypt nationalizes canal; (2)
8/2: Britain and France begin invasion planning; (3) 10/29: Israel attacks
across Sinai.

1972:172). The pattern bears a rough resemblance to the Cuban Missile
Crisis. The British and French, like the United States, reacted to the fait
accompli with a Bullying influence strategy and the Egyptians, like the
Soviets, responded with a Trial and Error influence strategy. Figure 4.3
suggests, particularly when the comparison with the Cuban crisis is borne
in mind, that the Suez war was not a case of a sudden surprise attack
occurring out of the blue but a crisis that steadily escalated to war over a
period of three months.

When Israeli-Egyptian actions are extrapolated from the larger crisis,
a different picture appears. The time series for Israeli-Egyptian exchanges
appearing in figure 4.4 depict a relatively low level of overt hostility
between the two parties until just before the beginning of the war at the
end of October. To place the difference in perspective, note that the maximum hostility score on the vertical axis in figure 4.4 is set at 100 to depict

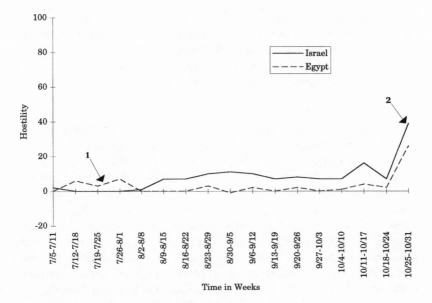

Fig. 4.4.   Suez Crisis, 1956 (Egypt-Israel)
Key dates are indicated with arrows: (1) 7/26: Egypt nationalizes canal; (2)
10/29: Israel attacks across Sinai.

variations in the magnitude of Egyptian-Israeli hostility that would not be
visible in the diagram if the maximum score were at 300 as in figure 4.3.

The low level of hostility on the part of Egypt, which reflects a period
of relative quiet on its border with Israel, is consistent with reports that
Nasser sought to avoid a confrontation with Israel at a time when he was
preoccupied with the canal crisis. Israel, conversely, was quietly preparing
to take advantage of the opportunity for a surprise attack, which was provided through its military alliance with Britain and France. With one
minor exception, the summary statistical measures of escalation in Israeli-
Egyptian actions, which appear in table 4.1, are all considerably lower
than those for any of the four Soviet-American crises.[4] But, while the
Israeli-Egyptian border clashes were in remission between the late summer
and early fall of 1956, the fedayeen raids intensified on Israel's eastern border with Jordan, and by mid-September border clashes broke out between
Israeli and Jordanian troops. The difference can be seen in a comparison

---

4. The exception is the rate of escalation indicator, which is slightly higher at 3.9 than
that for the Berlin Blockade at 3.4. But the low rate of escalation for the Berlin Blockade crisis is a function of an extended period of high hostility scores after the crisis became stalemated, whereas that for the Israeli-Egyptian actions in the Suez crisis reflects a low level of
activity.

of the time series in figure 4.4 with that for Jordanian-Israeli actions in figure 4.5. The Arab attacks on Israel had not abated during the Suez Crisis; only their locale had changed. When Israel called up its reserves on October 25, its Arab neighbors mistakenly assumed that the military preparations were aimed not at Egypt but at Jordan.

Reciprocity
The summary reciprocity statistics for Egypt and Israel, which appear in table 4.2, are consistent with the Egyptian-Israeli time series in figure 4.4. With such a low level of interaction between Egypt and Israel, it is not surprising that there is relatively little distance between the hostility scores of the two sides, which are both quite low. The direction score, which indicates the extent to which the two sides are responding in kind to each other's behavior, would be slightly above the sample median if the score from the Egyptian-Israeli actions in Suez were added to the sample of 34 crises in the appendix. The two sides were often moving in different directions—that is, as one was relatively quiet, the other was engaging in more contentious behavior. In this case, the statistical indicator reflects the sporadic and infrequent attacks across the Egyptian-Israeli border prior to late October. There is no sustained interaction, hostile or cooperative, between the two sides until the end of the crisis.

The quantitative data demonstrate that when the behavior that Israel and Egypt directed at each other is separated from the larger Suez Crisis, there really is no militarized crisis between Egypt and Israel until Israel launches its attack across the Sinai on October 29. The prior sporadic hostilities are at a lower level than those that had occurred, along with verbal threats of war from Egypt, on a fairly regular basis throughout the period since the 1949 armistice. The magnitude of hostility occurring between Egypt and Israel from July 26 to late October certainly is well within what Azar (1972:184) described as the "normal relations range" of hostility for these two states.

Nasser's seizure of the canal did not precipitate a crisis in Egypt-Israeli relations but a diplomatic opportunity for the Israelis to take military action to reverse Egypt's earlier encroachments on Israel's security and economic health and to strengthen its overall strategic and economic position in the region.

Influence Strategies

Egypt
Nasser's initial strategy was to gain control of the Suez Canal through a fait accompli and then stand firm without taking any additional actions

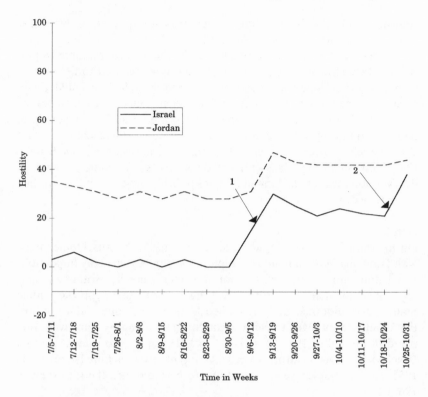

Fig. 4.5. Suez Crisis, 1956 (Jordan-Israel)
Key dates are indicated with arrows: (1) 9/13: beginning of border
clashes between Israeli and Jordanian troops; (2) 10/25: Israel calls up
reserves.

that would encourage the British and French to intervene militarily. The
Egyptian behavior following the nationalization of the canal, however, is
too inconsistent, and Nasser's responses to British and French demands
are too overtly defiant to fit the "firm but flexible" pattern of a Reciprocating influence strategy. Egypt's pattern of influence attempts more
closely resemble a Trial and Error approach to bargaining. The Egyptian
approach to Israel, however, most closely resembles a strategy of
Stonewalling.

As noted earlier, Nasser attempted to avoid any complicating confrontations with Israel during the crisis. Britain was the main enemy; Israel
was a secondary threat. By mid-October Nasser became convinced that
Britain would attack to regain control of the Suez Canal, but the Israeli

collusion with the British and French was unexpected (Calvocoressi 1967:45–46; Louis and Owen 1989:169).

When Israel launched its attack into the Sinai, Nasser adopted a passive military strategy. Egyptian forces were not prepared to fight a war with Israel, let alone the British and French as well. Nor could Egypt expect outside military intervention. Khrushchev made it clear to Nasser in a message at the beginning of the war that the Soviet Union would not intervene militarily. The Egyptian army retreated to the canal in the face of the Israeli invasion and then put up only token resistance to the British-French invasion forces. Nasser devoted his efforts to obtaining diplomatic intervention through the United Nations to bring pressure on the invading states to accept a cease-fire .

Israel

During the period preceding the Suez Crisis, the Arab refusal to negotiate with Israel made the pursuit of a diplomatic strategy virtually impossible. Israel stood alone. The Soviet Union was openly hostile; Britain was urging appeasement in the form of yielding territory to Egypt; the United States was standoffish; and the United Nations was unhelpful if not hostile. Contingency plans to capture the Strait of Tiran by force were prepared in the fall of 1955 (Avi-Hai 1974:132). There also is evidence that Israel was engaged in efforts to provoke Egypt into attacking Israel during 1955–56, but Nasser was too cautious to be lured into the trap (Dayan 1966).

By the fall 1956, with Egypt's Soviet arms becoming operational, the window of opportunity for a low-cost military campaign would soon close. Encircled, isolated, and faced with an implacably hostile adversary that was growing in strength, the Israelis seized the opportunity to improve their strategic and economic security militarily (see Dayan 1966:4; Eban 1972:134; Avi-Hai 1974:1350). The IDF would launch a surprise first strike to gain control of the Strait of Tiran and access to the Gulf of Aqaba to reopen shipping to the Persian Gulf and Asia. The strategic goals were to weaken Egypt and to stop the fedayeen raids from Gaza.

The Superpowers and the Suez Crisis

The United States

Nasser's nationalization of the canal presented a policy dilemma for the United States. On the one hand, Eisenhower (1965:41) wanted to stand by his British and French allies, but the United States, with its long history of opposition to colonialism, was opposed to any attempt to reverse Nasser's action through the use of force. But the most critical concern was the strategic importance of the Middle East in the Cold War struggle. The Eisenhower administration could not allow the Soviet Union to fill the power vacuum that the British departure would create.

The Americans attempted to work with their British and French allies to achieve a compromise settlement while issuing frequent appeals to all parties to refrain from war. U.S. Secretary of State Dulles's diplomatic efforts through the formation of SCUA and the United Nations were unsuccessful. When the U.S. government received reports in mid-October of Israeli mobilization, Eisenhower warned Israeli Ambassador Abba Eban against military action, and the president added that he would not be swayed by the sentiments of Jewish voters before the November elections (Eisenhower 1965:56). Direct warnings were also sent to Ben-Gurion on October 27 and 28 and to Nasser on October 29 (Eisenhower 1965:69–70, 74). It would not be the last time that Israel ignored American warnings against military action.

The Israeli offensive at the end of October transformed the American diplomatic strategy into one devoted almost exclusively to its Cold War competition with the Soviet Union for influence in the Middle East (Eisenhower 1965:83; Neff 1981:390–92). The United States acted immediately to seize the leadership role in United Nations efforts to halt the military hostilities in an effort to reduce the risk of Soviet military intervention and to preempt any Soviet attempt to lead the diplomatic effort to stop the war. When its October 30 Security Council initiative calling for a cessation of hostilities was blocked by British and French vetoes, the United States deserted its Western allies and moved the issue to the General Assembly.

The Soviet Union

Nasser's nationalization of the Suez Canal provided the Soviets with a golden opportunity to increase their influence in the Arab Middle East at the expense of the United States and its Western allies. The Kremlin took a strong diplomatic stand in support of Nasser's action and assumed the role of champion of Arab states against Western imperialists. Nevertheless, the Soviets had no interest in a direct military confrontation with the United States. The primary Soviet strategy, aside from continuing the military arms assistance that had been provided to Egypt over the previous year, was to attempt to mobilize world opinion on the Egyptian side.

When Israel launched its attack across the Sinai, the Soviets quickly labeled Israel the aggressor; otherwise, they remained diplomatically inactive during the early days of the war, when the United States seized the initiative. The Soviets were preoccupied with a crisis of their own—the uprising in Hungary. When that revolt was put down on November 5, Soviet Middle East diplomacy became more assertive. Late that day, Soviet Prime Minister Nikolai Bulganin sent separate letters to the British, French, Israelis, and Americans. The first two warned of Soviet rocket attacks against Britain and France if the war were not quickly stopped; the letter to Israel threatened the state's existence; that to the United States warned of the potential for the crisis to escalate into a third world war (Kissinger 1994:542–43; Brecher 1975:284). The Soviet threats came on the same day that the United Nations General Assembly, with American support, approved a United Nations peacekeeping force to patrol the Sinai following an Israeli withdrawal.

The Soviet threats almost certainly were bluffs. Khrushchev had warned Nasser that the Soviet Union would not become involved militarily. It is difficult to know how much effect Khrushchev's threats had on the resolution of the crisis, as the Americans already were putting strong diplomatic pressure on their allies to terminate the hostilities. At the least, the Soviet threats added some urgency to those efforts. The British, French, and Israelis agreed to the cease-fire on the next day. Perhaps most important, the threats' perceived effect encouraged Khrushchev to attempt verbal coercion in subsequent superpower crises (see chap. 3).

A proposal that accompanied Khrushchev's threats resurfaced in a subsequent Middle East crisis. The Soviet letters called for a United Nations peacekeeping force to halt the war and maintain a cease-fire, but the force proposed by the Soviets would include military units from each of the superpowers.[5] The UNEF peacekeeping force, which has served as the model for subsequent United Nations peacekeeping efforts, stipulated that the force would be composed only of troops from states that were neutral to the dispute and would exclude Security Council members. As I noted in chapter 3, the Soviets offered a similar proposal 16 years later, when Brezhnev threatened unilateral intervention during the 1973 Middle East Alert Crisis. Then, as in 1956, the United States opposed including troops from the superpowers in the peacekeeping force.

The combined diplomatic pressure of the two superpowers, with the United States leading the way in the United Nations, forced the British and French to withdraw their troops and to abandon their efforts to regain control of the canal. The occupying Israeli forces were replaced by the UNEF.

---

5. Khrushchev (1970:434) later stated that he consulted with Foreign Minister Molotov regarding the joint U.S.-Soviet peacekeeping action. Molotov reportedly told him that the United States would never consider such action against its allies, but Khrushchev thought that it would be worth making the proposal to embarrass the United States in the eyes of the Arabs.

Outcome and Lessons

The Suez Crisis was an unqualified disaster for Britain and France. They had been abandoned by their most important ally, had been outmaneuvered diplomatically by a Third World nationalist championing the end of colonialism, and had suffered an irreparable blow to their major-power status. U.S. diplomatic opposition to the British and French actions weakened the unity of the Western alliance. America's leadership in resolving the crisis, however, demonstrated that it had superseded the European powers as the leading Western influence in the Middle East. The Kremlin's strong support of Egypt significantly increased the Soviet Union's prestige and influence in the Middle East.

Despite the rout of the Egyptian army, Nasser emerged as the major diplomatic victor in the Suez Crisis. Egypt retained control of the Suez Canal, and the UNEF troops occupying the Sinai patrolled the area at Egypt's pleasure. Above all, Nasser had solidified his claim to the leadership of the Arab world by successfully challenging and diplomatically defeating Egypt's former colonial masters. But while his prestige soared, Nasser could not help but be aware of the disastrous performance of the Egyptian army.

Israel achieved a stunning military victory only to have the territorial fruits of the campaign wrenched away by diplomatic pressure. Some of its strategic objectives were achieved, however: there was a shift in the balance of power in Israel's favor, the Sinai was demilitarized, and the fedayeen raids were terminated. The Gulf of Aqaba was reopened to Israeli navigation, but the canal remained closed. Israel had been most successful in the pursuit of Ben-Gurion's long-term goal of achieving the reputation of the dominant military power in the region.

Egypt

The primary lesson that Nasser publicly drew from the crisis was that the age of European intervention in the internal affairs of Third World states was quickly ending (Calvocoressi 1967:58). He also realized that he now was the undisputed leader of the Arab Middle East and that his future actions would be judged with that responsibility in mind.

Strategically, the crisis should have driven home the reality of Egypt's military incompetence. Nasser, however, made no high-level changes in his military command. The same commanders who led the Egyptian forces in 1956 would still be in command in 1967. Nevertheless, Nasser was not blind to Egypt's relative military disadvantage vis-à-vis Israel, and as late as 1965 he was still warning other Arab leaders that a war against Israel would not be feasible until the Arab states were able to change the balance in military hardware and training.

Not only had the Egyptian army been routed by Israeli forces, but Khrushchev had made it clear in a letter to Nasser that Egypt could not expect the Soviet Union to come to Egypt's aid in any future wars with Israel. When Syrian leaders urged an attack on Israel in 1960, with the argument that any Western opposition would be met by a counterchallenge from the Soviet Union, Nasser countered the argument by retrieving Khrushchev's letter from a safe and showing it to the Syrians (Nutting 1972:170).

Israel

It is impossible to separate Israel's choice of a military strategy in 1956 from its recent history and that of its people. Ben-Gurion, who was Israel's first prime minister, could not help but be influenced by memories of the Arab attack on the new state of Israel in 1948. But the most common references in speeches by Israeli leaders were to World War II and the Holocaust. To justify a retaliatory raid in November 1955, Ben-Gurion told the Knesset, "What Hitler did to 6 million Jews in the ghettos of Europe, no persecutor of Jews will do to free Jews in their own homeland" (Avi-Hai 1974:128).

In a speech to the United Nations General Assembly immediately following the Suez war, Golda Meir described Nasser as a disciple of Hitler who was determined to annihilate Israel, and she noted that Egyptian troops were found with Arabic translations of *Mein Kampf* in their knapsacks (Meir 1973:93, 96). For the Ben-Gurion foreign policy–making team, memories of the Holocaust colored their view of interstate relations. The Suez experience could only confirm those views as well as Ben-Gurion's realpolitik.

Two more specific lessons were drawn from the Suez war. One was military, the other was diplomatic. The military lesson was that of the efficacy of a surprise first strike. Consequently, the IDF embarked on a program to strengthen its air force and armor units. The diplomatic lesson was that the success of the military strategy would require a supply of modern weaponry from a major power, specifically, the United States. Israeli policymakers also had acquired a new awareness of the pivotal role that the United States would play in any future Middle East crisis. After the Suez Crisis, the Israeli leadership became determined to improve the country's relationship with the United States.

In essence, the diagnostic lessons drawn by the two sides intensified the rivalry. The causal lessons were essentially military, although they had diplomatic implications. Nasser's recognition of Israel's superior military capabilities counseled avoiding the risk of war in a future crisis, whereas Israel's military success reinforced its belief in a strategy based on deterrence coupled with a willingness to launch a preemptive first strike. There was no evidence of learning directed to the management of future crises per se.

Six Day War Crisis, 1967

The Intercrisis Period, 1957–66

Thanks to the presence of the UNEF in the Sinai, the border between Egypt and Israel remained relatively calm and the Gulf of Aqaba remained open to Israeli shipping. Skirmishes continued along Israel's borders with Syria and Jordan, but the Arab cross-border raids and acts of terrorism and Israeli retaliations did not approach the intensity preceding the Suez war until the fall of 1966.

Egypt

Nasser remained in control of the Egyptian regime throughout the intercrisis period, but there was considerable turmoil at the top, largely because of personal animosity and political rivalry between Nasser and General Abdel Amer (el-Gamasy 1993:41). The Egyptian infrastructure and economy deteriorated, with the armed forces called on to undertake responsibilities ranging from public transport to supervision of the fisheries. The strength of the armed forces also was drained by five years of protracted guerrilla warfare in Yemen.

Nasser struggled, with minimal success, to unite the Arabs under Cairo's leadership and direction. Egyptian-Soviet relations, however, strengthened significantly. The Soviets funded the Aswan Dam project and sent a steady stream of arms to Egypt. Relations with the United States continued to deteriorate, particularly after the 1964 election, when President Lyndon Johnson's administration more openly supported Israel.

Nasser's regime remained implacably hostile to Israel. In addition to the public displays of anti-Israeli propaganda, Nasser devoted his foreign-policy efforts to building a wider political and military alliance with neighboring Arab states, promoting the cause of displaced Palestinian Arabs, and, with Soviet assistance, strengthening his armed forces.

Israel

The Labor Party remained in power in Israel throughout the intercrisis period, although Ben-Gurion resigned in 1963 and was replaced as prime minister by Levi Eshkol. The Eshkol government was something of a mix between hawkish holdovers from the Ben-Gurion government, such as IDF Chief of Staff Yitzhak Rabin, and relative doves, such as Eshkol and Foreign Minister Eban. Eshkol, who had a reputation for building consensus, was known for his skill in bargaining and conciliation. One of his first acts after taking office was to indicate his readiness to seek a negotiated settlement with Israel's Arab neighbors. But the Eshkol administration became more hawkish as the 1967 crisis unfolded. It added decidedly hawkish critics, such as Dayan, who became defense minister, and the Likud Party leader, Menachem Begin, to create a government of national unity on the eve of the Six Day War.

With relatively quiet borders, greater access to international shipping lanes, and completion of a major water project, Israel enjoyed an economic boom during the 10 years between the Suez and Six Day Wars. The Israeli leadership, however, held no illusions regarding the nature of the cold peace with its Arab neighbors. Israel used its new industrial strength and economic prosperity, along with arms purchases from the United States, to significantly strengthen its military capabilities.

The Superpowers

During the second half of the 1960s, the United States and the Soviet Union intensified their competition for influence in the Middle East. Soviet influence among the Arab states, particularly Syria and Egypt, had increased considerably following the Suez war. The Soviet leadership recognized, however, that the USSR's influence in Damascus and Cairo was based less on its ideological attractiveness to Arab regimes than on a realpolitik calculation of the Soviet Union's usefulness as a counterweight to American support of Israel. Thus, Soviet leaders pursued a policy of encouraging tension between the Arabs and Israelis to enhance Soviet importance to the Arabs while promoting the cause of Arab unity in a anti-Israeli, anti-Western front to weaken American influence. To strengthen their ties to Egypt, the Soviets encouraged Nasser to enter into a tighter alliance with Syria, with whom the Soviets enjoyed a close relationship.

The Kremlin, however, sought to maintain a ceiling as well as a floor on the level of Arab-Israeli tensions. The Soviet Union had no interest in seeing the conflict between Israel and the Arabs escalate to war, which would risk a superpower confrontation. Nevertheless, efforts to enlist Egyptian support of Syria in its conflict with Israel in the spring of 1967 had precisely that effect.

The Johnson administration in the United States was preoccupied with the war in Vietnam and domestic opposition to the war. American Middle East policy required walking a narrow line between courting better relations with the Arab states and remaining committed to Israel's security. Consequently, American diplomacy, unlike that of the Soviets, was directed toward the maintenance of a peaceful status quo and the reduction of Arab-Israeli tensions. Nevertheless, American-Egyptian relations had soured as Nasser extended his ties to the Soviet Union, while the United States drew closer to Israel in the years after the Suez Crisis.

Key Events

A crisis flared briefly between Israel and Egypt in January 1960, after an Israeli retaliatory raid against a Syrian village. In 1958 the states of Egypt and Syria had been joined as the United Arab Republic (UAR), and, as a consequence, Egypt had assumed some responsibility for Syrian security. In response to the 1960 Israeli raid, Nasser mobilized Egyptian forces and moved 50,000 troops into the Sinai.[6] When Israel responded with a countermobilization, Nasser withdrew the Egyptian troops. The "Rotem Crisis," however, would assume importance as a precedent and as a learning experience for both sides when Nasser sent Egyptian troops into the Sinai during the 1967 Six Day War.

Syria seceded from the UAR following a military coup in 1961. Nasser's attempts to initiate a countercoup failed, but Egypt soon became involved in another internal conflict. When a civil war broke out in Yemen in the fall of 1962, Egypt intervened on the side of pro-Nasserite forces who were challenging Yemeni royalists backed by Saudi Arabia. Before long a third of the Egyptian army was committed to what would turn out to be a draining and fruitless engagement.

The Palestine Liberation Organization (PLO) was formed out of various Palestinian splinter groups in May 1964. That fall, an Arab summit endorsed the establishment of the PLO as the first step toward the liberation of Palestine. At the beginning of 1965, Syrian-based guerrillas began attacks on Israel. Meanwhile, since 1963 tensions had been building between Israel and Jordan over Israel's alleged diversion of Jordanian water for Israel's industrial and agricultural development. Efforts to sabotage the pipeline led to raids and reprisals through the next three years. When Syria attempted to block the supply of water to Israel, the tension grew on Israel's borders with both Syria and Jordan.

At the third Arab summit in Casablanca in September 1965, Nasser warned other Arab leaders that war against Israel would be imprudent given the state of Arab weaponry and training. Nasser's warning gained

---

6. It could be argued that the Rotem incident should qualify as a militarized crisis, with the Egyptian and Israeli moves qualifying as displays of force by both sides. I have not included it because of it was so short-lived and was not treated as a serious threat of war by either side.

credence in May 1966, when the Israeli government announced that the United States had agreed to sell Israel tactical military aircraft. Nevertheless, Arab terrorist raids inside Israel and Israeli counterattacks against Syria and Jordan accelerated during the fall of 1966. Al Fatah, the faction of the PLO led by Yasir Arafat, claimed credit for the raids. The already high level of hostility between Syria and Israel had been increasing since the radical Ba'ath party seized control of Syria in a bloody coup in early 1966.

Crisis Structure

Egypt
Perceptions of Israeli intentions.   After the Suez war eliminated the threat of British reoccupation of Egypt, Israel assumed the role of Egypt's primary enemy. Nasser had no illusions about Israel's military capabilities, but the United States had assured him that Israel would not attack first (el-Gamasy 1993:33). By late 1966, however, Nasser became increasingly concerned about the possibility of an Israeli attack on Syria, which could drag Egypt into war (Nutting 1972:396–97).

   Egyptian interests.   Nasser pursued two potentially conflicting foreign-policy goals: to ensure the security of Egypt and to further his personal prestige and influence in the region. The first required avoiding another war with Israel until Egypt had grown strong enough militarily to be assured of victory. The second required that Egypt assume the leadership of the Arab campaign to regain all of the territory of Palestine. The two objectives came together in Nasser's plan to bring the armies of the countries bordering Israel together under a Cairo-led unified Arab command. The danger was that one of his more impetuous allies would provoke a war with Israel before the Arab armies were sufficiently united, equipped, and trained to achieve victory. But when Nasser urged caution in dealing with Israel, he weakened his claim to Arab leadership. As the 1967 crisis escalated, the Syrians and Jordanians accused Nasser of abandoning them and hiding behind the UNEF peacekeeping forces (Nutting 1972:392).

   Egyptian capabilities.   As late as the summer of 1965, Nasser indicated that it might take another five years for united Arab forces to be prepared for war with Israel (Eban 1992:330). In fact, at the outset of the 1967 crisis, the Arab forces were no match for the Israelis. A third of the Egyptian army remained bogged down in the war in Yemen; the rest were poorly trained, and the "united" Arab command was deeply fragmented. Nevertheless, as the crisis escalated, so did Nasser's estimate of Arab capabilities. The change apparently was related to overly optimistic reports from

Egyptian intelligence and his top military adviser, General Amer. There also may have been some wishful thinking on Nasser's part as he found himself trapped by the situation. As J. G. Stein (1991:137) aptly put it, Nasser's miscalculation of Egyptian capabilities was a consequence rather than a cause of his decision to escalate the crisis. But his advisers encouraged the misperception. According to el-Gamasy (1993:38–39), as Nasser was considering the fateful move of mining the Strait of Tiran in May 1967, he questioned Amer about the state of readiness of the Egyptian forces, and Amer replied, "I stake my neck on it. Everything is perfectly ready."

The superpower role was another element that affected Nasser's estimate of Egyptian capabilities as the crisis escalated. The diplomatic lesson that Nasser drew from the Suez Crisis was that the superpowers would intervene to prevent a full-scale war to avoid the risk of being drawn into it on opposite sides. The United States had been willing to reverse the military gains of its Western allies and Israel in 1956; Nasser reasoned that the United States would restrain Israel in 1967. Nasser believed American assurances that Israel would not fire the first shot, and he went out of his way to assure the Americans that Egypt also would not do so (see Nutting 1972:410). He would restrain the Syrians; the Americans would restrain the Israelis. Just as Syria would not go to war without Egyptian support, Israel, Nasser reasoned, would not be willing to a fight a two-front war without Western help (Nutting 1972:408).

Israel

Perceptions of Egyptian intentions.   Despite the bellicosity of Nasser's anti-Israeli rhetoric, the Eshkol government was aware of Nasser's view that war with Israel was to be avoided until the Arabs were able to build a military force "designed to be decisive in the relatively distant future" (Eshkol 1969:35–36). The prevailing view in Israel at the start of the crisis was that Nasser was not ready for war and would not allow Egypt to be dragged into one (Mor 1993:119). As its clashes with Syria escalated to a militarized crisis, Israel's leadership believed that Egypt's heavy military involvement in the civil war in Yemen would keep Nasser from intervening militarily (Brecher 1980:48).

Israeli interests.   Israeli foreign policy continued to be dominated by security concerns. Peace, that is, Arab acceptance of Israel's existing borders, was seen as dependent on Israel's military strength (Mor 1993:110). Given the size of Israel and its population, survival required sufficient military strength to deter the Arabs from attacking, or, if they did attack, to defeat them quickly and decisively with minimum casualties. Besides the geopolitical realities and the Arabs' expressed intentions, there was the memory of the Holocaust. Each of these factors reinforced the perception that a military defeat would mean the annihilation of Israel (see Brecher and Geist 1980:38–39).

Israeli capabilities.   The Israeli leadership was unanimous in its view that the IDF was capable of defeating any Arab coalition (Mor 1993:115; Brecher and Geist 1980:96–100). The issue was the cost of victory—specifically, Israeli casualties. Dayan (1976:392), who returned to the government as defense minister during the crisis, was confident that the IDF again would rout the Egyptians. But the Israeli leadership also agreed that the advantage that the IDF enjoyed at the time of the crisis would not last indefinitely. If a war with Egypt was part of Israel's future, it was in Israel's interest that it occur sooner rather than later.

Crisis Behavior

A week after Egypt and Syria signed their mutual defense treaty on November 4, 1966, three Israeli soldiers were killed when an Israeli detachment patrolling the border with Jordan ran over a land mine planted by Arab terrorists. Israel retaliated on the next day, November 13, by attacking the Jordanian village of Es Samu, a suspected terrorist base. The attacking force destroyed a number of houses and killed 18–20 Jordanians. Besides expressing outrage at Israel, the Jordanians criticized Egypt's failure to come to their aid. Jordanian and Syrian criticism of Nasser's failure to act as the putative leader of the unified Arab command intensified with the increase in Israeli retaliatory attacks in the early spring of 1967. When Israeli pilots flew directly over Damascus on April 7 and shot down six Syrian MiG fighter planes, the Syrians demanded to know why Egypt's air force remained on the ground. The pressure on Nasser grew as the raids and counterraids intensified along Israel's borders with Syria, Jordan, and Lebanon.

On May 11, Soviet President Nikolai Podgorny told a visiting Egyptian parliamentary delegation led by Anwar Sadat that Israel was massing troops along the Syrian border and was preparing to attack Syria sometime between May 18 and 21 (Golan 1990:58). When Nasser sent his chief of staff, General Muhammad Fawzi, to investigate on May 14, he found no evidence of the buildup; nevertheless, Egypt placed its forces on alert and activated its joint defense pact with Syria. On the next day, Egyptian troops began to cross the canal and move into the Sinai.[7]

---

7. After Nasser moved Egyptian troops into the Sinai, he stated in a May 22 speech that the main impetus for the Egyptian move was a May 12 statement by an Israeli official indicating that country's intentions to attack Syria and overthrow the Damascus regime. What was said and by whom remains a mystery. The most plausible explanation is that Nasser was

General Fawzi requested on May 16 that the UNEF troops be redeployed to allow Egyptian forces to occupy positions in the Sinai to protect Syria's border with Israel. Two days later a formal request was forwarded to United Nations Secretary-General U Thant. But instead of redeploying UNEF, Thant ordered a full-scale withdrawal of all UNEF forces from the Sinai.[8] Israel immediately placed its forces on alert and ordered a limited mobilization of reserves on May 19. By May 21 Egyptian forces had replaced the UNEF throughout the Sinai, including the strategically critical high ground overlooking the Strait of Tiran at Sharm al-Sheikh. The Israeli cabinet considered preparing for an attack but decided to try diplomacy first.

After hesitating for four days, Nasser took the fateful step of closing the Strait of Tiran to all shipping to and from Israel. As Nasser intensified his rhetoric as well as Egypt's physical threats against Israel, other Arab states rallied behind Egypt. Algeria and Morocco agreed to send forces to the region. By May 25 Jordan and Syria had mobilized, and an Egyptian armored division had been moved into the Sinai. On May 30 Jordan's King Hussein signed a mutual defense pact with Egypt and promised to place Jordanian troops under Egyptian command. Iraq signed a similar pact on June 4.

During late May, representatives of Egypt and Israel flew to the capitals of their respective superpower supporters. Both Johnson and Aleksey Kosygin warned their clients against attacking first (Laqueur 1969:157; Neff 1984:158–59). But Soviet Defense Minister Andrei Grechko assured the Egyptians of full Soviet support should Israel attack and of Soviet intervention if the United States entered the war (Parker 1993:31–32; Heikal 1978:180). When Israeli Foreign Minister Eban met with Johnson on May 26, the American president was more circumspect. The United States would wait to see how the United Nations Security Council responded to the crisis before pledging unilateral American action (Johnson 1971:293; Laqueur 1969:156). On May 27 Kosygin warned the United

---

referring to a public briefing by IDF Intelligence Chief General Aharon Yaariv, who referred to a military operation against Damascus as "the only sure and safe answer to the problem." Yaariv, however, went on to say that he did not find such a solution feasible and suggested limited military strikes to serve as a warning (Parker 1993:15–16, 38; Feron 1967). A UPI account attributed Yaariv's off-the-record remarks to an unnamed Israeli leader, and the Egyptians may have inferred that the comments came from Rabin. The most extensive recent account appears in Parker (1993:5–8).

8. The UNEF units were in the Sinai at the pleasure of Egypt, whose territory they occupied. When the Egyptians demanded their redeployment, Thant reasoned that UNEF's function as a peacekeeping unit would be seriously compromised. He appealed to Israel to accept the deployment of the forces to the Israeli side of the border, but Israel refused the request.

States that if Israel attacked first, the Soviets would be forced to support Egypt. Johnson strengthened the American warning to Israel to avoid attacking first (Neff 1984:158). Israel received a direct warning from the Soviet Union on June 1.

Israel nevertheless was moving toward plans to launch a preemptive attack, although once again the decision was delayed on May 28 while the Israelis waited to ascertain the results of a U.S. plan to mount an international armada to open the strait. On May 30 Eshkol declared the blockade of the Strait of Tiran an act of aggression. In response to growing public pressure, Eshkol formed a government of national unity on the next day, adding hawkish critics Dayan and Begin to the cabinet.

After securing Egypt's defense pact with Jordan, Nasser turned to diplomacy to solidify the new status quo. Egyptian forces in the Sinai took up defensive positions, and Nasser proposed that Vice President Zakaria Mohieddin visit Washington to discuss diplomatic solutions to the crisis. Mohiedden's visit, which was scheduled for June 7, never took place. On the morning of June 5 Israel launched a preemptive air strike against Egypt, effectively destroying the Egyptian air force on the ground. Combat on the ground began almost immediately, with Jordan entering the war in the east and Syria in the north. On June 6 Nasser asked the Soviet Union to intervene on the Egyptian side, but the Soviets, fearing a direct confrontation with the United States, refused (Parker 1993:33; Golan 1990:63). Instead, the Kremlin demanded an immediate cease-fire and Israeli withdrawal. Without mentioning Israeli withdrawal, the United States urged Security Council action to end the fighting. A unanimous Security Council resolution calling for a cease-fire was ignored by the Israelis, who enjoyed success on all three fronts. Six days after its first strike, Israel decisively defeated the armies of Egypt, Syria, and Jordan.

Patterns of Behavior

Figure 4.6 depicts the broader crisis between Israel and its three Arab neighbors (Jordan, Syria, Egypt) as well as guerrillas associated with one or another branch of the PLO. Figure 4.7 includes only the actions of Israel and Egypt. The rapid escalation of the crisis in May 1967 is the most striking feature of the time series of Arab-Israeli interactions depicted in figure 4.6. The increase in hostility is led by the Arabs, with Israel responding in kind and magnitude. In its final phase, the crisis preceding the Six Day War displays the rapid escalation and high reciprocity of a conflict spiral, or Fight model of crisis escalation. The overall rate (9.8) and intensity (43.61) of escalation for the Six Day War crisis are dampened by the extended period of moderate hostility preceding the final phase, but, as table 4.3 illustrates, in the last four weeks of the crisis the rate of escalation soars to 82 and the intensity of hostility jumps to 162.

It is clear from figure 4.6 that the Arabs were leading in escalating the level of coercion, with Israel responding in kind. The time series of Arab and Israel actions preceding the final phase of the crisis depicts a pattern in which the two sides alternate in moving to more accommodative or coercive behavior, although they appear to be fairly in sync with regard to the overall magnitude of hostility. As table 4.2 illustrates, the degree of reciprocity in Arab-Israeli actions during the Six Day War crisis is considerably higher than that for the Suez Crisis. Until May, when Israel issued sterner warnings with regard to retaliation against Syria for encouraging terrorist activities, there is a tit-for-tat pattern of Arab guerrilla raids and Israeli retaliations. Most of that activity, however, was occurring on Israel's borders with Syria, Jordan, and Lebanon. As figure 4.7 illustrates, the border with Egypt remained quiet.

It is useful to compare the differences between figures 4.6 and 4.7 with those between figures 4.3 and 4.4 for the Suez Crisis. With the exception of Nasser's rhetoric, there is little direct conflict between Israel and Egypt prior to the final phase of either of the two crises. In fact, from the late summer of 1966 to the sudden escalation of the crisis in May 1967, the Egyptian-Israeli border was the quietest it had been since the Suez war. Until their final phases neither the Suez nor the Six Day Crisis was an Israeli-Egyptian crisis. In both instances, one of the two long-term adversaries was drawn into an escalating dispute by military alliances with third parties who were embroiled in a dispute with the other. In the Suez Crisis, Israel agreed to a joint military operation with Britain and France; in the Six Day War crisis, Nasser's move into the Sinai was prompted by Egypt's commitment to defend Syria and Nasser's concern for his status in the Arab world.

There is, of course, a crucial difference between the two cases. The dramatic escalation of the crisis that occurs in the last month of the Six Day War crisis, which is depicted in figure 4.7, is absent from the time series of Egyptian-Israeli actions in figure 4.4. Israel launched a planned surprise attack on Egypt during the Suez Crisis in 1956. Nasser's motives in 1967 were more ambiguous, but his initial strategy was to employ a show of force to deter a potential Israeli attack on Syria. The movement of Egyptian troops into the Sinai, however, transformed the dispute into a rapidly escalating Egyptian-Israeli crisis. A comparison of the escalation scores for the aggregate of all participants in the dispute with those for just Israel and Egypt during the final month of the crisis is revealing. As table

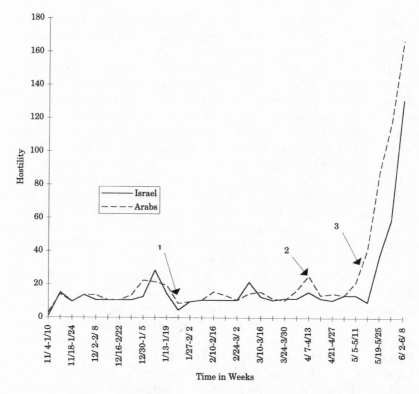

Fig. 4.6.   Six Day War Crisis, 1967 (Israel-Arabs)
Key dates are indicated with arrows: (1) 1/25: Israeli-Syrian border talks;
(2) 4/7: Israeli-Syrian air combat over Damascus; (3) 5/14: Egypt moves
troops into Sinai.

4.3 illustrates, the 1967 crisis became an Egyptian-Israeli crisis after May
12, with Egypt and Israel accounting for roughly two-thirds of the crisis
escalation. And, although the pattern depicted in figure 4.7 resembles the
tit-for-tat symmetry of a Fight, it is clear from figure 4.7 as well as the statistical summary in table 4.3 that Egypt led in the severity, intensity, and
rate of escalation.

The reciprocity scores that appear in table 4.2 are a bit deceptive
because, as in the Suez Crisis, the low direction and distance scores for
Egyptian-Israeli interactions are partially a function of the low level of
interaction between the two sides for much of the crisis. The distance
scores for the Suez Crisis and the Six Day War crisis are quite comparable
when measured over the entire course of each crisis. The Six Day War crisis, however, differs from the Suez Crisis in the last four weeks, when the

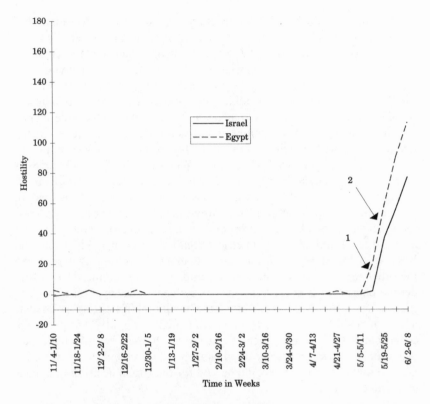

Fig. 4.7. Six Day War Crisis, 1967 (Israel-Egypt)
Key dates are indicated with arrows: (1) 5/14: Egypt moves troops into
Sinai; (2) 5/22: Egypt closes Strait of Tiran to Israeli trade.

TABLE 4.3. Six Day War Crisis Escalation Scores (May 12–June 6, 1967)

Crisis Participants	Escalation Scores		
	Magnitude	Intensity	Rate
All Participants	298	162	82
Arabs	167	103	42
Israel	131	59	41
Egypt-Israel	190	113	56
Egypt	113	71	31
Israel	77	43	25
Percentage of crisis hostility score	64	70	68

distance between the hostility scores of the two sides widens considerably.[9] The direction score (1.67) for the Six Day War crisis is considerably lower than that for the Suez Crisis (4.15), indicating that the two states are more in sync with regard to when they increase their contentious behavior.

In sum, the interaction between Israel and Egypt during the critical final four weeks of the crisis exhibits rapid and intense escalation in hostility along with considerable symmetry as the two parties become locked into increasingly coercive actions. There is a difference, however, in the magnitude of overt hostility exhibited by the two sides; Egypt continues to lead in escalating the level of coercion. When the Six Day War crisis is compared with the random sample of 34 militarized crises in the appendix, this incident ranks well above the median in escalation and at the median in reciprocity. That location places this crisis on the border between a crisis in which the escalating actions and counteractions of two determined adversaries resemble the symmetrical conflict spiral of a Fight and the Resistance model, in which one party assumes the role of aggressor and the other responds in a tit-for-tat but nonaggressive manner.[10] The borderline placement is consistent with the influence strategies employed by the two sides. Egypt led in escalating the hostility, but Israel responded at a level of hostility that came very close to matching Egypt's. The pattern is consistent with what one might expect when the party being challenged views the other side as implacably hostile but is confident of its own military capabilities. The same could be said for the Israeli decision to launch a preemptive attack.

Influence Strategies

Egypt

Nasser's approach to achieving his twin goals—leadership of the Arab world and elimination of Israel—without endangering Egyptian security was based on a plan to unite the Arab states under Egyptian command and to achieve military superiority over Israel. Given the strength and competence of the Arab forces relative to the IDF, patience was required.

Nasser's decision to sign a mutual defense agreement with Syria on November 4, 1966, was a risky departure from that strategy. Syria, particularly under the radical Ba'ath regime, was a potential loose cannon that might provoke an unwanted war with Israel; moreover, both the PLO and al-Fatah had their head offices in Damascus. The defense pact with Syria offered Nasser an opportunity to strengthen his claim to leadership in the

---

9. The distance score for the four-week period jumps to 27.5.

10. The Six Day War crisis, with a reciprocity score of –.34, would rank 17th among the 35 cases in the augmented sample, which would have a median score of –.19.

Arab world and a potential means of restraining Syria from impetuous actions that could lead to a war with Israel. The Soviets also encouraged the agreement as a means of restraining the radical Syrian regime (see Laqueur 1969:49). Unfortunately, the Egyptian commitment emboldened the Syrian regime to take greater risks.

During the winter and spring of 1967, the Syrian-Israeli border skirmishes intensified. The failure of the Egyptian air force to come to Syria's aid during the April 7, 1967, Israeli raid over Damascus was particularly embarrassing for Nasser, the self-proclaimed leader of the Unified Arab Command. These problems came as Nasser's prestige was slipping at home because of economic problems, the endless military campaign in Yemen, and the popular appeal of the Syrian-Palestinian formula of a popular liberation war. The latter was viewed as an alternative to Nasser's more cautious strategy of avoiding clashes with Israel while the Arab states strengthened and unified their military forces (Dishon 1971:185). When Nasser received Soviet reports of Israeli military activity along its border with Syria, coupled with Egyptian alarm at what were perceived to be public Israeli threats to invade Syria and overthrow the Damascus regime, he made the fateful decision to move Egyptian forces into the Sinai.[11]

The movement of Egyptian troops into the Sinai was designed as a military demonstration to deter an Israeli attack on Syria as well as a public demonstration of Nasser's resolve to shore up his shrinking prestige in the Arab world (see Mor 1993:127; el-Gamasy 1993:22). The letter to UNEF Commander Indar Rikhye did not demand the withdrawal of the UNEF forces but only a redeployment to allow Egyptian troops to be in a position to protect the Israeli-Syrian border. Egyptian forces initially were deployed in the center of the Sinai, rather than along the Egyptian-Israeli border, and received strict orders to avoid provoking Israel (Mor 1993:129; Nutting 1972:410). In fact, Israel was not alarmed by the initial moves.

Based on United Nations Secretary-General Dag Hammarskjöld's acquiescence during the Rotem Crisis in 1960, Nasser also had reason to believe that Secretary-General Thant would order the UNEF troops to

---

11. The Soviets knew the reports were fabricated but strongly supported the Syrian regime, which was the most actively pro-Soviet of all the Arab governments. During April and May the Ba'athist Syrian government had come under increasing internal threats at the same time that the border skirmishes with Israel intensified. The Soviets may have sought to activate the Joint Defense Pact to shore up the security of the Damascus regime by encouraging Egypt to bring pressure on Israel from the south and to exhibit additional military muscle to assist the Syrian government in meeting any domestic threats (see Dishon 1971:184, 189).

redeploy temporarily (see Mor 1993:132). When U Thant gave Nasser an all-or-nothing choice, Nasser had to decide between an embarrassing retreat and the more provocative move to remilitarize all of the Sinai, including Gaza and Sharm al-Sheikh. Nasser hesitated for four days and then made the fateful step toward war. During a Higher Executive Committee meeting to decide whether to close the strait, Nasser reportedly said that the decision to close the strait made war with Israel virtually certain.[12]

The quantitative analysis of Egyptian influence tactics classifies the Egyptian influence strategy as an escalating coercive Bullying influence strategy. Although the intentions behind Nasser's initial move into the Sinai may be described as consistent with a Cautious Bullying strategy, Egypt's subsequent moves, including Nasser's verbal threats, are consistent with a more aggressive Bullying strategy.

Bullying influence strategies most often end either in war or with the other party yielding, but the other party rarely yields when it is defending the status quo and believes it can match the military capabilities of the Bullying state (see Leng 1993: chap. 7). It is instructive to compare Nasser's behavior with the United States. Cautious Bullying strategy during the Cuban Missile Crisis. In that dispute, the United States was defending the status quo against an attempted fait accompli, which the U.S. government viewed as a threat to its security; in the Six Day War crisis, the party defending the status quo against an attempted fait accompli was Israel, the party being bullied. Moreover, unlike the Cuban Missile Crisis, the party being bullied in the Six Day War crisis also was the party with the advantage in military capabilities.

Both sides wished to avoid the costs and risks of war in the Cuban Missile Crisis. When the crisis threatened to escalate out of control, the United States communicated its concern to the Soviet Union and offered face-saving concessions. Conversely, there were no direct Egyptian-Israeli negotiations during the Six Day War crisis, and as the situation escalated, the signals Egypt sent—both through military preparations and rhetoric—indicated that they were preparing for an attack. It was an ill-advised strategy against a militarily superior adversary that recognized the tactical importance of striking first and that viewed war as less of a threat to its long-term security than acceptance of the situation created by Nasser's attempted fait accompli.

Nasser recognized that he was risking a war that he wished to avoid. But an escalating crisis can create its own momentum, and a number of

---

12. Sadat claimed that during the Higher Executive Committee meeting, Nasser estimated that the movement of Egyptian forces into the Sinai created a 50 percent possibility of war, but if Egypt closed the straits, then the likelihood of war was 100 percent (quoted in el-Gamasy 1993:27).

commentators have argued that the Egyptian actions became propelled by events (Yost 1968; Nutting 1972; Mor 1993). The complete UNEF withdrawal left a power vacuum in the Sinai. When Nasser came under strong Egyptian and Arab pressure to fill it, what began as an act of limited deterrence escalated to a gamble with Egyptian security in the interests of Egypt's—and Nasser's—reputations for resolve. Nasser's willingness to consider a diplomatic solution to the crisis shortly after Egyptian forces had solidified their positions in the Sinai along with their defensive placement and his instructions to avoid provoking the Israelis indicate that he was not planning to attack Israel (Mor 1993:140). Nevertheless, once Nasser mined the Strait of Tiran, he knew that he taken a fateful step toward war.

If the likelihood of war was high and Egypt's chances of achieving a military victory were not, the situation may have appeared less dangerous to Nasser because of a lesson that he drew from the Suez crisis 10 years earlier. According to Nutting (1972:408), Nasser was convinced that if Israel launched an offensive, the superpowers once again would act through the United Nations to stop the fighting and force a mutual withdrawal.

In sum, the escalation of the Six Day War crisis contained several pathological elements that can confound a realpolitik influence strategy: events running out of control, public pressures to take aggressive action, the national leader's concern with the state's—and his own—reputation for resolve, and the pressure of time. Each of these factors contributed to a Bullying influence strategy that in retrospect appears reckless. But another contributing factor was the experience of the superpower intervention in the Suez Crisis, which encouraged Nasser to underestimate the magnitude of the risk that he was taking. Based on that experience, Nasser counted on the superpowers to restrain Israel and mediate a crisis settlement for the crisis that would preserve some Egyptian gains.

Israel
The Eshkol government was no different from the Ben-Gurion government in believing that Israel's goal of gaining Arab acceptance of its existing borders was most likely to be achieved through a strategy of deterrence. If deterrence failed in the short run, the best long-term prospects lay in demonstrating Israel's decisive military superiority in action. A decisive military victory with few casualties would require the advantage of surprise that could come only by striking first.

The 1956 Sinai campaign demonstrated the effectiveness of seizing the military initiative with a sudden first strike, but the outcome of the war demonstrated the disadvantages of diplomatic isolation. The second component of Israel's deterrent strategy since the Suez war had been to seek closer ties with the United States to balance Soviet military aid and diplomatic support of Egypt and Syria. In the Cold War atmosphere that prevailed in the 1960s, as Nasser moved closer to the Soviet Union, Israel strengthened its ties with the United States. From the intense crisis period of May until its preemptive attack on June 5, the Israeli influence strategy combined responding in kind to Egyptian threats with attempts to seek American diplomatic assistance in reversing the Egyptian fait accompli. The empirical classification of Israeli influence attempts and responses to Egyptian actions is most consistent with a Reciprocating influence strategy.

Israeli policymakers believed that Egypt would not intervene militarily in the growing crisis with Syria because the Egyptian army was tied down by participation in the civil war in Yemen (Brecher and Geist 1980:48). When Nasser massed Egyptian troops and moved into the Sinai on May 14–15, Israeli policymakers drew an historical analogy to the Rotem incident of 1960, when Israel quickly responded with a show of force of its own, and Egyptian troops were withdrawn a day later (Mor 1993:120). Thus, the Israeli government's immediate response to the Egyptian movement into the Sinai in 1967 was to bring the IDF to an advanced state of readiness. Meanwhile, Israeli leaders attempted to enlist Western diplomatic support through the United Nations to pressure Egypt to withdraw its forces from the Sinai. Diplomatic efforts continued even after Nasser closed the Strait of Tiran on May 22, with Foreign Minister Eban traveling to Western capitals to solicit assistance. During a May 26 meeting with U.S. President Johnson, Eban thought he had received assurances that the United States would use all the means at its disposal, including unilateral action, to reopen the strait. Three days later the United States denied that it had made any commitment to unilateral action (Dishon 1971:200). When Israel's head of counterintelligence, Aluf Meir Amit, met with Johnson, Amit came away with the impression that if Israel decided to take unilateral action, the United States would not object (Brecher 1975:417; J. G. Stein 1991:145).

At this point in the crisis, the Israeli government was divided between doves, like Eshkol, who favored a diplomatic solution, and the general staff of the IDF, which argued that the blockade of the strait represented a test of the credibility of Israeli deterrence. Israel, the generals argued, could not maintain its credibility by relying on the diplomatic intervention of others (Brecher and Geist 1980:397; Maoz 1990:160).

By the time a national unity cabinet was formed on June 1, the Israelis had given up hope of effective American action to reopen the strait, the military was becoming increasingly concerned about Egyptian troop concentrations on the border, and Israeli intelligence reported that an increasing stream of Soviet arms was being delivered to the Egyptian forces. On June 4 the Israeli government decided to strike first.

As the crisis escalated, what began as a Reciprocating influence strategy became transformed into a decision to go to war. The final decision was influenced by a combination of internal and external pressures, but the memory of the 1956 Suez Crisis also played a role. Israeli policymakers were well aware that the Western powers, without the support of the Soviet Union, were unable to persuade Nasser to retreat from his Suez fait accompli in 1956. The Israelis did not have much faith in American efforts in a similar situation in 1967, especially after the U.S. government disavowed Johnson's earlier commitment to take unilateral action. When Dayan was added to the national unity cabinet, the man who was military chief of staff during the Suez campaign led the argument for a preemptive first strike. That argument was based on Israel's need to avoid heavy casualties in a protracted war and on the military success of Israel's surprise attack in 1956. Eban, who had served as Israeli ambassador to the United States in 1956, drew a different lesson from the Suez war. Another Israeli attack across the Sinai, he reasoned, would again brand Israel as the aggressor and bring another American-Soviet demand to retreat from any military gains (Laqueur 1969:141). Eban's views prevailed when he returned from Washington on May 27, but Dayan's arguments prevailed once it became clear that there would be no decisive U.S. action.

The Superpowers
The Johnson administration sought to dampen the crisis to avoid a war in which it would be forced to align itself against the Arabs and possibly find itself in a crisis with the Soviet Union. The United States relied primarily on multilateral diplomacy through the United Nations in an attempt to reinforce the legitimacy of the precrisis status quo and to keep the crisis from escalating to war. But when the United States failed to gain support for a multilateral force to reopen the Strait of Tiran, Johnson gave the Israelis the green light to preempt (Brecher 1975:417; J. G. Stein 1991:145).

As noted earlier, the Soviet strategy was to keep the Arab-Israeli conflict simmering without boiling over. The Soviets expected that increased tension would unite the Arabs against Israel and increase the influence of the Soviets as the counterweight to American support of Israel. The false Soviet report of the Israeli buildup of forces on the Syrian border in May 1967 appears to have been part of that strategy—that is, it was intended to encourage Nasser to draw closer to Syria in its escalating dispute with Israel. But when Nasser moved troops into the Sinai and the Egyptian-Israeli crisis rapidly escalated into a serious threat of war, the Soviets, while publicly supporting the Arabs, began privately to send more cautionary messages. While Defense Minister Grechko urged the Egyptians to stand firm and indicated to Egyptian military commanders that they would have the full support of the Soviet Union if Israel attacked first, Premier Kosygin warned the Egyptians as well as the Israelis against attacking first. According to Heikal (1978:180), Grechko told Egyptian War Minister Shamsedin Badran, "Stand firm. Whatever you have to face, you will find us with you. Don't let yourselves be blackmailed by the Americans or anyone else. . . . I want to make it clear to you that if America enters the war we will enter it on the other side."

When Israel attacked first, the Soviet leadership decided against military aid in favor of promoting a cease-fire; however, as the war progressed the Soviets became more alarmed. Kosygin warned Johnson on June 10 that the Soviets might have to take "independent action" if Israel continued to ignore calls for a cease-fire and expanded its military operations in Syria (Johnson 1971:301–2). The United States dispatched the Sixth Fleet to the Mediterranean to discourage Soviet intervention, but the United States also demanded that Israel immediately stop its attacks on Syria. Having already dealt the Arabs a stunning military defeat, Israel agreed to do so.

Neither the United States nor the Soviet Union wanted to be drawn into another war in the Middle East. During the crisis, both acted to restrain their allies from going to war by issuing strong warnings against striking first.[13] The desire to avoid war, however, did not restrain either superpower from providing military aid to the armed forces of its Middle East ally; the Soviets also offered military support if the United States entered the war.

Outcome and Lessons

What began as a military demonstration to deter Israel from attacking Syria propelled Nasser into a series of provocative actions that prompted an Israeli attack and a disastrous Egyptian defeat. Instead of reassuring Syria and solidifying his position in the Arab world, Nasser's actions resulted in Syria's loss of the Golan Heights, Israeli occupation of the entire West Bank territory, including East Jerusalem, the capture of Gaza, and the occupation of the Sinai to the edge of the Suez Canal. The Egyptian air force had been destroyed, and the remaining Egyptian troops were virtually without arms. Cairo could not have been defended if Israel had

---

13. After Eban reported to Johnson that Egypt was massing troops for an attack, Johnson informed Kosygin, who telephoned Nasser in the middle of the night on May 27 to warn against striking first. The U.S. ambassador delivered a similar message to Eshkol (Dishon 1971:199).

continued its offensive in Egypt. Egypt was left vulnerable and humiliated. Nasser offered to resign, but the Egyptian parliament rejected his offer.

Israel emerged with a decisive military victory in a war that it had not sought. A government whose foreign policy was focused on seeking security against Arab attack emerged from the Six Day War with the asset it most urgently needed—strategic depth. The control of the Sinai, the Golan Heights, and the West Bank of the Jordan, including Jerusalem, for the first time provided the advantages of physical barriers and substantial bargaining chips in any future efforts to seek peace with Israel's three most important Arab neighbors.

Egypt

On the surface, it would appear that the Egyptian government learned nothing from its defeat in 1967. As el-Gamasy (1993:78) put it, "The truth is that the defeat was rejected. It was never accepted by the Arabs, who refused to submit politically to Israel." Instead they committed themselves to regaining the lost territory by force, just as before the war they had committed themselves to eliminating the state of Israel by force. Two weeks after the defeat, Nasser was in the Soviet Union seeking long-term military assistance to achieve parity with Israel.

But the war did bring about an important change in Egyptian goals. Before 1967 the objective was the destruction of Israel, with little thought given to the vulnerability of Egypt itself. After 1967 there was a shift in priorities from seeking the destruction of Israel to regaining the Egyptian territory that was lost in the 1967 war. The significance of the shift in objectives, which would lead to an acceptance of the reality of Israel's permanence, would not be overtly recognized for several years, but the outcome of the 1967 war made it all but inevitable.[14]

There also was a certain amount of simple learning with regard to military strategy and preparedness. After the 1948 and 1956 wars, the Egyptian government was so obsessed with refusing to recognize Israel's existence that the Egyptians did not even attempt to analyze Israel's military capabilities and methods. After the 1967 war, however, a thorough assessment was begun (see Heikal 1975:241). That assessment ultimately led to the military preparation and strategy employed by Sadat in 1973.

Israel

The 1967 war reinforced the Israeli government's belief in the implacable hostility of the Arabs and the wisdom of the Israel's deterrent strategy of

---

14. During 1970 and 1971, articles in *Al Ahram* began to make the case for accepting the existence of Israel as a political reality and concentrating Egyptian efforts on regaining the territory lost in 1967, although Sadat continued to give speeches stating that Egypt's goal remained regaining all of the Palestinian territory (see Sachar 1981:183).

peace through strength. The outcome of the war had greatly improved Israel's strategic position and demonstrated yet again the IDF's superiority over Arab forces. The decisiveness of the victory suggested the efficacy of the use of force to further Israel's vital interests in the future. If any aspect of Israel's prewar strategy was discredited, it was Eban's search for a diplomatic solution. Hawkish critics claimed that Eban's mission had given the impression that Israel was irresolute and that it had invited pressures to compromise vital interests (see Dishon 1971:197).

As for the Arab land occupied by Israeli troops at the end of the war, the Israeli foreign ministry concluded that maintaining those boundaries would be essential to deterring Arab attacks in the future and to defending Israel should the Arabs not be deterred (Israel Ministry of Foreign Affairs 1972:25–27). Because the Arab hostility to Israel was assumed to be absolute and incorrigible, the adverse political effect of occupying Arab territory did not play a large role in the Israeli strategy. With more secure boundaries, the demonstrated superiority of the IDF over Arab challengers, and a de facto alliance with the United States, Israel's short-term security objectives had been satisfied. Perhaps some of the land might serve as a bargaining chip in seeking peace in the long run, but in the short-run the territory's value was strategic.

October War Crisis, 1973

The Intercrisis Period, 1967–72

The Six Day War, which ended in Israel's third decisive victory, made the Middle East war of October 1973 all but inevitable. Israel emerged from the Six Day War with a fourfold increase in the territory under its control; Egypt was faced with rebuilding its morale, its reputation, and its army after a devastating defeat that left Israeli troops in control of the Sinai and Gaza territories. In the period immediately after the war, the Israeli cabinet considered withdrawing from the Sinai and Golan in return for peace agreements with Egypt and Syria, but Israel's leaders changed their minds a few months later and began to build settlements in both areas as well as in the West Bank territory.[15] The Arab states met in Khartoum in September 1967 to issue what became known as the *three nos*: there would be no

---

15. The Israeli cabinet transmitted its initial intentions to the United States through Secretary of State Dean Rusk, but the United States apparently did not follow up on the proposal. Accounts appear in Eban (1977:435–36) and Elon (1996:26–27). Elon speculates that the United States was content to have Israel remain in the Sinai, with the Suez Canal closed, to force Soviet ships with military equipment bound for Vietnam to circumnavigate Africa.

peace, no recognition, and no negotiation with Israel until all the territory taken in 1967 had been returned.

Egypt

After Nasser died in 1970, Anwar Sadat was chosen as Egypt's new leader. Sadat lacked Nasser's charismatic qualities, but he also lacked the long list of enemies that Nasser had acquired among Western and Arab leaders. With fewer pretenses regarding his leadership position in the Arab world, and fewer enemies, Sadat had more room to maneuver diplomatically. Sadat initially faced a turbulent period internally with strong opposition from Nasserites in the cabinet, in particular his Marxist-Leninist vice president, Ali Sabri, a favorite of the Soviet leadership. But after successfully foiling a coup attempt that included Sabri in the spring of 1971, Sadat consolidated his control of the Egyptian regime.

Economically, the period between 1967 and 1973 was a continuation of a decade of austerity and sacrifice. The costs associated with industrial development, the Aswan Dam, and the war in Yemen had strained the Egyptian economy even before the 1967 war. Then, in the five years between 1968 and 1973, Egypt's military spending shot up to 26 percent of its national budget (Whetten 1974:164). The army remained in a state of almost constant mobilization, with conscripts training and maneuvering in the desert and engaging in cross-canal clashes with the Israelis. By the summer of 1973, there were serious signs of strain at every level (Heikal 1975:205).

Egypt's view of its relationship with Israel changed after the 1967 war. The existence of Israel gradually was accepted as a political reality. The government officially continued to proclaim its intention to reclaim all of Palestine, but the recovery of the Egyptian territory lost in the 1967 war was the first priority. Sadat embarked on a two-pronged strategy. On February 4, 1971, he announced a new diplomatic initiative, but at the same time he stepped up preparations for a military campaign to regain some of the territory by force.

Sadat also sought to open diplomatic relations with the United States as Egypt's relations with the Soviet Union deteriorated. The presence of thousands of Soviet military advisers, technicians, and other personnel inevitably led to tensions with Egyptian military leaders. But, beyond the day-to-day irritations, the memory of British colonial control over Egypt, reconfirmed by the Suez experience, provided an historical lesson of the need to guard against potential threats to Egypt's independence. Another source of friction was the Soviet diplomatic effort to restrain Egypt from attacking Israel to regain the Sinai territory. The Soviets, who put a higher priority on détente with the United States, resisted supplying Egypt with the sophisticated weapons needed to mount a successful campaign (Heikal 1975:160–67). On July 6, 1972, Sadat shocked everyone by expelling all 15,000 Soviet military advisers and personnel from Egypt. The move was designed to allow Sadat greater freedom of action in preparing for war and to pressure the Soviets, through the threat of a diplomatic move away from the Soviet camp to the United States, to supply the advanced weapons necessary for a military effort to regain territory in the Sinai (Lebow and Stein 1964:164).

Hafiz Ismail, Sadat's national security adviser, was sent to meet with Kissinger and Nixon in February 1973. Ismail, who asked the United States to use its influence to pressure Israel to return the Egyptian territory seized in the 1967 war, returned empty-handed to learn that the United States had agreed to sell advanced jet fighter planes to Israel. The visit, however, made an impression on the Kremlin leadership, which had received KGB reports about the trip (Lebow and Stein 1994:169).

The rise of Muammar al-Qadaffi, who seized power through a coup in Libya, added another complication to Egypt's relations with Israel. Qadaffi, who was leading a Nasser-style revolution backed by Libya's considerable oil revenue, became the loose cannon for Sadat that the Syrian radicals had been for Nasser. On more than one occasion, Sadat had to restrain his erstwhile ally from precipitous attacks on Israel.[16]

Israel

Between the Six Day and October Wars, Israeli leaders were content with the strategic status quo, which they confidently believed they could defend against any conceivable Arab attack. A new Israeli government, with Golda Meir as prime minister, was formed in December 1969. The Meir government was divided into hawkish, dovish, and moderate coalitions, led by Meir, Eban, and Dayan, respectively.

Israeli military activity was increasingly directed toward dealing with PLO terrorist activities. Improvements were made in the technological sophistication and overall strength of the IDF, with several major arms purchases from the United States. A set of fortifications, the Bar Lev line, was constructed in the Sinai. Israeli relations with the United States, which had been solidified during the Johnson years, remained strong through the

---

16. According to Heikal (1975:192), in April 1973 Qadaffi went so far as to issue an order to an Egyptian submarine commander to sink the British liner *Queen Elizabeth 2*, which was filled with Israeli tourists. The commander reported the order to Sadat, who canceled it. In early 1973, when Israel shot down a Libyan Airlines jet that had wandered over sensitive Israeli military installations in the Sinai, Qadaffi was ready to bomb Haifa in retaliation.

1968–73 period, although the Americans continued to urge Israel to consider a diplomatic settlement with Egypt.

The Superpowers

The policies of the superpowers were driven by three considerations: their competition for influence within the region, loyalty to their chief clients, and a mutual desire to avoid a war that could lead to a superpower confrontation.

The United States found itself cross-pressured between the demand to provide military and diplomatic assistance to Israel and the competition with the Soviets for influence among the Arab states. The best way to further both interests was through promoting better Arab-Israeli relations, and the best way to do so was through a peace settlement. The Nixon administration was active in mediation efforts in the period between 1969 and 1971 and in back-channel diplomacy with Egypt after Sadat expelled the Soviet advisers. Nevertheless, as the war of attrition led to increased tensions and conflict, the United States found itself increasing its military aid to Israel to remain a step ahead of the aid the Soviet Union provided to Egypt. Moreover, given Israel's support in the U.S. Congress, the Nixon administration could not pressure Israel to make the concessions necessary to obtain a peace settlement.

The Soviet Union likewise found itself caught between its policy of supporting the Arab cause against Israel, which meant upgrading military assistance to Egypt and Syria, and the desire to avoid another Middle East war. The Soviets were willing to urge the Egyptians to consider a peace settlement, but they were not willing to bully Nasser or Sadat for fear of losing the USSR's major Middle East client to the United States (Breslauer 1979:88–89). Instead, the Soviets attempted to demonstrate their loyalty to Egypt by increasing military assistance even after Sadat expelled the advisers and technicians.

Superpower détente gathered momentum in the early 1970s, reinforcing the mutual desire to avoid another Middle East war, but the competition for influence in the region did not lessen. Each side continued to provide the arms that would give its client greater confidence in its military capabilities.

Key Events

In November 1967, the United Nations Security Council passed Resolution 242, which called for a return of the Arab territories captured in the 1967 war in return for an Arab end to the state of belligerency, acknowledgment of Israeli sovereignty, guarantees of peace and security, and freedom of navigation through the Strait of Tiran and the Suez Canal. When United Nations mediator Gunnar Jarring met with the Israelis in December of that year, they insisted on direct negotiations with the Arab states as a prerequisite to considering the implementation of Resolution 242. Egypt insisted that Israel agree to return the occupied territories prior to any face-to-face negotiations. Jarring's efforts went nowhere.

Despite the one-sided outcome of the 1967 war and the presence of United Nations observers in the canal zone, there was no peace. The five years between the Six Day War and the October War were marked by military exchanges between Israel and Egypt, which reached the severity of an interstate war between 1969–70. Nasser launched Egypt's "War of Attrition," which consisted primarily of concentrated shelling of Israeli positions along the canal with occasional commando raids. Israel responded with tank attacks across the canal and "deep-penetration" air attacks on military and civilian targets inside Egypt. Although the ground combat forces of the two sides were not directly engaged, the war of attrition claimed more than 5,000 battle-connected deaths, mostly on the Egyptian side (Small and Singer 1982:94).

The United States and the Soviet Union held secret talks on the Egyptian-Israeli conflict during the fall of 1969, and a U.S. peace initiative through Secretary of State William Rogers was begun in December of that year. Both sides rejected the initiative, which involved the trade of land for a peace settlement. Rogers's second initiative, in June 1970, finally led to a cease-fire in August.[17] The Soviet Union proposed joint Soviet-American sponsorship of a comprehensive settlement of the Arab-Israeli conflict in September, but on September 28, 1970, shortly after that initiative was floated, Nasser died of a heart attack. Sadat succeeded Nasser over the Soviet-supported Ali Sabri.

Sadat declared 1971 the "year of decision" for the recovery of the Sinai and Gaza territories from Israel. In a speech to the Egyptian Assembly on February 4, he presented a proposal for an interim agreement under which Israel would partially withdraw from the Sinai in return for Egypt's reopening of the Suez Canal to Israeli shipping (Heikal 1975:116–18). During the spring, with the help of U.S. and United Nations mediation, the two sides came tantalizingly close to reaching an agreement that would trade a partial Israeli withdrawal as an interim step leading to Egyptian recognition of Israel in return for a complete Israeli withdrawal from the

---

17. The initiative was accepted unconditionally by Egypt in June, but Israel did not agree to accept the initiative until the Egyptian air defenses, with the assistance of Soviet military "advisers," became more effective in inflicting losses on attacking IDF planes.

Sinai. The initiative, along with the mediation efforts, collapsed in the summer of 1971.[18]

In January 1972, Meir stated that Israel had no intention of returning to its pre-1967 borders: it would keep all of Jerusalem, the Golan Heights, and Sharm al-Sheikh. Following Ismail's unsuccessful trip to Washington in February, Sadat declared that war with Israel was inevitable. The first major armed clash between the two sides since the 1970 cease-fire occurred on June 13, 1972, when Egyptian and Israeli planes engaged in an air battle over the Sinai. But when Sadat expelled the Soviet military advisers and personnel from Egypt on July 6, his intentions were misinterpreted by the Israeli leadership, which viewed it as evidence that Sadat was softening Egypt's position vis-à-vis Israel. Prime Minister Meir saw the move as opening the door to negotiations, and Defense Minister Dayan saw it as an opportunity to reduce Israeli forces along the canal.

Arab-Israeli tensions increased in September 1972 following a terrorist attack by the Palestinian Black September group on Israeli athletes at the Olympic Games in Munich. Israel responded with retaliatory raids on Palestinian camps in Syria and Lebanon. The shock that resulted from the Munich attack encouraged a shift in Israeli security concerns away from its security from attack by Egypt and Syria to antiterrorism (see Eban 1992:512). By the end of 1972, there had been 271 combat and terrorist incidents involving Israel, with 122 along the Syrian border and 60 in Gaza (Sobel 1974:23).

Crisis Structure

Egypt
Perceptions of Israeli intentions. The Egyptian leadership became convinced that Israel intended to consolidate the territorial gains of the 1967 war and to defend and fortify those territories in a long-term strategy of forcing the Arabs to accommodate themselves to the new status quo. Israel, in the view of Egyptian leaders, "would not budge unless it felt threatened by our armed forces" (el-Gamasy 1993:143). New Israeli fortifications and new settlements in the West Bank territory and the Sinai appeared to confirm those suspicions, as did the statements of Israeli leaders, such as those of Meir in January 1972. According to Heikal (1975:205), one of the most potent forces influencing Sadat's determina-

---

18. An excellent account of the mediation efforts and how they were perceived by the participant states appears in Maoz 1998.

tion to take forceful action was the "incredible arrogance of Israeli politicians."

Egyptian interests. Egypt's paramount foreign-policy goal was to regain the territory lost in the 1967 war. By the beginning of 1973, Sadat had given up on any hope of doing so through diplomacy. Egypt, he decided, could regain its lost territory only through force. Sadat's second priority was to restore Egyptian pride and prestige. Sadat reportedly told his associates, "I will not sit at a table with Israel while I am in such a humiliating position, because that means surrender" (el-Gamasy 1993: 150).

Egyptian capabilities. The combined Egyptian and Syrian military forces outnumbered those of Israel by three to one. They also enjoyed substantial numerical advantages in combat aircraft, tanks, artillery, and surface-to-air missiles (SAMs).[19] In the minds of the Egyptian command, the missiles were the key to success. The skill of Israeli pilots could make up for the numerical advantage enjoyed by Egypt and Syria in the air, but the SAMs provided by the Soviets could tilt the balance in favor of the Arabs (Sachar 1981:197).

After a thorough review of the operations in the 1967 war, Sadat had overhauled the Egyptian officer corps. By 1973 the Egyptian armed forces had mastered their new Soviet weapons, and months of practice had gone into rehearsing a cross-canal invasion. However, the state of readiness, which had continued since the 1967 war, drained away Egypt's material resources and military morale, while the public began to wonder if the Egyptian leadership had any real intention of fighting. Moreover, on the diplomatic front, Sadat had become increasingly worried that the Soviet-American détente could lead both superpowers to accept the status quo in the Middle East to avoid a confrontation (Lebow and Stein 1994:171).

Israel

Perceptions of Egyptian intentions.   Israel's leaders recognized that they had been wrong in accepting at face value the threats from Nasser that accompanied his actions during the Six Day War crisis. Sadat's rhetoric was seen as of a piece with that of Nasser, so Sadat's threats were dismissed as mere rhetoric for home consumption. As Quandt (1977:110–14) has pointed out, much of Egyptian foreign policy is certainly theater aimed at a domestic audience, but the focus on that aspect of Sadat's activ-

---

19. Combined Egyptian and Syrian aircraft equaled 860 to Israel's 480. Syria and Egypt had 3,200 tanks, many of the latest Soviet model, compared to 1,700 Israeli tanks, many of them obsolete. Egyptian-Syrian artillery outnumbered that held by Israel by four to one. The Egyptians also had several thousand new Sagger antitank rockets (Sacher 1981:197).

ity appears to have distracted the Israeli leadership from signals indicating the seriousness of Sadat's intentions and Egypt's preparations for war (Brecher and Raz 1977:481–82). Sadat was like the little boy who cried "Wolf!" The Egyptian leader threatened war so often without acting that the Israelis stopped paying attention. When Sadat's 1971 year of decision came and went with no Egyptian military action, Israeli political and military leaders treated Sadat's subsequent threats less seriously (see Brecher and Raz 1977:479; Kissinger 1982:460). When Sadat expelled the Soviet advisers, the Israeli government saw the action as an indicator that Sadat did not intend to start a war with Israel for several years (Brecher and Raz 1977:479). That the Soviet weapons remained, that Egypt renewed Soviet naval facility rights in December 1972, and that Soviet arms sales to Egypt increased significantly during 1973 did not change that perception.

Israeli intelligence also assumed that after Egypt's 1967 disaster, it would not attack unless it had achieved superiority in the air (Brecher and Raz 1977:480; Kissinger 1982:460). The assumption represents a case of one state assuming that another had learned a particular lesson from a previous conflict—that is, the critical role played by airpower in the Israeli victory in 1967. The Israelis, however, overlooked the possibility of substituting surface-to-air missiles for a superior air force. The Israelis also were convinced that if an attack did come, they would receive sufficient warning to prepare their defenses (see Meir 1975:359–60). In that case, they overlooked the lesson that Egypt did learn from the Six Day War: the tactical advantage of a surprise first strike.

Israeli interests. Security remained the primary focus of Israeli foreign policy. But with the dramatic military successes of the Six Day War and its resultant strategic territorial gains, Israeli leaders were confident that they could repel any conventional attacks from neighboring Arab states. The Meir government preferred the continued tensions that came with occupying strategically important Egyptian territory in the Sinai to a negotiated withdrawal and uncertain international guarantees.

There was one complicating consideration. Israel's long-term security depended on retaining U.S. diplomatic support and military assistance. To appease the United States, appearance of some flexibility on the territorial issues was required. The Meir government was willing to negotiate a limited withdrawal in the Sinai to appease the United States. The Israelis, however, would not return to the pre-1967 borders: they would retain the West Bank territory, including all of Jerusalem, the Golan Heights, and Sharm al-Sheikh (Sulzberger 1972).

Israeli capabilities. Israel's political and military elites were confident that the IDF's military superiority would be sufficient to deter Egypt and Syria from attacking. But if an attack did come, Israeli leaders had no doubt that the IDF would achieve a quick and decisive military victory, just as it had in 1967. A low-cost victory, which had resulted in large part from poor Arab military leadership and the advantages of surprise, was attributed almost wholly to the IDF's invincibility.

Crisis Behavior

On January 31, 1973, Egyptian and Syrian forces were placed under a joint military command to prepare for an attack on Israel. Two weeks later, on February 15, over the Gulf of Suez, Israeli and Egyptian fighter planes fought for the first time in eight months. The next week, Israel killed 108 civilians when it shot down a Libyan commercial airliner that had strayed over Israeli territory, including a militarily sensitive air base.

Most of Israel's attention, however, was directed toward its problems with Palestinian terrorist attacks. During the spring of 1973, Israel intensified its raids against suspected Palestinian terrorist groups in Gaza and Lebanon. That April a number of PLO factions agreed to unite under the leadership of al-Fatah's Yasir Arafat. There was a temporary rise in Egyptian-Israeli tensions in early May when Egypt's increased military activities in the canal area caused sufficient alarm for Defense Minister Dayan to order a partial mobilization of Israeli forces.[20] But when the perceived threat of war passed, the Israeli military command was criticized for the unnecessary cost of the partial mobilization, and the view that Egyptian military operations need not be taken seriously was reinforced among Israeli policymakers (see Brecher and Raz 1977:475–76). In fact, Egyptian and Syrian military leaders had met in early May to devise a plan for a coordinated attack on Israel in the fall. A few days later, Brezhnev and Gromyko warned Kissinger of the likelihood of war, but U.S. analysts dismissed the warning, which was repeated to Nixon in June, as "psychological warfare" (Kissinger 1982:461).

Egyptian and Syrian leaders met in Alexandria in August 1973 to determine the date for a coordinated attack on Israel in late September or early October. Egyptian and IDF fighter planes fought over the Gulf of Suez on August 9, and Egyptian and Israeli naval vessels exchanged fire in the gulf on August 13. A month later, the Israeli air force ambushed and

---

20. There was disagreement at the time with regard to the seriousness of the Egyptian military activities. Israeli intelligence sources had some evidence that May 15 had been selected as D day for an Egyptian attack across the canal, but in a meeting of Israeli leaders on May 9, military intelligence leaders rated the likelihood of war as low. Dayan nevertheless decided to order the mobilization of some reserve units and the reinforcement of fortifications in the canal area (see Black and Morris 1991:30; Brecher and Raz 1977:475–76).

shot down 13 Syrian MiG fighter planes. Egyptian and Syrian forces began to mobilize for war on September 21.

Final plans for an October 6 Egyptian-Syrian attack were completed on October 3. Even at that late date, Egyptian military movements were dismissed by the Israeli foreign office as "routine," and U.S. intelligence sources found the joint military movements of Egyptian and Syrian forces "coincidental" (Kissinger 1982:464). When the Soviet Union began airlifting all its dependents out of Egypt and Syria on October 3, American and Israeli intelligence services missed the event's importance. They viewed it as the result of a crisis in Soviet-Egyptian and Soviet-Syrian relations or of anticipation of hostilities that might be initiated by Israel (Kissinger 1982:466–67). The latter interpretation was encouraged by reports in the Arab press charging that Israel was preparing for war on the Syrian border.

Israeli Prime Minister Meir later recalled stating in a cabinet meeting on October 5, "Look, I have a terrible feeling that this has all happened before. It reminds me of 1967, when we were accused of massing troops against Syria, which is exactly what the Arab press is saying now" (Meir 1975:355–56). Meir still believed that war was highly improbable, but as a precaution, Israeli forces were ordered to stand at the highest state of alert. When the Israelis finally realized that Egypt and Syria were preparing for war, just a few hours before Egyptian troops crossed the canal, Meir assumed that the actions were preemptive, that the Arabs had become convinced that Israel, as in 1956 and 1967, was about to attack them. In the hours before the war, the Israelis enlisted the aid of United States in assuring the Egyptian and Syrian governments that Israel had no intention of taking offensive action.

The Egyptian assault began at noon on October 6 with an artillery barrage along the length of the canal and air strikes against Israeli air bases in the Sinai.

Patterns of Behavior

The evolution of the crisis between Israel and the Arabs is depicted in figure 4.8, which includes the interactions of Israel with Syria, Lebanon, and the PLO as well as with Egypt.

Escalation

Some useful insights into the behavior of the parties in the 1973 crisis can be gained by comparing figure 4.8 with figure 4.6, which depicts Israeli-Arab interactions in the 1967 crisis. In both crises the magnitude of hostility remains relatively low until it escalates dramatically in the last month.

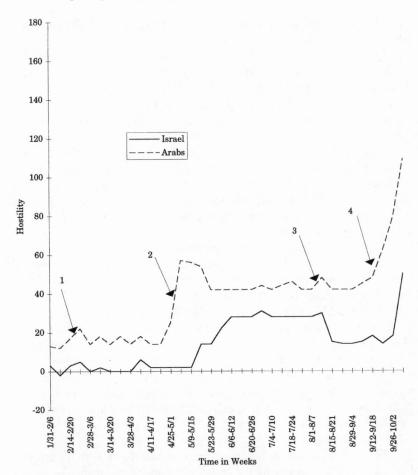

Fig. 4.8. October War Crisis, 1973 (Israel-Arabs)
Key dates are indicated with arrows: (1) 2/21: Israel shoots down Libyan
airplane; (2) 4/26–28: Israeli–Palestine Liberation Organization clashes;
(3) 8/9, 8/13: Egyptian-Israeli naval and air clashes; (4) 9/21: Egyptian and
Syrian mobilization.

There are, however, several important differences between the two crises.
Whereas the steep escalation to war occurs over a period of three and a
half weeks in the 1967 crisis and reaches a very high magnitude of hostility
before war breaks out, the escalation in the 1973 crisis occurs in just a two-
week period, with war occurring when the magnitude of escalation is just
a little over half that for the 1967 crisis (table 4.1). However, the intensity
of Arab hostility toward Israel over the course of the crisis preceding the

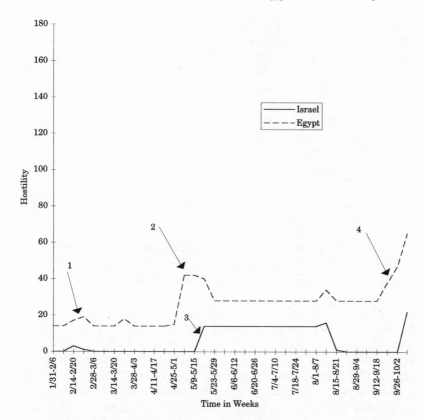

Fig. 4.9.   October War Crisis, 1973 (Israel-Egypt)
Key dates are indicated with arrows: (1) 2/15: Israeli-Egyptian air battle;
5/2: Egyptian maneuvers; (3) 5/17: Israeli partial mobilization; (4) 9/21:
Egyptian and Syrian mobilization.

rapid escalation in the final weeks is higher in 1973 than in 1967. If the
interactions of just Israel and Egypt in the 1973 crisis, which are depicted
in the time series in figure 4.9, are compared to those for 1967 (figure 4.7),
it is clear that Egypt played a more active role in the early phases of the crisis in 1973 than it did in 1967. In fact, the intensity score in table 4.1 for
Egypt in 1973 (26.42) is almost three times that for 1967 (9.48).

The 1967 crisis began primarily as an intensifying dispute between
Syria and Israel into which Egypt entered during the final phase. The crisis continued to escalate as the more aggressive party (Egypt) tried to
achieve its objectives without going to war and third parties pressed for a
mediated settlement until Israel decided to preempt. Table 4.4 contains the

escalation scores for the final phase of the 1973 crisis. A comparison of table 4.4 with table 4.3, which contains the scores for the final phase of the 1967 crisis, illustrates the difference between the final phases of the two crises. The scores for each of the escalation indicators for Egypt and Israel during the final phase of the 1973 crisis are less than half those for their counterparts for the 1967 crisis.

Even though the final escalatory phase of the 1967 crisis extends over a longer period of time than the final phase in 1973, the rate-of-escalation score for Egypt-Israel in 1967 (56) is three times greater than in 1973 (17). The 1967 crisis also reached far higher levels of intensity (113:41) and magnitude (190:69) before war broke out. In 1973 Egypt was engaged from the start in preparations for war with Israel, with intensified activity leading to Israeli responses at a somewhat lower magnitude of hostility. The short and relatively low intensity of escalation in the two weeks preceding the war reflects Sadat's planned surprise attack coupled with remarkably restrained Israeli responses. In sum, the 1967 crisis escalated to war; in 1973, Egypt launched a premeditated surprise attack.

Reciprocity

Another interesting comparison lies in the degree of reciprocity exhibited in the months prior to the final escalatory phase of the crisis. The Israeli-Arab interactions in the Six Day War crisis, which are depicted in figure 4.6, resemble a tit-for-tat pattern in which one side and then the other leads in increasing the magnitude of hostility from one week to the next. The pattern reflects Israel's long-standing policy of responding to Arab attacks or acts of terrorism in kind but with a greater degree of severity. In 1973 (figure 4.8) the pattern is different. Israel is responding in kind but at a lower magnitude of hostility; the Arabs lead in acts of hostility throughout the crisis. The visual pattern is supported by the statistical scores appearing in table 4.2. Most notable is the difference in the distance score for

TABLE 4.4.   October War Crisis Escalation Scores (September 21–October 6, 1973)

	Escalation Scores		
	Magnitude	Intensity	Rate
All Participants	137	94	28
Arabs	95	69	20
Israel	42	25	8
Egypt-Israel	69	41	17
Egypt	51	36	12
Israel	14	5	5
Percentage of crisis hostility score	50	44	60

Egyptian-Israeli actions in 1973 (20.56) versus that in 1967 (3.87). In 1973 Israel was responding in kind—the direction scores for the two crises are comparable—but not in magnitude. The restrained reaction pattern reflects Israel's satisfaction with the status quo, its preoccupation with PLO terrorism, and its confidence in its military superiority.

Based on a comparison with the larger sample of 34 crises in the appendix, the 1973 crisis falls below the sample mean on all three measures of escalation. While Sadat prepared the political and military groundwork for an eventual surprise attack, he worked hard diplomatically to keep his more belligerent allies, such as Syria and Libya, in check. Israel responded forcefully to terrorist attacks but responded in a restrained manner to the Egypt's military preparations. Sadat's careful crisis management occurred not out of a fear of war but to provide the best conditions for launching a surprise attack. Israel's restrained responses had more to do with an erroneous conception of Egyptian intentions and unwarranted confidence in its deterrent power than with fear of provoking a war with Egypt.

Influence Strategies

Egypt
Sadat moved to a more flexible influence strategy by accepting the permanence of the state of Israel and by switching Egyptian goals away from the elimination of Israel to regaining the Egyptian territory lost in the 1967 war.

The limited objective made it possible to devise a military strategy consistent with Egypt's military capabilities—that is, to achieve limited gains in the Sinai to rebuild Egyptian pride and inflict sufficient casualties on Israeli forces to create a more favorable environment for a negotiated return of all of the Egyptian territory. Part of Sadat's strategy was to shift the psychological balance in the Middle East away from the perception of the Arabs as impotent in the face of Israeli military superiority. "If we could recapture even four inches of Sinai territory . . . then the whole situation would change," Sadat argued (Sachar 1981:192). In carrying out the offensive, the Egyptians had learned from the Israelis the advantages of a surprise attack to achieve an initial advantage. Once across the canal, Sadat counted on American as well as Soviet diplomatic intervention to achieve a cease-fire and diplomatic discussions regarding the future of the Sinai.[21] As Kissinger (1982:460) later wrote, "Sadat aimed not for territo-

---

21. Ismail had been told during his February 1973 meetings with Kissinger and Nixon that the United States was ready to become actively involved in seeking a diplomatic solution in the Middle East (Kissinger 1982:460).

rial gain but for a crisis that would alter the attitudes in which the parties were then frozen—and thereby open the way for negotiations."

An empirical analysis of the Egyptian influence strategy places it in the Bullying category. The few influence attempts directed by Egypt to Israel are threats or shows of force; Egypt does not respond positively to any Israeli moves, and military activity and public statements are consistently hostile.

As the crisis evolved, many of Sadat's efforts were not unlike those of Nasser before the 1967 war: obtaining military alliances with Syria and Jordan, pressuring the Soviets for additional advanced weapons and military equipment, and accelerating the training of Egyptian forces. But Sadat's acceptance of the reality of Israel's status in the Middle East also led to a more careful analysis of Israeli military capabilities and tactics as well as a hard look at the 1967 war disaster.

Egyptian leaders drew three central lessons from the 1967 experience: the necessity of an adequate defense against the Israeli air force, the need for more intensive planning and training, and the strategic advantage of a surprise first strike. Sadat obtained Soviet SAMs to meet the first requirement, and Egyptian commanders conducted endless practices for a cross-canal offensive. The latter resulted in a textbook example of what has been called the "cry wolf" syndrome—repeated threats that are not converted into action reduce the defenders' attention (see Shlaim 1976:356). Sadat later claimed that the military activities were part of a "strategic deception plan" to overwhelm the Israelis with so many false alarms that they would ignore the preparations for the cross-canal attack in the early fall.

It is difficult to know just how calculated Sadat's actions were at the time, as opposed to an after-the-fact rationalization. A self-perception theorist might argue that Sadat based his subsequent perception of his actions as components of a carefully crafted strategy of deception on his observation of their consequences (see Bem 1972): "That is how it worked out, so that is what I must have been attempting to accomplish." The fits and starts in military preparations may have reflected indecision and the tension between internal political pressures to demonstrate resolve on the one hand and a prudential understanding of the military balance, coupled with Soviet efforts to restrain the Egyptians, on the other. There is, however, no doubt that, as D day approached in September 1973, the Egyptians engaged in a campaign of deception designed to mask their intentions through a flurry of diplomatic activities and to downgrade the capabilities of their forces through erroneous leaks to the press (Sachar 1981:198; Shlaim 1976:355). Whatever Sadat's intentions were at the time, there is no doubt that his actions had the desired effect on the Israelis.

Israel

The Israeli influence strategy during the crisis period falls on the border-line between Reciprocating and Stonewalling. The Israelis responded in kind to Egyptian threats, and there were Israeli counteroffers to Egyptian demands issued through the United Nations, a pattern that is consistent with a Reciprocating influence strategy. But the frequency of actions directed by Israel toward Egypt is low (see figure 4.9), and Israel offers no cooperative initiatives of its own. In addition, Israel's responses to Egyptian initiatives contain counterproposals, such as direct Egyptian-Israeli negotiations, designed solely for propaganda purposes. As discussed earlier, a case can be made that Israel was willing to offer territorial concessions in the Sinai to open shipping and gain some guarantee of its border with Egypt during the spring 1972 negotiations, but by 1973 the Israeli position had once again hardened. Israel's behavior during the 1973 crisis is consistent with the position of a state that is quite content with the status quo and confident of its ability to defend it.

If ever there was a case of a political belief system creating a predisposition to misinterpret new information in a disastrous way, it was in the Israeli response to Egyptian moves in the 1973 crisis. The Meir government continued the realpolitik approach to the Arab-Israeli conflict that had been followed by Ben-Gurion and by the government of national unity during the last month of the 1967 crisis. That approach in itself would not have led to the misperception of Sadat's intentions, but the Israelis knew that they had overdrawn the first analogy and overreacted to Nasser's threats in 1967. Now, oblivious to Sadat's more limited objectives, they made the opposite mistake and did not take his warnings of military action seriously enough. The Meir government placed Sadat into the same category as Nasser. Their mistake was the opposite of their predecessors, who saw Nasser as another Hitler.

The Superpowers and the 1973 Crisis

Soviet Union

To reduce the risk of losing their major Middle East ally to the United States, Soviet leaders found themselves supplying the means for Egypt to launch a war that would threaten the Kremlin's central foreign-policy goal—détente with the United States. To rationalize the contradiction between the two policies, the Soviet leadership apparently convinced itself that the arms shipments would lead to greater Egyptian dependence on the Soviet Union for military supplies, which, in turn, would lead to greater Soviet influence over Egyptian military decisions (Lebow and Stein

1994:171). The assumption was not unlike that made by Nasser in 1967, when he signed a defense pact with Syria in the mistaken belief that doing so would place him in a better position to restrain the Syrians.

Sadat interpreted the shipment of sophisticated weapons as a signal to go ahead with the Sinai campaign despite the Soviets' verbal protests. There also was a fundamental contradiction between the objectives of the two allies. Sadat wanted a crisis in the Middle East to prepare the diplomatic foundation for regaining the Sinai; Soviet-American détente was a potential obstacle to his objectives. Sadat feared that to further détente the Kremlin might agree to accept the territorial status quo in the Middle East (Sadat 1977:229). To add to the problem confronting them, the Soviets had no more confidence in Egypt's military capabilities than did the Israelis and the Americans. Immediately after Egyptian forces crossed the canal on October 6, the Soviets attempted to obtain a cease-fire before the war turned decisively in Israel's favor. On the evening of the first day of the war, the Soviet ambassador reported to Sadat that the Syrians, who were not doing as well in the fighting, already were willing to settle for their limited gains and accept a cease-fire. Sadat refused cease-fire proposals on the grounds that they did not call for a withdrawal of Israeli forces from all the territory captured in 1967 (Heikal 1975:212). The Soviets then began a large-scale airlift of new supplies to the Egyptian and Syrian forces.

The United States
The United States was pursuing seemingly contradictory objectives of its own. The White House was attempting to further détente with the Soviet Union while pursuing diplomatic initiatives to remove Soviet influence from the Middle East. Ismail's February 1973 visit to Washington, which followed the expulsion of the Soviet advisers, provided a welcome opportunity to promote the second objective, although the White House offered virtually nothing in return. "Politics know no ethics and it is not within the US brief to pay for anything which is offered freely," Kissinger is reputed to have told Ismail (el-Gamasy 1993:148). Kissinger's strategy was to avoid any new efforts at mediation until the United States could supplant Soviet influence in Cairo and the Egyptians moderated their demands (Kissinger 1982:1247). In the interim, the United States would rely on Israel's deterrent strength to maintain peace.

The United States remained committed to the defense of Israel and continued to supply the Israelis with sophisticated arms and fighter planes. The Americans were confident that Israel's demonstrated military superiority would be sufficient to deter an Egyptian or combined Arab attack. American intelligence agencies accepted Israeli intelligence's belief that Egypt would not attack without air superiority and that Syria would not attack without Egypt (Kissinger 1982:459–60). As noted earlier, American policymakers ignored Soviet warnings of an impending war in the summer and fall of 1973.

On the evening of October 6, after Egypt's surprise attack, Egyptian Ambassador Mohamed el-Zayyat met with Kissinger to emphasize the limited objectives of the Egyptian offensive. On the next day, the White House received the first of several communications from Egypt stressing Sadat's limited objectives (Kissinger 1982:481–82). Initially, the American leadership was confident that Israel, once fully mobilized, would achieve a quick victory. The resupply of arms to Israel was delayed for a week, as the U.S. Defense Department sought to avoid antagonizing the Arabs and Kissinger sought to avoid another quick, decisive Israeli victory. If a cease-fire could be achieved with Israel having gained the upper hand but with limited Egyptian gains in the Sinai to restore Arab pride, the United States thought it could broker a peace settlement (Kissinger 1982:493–95). But by mid-October, with continuing Egyptian gains and Israeli supplies running low, the United States decided to match the Soviets' massive airlift. The two superpowers were nearing a confrontation when Israel turned the tide of the war in its favor as IDF forces crossed the canal to envelop Egyptian forces on October 15.

Outcome and Lessons

Egypt did not achieve a military victory in the October War, but victory had not been Sadat's objective. The war was fought for psychological and diplomatic purposes: to restore Egyptian pride and to shake Israeli confidence in its invincibility by "bleeding the enemy" (Kissinger 1982:459–60; Heikal 1975:212). Both objectives were accomplished. Moreover, by carefully cultivating his relationship with the White House, Sadat enlisted U.S. support in pressuring Israel to move to a diplomatic settlement to return the Sinai to Egypt. The outcome was a diplomatic triumph for Egypt.

Israel achieved a military victory, but it was not a victory to be celebrated. For the first time, Israeli losses were heavy. How many more such wars could a country as small as Israel endure? As Eban (1992:540) later wrote, "Hardly anyone in Israel spoke of 'victory.' That word had been drained of its meaning. . . . A new psychological balance had been established."

Egypt

For the Egyptian leaders, the outcome of the 1973 war was a confirmation of Sadat's military strategy of limited objectives, careful preparation, and surprise attack. The diplomatic consequences, which included American efforts to solidify the cease-fire followed by Kissinger's intercession to bring about the disengagement accords of 1974, confirmed the wisdom of Sadat's political strategy of moving Egypt away from diplomatic dependence on the Soviet Union to a more cooperative relationship with the United States. Sadat understood that only the United States could bring to bear the diplomatic pressure to persuade Israel to withdraw from Egyptian territory.

Israel

The Israelis learned the reality of their military vulnerability. The era of quick, low-cost military victories ended when Egyptian forces broke through the Bar-Lev line of fortifications in the Sinai. For the first time Israeli leaders began to have second thoughts about the policy of deterrence and force instituted by Ben-Gurion in 1948.

The Israeli government also learned something about the risks associated with drawing historical analogies from experiences with past leaders and events. As a subsequent official Israeli investigation found, there was ample information of the impending Egyptian attack (see Shlaim 1976: 350).[22] The Agranat Commission of Inquiry placed a large part of the blame on the Israeli intelligence service's rigid adherence to what became known as the "conception": a set of beliefs regarding Egyptian and Syrian intentions. The decidedly realpolitik conception was quite simple: (1) Egypt would not go to war unless it achieved the capability to launch successful air strikes deep into Israeli territory to neutralize the Israeli air force; (2) Syria would not go to war without Egypt (Shlaim 1976:352). Israeli intelligence did not rule out the possibility of an Egyptian attack but they rated the probability as extremely low, and governments act on the basis of probabilities.[23]

The first assumption in the conception was based partly on the belief that Sadat would draw a military lesson from the 1967 campaign that would limit his options in 1973. This assumption overlooked the possibility of neutralizing the Israeli air force through other means—SAMs. But the conception also was based on the belief that Egyptian objectives had not changed from those of Nasser in 1967. Therefore Sadat would not

---

22. Shlaim 1976 provides a summary account of the Agranat Commission's findings as well as an analysis that demonstrates how a strongly held belief system led to misperceptions of Egyptian intentions.

23. It can be argued that because it was a probabilistic estimate, the intelligence services cannot be accused of being wrong, but that conclusion seems to put too fine a point on the analysis (see Maoz 1990:6).

launch an attack without a reasonable chance of achieving a complete victory. But Sadat was not Nasser and was not pursuing the same all-or-nothing military objective. Furthermore, when Israeli—and American—intelligence picked up indications that Egypt and Syria were preparing for war, the intelligence agencies assumed that the Arabs were preparing to defend themselves against an Israeli attack. It was a reasonable hypothesis that, given the experiences of 1956 and 1967, the Arabs would attempt to prepare themselves for another Israeli surprise attack. But the lesson that Sadat drew from those experiences was to launch a surprise attack of his own.

Finally, the perceived gap between Israeli and Arab military capabilities was inflated by the ease with which Israel achieved victory in 1967. When Sadat removed the Soviet advisers in 1972, the Israelis, remembering their easy victories in 1956 and 1967, underestimated the capacity of Egyptian technicians and troops to use the equipment that was left behind. The Israelis drew lessons from the 1967 crisis, but those lessons did not serve them well.

Conclusions

Patterns of Behavior

Although there are significant differences in the patterns of escalation and reciprocity from one crisis to the next, all four Egyptian-Israeli crises ended in war. If effective crisis management means the achievement of a peaceful settlement to the crisis, then it cannot be argued that any of the behavior changes led to more effective crisis management. On the other hand, within the structure of the Egyptian-Israeli relationship at the time, Egyptian President Sadat's strategy of limited war in 1973 represented a prudent combination of military force and diplomacy to prepare the groundwork for the return of the Sinai to Egypt. But before discussing the influence strategies of the rival states, it might be useful to review the patterns of behavior in the four crises.

When the Middle East crises are treated as dyadic disputes between Egypt and Israel, they are notable for the low magnitude of escalation prior to a short period of rapid escalation immediately preceding the outbreak of war. The reason for the pattern in the first three crises is not hard to find. None of them began as an Egyptian-Israeli dispute. Egypt did not become involved directly in the Palestinian conflict until the dispute was on the verge of war; the activity on the Egyptian-Israeli border was at its lowest level since the end of the Palestine War until Israel mobilized in the last week of the Suez Crisis; and Egypt did not play an active role in the Six Day War crisis until the final month before the outbreak of war.

The Suez Crisis was essentially a dispute between Egypt and Britain, with Israel taking advantage of collusion with Britain and France to launch a surprise attack in the Sinai. The Palestine and Six Day War crises both were instances where Egypt was drawn into crises generated by more radical Arab states. Only the 1973 crisis could be characterized as an Egyptian-Israeli dispute from beginning to end. The intensity of hostility early in the 1973 crisis is the highest of the four crises, but even in the 1973 crisis the hostility scores are well below those for the American-Soviet crises.

As in the cases of the Palestine and Suez Crises, the 1973 crisis ended in war not because the escalation of hostility between Egypt and Israel spiraled out of control but because one party decided on war before the crisis began to escalate. That the Arab states would attack the new Jewish state in Palestine in 1948 was a foregone conclusion as soon as the United Nations General Assembly voted for partition; the British-French decision to regain control of the Suez Canal by force was made before the crisis began to escalate, and Israel's decision to attack was based on the opportunity to act in concert with the British and French; Sadat decided on war in early 1973, well before that crisis began to escalate. The 1967 crisis is the only dispute in which a case can be made for a conflict spiral propelling the two sides to war.

Due to the rapid escalation during the last three weeks of the crisis, the 1967 crisis has the highest overall escalation score of the four Egyptian-Israeli crises. The pattern of escalation during that period approximates a conflict spiral. Once Egypt becomes an active participant in May, the crisis exhibits very high scores on all three escalation indicators (table 4.3) until the outbreak of war three and a half weeks later. The 1967 crisis also exhibits the high reciprocity in escalating hostile actions, or lock in, that is associated with a conflict spiral or Fight model of escalation (figure 4.7). The Six Day War appears to be the one case in which the spiraling escalation resulted in a war that had been sought by neither side.

The observed reciprocity in the actions of the two parties over the course of the four crises consists almost entirely of tit-for-tat coercive exchanges. Following the armistice accords at the end of the Palestine War, there were no direct negotiations between the two sides. Until Sadat reordered Egyptian priorities so that the return of the Egyptian territory occupied by Israel after the 1967 war took precedence over the recovery of all of Palestine, there was no common ground on which to negotiate.

Influence Strategies

Egypt and Israel's influence strategies over the four crises appear in table 4.5. In each of the four crises, at least one of the two parties employed an escalating coercive Bullying influence strategy; in two of the crises both parties used Bullying influence strategies. States are most likely to choose Bullying influence strategies when vital interests—territory and/or political independence—are at stake, and when they do, the crisis is highly likely to end in war (Leng 1993:151–53). The four Egyptian-Israeli crises fit the pattern. All four were cases in which vital interests were at stake and at least one of the parties employed a Bullying influence strategy.

Israel's choices of Bullying strategies in 1948 and 1956 were straightforward. Faced with an implacably hostile adversary determined to destroy the Jewish state, the Israeli government relied on military force. Although the predominant Israeli influence strategy in the 1967 crisis is Reciprocating, once the effort to obtain effective outside diplomatic intervention failed, the government turned to the use of force. The IDF's easy victory in 1967 reinforced the government's reliance on a military strategy.

Egypt used Bullying strategies in all but the Suez Crisis, when its preoccupation with the crisis with Britain and France encouraged Nasser's government to avoid creating a second crisis with Israel. Unlike Israel, Egypt did not have vital interests at stake in either the Palestine or Six Day War crises. In both cases Egypt's participation and the belligerency of its actions were prompted by pressures from its domestic constituency and, most important, the government's desire to assume or retain leadership of the Arab states.

The Egyptian government entered the Palestine crisis of 1948 intending to launch an attack on Israel, which explains Egypt's use of a Bullying influence strategy. But Nasser did not intend to go to war with Israel in

TABLE 4.5. Egyptian-Israeli Crises: Influence Strategies and Outcomes

Crisis	Influence Strategies		Outcome
	Egypt	Israel	
Palestine, 1948	Bullying	Bullying	War: Israeli victory
Suez, 1956	Stonewalling	Bullying	War: Israeli military victory, Egyptian diplomatic victory
Six Day, 1967	Bullying	Reciprocating	War: Israeli victory
October, 1973	Bullying	Reciprocating/ Stonewalling	War: Stalemate

1967. Nevertheless, he employed a Bullying influence strategy despite recognizing the advantage that Israel enjoyed in military capabilities.

The realpolitik logic behind a Bullying influence strategy is that the policymakers in the adversary state not only will respond to threats in a rational and prudent manner but also will be less risk-acceptant than the challenging party. But in 1967, Israel had an edge in motivation as the party defending the status quo against a fait accompli that presented a serious long-term threat to its security. States, like individuals, have been shown to accept greater risks to avoid losses than to achieve gains (Leng 1993: chap. 7; Kahneman and Tversky 1979; Farnham 1994). Given Israel's advantage in military capability, Nasser's military move into the Sinai and the mining of the Gulf of Aqaba posed greater costs and risks to Israeli security than did launching a preemptive military attack.

There are two plausible explanations for Nasser's choice of a Bullying influence strategy in 1967. First, he was under pressure both within Egypt and from other Arab leaders to take assertive action against Israel in the escalating crisis; consequently, his attempt to assume a leadership role led to the rapid escalation of the crisis. Second, Nasser drew lessons from his experience in the Suez Crisis in 1956 that encouraged him to accept the high risk of war in 1967.

Learning in the Egyptian-Israeli Crises

Egypt
The most significant diplomatic lesson that Nasser appears to have drawn from the Suez experience was that Israel, which had attacked in collusion with Britain and France in 1956, would not be willing to risk a two-front (Egypt and Syria) war in 1967 without Western help. Israel's only Western ally was the United States, and the Americans had told Nasser that they would restrain Israel from attacking first (Nutting 1972:398). To avoid war, Nasser went out of his way to assure the Americans and, through them, the Israelis, that he would not fire the first shot. As the British representative, Anthony Nutting, observed from his conversations with Nasser at the height of the 1967 crisis, "Living as he was in the atmosphere of 1956, Nasser refused to believe that he was seriously threatened by an Israeli attack" (Nutting 1972:408). Nasser correctly recognized after the Suez experience that the superpowers were now the key outside powers in the Middle East, but he overestimated the United States's influence over Israel. The lesson that Nasser failed to draw from the Suez Crisis and war was the most obvious one: following its low-cost military effort to improve its strategic position in 1956, Israel would not hesitate to use military force again if its long-term security were threatened.

Egypt drew three lessons from its disastrous defeat in the Six Day War. The first was a military lesson with a political consequence: Arab states could not achieve a complete military victory over Israel. The political consequence was a shift in strategic objectives from the recovery of all of Palestine to the recovery of the Egyptian territory lost in the 1967 war.

The second lesson was political but had a military consequence. After three decisive victories over Arab forces and significant territorial strategic gains, Israel had to be convinced of its military vulnerability before it would be willing to negotiate a return of the territory conquered in 1967. The military consequence was Sadat's plan for a limited war in the Sinai.

The third lesson was strictly military. Israel's successes in 1956 and 1967 had demonstrated the tactical advantage of a surprise first-strike attack. These lessons, along with Sadat's recognition of the key diplomatic role of the superpowers, especially the United States, in achieving a cease-fire and persuading Israel to negotiate a return of the Sinai and Gaza territories, led to his limited war strategy in 1973. Interestingly, Sadat's strategy's success ultimately depended on the same lesson that Nasser drew from the Suez Crisis—that is, the role of the United States in restraining Israel. But unlike Nasser, Sadat prepared the diplomatic ground for American support by offering the prospect of better Egyptian-American relations in the future and by carefully communicating his limited objectives to the United States.

Israel
Israel drew a simple realpolitik lesson from the Palestine War: the country's security depended on its military strength. The historical analogy to which Israeli leaders most often turned was the Holocaust. This time it was not the survival of the Jews that was at stake, but the survival of the Jewish state, which was isolated in a hostile Arab world.

The pivotal role played by the superpowers in determining the Suez conflict's outcome convinced the Israeli leadership of the importance of creating a good relationship with the United States, not only to obtain advanced weaponry but also to gain a diplomatic ally. The IDF's military success in the Suez campaign also convinced the Israelis of the advantages of a surprise first strike in future confrontations with the Arabs. That lesson was implemented in Israel's preemptive attack in 1967.

The IDF's dramatic victory in 1967 reinforced Israel's reliance on a military strategy for dealing with its Arab neighbors. There was little enthusiasm in the Meir government for returning the conquered territories to achieve a negotiated peace settlement with Egypt. Furthermore, the IDF's easy victory in 1967 led Israeli intelligence as well as Prime Minister Meir to underestimate Egypt's resolve in 1973.

None of the lessons drawn by either Egypt or Israel from their first three crises and wars was directed toward crisis management per se. There was little that could be learned from the first two wars, which were not preceded by extended Egyptian-Israeli crises, but even after the 1967 war, the two sides learned only from their war experiences. The lessons were essentially military, whether they were functional, as in the recognition of the tactical advantage of a first strike, or dysfunctional, such as Israel's complacency after its easy 1967 victory.

There is nothing in the behavior of the two sides prior to the end of the 1973 war to suggest that the governments of either Israel or Egypt changed their realpolitik views of their relationship. Within the bounds of realpolitik, however, Sadat drew lessons from the 1967 crisis and war that led to an effective strategy combining the use of force and diplomacy in 1973. Sadat had little choice but to attempt to change the situation given the collapse of the 1971–72 mediation efforts, Israel's satisfaction with the status quo, and its confidence in its military superiority. The only way in which Sadat could convince Israel to return the Sinai to Egypt was by creating a crisis that would convince Israel of its vulnerability.

The Superpowers

Neither superpower was deeply involved in the Middle East when the Egyptian-Israeli rivalry began in 1948. The Soviet Union took advantage of an opportunity to take a stand against Western imperialism during the Suez Crisis by opposing the Israeli, British, and French invasion, but by 1956 the USSR was also maneuvering to increase its influence among the Arab states in the region. The United States found itself in the awkward position of deserting its Western allies as it attempted to seize the United Nations leadership role in achieving a cease-fire. Although the two superpowers were ostensibly on the same side during the Suez Crisis, their policies were driven by their Cold War competition for influence in the region. An interesting aspect of the Suez crisis from the Soviet perspective is that Khrushchev's rocket-rattling effort to bully the British and French, which he considered successful in bringing about a cease-fire, probably encouraged his bullying over Berlin a few years later. The Soviet suggestion that the United States and Soviet Union send in a joint peacekeeping force to guarantee the cease-fire resurfaced during the 1973 Alert Crisis. Brezhnev accompanied his demand with the warning of possible Soviet unilateral action, as Khrushchev had done in 1956.

The Soviets sent mixed signals to Egypt during the 1967 and 1973 crises. In both instances they cautioned the Egyptians against going to war while providing them with the military means to do so. Soviet influence among the Arab states increased as the Arab-Israeli rivalry intensified, but the Kremlin did not want the rivalry to escalate to a war that could lead to a superpower confrontation. The United States, conversely, attempted throughout to reduce tensions between the two Middle East adversaries so that support for Israel would not stand in the way of improved relations with Arab states in the region. The United States nevertheless became a major supplier of military equipment to Israel and its primary, albeit unofficial, ally.

In the end, neither superpower was able to restrain its client from going to war. The United States could not restrain Israel from attacking first in 1967; the Soviets could not restrain Sadat from going to war in 1973. In both crises, the arms supplied by the United States and the Soviet Union encouraged their respective clients to launch surprise attacks. The superpowers managed to avoid a direct confrontation during the short 1967 war, although Soviet Premier Kosygin warned American President Johnson four days after the war began that the Soviets might have to take unilateral action if Israel continued to ignore calls for a cease-fire. Despite the attempt at superpower collaboration to achieve a cease-fire in the 1973 war, the breakdown in the cease-fire resulted in another Soviet threat of unilateral action and the Alert Crisis.

In sum, throughout the Egyptian-Israeli rivalry the superpowers were caught between their Cold War competition for influence in the strategically important region, which required military assistance to their most important clients, and the desire to avoid the risks of a superpower confrontation growing out of a Middle East war. For each superpower, the first consideration took precedence over the second.

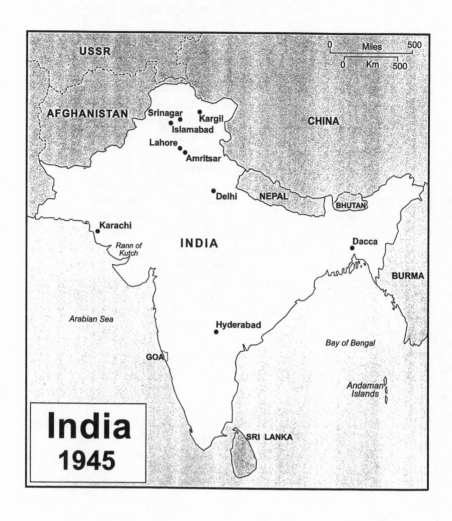

India 1945

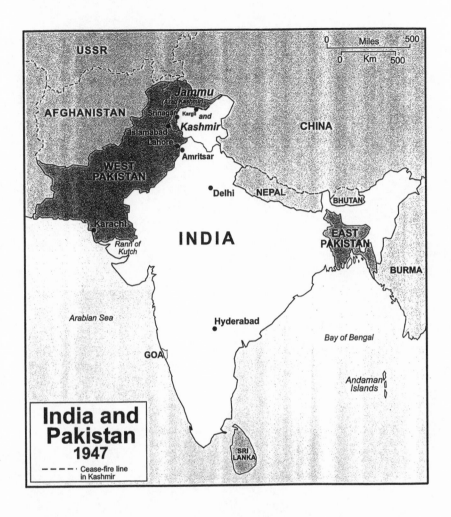

CHAPTER 5

The Indo-Pakistani Rivalry

When India achieved its independence from Great Britain on August 15, 1947, the new entity was divided into two states, India and Pakistan. The partition and the communal violence that accompanied it led to a bitter rivalry that produced four militarized crises between 1947 and 1971. Two of the crises ended in wars. The other two led to hostilities that stopped short of war between India and Pakistan, although the first Kashmir Crisis did result in an extrasystemic war that pitted Kashmiri forces backed by India against invading irregular forces from Pakistan (see Small and Singer 1982:99).

The intensity of the rivalry and the gravity of the territorial issues at stake bear strong resemblances to the Egyptian-Israeli crises. There also are some intriguing similarities between the two rivalries in the strategies pursued by the rival states and the lessons that they drew from their crisis experiences.

Like those in the Egyptian-Israeli rivalry, the four Indo-Pakistani crises focused on territorial issues, although neither party began the rivalry intent on eliminating the other. Unlike the Egyptian-Israeli rivalry, in the first three Indo-Pakistani crises, the smaller state, Pakistan, assumed the role of challenger. Faced with a stronger power satisfied with the status quo, Pakistan deliberately generated crises in the hope of forcing negotiations through outside intervention. Like Egypt, the Pakistani government drew lessons from the diplomatic intervention of major powers that encouraged the acceptance of high risks in subsequent crises.

The final Indo-Pakistani crisis differs from the others. It grew out of the separatist movement in East Pakistan that led to the birth of Bangladesh, and India led in escalating the crisis to war. The Bangladesh war ended in a decisive Indian military victory and the dismemberment of Pakistan. It did not end the rivalry.

Background

Despite the efforts of the nonviolent revolutionary leader, Mohandas Gandhi, to create a unified India, the conflict born out of religious differences between the majority Hindus and the Muslim minority forced the creation of the two dominions. Communal conflict between the Hindus and the Muslims can be traced back to the Muslim invasions and forced religious conversions that occurred centuries earlier, but the more immediate issue at the end of World War II was the Muslim fear of political domination in a state with a three-to-one Hindu majority.

Britain's intention to grant independence to India was announced as World War II drew to a close. But several conferences between 1945 and the summer of 1947 foundered amid the waves of the ongoing conflict between the Congress Party's Jawaharlal Nehru, who became the interim prime minister, and Ali Jinnah, the leader of the Muslim League. Since 1940 the Muslim League had led the cause for a separate Muslim state. By the spring of 1947, the last British governor-general, Lord Mountbatten, announced that his government would transfer power to two separate states. Pakistan was created out of the predominantly Muslim provinces of Punjab, the Northwest Frontier, and Sind in the west and East Bengal in the east. It was a divided state. Nearly 1,000 miles of Indian territory separated East Bengal from the provinces in the western half of Pakistan.

The partition of India led to massive population shifts and widespread communal violence. Millions of Muslims and Hindus left the states in which they were a minority, and hundreds of thousands were slaughtered in the communal violence that accompanied partition. When the British left India in August 1947, there were 600,000 dead and 10 million refugees. The communal violence and nationalistic fervor following the separation further exacerbated the tensions that existed between the two religious communities before partition.

The British left it to each of the more than 500 former princely states to decide whether they would accede to India or Pakistan or become independent. Only three states opted for independence: Junagah, Hyderabad, and Kashmir. Kashmir, which both India and Pakistan viewed as strategically vital to their security, became the focal point of ongoing Indo-Pakistani rivalry. The Kashmir dispute produced the first Indo-Pakistani crisis in 1947–48 and a war in 1965. A crisis over an uninhabited bit of land called the Rann of Kutch led to hostilities between Indian and Pakistani forces in the spring of 1965. In 1971 a civil war between East and West Pakistan led to a major Indo-Pakistani war. The dispute over the Rann of Kutch territory was settled with British mediation. The 1971 dispute was resolved by an Indian military victory and the birth of the state of Bangladesh. But Kashmir's status remains unresolved a half century after it led to the first Indo-Pakistani crisis.

First Kashmir Crisis, 1947

Like the larger Indian subcontinent, the population of Kashmir was divided along sectarian lines. Kashmir's population was 77 percent Muslim and 20 percent Hindu, but its government was led by Maharaja Hari Singh, a Hindu who had ties to India's Congress Party and a close personal relationship with Nehru. When Britain granted independence to India and Pakistan on August 15, Singh negotiated a "standstill" agreement with Pakistan, which provided for Kashmiri independence while the princely state decided whether it wished to accede to India or Pakistan or remain independent. Singh attempted to conclude a similar agreement with India, but India, with an eye toward the consequences of a referendum in the predominantly Muslim state, refused. In the meantime, Jinnah and a group of his followers from the Muslim League had arrived in Kashmir to popularize the cause of Muslim unity and to arouse the passions of the Muslim majority.

The Pakistani government expected Kashmir to accede to Pakistan shortly after independence, but Singh sought to take advantage of the standstill agreement to allow sufficient time to negotiate a degree of autonomy. As the weeks passed without a decision by Singh, the Pakistani leadership became more and more distrustful of the maharaja's intentions. The Indian government, meanwhile, worried that the Muslim unrest within Kashmir would undermine the authority of the Kashmiri regime and reduce the prospects for accession to India. Kashmir, in fact, was being drawn into the communal violence that raged throughout much of India and Pakistan. When a Muslim rebellion in Jammu was brutally put down by the Kashmiri government in October 1947, Muslim Pathen tribesmen from West Pakistan invaded and threatened to overpower Kashmir's defenses.

Crisis Structure

India
Perceptions of Pakistani intentions.   The Indian government's distrust of the Pakistani leadership dated back to disputes that occurred during the struggle for independence, when the Muslim League insisted on the creation of a separate Muslim state. The distrust was exacerbated by Pakistani pressures on Kashmir to accede to Pakistan. When the Pathen tribesmen attacked on October 22, the Indian government was convinced that the Pakistani government was behind the invasion (Wirsing 1994:41; S. Gupta 1966:103). Pakistan's objective, in the view of Indian leaders, was

to topple the Kashmiri government and replace it with a Muslim leadership favorable to accession to Pakistan. By late September, the Indian defense ministry reported receiving information of Pakistani plans for military intervention in Kashmir (Wirsing 1994:48).

Interests. Indians have a strong sentimental attachment to Kashmir, with many of India's most influential elites having come from the princely state. Kashmir's importance to India, however, went beyond sentimental attachments. Kashmir was strategically situated along India's northern border with China as well as with Pakistan. For India, control of Kashmir was a vital security interest. There also was the deeper Indo-Pakistani conflict over partition and the Indian ideal of a single secular state. As Nehru put it, "We cannot give up the basic ideal which we have held so long and on which the whole conception of our state is founded" (Korbel 1966:43). The loss of Kashmir to Pakistan would be another loss to religious separatism.

Capabilities. Indian Prime Minister Nehru had the diplomatic advantage of friendly relationships with Kashmir's two most influential leaders, Maharaja Singh and the nationalist leader, Sheikh Abdullah. The three leaders shared coincidental interests in blocking Kashmir's accession to Pakistan. The maharaja worried about the fate of Kashmir's Hindu minority as well as his personal future should Kashmir be incorporated into Pakistan. Abdullah, who was the most popular political figure in Kashmir, was a staunch advocate of Kashmiri independence. Abdullah also had a long-standing cordial relationship with Nehru, and held a deep animus toward the Muslim League (Korbel 1966:70–72). Kashmir's Muslim majority, conversely, was divided between those who favored accession to Pakistan and those who favored independence.

India's army numbered about 200,000 compared to Pakistan's 55,000 (Choudhury 1968:67). Pakistan, however, had a logistical advantage owing to the proximity of the fighting area. Indian forces had to traverse a long mountain road that was virtually inaccessible in winter to reach Kashmir by land. Despite the numerical advantage enjoyed by their forces, the Indian leadership did not expect to achieve a quick and easy victory in a war with Pakistan. They also realized that the Kashmiri defense forces alone were no match for a Pakistani invasion.

Pakistan
Perception of India's intentions. The Pakistani leadership's perceptions of India's intentions in Kashmir were a mirror image of those held by the Indian leadership. Pakistani policymakers were convinced that India was determined to secure the accession of Kashmir to the Indian union and that these efforts had the support of Maharaja Singh (see Choudhury

1968:98; Hasan 1966:80). When Indian troops entered Kashmir, Pakistani Prime Minister Liaquat Khan claimed that India had been intending all along to occupy Kashmir (India, Government 1947–48:62–65).

Interests. If the Indian leadership considered control of Kashmir to be a vital security interest, it was a matter of survival to Pakistan. Pakistani military analysts believed that Indian control of Kashmir would make Pakistan all but indefensible (Choudhury 1968:90). As vital as Kashmir was to the security of India, it was more important to Pakistan's existence.

In addition to Kashmir's strategic importance, more than three-fourths of the Kashmiris were Muslims. Having fought so hard for a separate state for the Muslim minority of India, the loss of Kashmir to India would represent a significant defeat to Jinnah and other members of the Muslim League. From the Pakistani perspective, Kashmir was territory worth fighting for.

Capabilities. The Pakistani leadership recognized the diplomatic advantage that India enjoyed through Maharaja Singh's close relationship with Nehru and the Congress Party. But opposition to the maharaja and civil unrest had been increasing since independence. By the fall, there were full-scale revolts under way in Jammu and Poonch. Pakistan's capacity for political influence among the populace in Kashmir was weakened, however, in October, when the maharaja ordered Sheikh Abdullah's release from prison. The popular leader of the Kashmiri independence movement posed another political threat to Pakistan's hopes for the accession of Kashmir.

Despite having a nearly four to one disadvantage vis-à-vis India, Pakistan's military leadership was relatively confident regarding their chances on the battlefield (Blinkenberg 1972:85). The logistical advantage, with the coming winter season, was one reason for the confidence; another was the low opinion of India's military competence and motivation. Nevertheless, Prime Minister Liaquat Ali Khan was well aware of the potential consequences of the numerical disadvantage facing the Pakistani army (Choudhury 1968:200).

Crisis Behavior

Narrative Summary
Early in the fall of 1947, Muslim refugees fleeing the civil strife in Jammu and Poonch arrived in Pakistan with stories of atrocities, including the mass murder of Muslims by Kashmiri government forces. Tensions increased between the governments of Pakistan and Kashmir, with Pakistan accusing Kashmir of genocide and Kashmir accusing Pakistan of

supplying military support to insurrectionists. On October 15, the maharaja asked for an impartial inquiry, but he warned that Kashmir might need to seek outside assistance, presumably from India, in putting down the revolts.

When the threat was repeated three days later, Jinnah charged the maharaja with seeking a pretext for Indian military intervention as the first step toward accession to India (Korbel 1966:69). On October 22 Pathen tribesmen from the Northwest Frontier province of Pakistan invaded Kashmir and overran the state defenses. By October 26, Pathen forces were advancing on Srinagar, the capital of Kashmir. Meanwhile, Kashmiri troops, along with mobs of Sikhs and Hindus, went on a rampage of killing and looting against Muslims. Within a few days more than 100,000 Muslims from Kashmir had fled into Pakistan.

Maharaja Singh appealed to India for military help on October 24. The Indian government was willing to send the aid to Kashmir, but Lord Mountbatten, who was now the governor-general of India, warned against violating Kashmir's neutrality and inviting direct intervention by Pakistan. According to Mountbatten, intervention could be justified legally only if Kashmir acceded to India. India immediately dispatched a representative to the maharaja to suggest accession. The maharaja was desperate for Indian military assistance and Nehru and Menon made it clear that signing the instrument of accession was a prerequisite to obtaining that assistance (Jha 1996:137).[1] No attempt was made to consult with Pakistan over the escalating crisis. On October 26, the maharaja signed an instrument of accession to India. Mountbatten accepted the accession as provisional, pending a plebiscite to determine the will of the people once law and order had been reestablished (India, Government 1947–48:46–48). Indian troops were airlifted to Srinagar on October 27.

Jinnah, who was now the governor-general of Pakistan, started to order Pakistani troops into Kashmir on the next day, but on the urgent advice of his military command, he rescinded the order in favor of requesting consultations with India. Pakistan also declared the accession of Kashmir to India to be illegal. Jinnah and Mountbatten met in Lahore on November 1, at which time both parties agreed that Kashmir's accession to India or Pakistan should be settled by a plebiscite. The two sides, how-

---

1. The timing of the maharaja's signing of the instrument of accession and the intervention by Indian forces has remained cloudy. The maharaja's signature on the instrument of Accession is dated October 26, one day before Indian troops were airlifted into Kashmir; however, two persons involved in the situation at the time have since written that the maharaja actually signed the instrument of accession shortly *after* the beginning of the Indian intervention (Mahajan 1963:151–52; Singh 1982:57–59).

ever, could not agree on the modalities for conducting the plebiscite. Consequently, the agreement on a plebiscite was in principle only.

India rejected a Pakistani proposal for an immediate cease-fire and withdrawal of all outside forces from Kashmir. Two weeks after the talks broke up, Liaquat Khan accepted the Indian plan for a United Nations–directed plebiscite and proposed that the United Nations intervene to stop the fighting and arrange the withdrawal of all outside forces from Kashmir. Nehru responded a week later on November 21 by rejecting the proposed United Nations intervention. Then, in mid-December, he modified his position by agreeing to seek United Nations diplomatic assistance in resolving the conflict. On New Year's Day 1948, India asked the Security Council to deal with the crisis as a threat to international peace "owing to the aid which invaders, consisting of nationals of Pakistan and of tribesmen are drawing from Pakistan for operations against Jammu and Kashmir" (United Nations Security Council 1948: document 628). The message went on to threaten Indian military action within Pakistan should Pakistan not cease its aid to the raiders. Liaquat Khan responded on January 3 by accusing India of attempting to annex Kashmir as the first step in a plan to eliminate Pakistan as an independent state.

The United Nations formed the Commission on India and Pakistan (UNCIP), which was charged with mediating a cease-fire and negotiations to resolve the dispute in Kashmir. On April 11, the Indian army launched a major new offensive in Kashmir, which swelled the stream of refugees fleeing into Pakistan. Both sides rejected UNCIP proposals for a cease-fire, however, and the fighting continued. On May 11, the Pakistani government sent its regular forces into defensive positions in Kashmir alongside the tribesmen and rebels (see Wirsing 1994:54). Then, on August 13, the UNCIP finally managed to broker an agreement on a cease-fire, which took effect on January 1, 1949. The cease-fire called for the withdrawal of all Pakistani troops and "the bulk" of Indian forces from Jammu and Kashmir. Pakistan named that part of Kashmir that remained under its control Azad Kashmir, or "free Kashmir." Principles, albeit somewhat vague, for holding a plebiscite in Kashmir were agreed upon on January 5, 1949.

Outside of their activities in the United Nations Security Council, the role of the two superpowers in the First Kashmir Crisis was minimal. Both were preoccupied with the Cold War in Europe, and the United States was happy to defer to Great Britain in United Nations Security Council discussions. When Indian and Pakistani representatives requested that an American be appointed to mediate the dispute, the United States urged the parties to accept the mediation of Great Britain (McMahon 1994:30). During the crisis, however, the American representatives pushed for a plebiscite in Kashmir, an action that cheered the Pakistanis and irritated the Indians, who opposed the plebiscite. Nehru pointedly told U.S. Ambassador Loy Henderson that the Indian leader was tired of receiving moralistic lectures from the United States (McMahon 1994:34–35).

Patterns of Behavior

Figure 5.1 presents the time series for the weighted actions of India and those directed by Pakistan either to India or, early in the crisis, to Kashmir.[2] The pattern of behavior exhibited in figure 5.1 approximates that of a Fight—that is, a rising spiral of hostility with the adversaries responding in kind and magnitude to each other's escalating hostility. A rough sense of how the escalation of the crisis compares to militarized crises more generally can be obtained by comparing the escalation and reciprocity scores from the First Kashmir Crisis, which appear in tables 5.1 and 5.2, to those in the larger sample of crises in the appendix. The First Kashmir Crisis is well above the median in both escalation and reciprocity.

The rate of escalation is fairly high, but the magnitude and intensity of the escalation are what stand out. The First Kashmir Crisis ranks third

TABLE 5.1.   India-Pakistan: Escalation Scores

Crisis	Magnitude Score (Rank)	Intensity Score (Rank)	Rate Score (Rank)	Rank India-Pakistan Crises	Rank in Larger Sample
First Kashmir	307.00 (6)	180.70 (2)	4.60 (12)	2	5
India	163.50	92.30	2.50		
Pakistan	143.50	88.40	2.10		
Rann of Kutch	106.50 (17)	47.74 (16)	2.31 (14)	4	17
India	52.00	23.44	1.23		
Pakistan	54.50	24.30	1.08		
Second Kashmir	139.50 (13)	21.83 (25)	3.87 (13)	3	18
India	70.00	10.14	1.94		
Pakistan	69.50	11.69	1.93		
Bangladesh	318.00 (6)	101.29 (7)	7.99 (10)	1	6
India	184.00	63.97	4.73		
Pakistan	134.00	37.50	3.26		
Mean Score	217.75	87.89	4.69		

2. Actions directed by the government of Pakistan toward the government of Kashmir are included on the grounds that these actions were viewed by India as hostile actions directed at India as well. The actions taken by unofficial groups, including the invading Pakistani tribesmen, are not included.

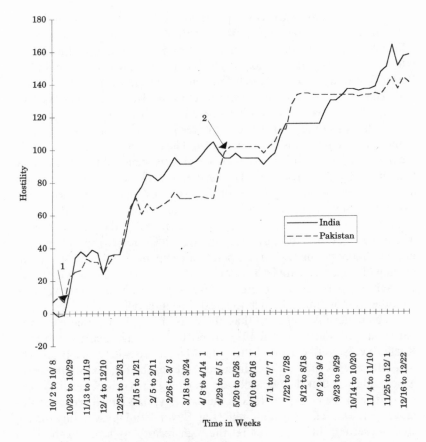

Fig. 5.1. First Kashmir Crisis, 1947–48
Key dates are indicated with arrows: (1) 10/22: Pathen tribesmen invade Kashmir; (2) 5/9: Pakistani regular forces join tribesmen and rebels in Kashmir.

in magnitude and second in intensity among the 12 crises in the three rivalries. Only the Berlin Blockade and the Bangladesh Crises exhibit a higher magnitude of escalation, and only the Berlin Blockade has a higher intensity score. The rate of escalation would rank fourth among the 12 crises. Like the Berlin Blockade Crisis, the high escalation scores are remarkable for a crisis that does not escalate to war between the two states.

The escalation scores suggest that the Berlin Blockade and First Kashmir Crises were disputes in which the parties were willing to accept a high degree of hostility without crossing the threshold to war. In these crises as well, the rival states were uncertain about the balance in capabilities, and neither was ready to accept the costs of a full-scale war. India and Pakistan also were restrained from fighting each other by an outside influence—the command of both armies by British officers who had no interest in fighting each other. It also should be noted that, unlike the Berlin Blockade Crisis, although India and Pakistan avoided direct combat, there were sustained hostilities in the First Kashmir Crisis between Kashmiri forces backed by India and the Pathen invaders.[3]

Fights are notable for the degree of reciprocation, or tit for tat, shown in the conflictual actions of the two sides. The closeness of the two sides in the magnitude of hostility as the crisis evolves is remarkable in light of the high intensity of interaction. The distance score, which measures how close together the hostility scores of the two sides are as the crisis evolves, would rank seventh if the First Kashmir Crisis scores were added to those in the sample of 34 crises in the appendix. Conversely, the direction score, which indicates the extent to which the two sides are in sync as they each move to more conflictual or cooperative behavior, would fall below the median of the larger sample. The combination suggests a tit-for-tat pattern wherein one party takes a more coercive action at one time interval with the other responding in kind at the next time interval.

The pattern is similar to that observed in Egyptian-Israeli behavior, particularly in the 1967 and 1973 crises. But the reciprocity in the First Kashmir Crisis differs from the Egyptian-Israeli crises in two respects. The first difference is the very low distance score for the First Kashmir Crisis, which indicates that the two sides are matching each other's hostility over the course of the crisis, whereas in the two Egyptian-Israeli crises the distance score was relatively high, reflecting Egypt's lead in escalating the crisis. The second difference is that the high reciprocity score in the First Kashmir Crisis reflects some mutual moves to accommodation, in the form of direct negotiations, as well as coercion. In that sense, the First Kashmir Crisis departs from a classic Fight, or conflict spiral, in that the two parties are not locked into exclusively conflictual behavior.

The overall impression given by the escalation and reciprocity scores as well as by the visual pattern in figure 5.1 is that of a crisis in which the two parties alternated between proposing and rejecting solutions to the dispute while continuing to match each other in escalating the magnitude of hostility. The pattern suggests a mutual determination to demonstrate resolve and to respond in kind to any attempts by the other to take advan-

---

3. The 1,500 casualties were sufficient for Small and Singer (1982:99) to classify the war as extrasystemic—that is, as an international war in which there are not members of the interstate system participating on both sides. Indian and Pakistani troops avoided direct combat with each other.

tage of the situation, along with a willingness to participate in a search for a peaceful resolution of the crisis.

Communication and Negotiation

Despite the ambiguous role of Pakistan in the Pathen invasion of Kashmir in October 1947, there was no direct communication between India and Pakistan in the critical period between the invasion and India's intervention. But with the urging of Great Britain, the two sides did meet to attempt to find a negotiated resolution to the crisis in early November 1947. Additional meetings occurred sporadically over the next three months. The meetings, however, degenerated into sessions dominated by exchanges of accusations. After unsuccessful attempts in early February 1948, the direct negotiations came to a virtual halt. The cease-fire agreement reached in August 1948 was based on a United Nations Security Council plan that was negotiated separately with each party. In a dispute marked by mistrust and misperceptions on both sides, the parties, which had so recently been members of the same dominion, consulted or negotiated with each other on only 18 of the 443 days of the crisis.

Influence Strategies

The predominant influence strategy for each of the two sides is best described as Cautious Bullying. As with a Bullying strategy, a Cautious Bullying influence strategy consists primarily of escalating coercive influence attempts, but the party employing the strategy is willing to negotiate, avoids direct hostilities with the other side, and avoids pushing the other party into choosing between war and surrender.

Both India and Pakistan relied primarily on escalating coercive influence attempts, but they were applied with caution. Protests were followed by verbal threats, which were augmented by displays of force and ultimately the use of force. Escalatory moves, however, were implemented gradually. Indian and Pakistani troops in Kashmir avoided direct confrontations with each other, and attempts to achieve a negotiated settlement, either between the two sides or through the mediating efforts of the United Nations, continued throughout the crisis. Given the two sides' shared hostility and the interests at stake, the mutual restraint seems remarkable, but it may have had more to do with the residual British presence than with moderation on the part of the national leaders. The commanders of both national armies were still British officers who had no interest in finding themselves at war with each other and who remained in frequent communication throughout the crisis (see Lamb 1966:54).

India

In the early fall of 1947, the Indian leadership received reports of a potential Pakistani intervention in Kashmir and began to prepare contingency plans for a counterintervention (see Wirsing 1994:48–49). Fearing that Pakistan might intervene in the late fall to take advantage of the inaccessibility of Kashmir to Indian troops in the winter, Prime Minister Nehru urged his deputy, Sardar Patel, to "force the pace and to turn events in the right direction . . . so as to bring about the accession of Kashmir to Indian Union as rapidly as possible" (Das Gupta 1968:49). Nehru's strategy was to accomplish the accession to deter Pakistan from attempting a military intervention. Should Pakistan not be deterred, Kashmir's accession to the Indian union would provide the political and legal grounds for an Indian counterintervention.

The Indian government was convinced that Pakistan had orchestrated the actions of the Pathen tribesmen who invaded Kashmir. Some Indian leaders even assumed that Pakistani military objectives extended beyond Kashmir. One of Nehru's advisers, recalling past Muslim invasions, commented, "Srinagar today, Delhi tomorrow" (V. P. Menon, quoted in Wirsing 1994:40). The Indian political leadership favored intervening immediately, but the governor-general, Lord Mountbatten, insisted on first obtaining the provisional accession of Kashmir to India. Mountbatten exerted a moderating influence to balance the hawkish views of Nehru's advisers, most notably Patal, who, along with his deputy, V. P. Menon, favored a purely military response. He believed that negotiations with the Pakistanis would merely signal Indian weakness. Nehru nevertheless agreed to the November 1 meeting in Lahore and sent a telegram to Liaquat Khan to assure him that India would withdraw its troops as soon as peace and order were restored (Burke 1973:27).

The Indian strategy for the remainder of the crisis was to use military muscle to take advantage of the opportunity for influence that the occupation of Kashmir provided and to pursue diplomacy to bring an end to the fighting. Once a cease-fire had been achieved, with Indian troops remaining in Kashmir to maintain order—and India's influence over events in Kashmir—India was willing to submit the accession question to a plebiscite under United Nations supervision (Wirsing 1994:56). India's acceptance of a referendum to decide Kashmir's future was based partly on the popularity of Abdullah, a staunch opponent of the Muslim League, who was now the head of the emergency interim government in Kashmir, and partly on the anti-Pakistani sentiment that had grown out of the October invasion. Nehru also attached stringent conditions to his acceptance. A "prolonged period of adjustment" would be necessary to obtain the peace and order necessary for a reasoned judgment by the people before a plebiscite could be held. In the meantime, the Abdullah government would remain in place (Korbel 1966:310).

Pakistan

Prior to the invasion of the Pathen tribesmen, Pakistani foreign policy appeared to be working at cross-purposes. While Prime Minister Liaquat Khan pursued a diplomatic effort to persuade the maharaja to accede to Pakistan, Jinnah, the Muslim League leader who now was governor-general of Pakistan, was in Kashmir, where he was politically agitating for the overthrow of the maharaja's regime. When the maharaja began his crackdown on suspected Muslim opponents, Jinnah and his associates actively supported the Kashmiri insurrectionists (see Korbel 1966:67–70). As Liaquat Khan was agreeing to the standstill agreement that would guarantee Kashmiri independence until the maharaja decided the issue of accession, Jinnah was pursuing a strategy certain to increase the maharaja's distrust of Pakistani intentions.

Whether the government of Pakistan was behind the October invasion of the Pathen tribesmen, as an Indian white paper (India, Government 1947–48) charged, or whether the invasion was a spontaneous reaction by traditionally well armed and bellicose Pakistani tribesmen outraged at the reports of atrocities against Muslims, as the Pakistanis claimed (see Choudhury 1968:111), remains unclear to this day. As the author of a recent account put it, "There is dispute about the number of tribesmen involved, about who supported them, certainly about motives, about things they did, and about the dates on which they supposedly did them. . . . There is nothing even remotely resembling a consensus" (Wirsing 1994:39). The most plausible speculation is that of Joseph Korbel, the first director of UNCIP. Korbel (1966:95) surmised that although the Pakistani leadership did not initiate or direct the invasion, Pakistani officials in the Northwest Frontier province provided encouragement and material assistance.[4] In any event, when India intervened in Kashmir following the invasion of the Pathen tribesmen, the Pakistani government viewed the Indian intervention not only as a threat to Pakistan's aspirations in Kashmir but also as a direct threat to the survival of Pakistan itself.

The hawkish Jinnah gave orders for the Pakistani army to attack Kashmir in full force. The potentially disastrous action was delayed and the order was eventually rescinded by the efforts of Pakistan's British military commanders and Prime Minister Liaquat Khan, whom Jinnah had

---

4. Korbel's surmise is plausible given the fierce independence of the already well armed and bellicose tribesmen. There also is evidence of the appearance of some Pakistani army "volunteers" in support roles, but there is no evidence of Pakistani planning or direction of the attack (see Korbel 1966:74–75).

not consulted (see Blinkenberg 1972:103). Liaquat Khan attempted diplomacy, first through direct negotiations with India in early November 1947 and then by appealing to the United Nations to intervene. Figure 5.1 suggests the reactive character of Pakistani diplomacy during the first six months of the crisis, until Pakistan decided to commit its troops to defensive positions within Kashmir in May 1948. The Pakistani military initiative was largely in response to the economic and social effects of a huge flow of refugees, especially from the Poonch area of Kashmir in the spring of 1948. The troops established a defense line in the Uri-Poonch area and carefully avoided any direct contact with Indian forces.

Pakistan appealed to the Security Council with the claim that the struggle in Kashmir was an Indian attempt to roll back partition—that is, to strangle the infant state of Pakistan. As a bargaining tactic, the Pakistani appeal to a higher authority, with the issue presented in moral terms, attempted to redress the imbalance in bargaining power enjoyed by India. Pakistan, however, was unable to obtain United Nations military intervention.

Short of attaining such intervention, Pakistan's diplomatic initiatives sought to obtain a cease-fire, the withdrawal of Indian forces from Kashmir, and a United Nations–supervised plebiscite to determine Kashmir's future. But by the summer of 1948, the Pakistani interest in a plebiscite had cooled, perhaps because of concern over the popularity of Sheikh Abdullah and the growing nationalist sentiment in Kashmir (see Blinkenberg 1972:130; Brines 1968:89). Meanwhile, the ongoing fighting in Kashmir created an unmanageable refugee problem and growing economic instability in Pakistan. Consequently, in the summer of 1948, Pakistan agreed to a cease-fire at the end of the year but rejected the UNCIP plan for the proposed plebiscite.

During the fall of 1948, as Indian forces achieved major military successes in Kashmir, the economic instability in Pakistan worsened. When the stridently anti-Hindu Jinnah died in September, the major internal obstacle to an agreement was eliminated. On January 5, 1949, Pakistan accepted the United Nations plan for the postwar political settlement as the best deal it could get.

Summary

Both sides viewed themselves as defending the status quo with vital security interests at stake. Each pursued a Cautious Bullying strategy, with a mix of military and diplomatic actions. Pakistan, which was the weaker party, also resorted to appealing to a higher authority, the United Nations Security Council, in an attempt to redress the imbalance in bargaining power. It is remarkable that the crisis did not lead to war between India and Pakistan given the seriousness of the stakes, the tendency of both governments to suspect the worst of the other, the high level of escalation, and the ongoing hostilities. Three factors appear to have prevented the crisis from crossing the threshold to an interstate war: (1) the fortunate coincidence of British military commanders, with good relations with each other and an interest in moderating the conflict, at the heads of both armies; (2) an imbalance in military strength favoring a party with limited military objectives; and (3) the diplomatic intercession of influential third parties with an impartial interest in terminating the crisis.

Outcome and Lessons

The United Nations Security Council's cease-fire proposal attempted to bridge the interests of both sides. Provisions for holding a referendum to determine Kashmir's ultimate future, however, were elaborate and vague. Most important, there was no timetable for arranging the promised plebiscite. The dispute over Kashmir was not resolved: division and distrust between the Pakistanis and Indians worsened.

India

When the cease-fire was implemented at the end of the year, most Indians viewed it with a sense of relief (Blinkenberg 1972:132). Indian forces had been militarily successful in Kashmir, and war with Pakistan had been avoided. Diplomatically, India had achieved most of its objectives. The "provisional" accession of Kashmir to India remained in place, along with the pro-Indian "emergency" government of Sheikh Abdullah; the Pathen invaders, along with most Pakistani forces, would be withdrawn, but a contingent of Indian troops would remain in Kashmir; and no date had been set for a referendum on Kashmir's future.[5] These gains were tempered by the fact of the war itself and by awareness of its consequences for future Indo-Pakistani relations.

India's presumed military superiority over Pakistan convinced Indian leaders that India enjoyed military hegemony on the subcontinent. As a consequence, the Indian government devoted only minimal attention to strengthening its military forces in the years following the crisis. The major

---

5. The Indian leadership objected to provisions to insure an impartial plebiscite under United Nations supervision and those provisions allowing some Pakistani troops to participate in a pacification program in Kashmir.

diplomatic lesson that Indian leaders drew from the crisis was that the Pakistanis were too unreasonable or too hostile for the two parties to achieve any settlement of outstanding issues through negotiation (see S. Gupta 1966:139).

Pakistan

Pakistan was not pleased with the inequality in the withdrawal of forces, which left an Indian military contingent in Kashmir, or with the continuing authority of the Abdullah government. The Pakistani leadership drew some consolation from the role played by the United Nations in negotiations for a promised plebiscite in Kashmir. Nevertheless, prior to the crisis Pakistan had expected that Kashmir would voluntarily accede to Pakistan. Viewed from that perspective, the outcome of the crisis could not be viewed as a success.

Despite the military restraint shown by India during the hostilities, the Pakistani leadership was convinced that India's long-term goal was to reverse the partition of the subcontinent by force (Blinkenberg 1972:111). These fears were exacerbated by India's actions in the states of Hyderabad and Junagadh, where Muslim attempts to accede to Pakistan were put down by force. The main lesson that Pakistani leaders appear to have drawn from the First Kashmir Crisis was military: Pakistan's survival required building an army capable of competing on even footing with India. As in the case of India, the distrust and hostility that had been hardened by the crisis and war virtually eliminated any prospects for a negotiated settlement of outstanding differences. Pakistan's only perceived diplomatic option was to compete with India in pleading its case to powerful third parties.

During a prayer meeting on December 29, 1948, just prior to the institution of the cease-fire, Gandhi exclaimed: "Will not the Pakistani Government and the Union Government close the ranks and come to an amicable settlement with the assistance of impartial Indians? Or, has impartiality fled from India?" (Pyarelal 1958:498). The answer was all too obvious.

Rann of Kutch Crisis, 1965

The Rann of Kutch Crisis would seem to be a classic example of how mutual animosity and distrust can create crises out of disputes over goods of no real consequence to either party. But from the perspectives of crisis bargaining and learning, it is a more complex case that suggests some interesting comparisons to crises in the other two rivalries. In the Rann of

Kutch Crisis, Pakistan combined force with a diplomatic strategy that relied on outside intervention that held some resemblance to Sadat's strategy in the 1973 Egyptian-Israel crisis. Ayub Khan's government also was encouraged by its success in the Rann of Kutch Crisis to devise a similar but higher-risk strategy in the Second Kashmir war, much in the manner that Khrushchev's successful installation of the Berlin Wall led to his higher-risk attempt to achieve a fait accompli in Cuba.

The Intercrisis Period, 1948–65

Sisson and Rose (1990:275) neatly summarize the relationship between India and Pakistan in the years between the First Kashmir and Rann of Kutch Crises: "Each side viewed the intentions and motivations of the other as fundamentally hostile. . . . Neither accepted the other as acting in good faith, but rather in a way designed to do the greatest harm to the interests of the other."

Following the Kashmir cease-fire, several United Nations efforts failed to reach agreement on demilitarization followed by a plebiscite in Kashmir. Military representatives of the two sides agreed on the cease-fire line in Kashmir on July 27, 1949. But the next month a United Nations proposal for arbitration was rejected, as was a subsequent United Nations proposal in December 1949.

The Kashmir issue continued to poison Indo-Pakistani relations. Pakistan rejected a 1949 Indian proposal for a mutual no-war declaration on the grounds that such a pledge could not be made while India continued its control of Kashmir. In 1951 Kashmir held its first statewide elections, and Sheikh Abdullah's party resoundingly defeated pro-Pakistani candidates. Until 1953 Nehru continued in principle to support public elections to decide the ultimate future of Kashmir, but a combination of influences prompted him to change his policy in 1954. Those influences included pressure from right-wing opposition parties that wished to integrate Kashmir into India, growing anti-Indian sentiment within Kashmir following the arrest of Sheikh Abdullah in March 1953, and, not least, concern over the military aid Pakistan received through its ties with the United States (see Jha 1972:359). In March 1954, Nehru concluded that Indian forces would need to be retained indefinitely in Kashmir to meet any new threats from Pakistan. Abdullah, who remained incarcerated until 1958, was replaced in Kashmir by a more reliably pro-Indian regime, which in 1957 confirmed the earlier provisional accession to India.[6]

---

6. Abdullah was convicted of treason in 1953, released in 1958, and convicted again in the same year for attempting to overthrow the Kashmiri government.

An uneasy relationship prevailed along other portions of the Indo-Pakistani border as well. There was a minor border clash in 1956 in the Rann of Kutch, which turned out to be an early precursor to the 1965 crisis. In October 1959, however, the two sides managed to reach final agreement on the status of India's eastern border with Pakistan. No less important, each party committed itself to accept arbitration of any future border disputes that could not be resolved by negotiation. The arbitration agreement became the basis for the settlement of the Rann of Kutch dispute in 1965.

Nehru's Congress Party remained solidly in control in India, with Nehru serving as prime minister and foreign minister through 1964. But Pakistan's Prime Minister, Liaquat Ali Khan, was assassinated in 1951. Pakistan then went through an extended period of political instability, which included increasing political tensions between East and West Pakistan. Ayub Khan assumed power in a bloodless coup in October 1958. That Pakistan was now controlled by a military dictator worsened relations with India and strengthened the position of those in Kashmir who favored permanent accession to India.

Relationships with the Superpowers and China

During the 1950s, India's Nehru became a leader of the nonalignment movement of states seeking an independent course free of entanglements in the Cold War. Pakistan, conversely, actively sought and obtained defensive alliances with its Western neighbors. In 1954 Pakistan signed a mutual security agreement with the United States that led to the acquisition of American military hardware and technical assistance. Pakistan further tightened its relationship with the West by joining the Southeast Asian Treaty Organization and the Baghdad Pact. The United States and Pakistan signed a more extensive bilateral defense accord in March 1959.

Nehru's espousal of nonalignment as the best way to maintain peace in South Asia led him to oppose Pakistan's alliance with the United States on ideological grounds, but he was more concerned with its effect on the military balance between India and Pakistan.[7] American aid to Pakistan, which the United States intended as a deterrent to the Chinese and Russians, encouraged India to seek military support from the Soviet Union.

The Soviet Union had originally had been hostile to Nehru's policy of nonalignment, but this attitude began to shift in the early 1950s, when India refused to join the West in condemning the Chinese entrance into the

---

7. The positions of the two sides are stated clearly in a December 1953 exchange of letters between Nehru and Pakistani Prime Minister Muhammed Ali Bogra (see Hasan 1966:344–448).

Korean War and supported the seating of the People's Republic in the United Nations. Following Stalin's 1953 death, the Soviets pressed for a stronger friendship. India and the Soviet Union shared a common interest in balancing against Pakistan, with the Soviets concerned about the security of their client regime in Afghanistan. After an exchange of visits between Nehru and Khrushchev in 1955, Khrushchev announced his support of India's position on Kashmir and initiated a program of economic and technological assistance to India.

The American alliance with Pakistan had grown out of the Truman administration's concern in the early 1950s over growing instability in the Middle East as well as competition with the Soviet Union and China on the Indian subcontinent. British influence throughout the area was rapidly declining, with Soviet influence growing in critical states such as Egypt and Iran. Pakistan was strategically placed to be an important component of an American effort to build a new security system in the region. To obtain an alliance commitment from Pakistan, the Truman administration was willing to accept what it perceived to be the temporary cost of antagonizing India. The relationship between the United States and India worsened during the Eisenhower administration, when U.S. Secretary of State John Foster Dulles's rigid Cold War views clashed with Nehru's policy of nonalignment.

When the Kennedy administration entered office in 1961, it held less rigid views regarding Cold War allegiances. Kennedy worked to improve American-Indian relations, particularly in light of China's growing power. The Johnson administration, which took office following Kennedy's assassination in November 1963, did not hesitate to express its displeasure at Pakistan's growing friendship with China. Although the United States did not abandon its Pakistani commitments, it began to supply aid to India as well.

At the beginning of 1965, India was receiving military aid from both the Soviet Union and the United States. Pakistan, meanwhile, improved its relations with the Soviet Union and, on April 8, 1965, the Soviets agreed to supply technical aid to Pakistan. The superpowers now were engaged in a competition for influence in South Asia where each was assisting both contending parties.

As the Rann of Kutch Crisis unfolded, American-Pakistani relations were strained. The United States was growing increasingly angered over Pakistan's warm relations with China, while the Pakistani leadership was furious over the new American relationship with India (see McMahon 1994:318). During the course of the Rann conflict, India complained that Pakistan was using American-supplied Patton tanks. The United States demanded that Pakistan desist using equipment that the United States had intended only for defense against China, which ironically was now Pakistan's staunchest supporter. India blamed the United States for the appearance of the tanks in the conflict; the Pakistanis reacted with anger when the United States demanded that Pakistan stop using them. These events weakened the credibility of the United States to mediate the dispute. As in the first Kashmir Crisis, the United States withdrew from an active role in the Rann of Kutch Crisis and supported British mediation efforts.

Soviet friendship with India served several purposes. First, it was a natural counterpoise to the American alliance with Pakistan and a potentially larger Western anticommunist bloc in South Asia. Second, the association with India provided a deterrent to any Pakistani adventures in Afghanistan. The third consideration, which surfaced as the Soviet-Chinese split became overt in the early 1960s, was to provide a deterrent to Chinese expansion in South Asia. When India accepted large-scale American aid in its hostilities with China in 1962, the Soviets remained silent (A. Stein 1969:270). The Soviets began to move to a friendlier relationship with Pakistan in the 1960s less as a counterbalance to the United States than as a means of weakening the Chinese-Pakistani relationship.

By the time of the crisis in the Rann of Kutch, Pakistan was in a defensive alliance with the United States, from which Pakistan had received considerable military aid, but at the same time Pakistan was pursuing new friendships with the principal U.S. adversaries—China and the Soviet Union. India, which saw itself as a leader of the nonaligned nations, had a long-standing friendship and aid pact with the Soviet Union but now was enjoying similar favors from the United States. The only Indian-Pakistani third-party relationship with no cross-cutting ties was that with China. The Chinese were tightening their friendship with Pakistan as their rivalry with India intensified. In fact, the United States and the Soviet Union now shared a common interest in weakening China's power and influence in South Asia.

Tensions over the Indo-Chinese border reached a crisis stage in 1959, when Indian troops launched unsuccessful raids on Chinese positions along the northeast frontier. Attempts to reach a border settlement in April 1960 broke down. Then, after a number of Indian provocations, China attacked across the border in October 1962. After quickly overwhelming the Indian forces, the Chinese proclaimed a unilateral cease-fire and withdrew. The border issue remained unsettled, but the outcome was a blow to India's prestige, particularly its military reputation. Pakistan moved to improve its relations with China. By December 1962, China and Pakistan announced that they were in "complete agreement" on their shared border in the Himalayas.[8] Then in March 1964, when Pakistan and China signed a final agreement on the demarcation of their boundary, China announced that it supported Pakistan's claim that the Kashmir problem should be settled through a plebiscite. Six months later, China detonated its first nuclear bomb.

During the 1963–65 period, Indo-Pakistani relations also deteriorated. The new Pakistani-Chinese friendship added to the tensions, as did the increasing Western military aid to India, which not surprisingly found its way to the border with Pakistan. Several rounds of ministerial talks on Kashmir in 1963 went nowhere. Then in December 1964 India abolished the special status of Kashmir under the Indian constitution. The action eliminated any remaining Kashmiri autonomy.

In the spring of 1965, after being enthusiastically received in China, Ayub Khan ended his trip with a visit to the Soviet Union, which also agreed to sell arms and supplies to Pakistan. It was in this atmosphere that a border incident occurred on a desolate patch of land called the Rann of Kutch in the spring of 1965.

Crisis Structure

Pakistan
Perception of Indian intentions.   Other than Kashmir, by the 1960s the Sind-Kutch border was the only unresolved territorial issue between India and Pakistan. The Pakistani leadership remembered how India had forcibly achieved the accession of Hyderabad and Junagadh as well as Kashmir's continued occupation. India retained a military post in the northern half of the Rann, which Pakistan claimed India had seized in 1956. The Pakistani leadership surmised that India intended to acquire all of the Rann through a military fait accompli, although there had been no significant Indian military activity in the area in recent years.

Pakistani perceptions of Indian intentions in the Rann are best understood within the context of Pakistan's view of India as a state with the long-term goal of reuniting the subcontinent under its control. During 1963 and 1964, in the light of a major expansion of the Indian army, which was a direct response to its embarrassing military defeat in the 1962 conflict with China, Ayub Khan made several speeches denouncing the expansion as the prelude to an attack on Pakistan (Das Gupta 1968:301).

Interests.   The Rann of Kutch was of no strategic value to Pakistan other than within the broader framework of a continuing struggle to

---

8. As much as the United States deplored the growing friendship between Pakistan and China, the changed relationships resulted in Pakistan replacing India as the main conduit between the Western powers and the Chinese. British contacts with China in 1965 were initiated through Pakistan, as was Kissinger's 1971 visit.

defend every inch of territory against Indian advances.[9] The Rann, however, did offer a relatively low-risk opportunity to test Indian resolve as
well as the military capabilities of the expanded and rebuilt Pakistani army
(see Jha 1972:205–6; Feldman 1972:133). As such, it also afforded a testing
ground for possible future efforts in Kashmir. In addition, there were reputational stakes in the outcome of the Rann dispute. A military or diplomatic success, even a minor one, would strengthen the morale and credibility of the Pakistani military forces as well as the prestige and political
power of Ayub Khan's regime.

   Capabilities.   India's immovable stance with regard to any revision
of the Rann of Kutch borders left Ayub Khan's government with military force as its only option. As a result of U.S. military hardware and
technical assistance, Pakistan's leaders believed that its forces could
match those of India in a limited conflict (Feldman 1972:136). The theater in which they would be operating also favored the Pakistanis, who
would have the advantage of transporting their troops and weapons as
well as maneuvering their armor on higher and drier terrain. Finally, the
Pakistani perception of the fighting abilities of the Indian army dropped
considerably after India's poor showing against the Chinese in the 1962
border conflict.

India

Perceptions of Pakistani intentions.   Pakistan's foreign and military policies since the end of the First Kashmir war added to the Indian leadership's distrust of the intentions of its former countrymen. Pakistan had
refused to agree to a mutual no-war pledge, had used outside aid to
undergo a massive military buildup, had signed a military alliance with the
United States, and had embarked on a courtship of China. The last action
was especially disturbing. When the crisis in the Rann of Kutch broke out,
some Indian policymakers suspected that the Chinese had egged on the
Pakistanis (see Lamb 1966:117).

   The other issue lurking in the background was Kashmir. Pakistan's
leadership made no secret of its intention to gain control of Kashmir by
whatever means. The fighting in the Rann was perceived as a test of India's
resolve and the credibility of its military forces, perhaps in relation to a
future challenge over Kashmir. At the outset of the Rann of Kutch Crisis,
one Indian policymaker remarked "There [are] people and countries who
only understand the language of strength and toughness. Pakistan [is] one

---

   9. Pakistan, like India, had minor oil interests in the Rann, but they did not appear to
be of much significance to the larger interests of either side (see Das Gupta 1968:341; Jha
1972:205–6).

of those."[10] This perception was strengthened by the nature of the Pakistani regime, which Nehru had called a "naked military dictatorship [that] always has inherent in it risks and dangers of individuals acting on moods" (Blinkenberg 1972:223).

Interests. Indian interests in the Rann of Kutch dispute were primarily reputational. There were no vital strategic interests at stake. The Rann was a desolate area that was flooded in the rainy season and barren in the dry season. Conversely, the Indian government saw itself as defending the status quo against a military challenge from Pakistan. The dispute was viewed as a test of Indian resolve.

The reputational stakes were particularly high for Prime Minister Lal Bahadus Shastri's government and for the new prime minister, who had taken office following Nehru's death less than a year earlier. Shastri already was under attack by opposition hawks for not taking a tough enough stand against Pakistan. Domestic problems also plagued the government. Language riots had broken out in provinces resistant to central control; there were serious economic problems, including severe food shortages that threatened famine in some areas. The Rann of Kutch Crisis presented a challenge to Shastri's reputation for resolve, but it also provided an opportunity. By acting forcefully in the Rann dispute, Shastri could reduce the political costs of his failure to solve India's domestic economic problems by demonstrating his resolve in dealing with Pakistan.

Capabilities. The Indian army enjoyed better than a three-to-one manpower superiority over Pakistan. Even with a sizable portion of India's forces deployed on the border with China, India still enjoyed a two-to-one local advantage (see Kaul 1971:17). Conversely, as a result of U.S. military aid, Pakistan had superior weaponry and extensive training in putting it to use. The terrain in the Rann also placed India at a significant disadvantage. Pakistan held the high ground, whereas the Indian terrain in the Rann was marshy, which ruled out the use of tanks, and during the rainy season between May and October it was a virtual swamp. The roads into the area were unreliable, and there were no rail connections (see Jha 1972:208; Kaul 1971:20; Blinkenberg 1972:246). If India was going to fight a war with Pakistan, its military leaders preferred to do so somewhere else.

Crisis Behavior

The Sind-Kutch boundary had been in dispute since 1948. India was satisfied with the status quo, whereas Pakistan sought to have a joint

---

10. H. R. Gupta (1969:183) cites this remark, attributed to H. R. Chagla, the education minister, as typical of Indian policymakers' viewpoint in April 1965.

boundary commission investigate claims to territory held by India. The dispute was not submitted to arbitration, as required by the 1959 agreement for unresolved boundary issues, because India insisted that there was no legitimate reason to dispute the boundary.

The crisis began in January 1965, with each side charging the other with incursions or interference with patrols along the border (see Blinkenberg 1972:246; Jha 1972:196–97). As with the First Kashmir dispute, who did what and when is not clear. Over the next three months there were several protests from each side. At least one Pakistani researcher (Choudhury 1968:289) claims that Indian troops launched an attack on a Pakistani post in early April, but that incident has not been substantiated by other sources.

It is undisputed that on April 9, two days after proposing negotiations to resolve the dispute, Pakistani regular forces crossed the border and attacked an Indian outpost. On the same day, Pakistan's foreign office called for an immediate cease-fire and peaceful solution to the dispute. India issued a protest and immediately deployed troops in the region. Another Pakistani proposal for a cease-fire to be followed by an investigation to restore the status quo ante was issued on April 13 and accepted in principle by India on the following day, provided Pakistan withdrew from the occupied areas. A second Pakistani offensive, launched on April 18, was followed by a new Pakistani peace proposal for a cease-fire and negotiations. The proposal was rejected by India, which claimed that Pakistan was attempting to include well-established Indian territory within the "disputed" territory to be negotiated. Pakistan launched a new offensive, which included U.S.-supplied Patton tanks, on April 24. India placed all of its forces on alert, and Shastri threatened military action against Pakistan on a battleground of India's own choosing, such as a direct attack against Pakistan proper. Ayub Khan warned of a "general and total war between India and Pakistan" (Choudhury 1968:290).

Both the United States and the Soviet Union, given their coincidental interests in friendship with both sides, urged the parties to seek a peaceful settlement, but Great Britain assumed a more active diplomatic role in achieving a cease-fire. On April 28, British Prime Minister Harold Wilson offered to mediate the dispute and proposed an immediate informal lull in the fighting to be followed by a formal cease-fire. Pakistan initially rejected the British proposal on the grounds that it favored the Indian interpretation of the status quo ante. A lull in the fighting nevertheless occurred following a formal British proposal on May 4. With the help of British mediation, agreement was reached on June 30 on a cease-fire and the submission of the boundary dispute to arbitration, in accordance with the 1959 agreement for the resolution of border issues. The cease-fire went into effect immediately, and the crisis was effectively over. The border dispute finally was resolved on February 19, 1968, when a three-person panel of arbitration returned the area to the status quo ante except for a portion of the area over which Pakistan had fought.[11]

Patterns of Behavior

Figure 5.2 presents the time series of weekly aggregated hostility scores for the two sides over the course of the crisis. Three things are immediately apparent from figure 5.2. The first is that despite the military hostilities that figured so prominently in the crisis, the escalation is well below that of the First Kashmir Crisis and it is confined to a relatively short period.[12] If the Rann of Kutch Crisis were added to the sample of 34 crises in the appendix, this crisis would rank close to the sample median on all three measures of escalation (table 5.1), despite the outbreak of military hostilities.

A second striking feature of figure 5.2 is the high degree of reciprocity in the actions of the two sides. The dotted and solid lines representing the hostility scores of the two sides remain very close together, if not overlapping, throughout most of the crisis. In fact, the composite reciprocity score for the Rann of Kutch Crisis (table 5.2) would rank third in reciprocity among the 34 crises in the appendix.

A third feature to the pattern in figure 5.2 is that, with the exception of a short period in late March, Pakistan remains in the lead in escalating the level of hostility throughout the crisis. The Pakistani lead is greatest during the period when the crisis escalates most rapidly—that is, after the Pakistani attack on April 9. That Pakistan led in escalating the crisis is not surprising given that the Pakistanis were challenging the status quo. In the 1947 crisis, once the Indian army intervened in Kashmir, the Pakistani behavior was largely reactive; India controlled the evolution of the crisis. In 1965 Pakistan leads in both escalating the crisis and in diplomatic initiatives.

The frequency of Pakistani proposals to reach a negotiated settlement

---

11. The panel consisted of an Iranian diplomat chosen by Pakistan, a Yugoslav judge chosen by India, and the chairman, a Swedish judge, Gunnar Lagergren, chosen jointly.

12. In two earlier studies in which this crisis was included, I identified the outcome as a war because of the military offensives launched by both sides and the casualty figures given by some sources. It appears, however, that the total casualties suffered by both sides remained under the Singer and Small (1972) criterion of a minimum of 1,000 battle-related deaths to qualify as a war. The most cited estimates are approximately 100 casualties on the Indian side and approximately 350 Pakistani casualties. Consequently, I have changed the categorization of the outcome of the Rann of Kutch crisis from a war to a compromise settlement.

is another important behavioral pattern that is not visible in figure 5.2. Pakistan's first proposal for high-level negotiations came on April 7, two days before its attack in the Rann. A second proposal was sent on the day of the attack. After India rejected both proposals, Pakistan presented additional offers to negotiate on April 12, 13, 17, and 23 before Britain offered to mediate on April 28. India rejected Pakistan's diplomatic initiatives because Pakistan was proposing to negotiate a revision, in Pakistan's favor, of boundaries that India contended were firmly in place before Pakistan began its challenge in the Rann. The Indian foreign office responded that Pakistan's April 23 proposal was "fantastic and baseless" (Jha 1972:203).

The pattern of behavior in the Rann of Kutch Crisis contains intriguing similarities to the Egyptian-Israeli crisis leading up to the Yom Kippur War of 1973. A series of low-level clashes was suddenly followed by a military attack from the party challenging the status quo—that is, Egypt in 1973 and Pakistan in 1965. The hostilities were relatively short-lived, with a cease-fire arranged by outside powers in both crises. There are, of course, important differences between the two crises. The most notable difference is that the hostilities in the 1973 crisis escalated to war. Unlike the Pakistanis, Sadat was not ready to accept a cease-fire when Egypt was enjoying success on the battlefield. However, Sadat maintained close communication with both superpowers throughout the crisis and communicated to each of them that his objectives were limited. When the United States and Soviet Union brokered a cease-fire proposal just as the war was turning in Israel's favor, Sadat quickly accepted the plan. The Pakistani government signaled its willingness to accept a cease-fire and to negotiate a readjustment of the boundary in the Rann of Kutch throughout the crisis. The similarities become even more striking when the influence strategies employed by Egypt and Pakistan are considered.

TABLE 5.2.   India-Pakistan: Reciprocity Scores

Crisis	Reciprocity Indicators			
	Direction Score (Rank)	Distance Score (Rank)	Rank in India-Pakistan Crises	Rank in Larger Sample
First Kashmir	3.90 (18)	3.80 (7)	2	13
Rann of Kutch	2.19 (6)	0.85 (2)	1	3
Second Kashmir	4.57 (20)	1.55 (4)	3	14
Bangladesh	3.14 (11)	26.29 (24)	4	17
Mean Score	5.01	8.12		

Influence Strategies

Pakistan

Pakistan began with a Bullying strategy but switched to what might be better described as a Reciprocating influence strategy.[13] Early in the crisis, it is difficult to determine which side is responsible for the sporadic clashes on the Rann border, but Pakistan's sudden attack on April 9 is consistent with a Bullying influence strategy. After April 9 the pattern is more consistent with a Reciprocating influence strategy: demonstrations of firmness followed by offers of cooperative initiatives and responses in kind to cooperative initiatives or to mediation efforts by third parties.

The prevailing interpretation of Pakistan's influence strategy during the Rann of Kutch Crisis is that it was a probing exercise designed to test India's preparedness and the comparative capabilities of the Pakistani army in limited hostilities with India as a prelude to a major military effort in Kashmir (Jha 1972:205–6; Blinkenberg 1972:249; Feldman 1972:133).

But there was a diplomatic component to Ayub Khan's strategy that bore a striking resemblance to that employed by Sadat in the Middle East crisis of 1973. Ayub Khan, like Sadat, needed a crisis to create a situation that would convince an adversary content with the status quo to negotiate. After meeting a stone wall in his attempts to achieve a negotiated readjustment of the border, Ayub pursued limited military action to create a crisis that would lead to meaningful negotiations through the intervention of concerned third parties. The diplomatic intervention of an influential outside power, as in Sadat's strategy in 1973, became a critical component of Pakistan's success both in obtaining its limited military gains in a negotiated settlement and in keeping the fighting limited. The British cease-fire was an essential component of the success of Ayub's strategy in 1965, just as the American-Soviet sponsored cease-fire was essential to Sadat's diplomatic success in 1973. The Pakistani leadership may have remembered the active diplomatic role played by the major powers in the first Kashmir Crisis and may have counted on similar intercessionary efforts in the Rann crisis. The strategic interests at stake for Ayub Khan were not comparable to those that motivated Sadat—a minor border adjustment in a desolate area versus a major portion of Egyptian territory—but both operations prepared the ground for negotiations that adversaries had steadfastly rejected.

This strategy was consistent with the numerous proposals for a negotiated settlement that were publicly submitted by Pakistan as the crisis

---

13. The operational indicators (see chap. 2) of Pakistan's predominant influence strategy place it on the borderline between Bullying and Reciprocating.

escalated. Like Sadat in 1973, Ayub's immediate goals were to achieve a modest military victory and to create a better negotiating situation.

India

When Pakistan challenged India militarily, the Indians responded in kind, as figure 5.2 illustrates. India's influence strategy is best described as Cautious Bullying. India's responses to Pakistan's challenges, including the use of force, are consistent with either Bullying or Reciprocating, but the consistent rejection of Pakistani offers to negotiate and the absence of any accommodative initiatives are inconsistent with a Reciprocating strategy.[14] The pattern is consistent with that of a state taking an uncompromising stand to preserve the status quo but prudently avoiding escalating the crisis to war.

Indian commanders did not view their army as enjoying a local military advantage when hostilities broke out in the Rann. Thus, while India had no interest in opening negotiations over the Rann of Kutch boundaries, it also did not want to fight a war there. After the Pakistani offensives in April, Shastri warned Pakistan that India would not hesitate to take military action on a battleground of India's choosing (Choudhury 1968:290). But by this time both the United States and the Soviet Union were urging military restraint and a negotiated settlement (Jha 1972:210–11). When Britain pressed for a cease-fire, Shastri had little choice but to accept. That the Indian strategy was restrained can be credited largely to Shastri's prudence, but it also was influenced by pressures from its two main suppliers of military assistance, the Soviet Union and the United States.

Summary

Resolving a dispute through negotiation requires that both parties wish to change the status quo and that each party recognizes that doing so requires cooperation with the other. If either party is content with the status quo or believes that it can unilaterally achieve the changes it desires, then a negotiating situation does not exist. At the beginning of 1965, the Indian government was satisfied with the status quo in the Rann of Kutch as well as Kashmir. India had no interest in opening negotiations over the status of either territory, much less submitting the issue to arbitration. Consequently, India brushed aside Pakistan's demands for negotiations over the status of the Rann borders. Ayub's regime created a crisis to alter the sta-

---

14. It can be argued that India did not respond to any of Pakistan's proposals for negotiation because the proposals were unreasonable. The categorization of the influence strategy is intended strictly as a descriptive device; it is not intended to be evaluative.

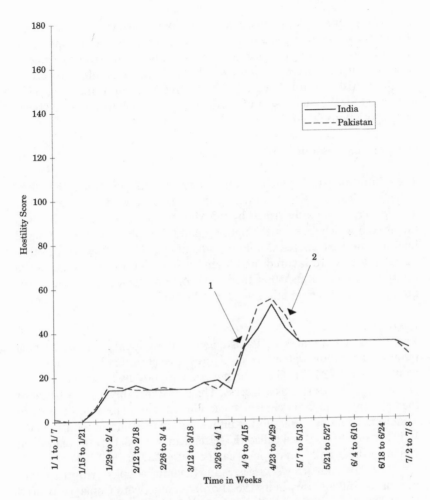

Fig. 5.2. Rann of Kutch Crisis, 1965
Key dates are indicated with arrows: (1) 4/9: Pakistan launches attack on
Indian positions on Rann border; (2) 5/4: India and Pakistan begin cease-
fire in response to British proposal.

tus quo and force negotiations. The success in doing so without having the hostilities escalate to a general war, however, depended on the diplomatic intervention of major powers and the restraint of the Shastri government. Ayub's challenge succeeded in moving India from stonewalling to accepting the British call for a cease-fire and agreeing to implement the 1959 agreement for the submission of border disputes to arbitration when bilateral negotiations failed.[15]

Outcome and Lessons

The arbitration panel, which announced its decision on February 19, 1968, upheld the Rann of Kutch borders prior to the crisis with the exception of a region predominantly visited by the Muslim Sind population. That was the area in which most of the fighting had taken place, and it contained high ground that offered a military advantage to its possessor. In other respects, the award favored the Indian position, but the precedent of the arbitration, and the fact that there was some movement from the status quo, were major diplomatic gains for Pakistan.

Pakistan

There was unhappiness in Pakistan over the tribunal's award, which required the withdrawal of Pakistani forces from territory held in the short conflict (Jha 1972:217). The Ayub government, however, viewed the overall outcome of the crisis as a success. The Pakistani army had the better of the fighting; the military challenge had altered the situation sufficiently to create a negotiating situation that ultimately led to arbitration through the 1959 accord. Ayub Khan called the settlement a "model for the manner in which all India-Pakistan disputes can be settled" (Jha 1972:223).

The Pakistani army's successes in Kashmir, coupled with the weakness of the Indian army in its 1962 border conflict with China, convinced the Pakistani leadership that, despite India's numerical superiority, Pakistan could prevail in a larger war (Gauhar 1996:211). There is no doubt that the military successes were a large factor in Pakistan's plans for a challenge over Kashmir later that summer.[16] Within the larger citizenry,

---

15. The cease-fire agreement prescribed bilateral negotiations. If those negotiations failed to achieve an agreement within two months, then the 1959 agreement to submit the dispute to a panel of arbitration would be implemented. After a foreign ministers' meeting at New Delhi scheduled for August 20, 1965, was canceled, the matter was automatically submitted to arbitration.

16. The most direct evidence appears in the accounts of Ayub's information minister, Gauhar (1996:203–16). Others who have reached the same conclusions include Schofield (1996:201); Blinkenberg (1972:246–47); Feldman (1972:135); Kaul (1971:20); and Akbar (1991:170).

calls for a jihad, or holy war, to liberate Kashmir provided additional impetus to pursue a military strategy. Added to these factors was Ayub's personal belief that the Hindu population of India was pacifist by nature (see Gauhar 1996:203).

Another lesson from the Rann crisis was that it was not necessary to achieve a complete military victory but only to prolong the fighting until concerned third parties interceded to arrange a cease-fire and a diplomatic settlement. Both superpowers had pushed for a diplomatic settlement, and China remained solidly behind Pakistan. Based on Pakistan's experiences in the 1947 and 1965 crises, Ayub reasoned that if Pakistan created a military crisis in Kashmir through fostering internal instability, the major powers would intervene diplomatically, India could then be pressured to submit the matter to mediation and, even, given the Rann precedent, to arbitration (see Gauhar 1996:216).[17] As noted earlier, the strategy is remarkably similar to that employed by Sadat in the Middle East crisis and war of 1973. But it should be noted that the expectation of major-power intervention to prevent the escalation of hostilities to a general war resembles the lesson that Egypt's Nasser unwisely drew from his experience in the 1956 Suez Crisis.

India
The Indian decision to accept the cease-fire and eventual arbitration was prudent under the circumstances, but Shastri was severely criticized by the political opposition in India, which was still smarting from the country's embarrassment at the hands of the Chinese. Although the arbitration tribunal's award largely favored the Indian position, many Indians, including some in the government, were unhappy with its compromise character as well as with the arbitration precedent. Those who remained unhappy over the United Nations' mediation efforts in the first Kashmir Crisis referred to the Rann award as "another eye opener" and vowed to oppose the submission of any future dispute to an international body (see Kaul 1971:20).

Indian policymakers viewed Pakistan's challenge in the Rann as a deliberate test of India's military preparedness and its political resolve (Blinkenberg 1972:246–47). The outcome was a blow to the Indian reputation for resolve, the consequences of which were likely to be harmful. Overall, despite an arbitration award that largely supported the Indian position, the Indian government could not help but view the outcome of the Rann crisis as harming its military and political reputations.

---

17. Gauhar was a confidant of Ayub. Gauhar 1996:203–16 quotes an August 29, 1965, directive from Ayub to his foreign minister, Bhutto. Analysts such as Feldman (1972:141) have speculated on similar reasoning by Ayub, but Gauhar's account offers direct evidence.

As with Pakistan, the first lesson Indian leaders drew from the Rann crisis was military. Despite its numerical military superiority over Pakistan, India had to be better prepared in the future. The serene sense of invincibility that India enjoyed after its experience in the First Kashmir war had evaporated after being militarily embarrassed by China and now Pakistan. A second lesson was that of skepticism regarding the submission of future disputes with Pakistan to international bodies, as noted previously. But for India, the principal lesson from the Rann experience was to improve its military preparedness.

Second Kashmir War, 1965

Kashmir in 1965

One of the tactics available to the weaker party in an ongoing dispute is to attempt to enlist the support of powerful third parties, often in the name of equity or justice. During the 16 years between the two Kashmir wars, Pakistan attempted to bring diplomatic pressure on India by internationalizing the issue, but the Indian government could not be budged. Despite a number of diplomatic initiatives, including a long round of ministerial talks in 1963, and discussions in the United Nations Security Council in 1964, no real progress was made in resolving the Kashmir dispute.

Tension over the issue increased after India declared president's rule over Kashmir in December 1964. The directive abolished Kashmir's special status within the Indian union and allowed the federal government to dismiss the state government of Kashmir and establish martial law in the event of an emergency. Sheikh Abdullah, who had been a close friend of Indian Prime Minister Nehru until his death in May 1964, became increasingly alarmed over the Shastri government's determination to absorb Kashmir into India. Abdullah traveled to China in February 1965 to solicit support for Kashmiri independence. When the sheikh returned in May, the Indian government ordered his arrest for condoning the Chinese aggression against India in 1962 and accused him having become an agent of the Pakistanis. The sheikh's arrest set off widespread protests in Kashmir, including riots and a general strike on May 14. By early June, Kashmiri opposition forces had mounted a sustained nonviolent civil disobedience movement.

These events occurred as India and Pakistan were struggling to bring an end to the Rann of Kutch Crisis. Clashes between Indian and Pakistani troops along the Kashmir border, which began in January 1965, continued sporadically throughout the Rann of Kutch Crisis.

The Superpowers

Relations between the superpowers and the protagonists in the Indo-Pakistani rivalry did not change appreciably in the few months between the Rann of Kutch Crisis and the Second Kashmir Crisis. The Johnson administration in the United States remained preoccupied with the escalating war in Vietnam, and during the summer of 1965, plans were under way for a major increase in American ground forces. The growing American participation in the Vietnam War increased the danger of Chinese intervention. The Soviets, meanwhile, were engaged in competing with the Chinese for influence among the communist regimes of East and Southeast Asia, including North Vietnam. After a visit to Moscow in May 1965, Indian Prime Minister Shastri joined Soviet Premier Aleksey Kosygin in denouncing the American bombing of North Vietnam and in calling for an end to the conflict based on the 1954 Geneva Accords.

The superpowers were on opposite sides in the both the Vietnamese and Indo-Pakistani disputes, but the United States and the Soviet Union shared a desire to limit Chinese influence in both conflicts. When the Chinese accused the Indians of provocations along the Indian border in September 1965, China received separate warnings against taking military action from each of the superpowers (see Donaldson 1974:206; Griffith 1967:115). By 1965 the superpowers shared a mutual interest in preserving stability on the Indian subcontinent and in keeping the Indo-Pakistani dispute over Kashmir from escalating. When the crisis escalated toward war, the United States and Soviet Union collaborated in pursuing a mediated solution.

Crisis Structure

Pakistan
Perceptions of Indian intentions.   The Pakistani leadership's perceptions of Indian intentions had not changed: India's immediate objective was to secure the permanent accession of Kashmir to India and India's long-term goal was to reunite the subcontinent under Hindu rule (Gauhar 1996:211; Hasan 1966:440, 452). The Pakistani leadership's perception of Indian intentions vis-à-vis Kashmir had been reinforced by Indian diplomacy. President Ayub Khan saw no prospect of persuading India to bend on the Kashmir issue. On the other hand, the Rann of Kutch experience had strengthened Ayub's belief that "the Hindu had no stomach for fight" should Pakistan turn to military means (Gauhar 1996:203).

Interests.   By 1965 a hawkish parliament, the Pakistani public, and the leadership of Azad Kashmir pressured Ayub Khan to gain control of

Kashmir through whatever means were necessary. The mood in Pakistan was summed up by a member of parliament who exclaimed in exasperation, "You may have any foreign policy you like. Instead of three pacts you may have thirty or even three hundred. I have nothing to do with them. I only want you to regain Kashmir for me" (S. Gupta 1966:452). Besides self-defense, and not incidentally because of it, the accession of Kashmir was Pakistan's first and most vital foreign-policy goal.

Capabilities.   As noted earlier, by the spring of 1965 the Pakistani leadership was convinced that its interests in Kashmir could not be achieved diplomatically. India was satisfied with the status quo, and the most influential Kashmiri, Sheikh Abdullah, favored independence (Feldman 1972:149–50).

Militarily, India continued to enjoy a more than two-to-one manpower advantage over Pakistan. With more advanced Soviet and now American military aid flowing into India, the time would soon come when Pakistan would no longer have a military option in Kashmir. At the moment, however, Pakistan believed that its army was qualitatively superior to India's. The Indian army had performed poorly in the border hostilities with China, and Pakistani forces demonstrated their superiority over those of India in the Rann of Kutch Crisis. The latter had led to increased confidence—in fact, overconfidence—in the comparative capability of the Pakistani army (Barnds 1972:203). As the director of Pakistani military operations, General Gul Hassan, put it, "the high command was intoxicated by our showing" (Gauhar 1996:203). India's internal political problems—the death of Nehru, language riots in March, food riots in July—added to the confidence of Pakistani leaders (Jha 1972:329–30).

The Pakistani leadership also had become convinced that Kashmir, with the right push, was ready for a popular uprising against Indian rule. Tensions had been high since the arrest of Abdullah in May; guerrilla activities had begun in some remote provinces. If Pakistan were ever going to take military action, now was the time, Foreign Minister Zulfikar Ali Bhutto argued in a letter to Ayub (Gauhar 1996:211).

Since 1947 Pakistan had engineered defensive alliances with the United States, a strong friendship with China, and, most recently, a good relationship with the Soviet Union. If the hostilities did expand into a full-scale war, the Pakistani leadership believed it had reason to expect that the major powers on the United Nations Security Council would intervene to achieve an early cease-fire and a negotiated settlement. In the minds of the Pakistani leaders, the military-diplomatic situation in the summer of 1965 offered excellent prospects for a limited war to force the Kashmir issue to the forefront of the international agenda.

India

Perceptions of Pakistani intentions.   India recognized the strategic importance of Kashmir to Pakistan and its leadership's unrelenting determination to obtain Kashmir's accession to Pakistan. The predominant view in
the Indian government was that the Rann of Kutch dispute had been a
pretext for a test of Indian military preparedness and resolve in preparation for a military challenge in Kashmir. When Pakistani irregulars
crossed the cease-fire line in August 1965, the Indian government viewed
the action as the beginning of a full-scale attack (Das Gupta 1968:345).

Interests.   The Indian diplomatic position on Kashmir had only
hardened since the First Kashmir war. With the exception of the small part
of Kashmir, Azad Kashmir, on the Pakistani side of the 1948 cease-fire
line, the accession of Kashmir into the Indian union had become virtually
permanent. India not only was content with the status quo in Kashmir; it
also viewed the status quo as vital to Indian security. Moreover, Indian
leaders believed that after the public criticism that they received for accepting the cease-fire in the Rann of Kutch Crisis, their domestic reputation
for resolve demanded that they react forcefully to any future Pakistani
challenge (see Lamb 1966:121). Any attack on Kashmir, the Shastri government warned, would be treated as an attack on India proper (Blinkenberg 1972:260).

Capabilities.   After the military embarrassment at the hands of
China, India's leaders became aware of the need to improve India's military weaponry and the competence of its armed forces. Besides pressing
for more aid from the Soviet Union, India turned to the United States for
additional military assistance. By August 1965, India's sole remaining military concern was the Pakistani advantage in armor (Kaul 1971:31). Otherwise, despite the Rann of Kutch experience, Indian leaders were
confident that with better preparation and more suitable terrain, they
would prevail over Pakistan. Plans for a counteroffensive in response to a
Pakistani attack in Kashmir were in place. On balance, Indian leaders
were confident that they could defend their position in Kashmir, albeit at
the cost of a major war and the potential risk of Chinese intervention.

Crisis Behavior

India's declaration of President's Rule on December 21, 1964, reignited
the flames of the Kashmir conflict. The tensions that followed led to sporadic border clashes in January and during the spring of 1965.

The early phase of the second Kashmir Crisis intersected at several
points with the Rann of Kutch Crisis and involved hostility between the
Indian government and Kashmiris as well as between India and Pakistan.

During April, as India and Pakistan were preoccupied with the escalating hostilities in the Rann of Kutch Crisis, there was a lull in activity along the Kashmir cease-fire line. But on May 4, the first day of the informal cease-fire in the Rann, Indian and Pakistani troops once again clashed on the Kashmir border. When Abdullah was arrested on May 8, violent demonstrations occurred throughout Kashmir, and a weeklong strike was declared on May 14. Thus, there was an internal crisis between Indian government forces and Kashmiri nationalists within Kashmir as Indo-Pakistani tensions grew in the spring of 1965.

On May 15, in response to Pakistan's seizure of a military post in the Rann of Kutch, Indian troops crossed the Kashmir cease-fire line to establish two military outposts at Kargail on the Pakistani side of the line. Two days later, the president of Azad Kashmir declared that his people were ready for war against India (Das Gupta 1968:344). Pakistan responded to the Indian actions on May 22 by firing mortar rounds across the border and by a military overflight of Indian territory. Troops from both sides clashed on the border on May 24 and 28. By the end of the month, a United Nations military observer in Kashmir reported that military activity on the Kashmir cease-fire line was the most intense it had been since the line was established in 1949.

When the Rann of Kutch cease-fire went into effect in early June and Pakistan withdrew from the disputed military post in the Rann, India withdrew its forces from Kargail. As a result, the hostilities along the cease-fire line de-escalated, although sporadic clashes occurred through June and July. Then, on August 5, Pakistani troops dressed in civilian clothes crossed the cease-fire line.[18] The infiltrators sought to join with rebel forces within Kashmir in an attempt to participate in the disruptions that had continued since Abdullah's arrest and detention. The Indian government, however, interpreted the action as a "thinly disguised armed attack," and Shastri publicly threatened that "force would be met with force" (Das Gupta 1968:345). On August 15, Indian forces crossed the cease-fire line and reoccupied the Pakistani posts in Kargail. Pakistani Foreign Minister Bhutto vowed that India's threats of war would not deter Pakistan from providing support for the Kashmiri "freedom fighters" (Jha 1972:318). On August 24 Indian troops again crossed the cease-fire line, this time in full strength into the Uri-Poonch area. Pakistan responded, on September 1, with an attack across the cease-fire line into Jammu. The

---

18. Pakistan denied any direct involvement, whereas India claimed to have found documents indicating that the operation had been planned by Pakistan in March 1965. With the publication of Gauhar's (1996) memoir, there now is no doubt that the operation was planned and orchestrated by the Pakistani government.

Indian air force went into action on the same day. The Second Kashmir war had begun.

On September 3, Secretary-General U Thant brought the matter to the attention of the United Nations Security Council, which quickly passed the first of several resolutions calling for a cease-fire. But by now there was a full-scale war, and on September 6, Indian troops, fulfilling Shastri's Rann of Kutch promise to strike at a place of his own choosing, invaded Lahore, a major Pakistani city on the northwest border with India. When a Pakistani counteroffensive ground to a halt on September 11, the leadership met to consider a cease-fire (Gauhar 1996:231).

China denounced what it described as Indian aggression and threatened to intervene. The United States suspended all military aid to both sides, and the Soviet Union offered its good offices to bring the warring parties together. All three actions were significant. The Chinese threat, which became an ultimatum on September 16, put pressure on India, which was enjoying success on the battlefield. The cutoff of American aid meant that Pakistan, which was militarily dependent on the United States, could not sustain a long war. The Soviet offer became the basis for mediation by Soviet Prime Minister Kosygin four months later.

A United Nations Security Council resolution calling for a cease-fire and withdrawal of troops to positions held before August 5 was accepted and put in place on September 22, but it was marred by frequent violations. Peace talks finally began on January 4, 1966, and were completed on January 10. The Tashkent Declaration provided for the withdrawal of forces to the pre–August 5 borders in Kashmir and pledged the two sides to resolve their differences peacefully. The only mention of the long-term status of Kashmir was the statement that "each of the sides set forth its respective position" (*New York Times* 1966).

Patterns of Behavior

Despite efforts to maintain strict operational rules in constructing statistical measures for comparative purposes, there inevitably are some difficult decisions requiring subjective judgments. One of the most difficult in conducting empirical comparisons of crises is that of choosing the boundaries of particular crises—that is, when they begin and end and what actions to include. The Second Kashmir Crisis presents some of the most difficult problems in this study. The first judgment is when to mark the start of the crisis. As figure 5.3 illustrates, relatively sustained hostility between the two sides does not begin until May 1965, following the arrest of Sheikh Abdullah.

However, a strong case can also be made that the action precipitating

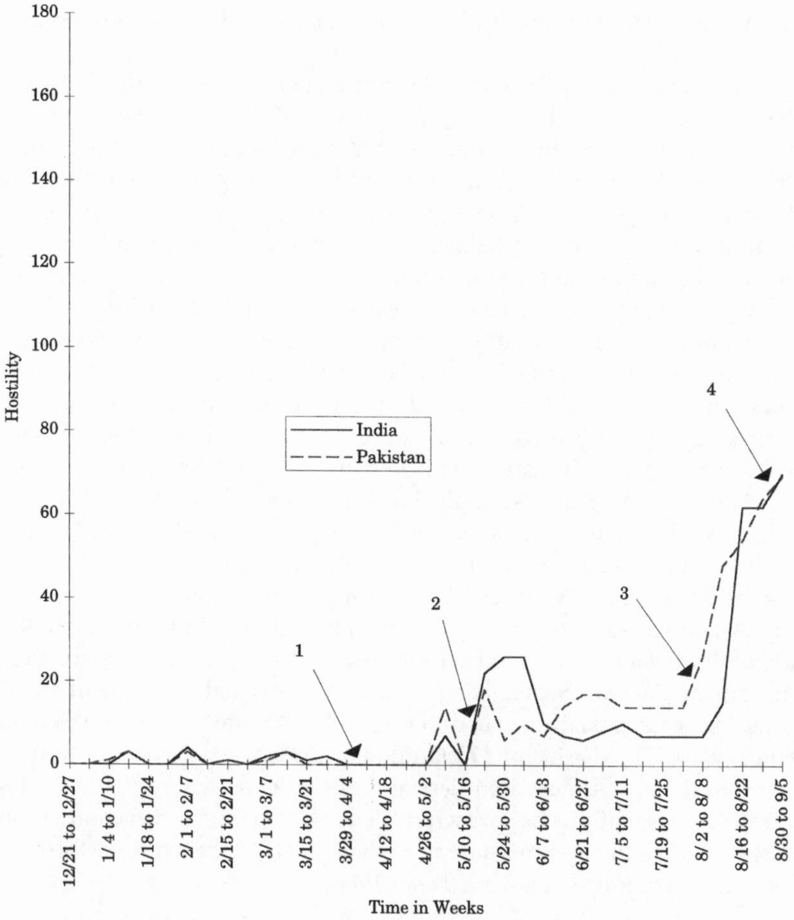

Fig. 5.3.   Second Kashmir Crisis, 1965
Key dates are indicated with arrows: (1) 4/8: Pakistan attacks in Rann of Kutch; (2) 5/17: India establishes posts in Kargail, across the Kashmir cease-fire line; (3) 8/5: Pakistani irregular forces cross the cease-fire line in Kashmir; (4) 9/1: start of Second Kashmir war.

the crisis between India and Pakistan was India's December 21, 1964, declaration of president's rule in Kashmir. That action was followed by a series of clashes in January. The President's Rule declaration convinced the Pakistanis as well as Abdullah that India intended the 1947 provisional accession of Kashmir to India to become permanent. The declaration also prompted Abdullah's trip to China to elicit support for Kashmiri independence, which resulted in his subsequent arrest. Moreover, as noted earlier, beginning in April there are important linkages between events in the Rann of Kutch Crisis and the escalation of the Kashmir Crisis. For these reasons, I have identified the beginning of the crisis as December 21, 1964.

The crisis ends or is transformed into a more severe category of dispute when it escalates to war. I have chosen the end date of the crisis as September 1, 1965, when the Indian and Pakistani regular forces become engaged in combat for the first time. Even though the Pakistani irregulars crossed the cease-fire line three weeks earlier, there was very little military action and no direct combat involving the regular forces of India and Pakistan prior to September 1.[19] A third decision is whether to include the interactions of the two parties in the Rann of Kutch Crisis as part of the Second Kashmir Crisis. I have not done so on the grounds that the actions in the two crises were directed at different issues.[20]

The time series in figure 5.3 reflects the events detailed earlier. The sporadic clashes along the border between January and March are reflected in the modest bumps in the hostility scores during those months. There is a lull in April, during the intense early phase of the Rann of Kutch Crisis, but the hostility levels spike in late May, following the arrest of Abdullah and the Indian seizure of military outposts in Kargail. The Indian lead in hostility during May is somewhat misleading, because it largely reflects its seizure of the two outposts in Kargail, which was in response to Pakistani actions in the Rann, which are not included in figure 5.3. Pakistan takes the lead in hostile activity during June with its movement of troops to the Kashmir border.

The pattern of escalation can be divided into two parts. The intensity, rate, and magnitude of escalation remain at a relatively low level until May, when the clashes between the two sides grow in intensity. Then, in August, with the infiltration of the Pakistani irregulars, the crisis exhibits the high reciprocity and high escalation of a conflict spiral, or Fight. The overall escalation and reciprocity scores in tables 5.1 and 5.2 also place the crisis in that category, although barely. As in the other two Indo-Pakistani crises, the distance indicator of reciprocity indicates that the two sides are

---

19. Most analysts mark the beginning of the war as September 1 (see Wirsing 1994:266; Choudhury 1968:295; Das Gupta 1968:347). The Correlates of War date for the onset of war is August 5, 1965, but, for the reasons mentioned in the text, I think that is too early.

20. To cite the most problematic of those decisions, the Pakistani seizure of two posts within the Rann is treated as part of the Rann of Kutch crisis but not as part of the Second Kashmir crisis. When India responded by seizing three posts on the Kargail sector across the Kashmir cease-fire line, the actions were included in both the Rann and Second Kashmir crises on the grounds that these incidents became a major issue in the settlement of the Rann crisis but were directly related to the escalation of the Kashmir dispute as well.

exhibiting very similar mixes of cooperation and conflict over the course of the crisis, but the direction indicator suggests that the two sides are often moving in opposite directions along those two dimensions. As figure 5.3 indicates, the high direction score is obtained primarily from the actions of the two sides prior to the Pakistani incursion on August 5, and it reflects alternating displays and uses of force. There are no accommodative initiatives from either side. The communication between the two sides consists solely of threats, displays, and uses of force.

It is instructive to compare the pattern of escalation in figure 5.3 with that for the First Kashmir Crisis in figure 5.1. The 1947 crisis effectively began with the invasion of the Pathen tribesmen on October 22 and then escalated rapidly, with India and Pakistan alternating in leading in escalation throughout the course of the long crisis. Both the escalation and the reciprocity scores for the First Kashmir Crisis in tables 5.1 and 5.2 are high, depicting a Fight pattern of escalation. Nevertheless, there are several times during the crisis when the magnitude of escalation for one or both sides declines, indicating efforts to obtain a negotiated settlement.

The pattern for the Second Kashmir Crisis in figure 5.3 is similar in the short period following the incursion by Pakistani irregulars to the outbreak of full-scale war. Although the overall escalation scores for the Second Kashmir Crisis are considerably lower than those for the First Kashmir Crisis, the rate and intensity of escalation following the incursion of Pakistani irregulars in 1965 exceed that for the period after the incursion of the Pathen tribesmen in 1947. Pakistan leads in the escalation of hostility throughout the postincursion period in 1965 until the Indian army is fully engaged in the war itself, and the war occurs at a relatively low magnitude of escalation.

There are two significant differences between the behavior patterns in the two crises. The first is that the Second Kashmir Crisis quickly escalates to a full-scale war, whereas the First Kashmir Crisis continues to escalate to a high magnitude and at a high degree of intensity without crossing the threshold of a full-scale Indo-Pakistani war. The second difference is the total absence of any direct negotiation between the two adversaries in the Second Kashmir Crisis.

The reason for the last two behavioral differences is not hard to guess. In 1947 policymakers in both India and Pakistan, especially the British commanders of each side's military forces, were intent on avoiding a war. In 1965 the Pakistani government sought to destabilize Kashmir, preferably without going to war with India, but both Pakistan and India were primed for war if the situation warranted it. Figure 5.1 demonstrates that states—even those with the intense hostility that existed between Indians and Pakistanis following the communal violence associated with the partition of India—are capable of managing an extended crisis with very high escalation when leaders on both sides wish to avoid war. Figure 5.3 illustrates how little it takes to spark a war when both sides are ready for it.

Influence Strategies

All three operational indicators place the influence strategies of both parties in the escalating coercive Bullying category. Each side relied solely on coercive inducements and responded to the other in kind, and, as noted previously, neither offered any accommodative initiatives. The operational classifications are consistent with the descriptive accounts provided by virtually all observers.

Pakistan

By 1965 the Pakistani government had exhausted virtually every diplomatic means of attempting to gain the accession of Kashmir. India would not negotiate or consider a plebiscite in Kashmir. Pakistan's efforts to internationalize the issue by appealing to the United Nations or to the country's Western allies had not succeeded in moving the Kashmir issue to the top of their agenda. Conversely, for the reasons mentioned in the section on capabilities, the Ayub regime's perception of its comparative military capabilities had become favorable—unrealistically so.

Ayub sought to take advantage of the unrest following Abdullah's detention by provoking a crisis within Kashmir. His plan was to have guerrillas infiltrate into Kashmir to promote a popular uprising. The political instability in Kashmir and the resulting risk of an Indo-Pakistani war, with the added possibility of Chinese military intervention, would bring the issue to the top of the superpower agenda. If India intervened militarily, the unrest could develop into a civil war, which would justify outside intervention, perhaps through the United Nations (see Feldman 1972:141). In a directive to Bhutto and the military commander in chief, General Musa, Ayub stated that his objective was "to take such action that will defreeze the Kashmir problem, weaken Indian resolve and bring her to the conference table without provoking a general war" (Gauhar 1996:216).

If the military hostilities nevertheless escalated to a direct confrontation between Indian and Pakistani troops, Pakistani leaders were confident of their army's capabilities. India also would be confronted with the threat of Chinese intervention in support of Pakistan. And, according to Foreign Minister Bhutto, the Chinese threat was the key to obtaining American diplomatic intervention to obtain a cease-fire (quoted in Gauhar 1996:231). When the major powers or the United Nations applied diplomatic pressure to achieve a cease-fire, the Pakistanis would insist that the entire Kashmir question be reopened.

As the crisis unfolded, the Pakistani leadership was considerably more risk acceptant than in the First Kashmir Crisis. Ayub urged his military commanders to "go to the jugular" in seizing the strategic town of Akhnur, even at the risk of war with India.[21] He left it to the hawkish Bhutto to choose the time and place to deliver "a couple of hard blows to the Hindu" (Gauhar 1996:218). Unlike in the First Kashmir war and the Rann crisis, Pakistan did not push for immediate negotiations. During August and the first week in September, Pakistan relied solely on its military to improve its bargaining position in Kashmir. But after the Indian invasion of September 6 resulted in military setbacks, Pakistan prudently chose to accept a cease-fire that had been arranged by the United Nations Security Council. Unfortunately for Ayub, Pakistan had to do so with no guarantees that the Kashmir question would be reopened. To make matters worse, the United States was content to let the Soviet Union take the lead in mediating the crisis.

India

Following the Rann crisis, Shastri came under considerable pressure from parliament and the military to take a tougher stand in any future crisis with Pakistan (see Lamb 1966:121). When Pakistani irregulars crossed the cease-fire line into Kashmir on August 5, more than 100,000 people marched to the Indian parliament building to demand that India respond forcefully.

The Indian leadership drew a historical analogy to the 1947 infiltration by Pathen tribesmen, which was successfully halted by Indian military intervention (Jha 1972:322). Therefore, Indian leaders prepared a similar strategy in 1965. India expected the Pakistanis to exercise caution, as they did during the 1947 crisis; consequently, India largely ignored the Rann experience and its lesson that India must acknowledge Pakistan's improved military capabilities and self-confidence. As a result, India was not prepared for the major Pakistani offensive that followed. When Pakistani tanks rolled across the cease-fire line and struck "at the jugular" in Akhnur on September 1, the attack far exceeded Indian expectations. Shastri responded by ordering the invasion of Lahore on September 4. Then, when the United Nations Security Council pushed for a cease-fire in mid-September, India quickly accepted, provided that there were no conditions requiring a reopening of the issue of the status of Kashmir.

---

21. Akhnur was in the Chamb district, where the cease-fire line was quite close to the international border as well as to the main line of communication between Jammu and Srinagar.

Outcome and Lessons

The termination of the Second Kashmir war contains some interesting similarities to the 1973 Middle East war. In both instances the challenger (Pakistan, Egypt) was willing to fight a limited war to achieve the conditions for a negotiated settlement that would be achieved through the diplomatic intervention of the major powers, presumably through the United Nations. Neither country communicated directly with its adversary, only through the major powers. Both Pakistan and Egypt insisted that any cease-fire include provisions for more extensive negotiations to resolve the larger issue at stake. Egypt was more successful than Pakistan in achieving the latter, although when the tide of battle turned against them both settled for less than they had hoped to achieve diplomatically. Finally, in both instances, a coincidence of interests led the superpowers to cooperate in limiting the escalation of the war and achieving the cease-fire. In the Middle East war, both sides were competing for influence in Egypt, and each sought to avoid a superpower confrontation. In the Second Kashmir war, the superpowers were competing for influence with both parties, and neither wished to alienate either India or Pakistan. An added twist to the Second Kashmir war was that both the United States and the Soviet Union sought to avoid the consequences of a Chinese military intervention.

After the signing of the Tashkent Declaration on January 10, the withdrawal of troops to the pre–August 5 borders, along with an exchange of prisoners of war, went smoothly. However, ministerial meetings on the larger issues confronting India and Pakistan, which were held in March, made no progress.

Pakistan

Ayub Khan's government attempted to portray the Tashkent outcome as a success: the larger Indian army had been fought to a stalemate, and the Indian hold on Kashmir had been challenged. There certainly was less reason to fear that India would militarily threaten Pakistani independence. But Pakistan's military challenge had failed to secure any new gains in Kashmir, and Ayub and Bhutto's diplomatic efforts had failed to reopen discussions on Kashmir's future. The public took a less positive view of the outcome. Antigovernment riots broke out in Lahore and Rawalpindi, and Ayub's popularity plummeted.

The Second Kashmir war provided several lessons for the leaders of West Pakistan. The first was that despite all of its efforts at improving its military capabilities since 1947, Pakistan could not defeat India in a general war. The second lesson was that the potential for Chinese intervention on Pakistan's side could prove to be a powerful deterrent to Indian aggression in the future. The third lesson concerned the behavior of the major powers. On the one hand, they had once again intervened to engineer a cease-fire before the war got out of control. On the other hand, the behavior of the United States was more evenhanded than the Pakistanis had expected or hoped. The Pakistani government began to view the interests of the superpowers as that of avoiding a major conflagration as opposed to supporting their respective allies. That judgment would play a significant role in the diplomatic strategy pursued by the Pakistani government in the 1971 Bangladesh Crisis.

Perhaps the most telling lesson drawn from the Second Kashmir war, however, occurred in East Pakistan. Once the war began, India was able to block all communication between East and West Pakistan. East Pakistan remained out of the war, largely because of India's fear of triggering Chinese intervention, but East Pakistan's insecurity became obvious. With its isolated geographical position and meager defenses, it was completely vulnerable to an Indian attack. The awareness of this vulnerability in any future Indo-Pakistani conflict added fuel to the arguments of those who sought Bengali independence.

India

India's leaders viewed the outcome with mixed feelings. The army had acquitted itself well, but the war also had demonstrated the strength of Pakistan's forces and raised the specter of Chinese military intervention. The Tashkent Declaration neither confirmed nor challenged the status quo in Kashmir, but the long-term effect was to harden the cease-fire line into something akin to an international border between India and Pakistan. In that respect, the outcome of the Second Kashmir Crisis was not unlike that of the Berlin Wall Crisis: the temporary dividing line within the disputed territory hardened into a seemingly permanent border.

The Second Kashmir Crisis reinforced the Indian belief that Pakistan could not be trusted to respect the status quo. It also reinforced the view in India that differences with Pakistan could not be resolved through negotiation. Conversely, the war had allowed India to regain confidence in its ability to meet any future Pakistani military challenge. That confidence was tempered by the specter of potential Chinese intervention.

Overall, the outcome of the Second Kashmir war can be classified as a compromise. The cease-fire brought the war to an end, and the Tashkent talks terminated the crisis, although the larger dispute over Kashmir remained unsettled. Perhaps the best short description is that of Burke (1973:336–37), who described the Second Kashmir war as having "a sobering effect on both countries."

Bangladesh Crisis and War, 1971

The Bangladesh Crisis grew out of a civil war between West Pakistan and Bengali separatists in East Pakistan. Unlike the previous three Indo-Pakistani crises, India was the challenger, as it actively supported the Bengalis. It also was the first of the crises to end in a decisive military victory for one rival, India. Despite these differences, the strategies pursued by India and Pakistan during the crisis reflected lessons drawn from their previous crises and from the Second Kashmir war.

The union of East and West Pakistan had been tenuous from the start. The two halves of the country were separated by 1,000 miles of Indian territory, economic disparities, and cultural differences. The one element that the two regions shared was their common faith, Islam. That commonality was sufficient to form the union in 1947 under Jinnah's charismatic leadership, but Jinnah was long dead by 1966. The natural barriers to a unified nation were exacerbated by the East Pakistanis' perception that they were treated as second-class citizens by the government in the west. Worse, the easterners were being economically exploited and politically marginalized.[22] Added to these long-standing grievances was the sense of isolation and vulnerability that East Pakistanis felt during the 1965 war. If West Pakistan was unable or unwilling to protect them from India, why not achieve greater security by seceding from West Pakistan and forming more friendly relations with India?

The Intercrisis Period, 1966–71

As India and Pakistan were beginning to withdraw their forces from Kashmir, the seeds were planted for the Bangladesh Crisis and war. On February 12, 1966, Sheikh Mujibur Rahman, president of the Awami League, an East Pakistani separatist group, issued a six-point program that would grant local autonomy to East Pakistan. Ayub Khan immediately denounced the plan, declaring that Pakistan would accept the challenge of civil war to preserve political unity. West Pakistani police arrested Rahman sheikh in mid-April, which set off mass demonstrations in East Pakistan. Rahman was held prisoner on charges of participating in a conspiracy against the Pakistani government until the charges were dropped almost three years later, on February 22, 1969.

During the period between 1966 and 1970, both India and Pakistan

---

22. Pakistan's major exports, tea and jute, came from East Pakistan, but the revenues went primarily to West Pakistan. East Pakistan comprised 60 percent of Pakistan's total population, but positions in the government and military were staffed almost exclusively by westerners.

faced considerable internal instability. Just 10 hours after the signing of the Tashkent Declaration, Shastri was felled by a heart attack, and Indira Gandhi replaced him as prime minister. The Congress Party, however, remained firmly in control in India, with Gandhi handily winning reelection in 1967. During the second half of the 1960s India struggled with serious economic problems, including severe food shortages. When Sheikh Abdullah was released from his latest detention in 1968, he provided a focus for growing resentment over Indian control over Kashmir. A "State People's Convention," held in Srinagar in October 1968, was attended by several hundred politicians and concluded that the final solution for Kashmir must be self-determination.

Along with the growing demand for autonomy from East Pakistan, Ayub Khan's government faced new political challenges in West Pakistan. Ayub survived a heart attack, followed by an attempted coup in January 1968, and an assassination attempt that November. By March 1969, however, the domestic turmoil persuaded Ayub to step down as president and to hand over power to the army commander in chief, Yahya Khan. Yahya immediately imposed martial law, but by the end of the year he had restored the parliamentary system in Pakistan, including the participation of opposition parties.

Relations with the Superpowers

Superpower competition for influence in South Asia continued between the Second Kashmir and Bangladesh wars, but now superpower relations with India and Pakistan were also affected by the triangular relationship among the United States, Soviet Union, and China. The Soviet friendship with India began as a natural offshoot of the USSR's rivalry with the Americans, but by 1965, India had become an even more important component of the Soviet Union's increasingly competitive relationship with China. Better Soviet relations with Pakistan would weaken Pakistani ties to both the United States and China. Thus, the Soviet Union agreed in the summer of 1966 to supply military and economic assistance to Pakistan as well as to India.

The Soviet diplomatic success at Tashkent raised the Brezhnev regime's perception of its leadership role in Asia. During 1968 and 1969, the Soviets visited Asian capitals to discuss prospects for a "collective security" system for Asia. The proposal, which was rather vague, received a cold shoulder from most Asian leaders, who had no interest in tying themselves to a Soviet alliance, and the plan was soon abandoned. But it outraged the Chinese, who saw it as an anti-Chinese military alliance with India as the centerpiece. The United States saw the proposal as an attempt to counter American influence in the area. The initiative came at a time when the Soviets were engaged in increasingly severe border clashes with the Chinese and were establishing a naval presence in the Indian Ocean for the first time.

Conversely, the Soviet mediation at Tashkent, with American approval, underlined the coincidence of Soviet and American interests on the Indian subcontinent. Both superpowers were anxious to reduce the tensions between India and Pakistan, and both the United States and the Soviet Union saw the containment of China as the first priority in the region (see McMahon 1994:334). The Johnson administration returned to a policy of supplying aid to both India and Pakistan. But in the aftermath of the American arms embargo during the Second Kashmir war, Pakistan was edging away from its close alliance with the West. After talks with Kosygin in the spring of 1968, Ayub demanded that the United States remove its strategic listening post at Peshawar, which had been a source of tension with the Soviet Union. China, meanwhile, was tightening its friendship with Pakistan. A Pakistani-Chinese economic agreement was signed in 1966. In November 1970, after an extended visit by Yahya Khan to Beijing, the two countries announced their mutual support for the "liberation" of Taiwan, Vietnam, and Kashmir.

By 1970 Pakistan had assumed a new role in its relationship with the United States, becoming the go-between in the thawing of American-Chinese relations (Kissinger 1979:857). The Nixon White House was placing increasing importance on the American friendship with Pakistan as an entrée to better relations with China, which could place the United States in the enviable position of being the only one of the three major powers to have good relations with the other two. At the same time, the U.S. State Department was pursuing better relations with India to provide a counterweight to Chinese influence in the region.

The net effect of this maneuvering was to increase the interest of each of the superpowers in avoiding another Indo-Pakistani war. Neither the United States nor the Soviet Union wanted to be forced to choose sides, thereby alienating either India or Pakistan, and the superpowers did not want to risk the possibility of being drawn into a confrontation with each other or with China. China, for its part, did not want its informal alliance with Pakistan to draw it into hostilities that could escalate to a confrontation with either superpower. In 1970 the United States and the Soviet Union were well into negotiations for the SALT I accord, which would be the centerpiece of their efforts to build détente. By the spring of 1971, China had made its first tentative contacts, through an invitation to an American table-tennis team, to normalize its relations with the United States. That summer, the United States announced that Nixon's national security adviser, Henry Kissinger, would make the first official American visit to the People's Republic. None of these parties wanted a war in South Asia to upset these delicate diplomatic efforts.

Seeds of the Crisis
On November 13, 1970, East Pakistan was assaulted by one of the worst cyclones in history. Between 1.5 and 2 million people died from the effects of the storm. While the West Pakistani government responded in a slow and apathetic manner, India offered emergency relief. Two weeks passed before Prime Minister Yahya Khan visited the scene of the disaster. When general elections were held throughout Pakistan on December 7, Sheikh Mujibur Rahman's Awami Party not only won an impressive victory in East Pakistan but emerged with the majority of seats in the Pakistani National Assembly.[23] The net effect was that Rahman would be elected prime minister when the assembly next met. Rahman promptly announced that he would not compromise on the Awami League's six-point program for autonomy for East Pakistan.

Yahya Khan found his government caught between Rahman's demands for autonomy and the strong nationalist position of the opposition People's Party (PPP) in West Pakistan, which was led by the former foreign minister, Bhutto. On March 6 Yahya Khan declared that he intended to preserve Pakistan's "complete and absolute integrity," by force if necessary. He then appointed General Tikka Khan, a notorious hard-liner, as governor of East Pakistan. On March 8 the Awami League responded by launching a civil-disobedience movement, which included a general strike.[24] Confronted by an East Pakistani majority and the threat of an assembly boycott by the PPP, which held a majority of the West Pakistani seats, Yahya indefinitely postponed the beginning of the parliamentary session. Talks between Yahya Khan and Rahman got nowhere. Two weeks later, on March 25, General Tikka Khan's troops killed 115 people in a confrontation with East Pakistani protesters.

Meanwhile, an airliner hijacking had further soured Indo-Pakistani relations. On January 30, two Kashmiris hijacked a commercial Indian flight and forced it to land in West Pakistan. After the passengers and crew were released and the Pakistani government granted political asylum to the hijackers, the hijackers blew up the plane in a well-staged event that was shown on Pakistani television. Indian Prime Minister Gandhi held the Pakistani government responsible and responded on February 4 by ban-

---

23. Rahman's Awami League won 169 seats to the 90 seats won by Bhutto's People's Party.

24. The major weapon in the civil-disobedience campaign was a general strike, but it should be noted that the actions of the separatists went beyond the Gandhian notion of civil disobedience to include rioting and the destruction of property owned by West Pakistanis.

ning overflights from East to West Pakistan. The ban was lifted when Pakistan agreed to pay compensation for the destroyed aircraft, but the incident added to the tension between the two sides. A West Pakistani commission of inquiry into the incident claimed, on April 15 that the whole affair had been engineered by Indian intelligence as a means of aiding the secessionist movement in East Pakistan (Blinkenberg 1972:307; Khan 1973:133).

The Crisis Structure

Pakistan
Perceptions of Indian intentions. The Pakistani leadership had not changed its belief that the Indian government was bent on destroying the state of Pakistan to reunite the subcontinent under Hindu rule (Sisson and Rose 1990:44; Cheema 1997:54). Thus, it is not surprising that the Pakistanis were convinced that India was actively encouraging and assisting the Awami League's secessionist movement in East Pakistan (Pakistan, Government 1971). When the rioting broke out in East Pakistan, Yahya Khan accused India of colluding with those inflaming the situation (Sisson and Rose 1990:170). Yahya Khan's suspicions appeared to be confirmed in the late spring, when the Indian army assumed responsibility for training and equipping the Mukti Bahini, the Awami League's guerrilla forces.

As the crisis in East Pakistan escalated to a civil war, the Pakistani leadership became convinced that India was preparing for an attack (Sisson and Rose 1990:4–5). Pakistani military intelligence, however, was under the impression as late as December 1971 that Indian military objectives were limited to seizing a small portion of East Pakistan along the Indian border (see Khan 1973:166–67). The Pakistani leadership began by overestimating India's hostile intentions and ended by underestimating India's military objectives.

Interests. For the Pakistani leadership, the interests at stake were enormous: the territorial integrity of Pakistan itself and the government's survival. Both the Bengali rebels' secessionist movement and India's armed forces threatened those vital interests. Just one day prior to the Indian offensive in November, Yahya Khan declared that Pakistan would defend its "honor and territorial integrity at any cost" (Sisson and Rose 1990:227).

Capabilities. As in its previous conflicts with India, the Pakistani army was overwhelmingly outnumbered by the Indian forces. It now suffered a disadvantage in arms and equipment as a result of a six-year American embargo on arms sales to both sides. (India continued to receive military assistance from the Soviet Union.) The strategic balance was further skewed by the separation of East and West Pakistan. India controlled the 1,000 miles of territory between the two Pakistans and came close to dominating the airspace as well. If that were not enough of a disadvantage, the Pakistani army would be fighting in hostile territory in East Pakistan, with an uncooperative indigenous population and active guerrilla opposition.

The Pakistani government was dominated by the military in 1971. The military command's beliefs in the superior fighting abilities of their Muslim troops versus India's Hindus continued to color their judgment of the military balance (Sisson and Rose 1990:223–24). That view had been reinforced by the Pakistani military success in the Rann of Kutch Crisis and the early offensive successes in the Second Kashmir war. Nevertheless, the military command was aware that an Indian invasion of East Pakistan would present an almost impossible strategic and logistic problem (Khan 1973:147–58).

India

Perception of Pakistani intentions.   Nothing had happened between 1965 and 1971 to dampen Indian impressions of Pakistani hostility. The tensions were exacerbated in January 1971 with the Pakistani government's handling of the hijacking of the Indian Airlines plane that was forced to land in Lahore. But India's involvement in the 1971 dispute between West and East Pakistan resulted from India's internal crisis created by the influx of East Pakistani refugees and from the opportunity to severely weaken Pakistan that the East Bengali secessionist movement afforded. Unlike the three previous crises with Pakistan, the Indian leadership did not perceive Pakistan to be a military threat to India in 1971. Rather, the consequences of the Pakistani civil war threatened India's economy and social stability.

Interests.   The refugee influx, which reached more than eight million by the summer of 1971 and eventually swelled to nearly 10 million, became an intolerable financial and social burden that threatened India's stability. Conversely, the crisis in East Pakistan provided an excellent opportunity for India to cripple its main adversary and improve its own security by assisting the Bengali rebels in achieving independence. A friendly Bangladesh would not only strengthen India vis-à-vis Pakistan but would also strengthen India's strategic position vis-à-vis China. As an Indian defense analyst wrote at the time, it was "an opportunity the likes of which will never come again" (Holmberg 1997:21–25; Sisson and Rose 1990: 149–50).

Capabilities.   The Indian military advantage over Pakistan was described in the previous section on Pakistani capabilities. That imbalance was partially offset by the threat of Chinese military intervention on the

Pakistani side. But in July the Indian government obtained a copy of a letter from China to Pakistan stating that Chinese assistance to Pakistan in a war with India would be limited to political support (Sisson and Rose 1990:199). India almost immediately moved three divisions from its border with China to its border with East Pakistan. The Soviet-Indian Treaty of Peace and Friendship, which was signed in August, provided added reassurance about the risk of Chinese intervention as well as India's military position vis-à-vis Pakistan. The agreement called for the shipment of additional military hardware to India and the cessation of Soviet military aid to Pakistan. Following the agreement, Prime Minister Indira Gandhi spoke with increasing confidence of India's ability to prevail in a military confrontation with Pakistan (see Jha 1972:403–4). But as an added precaution, the Indian attack on Pakistan was delayed until November so that it would be logistically difficult for the Chinese to attempt a military intervention across the Himalayas (Kissinger 1979:856).

In addition to its overall military superiority over Pakistani forces, India enjoyed an immense logistical advantage along the East Pakistan border. That advantage allowed India to provide sanctuaries in West Bengal to the Mukti Bahini guerrillas, who now numbered more than 150,000, and to provide them with weapons and military training for their forays into East Pakistan.

These factors—the image of Pakistan as an implacable enemy, a growing crisis coupled with a strategic opportunity, and overwhelming military superiority—encouraged India to pursue a strategy based on military coercion including, if necessary, war.

Crisis Behavior

When the Awami League won a National Assembly majority in the December 1970 elections, Sheikh Mujibur Rahman and his followers believed that East Pakistani autonomy might be achieved peacefully. Yahya Khan's pledge to use the military if necessary to preserve the union, his appointment of the ruthless General Tikka Khan as governor of East Pakistan, and his indefinite postponement of the assembly session threw cold water on those hopes. Low-level clashes between East Pakistani separatists and West Pakistani troops occurred throughout March. After General Tikka Khan's troops fired on East Pakistani civilians on March 25, Yahya defended the action on the grounds that Rahman's civil disobedience movement was "an act of treason [that] created turmoil, terror, insecurity, and murders" (Pakistan, Government 1971). On March 27, Sheikh Rahman declared East Pakistan the Sovereign Independent People's Republic of Bangladesh. He was arrested on the next day, but his followers formed a provisional government, and the civil-disobedience movement in East Pakistan escalated to armed rebellion.

India had banned the overflight of Pakistani military aircraft on March 15. During that month India began a substantial buildup of its military forces along the border with East Pakistan, as Pakistani army and rebel forces engaged in numerous clashes along the border area. By the end of the month, the Indian parliament was expressing its "solidarity" with the Bengali secessionist movement, and the government was calling for United Nations actions to restrain the West Pakistani forces (Blinkenberg 1972:314). West Pakistan protested India's interference in Pakistani internal affairs. On April 3 West Pakistan charged that Indian warships were harassing Pakistani merchant vessels and that India was providing arms to the rebels. China seconded the charges. On April 12 the Soviet Union sent representatives to meet with both India and Pakistan in an effort to avoid a direct confrontation.

The West Pakistani attempt to put down the revolt in East Pakistan was brutal even by twentieth-century standards, with widespread reports of atrocities. On April 15 India accused Pakistan of committing genocide. The Indian government also asserted that Pakistani forces had fired across the border into India. Four days later, Pakistan accused India of attacking a border post in East Pakistan. India made similar charges on April 27. Similar military incidents occurred throughout the crisis. By the end of April, India had fortified its border with East Pakistan, and the Indian army was garrisoning and training the Mukti Bahini guerrillas. Diplomatic relations between India and Pakistan continued to worsen. When Pakistan attempted to replace a Bengali diplomatic representative in Calcutta with a West Pakistani, India rejected the new representative's credentials. West Pakistan responded on April 26 by closing the mission.

The tide of refugees from East Pakistan into India became a serious social and economic burden for the Indian government. Besides the high costs of feeding and housing the refugees, the influx created social problems in the northeastern provinces of Tripura and Meghalaya, where the numbers of refugees threatened to upset the internal balance of tribal political groups (Sisson and Rose 1990:181). On May 24 Prime Minister Gandhi informed parliament that if the international community did not act soon to stop the influx of refugees and provide conditions for their return to their homes, India would be forced to "take all measures as may be necessary to ensure our own security and the preservation and development of the structure of our social and economic life" (Sisson and Rose 1990:153). By late May an estimated three million refugees had swarmed into India to escape what had become a massacre by West Pakistani troops.

The Mukti Bahini rebels, however, continued to achieve their share of victories against the Pakistani regular forces, partly as a result of the Indian army's training and material assistance. When the United Nations offered to send observers to the border, India rejected the plan and ordered other foreign-assistance agencies to leave.

On April 15 the Awami League declared the independence of the new republic of Bangladesh. As the civil war intensified, Gandhi vowed that India would not let Bangladesh die (Jha 1972:400). Reports of Pakistani atrocities and the plight of the refugees created a wave of pro-Bangladeshi sympathy and support for the Indian position in world opinion, especially in the United States, where the press and Congress attacked the Nixon administration's support of Pakistan (Kissinger 1979:858–59).

By the end of July, Yahya was issuing warnings to India that any attempt to seize all or part of East Pakistan would result in general war (Jha 1972:400–403). By that time, however, the Indian government had reached the conclusion that a military showdown was all but inevitable (Sisson and Rose 1990:189; Kissinger 1979:860–61). India rejected a mid-July American effort to offer its good offices. In an August 4 press conference, President Nixon declared his support for Pakistan while urging restraint by both sides (Nixon 1971:189).[25] A week later, India and the Soviet Union signed their Treaty of Peace, Friendship, and Cooperation. A Bangladeshi diplomatic mission was opened in New Delhi. On the same day, August 30, Pakistan put Sheikh Mujibur Rahman on trial for treason.

Clashes along the Indian–East Pakistani border intensified during September, with the Mukti Bahini rebels attacking West Pakistani troops from sanctuaries within India. The influx of refugees had reached eight million and was costing India approximately $25 million a day (Jha 1972:404). On September 1 Indian forces were placed on alert. Three days later Pakistan moved additional forces into position on the West Pakistani border with India. India responded in kind on September 9. In late September Gandhi visited Moscow and received promises of an airlift of military supplies in the event of the outbreak of war. During October and November, India moved more of its own troops to the border with East

---

25. According to Kissinger (1979:864–65) there was a serious division between the State Department and White House. The State Department supported the Indian position and urged intervention on the Indian side with the Soviet Union if China entered an Indo-Pakistani war. The White House, however, leaned toward Pakistan. Nixon distrusted the Indian government, and Kissinger wanted to protect the diplomatic opening to China. The United States did provide India with more than $70 million in aid for the refugees.

Pakistan to supplement the rebel forces. Yahya Khan complained that India was preparing a war of aggression to break up Pakistan. On October 17 he proposed that troops from both countries be withdrawn from the East Pakistani border. Gandhi rejected the proposal on the same day and warned that if a war occurred, India would not withdraw from any conquered territory in Pakistan.

During the late summer and early fall, the United States attempted to mediate. After discussions with the Indian ambassador, D. C. Jha, the United States acted as an intermediary between Pakistan and the provisional government of Bangladesh. These efforts, which took place sporadically through September and early October, initially yielded a modest softening of the positions of the two sides, but the talks broke off as the Indo-Pakistani crisis escalated (Kissinger 1979:869–73). Meanwhile, Gandhi met with Soviet Foreign Minister Gromyko in New Delhi, where Gromyko promised to airlift additional military supplies to India in the event of a war with Pakistan and/or China.

The U.S. government, meanwhile, was under extreme domestic pressure to extricate itself from the unpopular war in Vietnam. President Nixon hoped to avoid having to support another unpopular and weak ally in an Indo-Pakistani war. Consequently, Nixon and Kissinger attempted to collaborate with the Soviet Union in achieving a compromise settlement. Kissinger made an appeal through Soviet Ambassador Anatoly Dobrynin on October 9, but the Soviets were not willing to pursue any option other than independence for Bangladesh (Kissinger 1979:874). Gandhi met with Nixon in Washington on November 4 and 5, but the talks yielded no progress, despite a Pakistani offer, transmitted through Nixon, for a phased withdrawal from the East Pakistan border beginning with a unilateral withdrawn by Pakistan (Kissinger 1979:881–83; Sisson and Rose 1990:226–27).

Indian military forces were placed on full alert on October 18, and Pakistan followed suit three days later. On the same day, United Nations Secretary-General Thant offered to mediate the crisis. India called up its reserves the next day. New clashes occurred on October 24 and 25 along the East Pakistani border and along the Kashmir cease-fire line. On November 1 the Soviets began airlifting military supplies to India. Indian forces advanced into East Pakistan, clashed with Pakistani troops on November 9, and then withdrew. Another clash occurred on November 16. On November 18 India rejected Thant's offer to mediate. On the night of November 20–21, several Indian units launched simultaneous attacks across the border in East Pakistan. This time they did not withdraw after the attacks. The war had begun. Pakistan pursued international diplomatic assistance through the United States and the United Nations before responding in force with air and ground attacks, including attacks along the western Indo-Pakistani border on December 4. The United States dispatched the USS *Enterprise* to the Bay of Bengal, but the war was over by the time the ship arrived. The Indian forces achieved a decisive victory, and the new state of Bangladesh was born on December 18, 1971.

Patterns of Behavior

Figure 5.4 presents the time series of weekly hostility scores for India and Pakistan over the course of the crisis.[26] The time series in figure 5.5 includes West Pakistan's interactions with the Awami League and Mukti Bahini in East Pakistan as well as West Pakistan's interactions with India.

When the crisis is treated simply as a dyadic dispute between India and Pakistan, India leads in escalating the hostility, with Pakistan responding in kind but at a lower magnitude throughout the crisis. Even as a strictly dyadic crisis, the escalation scores on all three indicators in table 5.1 are high, with the composite escalation score the highest for the four Indo-Pakistani crises. One reason for the high escalation is that both sides were interacting with the other almost exclusively through military actions. There was no direct negotiation. The dominant pattern throughout is for a display or use of force by India to be reciprocated by Pakistan.

That pattern is reflected in the reciprocity score appearing in table 5.2. The two sides are relatively in sync in the direction in which they are moving—that is toward more or less hostility—but there is a considerable distance between the magnitude of hostility displayed by India and that shown by Pakistan over the course of the crisis. For that reason, the Bangladesh Crisis has the lowest composite reciprocity score of the four Indo-Pakistani crises. In fact, if the Bangladesh Crisis were added to the sample of 34 cases in the appendix, it would rank eleventh on the direction indicator but twenty-fourth on the distance indicator of reciprocity. The two indicators confirm the visual impression from figure 5.4: India consistently leads in escalating the crisis, and there is a consistently upward trend in hostility with a high rate of escalation in the last month of the crisis.

The overall pattern of a low composite reciprocity score and high escalation would classify the behavior pattern as Resistance, a crisis in

---

26. The starting date for the crisis is March 1, 1971, when Yahya Khan declared that the National Assembly meetings scheduled for that month would be suspended indefinitely. Figures 5.4 and 5.5 carry the crisis through December 4, when Pakistan declared war on India, one day after Small and Singer's (1982) date for the onset of the Bangladesh war. A case can be made that the crisis was transformed into a war on November 20–21, when India launched its offensive into East Pakistan, but the Pakistani government initially treated the action as another border incursion (Sisson and Rose 1990:228).

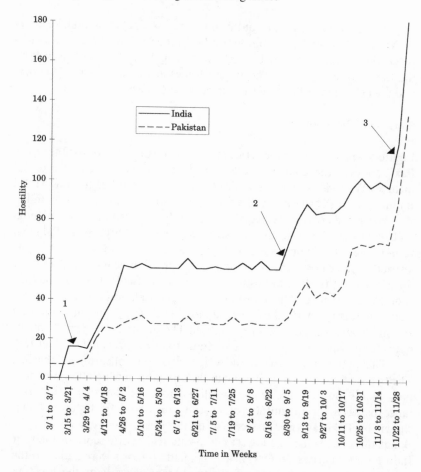

Fig. 5.4. Bangladesh Crisis, 1971 (India-Pakistan)
Key dates are indicated with arrows: (1) 3/25: India begins troop buildup
along East Pakistani border; (2) 9/1: India places forces on alert and calls
up reserves; (3) 11/21: Indian offensive into East Pakistan.

which one side (India) is leading in escalating coercion while the other
(Pakistan) responds in kind.

Figure 5.5, which includes the actions exchanged between Pakistan
and the East Bengali rebels as well as those between India and Pakistan,
provides a different perspective on the crisis. As figure 5.5 illustrates, the
early part of the crisis is dominated by Pakistan's attempts, beginning in
late March, to put down the secessionist movement by force. Those activities drop off in late May, when the West Pakistani forces successfully drive

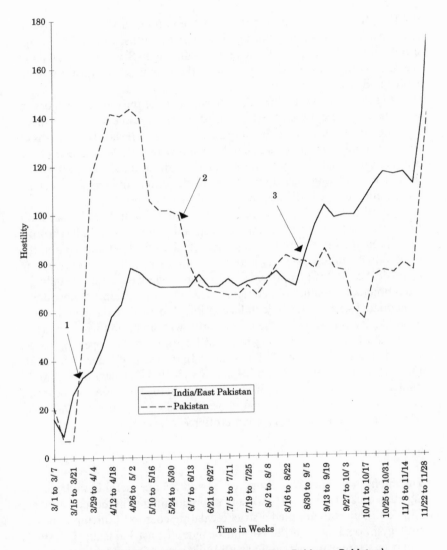

Fig. 5.5. Bangladesh Crisis, 1971 (India and East Pakistan–Pakistan)
Key dates are indicated with arrows: (1) 3/25: Yahya Khan orders Pakistani army to put down East Pakistani rebellion; (2) 5/30: East Pakistani rebellion put down, rebels forced into sanctuaries in India; (3) 9/1: India places forces an alert and calls up reserves.

the East Bengali guerrilla forces across the border into India. There is a relative lull in that activity during the summer months, although the magnitude of hostility remains fairly high. Beginning in September, India and the East Bengali rebels rapidly escalate the magnitude of hostility, with Pakistan delaying its responses.

Figure 5.5 shows the two-dispute character of the crisis, which began with the dispute between West and East Pakistan and ended as an Indo-Pakistani crisis. A comparison of the time series for the last two months of the crisis depicted in figures 5.4 and 5.5 shows that the final phase of the crisis was dominated by exchanges between India and Pakistan, with India leading in escalating the magnitude of hostile actions and Pakistan seeking an accommodative settlement in the final two months.

Another interesting feature of both figures 5.4 and 5.5 is that Pakistan, which continued to attempt to avoid another war with India through the diplomatic intervention of third parties, lags well behind India in the escalation of military activity until the outbreak of full-scale war. During October West Pakistan initiated some accommodative moves—including a reduction in the conflictual action directed at East Pakistan—to encourage a negotiated settlement, while India continued to escalate the magnitude of hostility. By this stage in the crisis, India was preparing for war, while West Pakistan was attempting to avoid it, primarily by appealing to the United States to intervene diplomatically. In the week of November 15–21, India's hostility score is 98, while Pakistan's is 69; in the next week, India's jumps to 120, and Pakistan's increases to 90; in the final week of the crisis, November 29–December 5, India's hostility score is at 180, while Pakistan, which has not yet launched a counteroffensive, is at 134.

Influence Strategies

The different perspectives of figures 5.4 and 5.5 are useful in understanding the classification of Pakistan's predominant influence strategy. Although Pakistan adopted a strict escalating coercive Bullying influence strategy in dealing with the Awami League in East Pakistan, Pakistan's influence strategy for bargaining with India is more consistent with a firm-but-flexible Reciprocating influence strategy. As noted in the previous description of the patterns of behavior, Pakistan's coercive actions toward India occurred in response to Indian attempts at coercion and did not threaten offensive action against India. Moreover, Yahya Khan's government initiated accommodative moves toward the end of the crisis. Yahya replaced General Tikka Khan with a civilian governor of Bangladesh on September 1. On September 5 Yahya extended the amnesty for refugees and commuted the death sentence against Sheikh Mujibur Rahman. The Awami League's leaders initially indicated that they would settle for internal autonomy without demanding full separation from Pakistan, but in the wake of the Pakistani atrocities and the prospect of Indian military intervention, the league toughened its position to demand complete independence and amnesty for Rahman. By October 20 the Bangladeshi representative indicated to the United States that he was no longer interested in contacts with West Pakistan (Kissinger 1979:872–73).

India employed a coercive Bullying influence strategy in dealing with Pakistan. The detailed descriptions of the influence strategies of the two sides begins with Pakistan, as the crisis began with its dispute with the Awami League.

Pakistan
Yahya Khan and his advisers believed that Pakistan's territorial integrity demanded that they quash the secessionist aims of the Awami League in East Pakistan, but the security of West Pakistan counseled against war with India. Consequently, the government pursued a dual strategy of attempting to crack down militarily on the secessionist movement in East Pakistan while attempting to restrain India from intervening on the side of the Awami League. The Pakistani government was convinced that without Indian intervention, the Bengali secessionist movement ultimately would be crushed (Sisson and Rose 1990:222). Avoiding Indian intervention was another matter. The Pakistani government's strategy was to appeal to the major powers to restrain India. Although Britain and the Soviet Union respectively had mediated the last two Indo-Pakistani crises, Yahya Khan's government placed most of its hopes on U.S. diplomatic intervention.

Yahya Khan was in contact with the White House throughout the evolving crisis, particularly as it escalated toward war in November. At that point, he accepted an American suggestion for a unilateral withdrawal of forces from East Pakistan's border with India. Even after the Indian offensive of November 21, Yahya continued to attempt to avoid war through American mediation efforts. If India did intervene militarily in East Pakistan, Yahya and his advisers were convinced that international pressure would bring about an early cease-fire and insistence on the withdrawal of Indian forces from Pakistani soil (Sisson and Rose 1990:223).

The Pakistani leadership's faith in outside intervention stemmed from its experiences in the first three crises. Outside intervention could either prevent the crisis from escalating to war or, if necessary, bring about an early cease-fire before the Indians could achieve a military victory.[27] Their expectations were not unlike the lesson that Nasser drew from the Suez

27. Reference to the lessons drawn from major-power intervention in previous crises appears in interviews with makers of Pakistani foreign policy that were conducted by Sisson and Rose (1990:222).

Crisis of 1956, which served him so poorly in 1967: the great powers would intervene to contain the war and prevent Egypt (or Pakistan) from suffering any permanent loss of territory. Yahya Khan was more active than Nasser in seeking international diplomatic intervention, and Yahya did not deliberately inflame relations with India as Nasser did with Israel.

As figure 5.4 illustrates, Pakistani hostility toward India was primarily reactive, whereas Egypt led in escalating the 1967 crisis with Israel (figure 4.6). But like Nasser's move into the Sinai, General Tikka Khan's brutal actions in East Pakistan set in motion a spiral of escalating hostility and violence that propelled the two sides to war. Egypt's move into the Sinai led to the occupation of Sharm al-Sheikh and the mining of the Strait of Tiran. West Pakistan's military actions in East Pakistan led to a civil war, which in turn produced the massive flow of refugees into India. In 1967 the Israeli government finally decided that given its military superiority, the costs and risks of war were preferable to the long-term economic and security consequences of Egypt's military fait accompli.

In 1971 the Indian government made a similar calculation when it weighed the long-term economic and social costs of dealing with the refugees and the continued presence of the radical Mukti Bahini in India against a war that India believed it could win easily (Barnds 1972:242; Sisson and Rose 1990:149–50). By the late spring of 1971, the U.S. government received intelligence reports that India was making plans for a "lightning Israeli-type attack" to seize control of East Pakistan (Kissinger 1979:856). Both Nasser and Yahya Khan overestimated the diplomatic influence that the superpowers were able or willing to exert on Israel and India.

India

India's first objective was the return of the refugees to East Pakistan. The refugees, though, would not return unless they could be assured of their safety. Safety meant a pro-Bengali, pro-Hindu regime in East Pakistan. The second Indian objective was to take advantage of the opportunity to create such a regime under the control of the Bengali rebels in East Pakistan.

The initial Indian diplomatic strategy had two tracks: (1) to persuade other governments, including the superpowers, to bring international pressure on Pakistan to provide political autonomy to East Pakistan, presumably under the control of Mujibur Rahman's Awami League; and (2) to add military pressure by providing advice and assistance to the Mukti Bahini forces operating out of sanctuaries in India and by threatening direct military intervention (see Sisson and Rose 1990:186–89).

New Delhi sent a number of diplomatic representatives out to tour the capitals of influential states around the world in the early summer and again in September to pursue the first objective. Gandhi also intended to press India's case in the United Nations General Assembly when it met in October. Like Pakistan, India attempted to internationalize the dispute but did so for a different purpose. India hoped to sway world opinion to persuade Pakistan to grant autonomy to Bangladesh, but if that effort failed, the Gandhi government would settle for neutralizing opposition to the use of military force (Sisson and Rose 1990:188). By mid-July the Gandhi government was preparing plans for a military solution (Sisson and Rose 1990:206–8). By the time Indian diplomats were presenting their case to national leaders in September, New Delhi was readying its troops for war.

Negotiations

Despite their intensive efforts to internationalize the conflict and to gain the diplomatic support of third parties, neither Pakistan nor India seriously considered direct negotiations. By 1971, after their three previous crises had escalated to military hostilities, both sides were convinced that nothing could be gained by direct negotiations. Efforts by third parties to arrange negotiations between Yahya Khan and Indira Gandhi went nowhere. One lesson that the two sides drew from their enduring rivalry was that there was little to be gained from direct negotiations.

Outcome and Lessons

When the fighting stopped on December 18, the entire Pakistani army in East Pakistan, some 93,000 troops, surrendered itself and its equipment to India. India had been midwife to the birth of a new country, had decisively defeated and permanently weakened its main adversary, and possessed an entire army and its weaponry. Pakistan was devastated, both physically and emotionally. Sheikh Mujibur Rahman became the first prime minister of Bangladesh, whose independence quickly received official recognition from the international community.

Kashmir

The Bangladesh issue had been settled; the only outstanding issues remained the return of prisoners of war and, of course, Kashmir. When the new Pakistani prime minister, Bhutto, sought negotiations to obtain the return of the prisoners, India agreed only on the condition that the agenda included Pakistani recognition of Bangladeshi independence and a settlement of the Kashmir dispute. The negotiations, including direct private discussions between Gandhi and Bhutto, were held in Simla, where a new accord on Kashmir was reached on July 3, 1972. The accord confirmed the current cease-fire line in Kashmir, which had shifted in India's favor during the course of the war. But there was no resolution of the larger issue of Kashmir's future. The Simla Accord stated only that the temporary cease-fire line in Kashmir would be "respected by both sides without prejudice to the recognized position of either side."[28] What Bhutto accepted at Simla was nothing more than a realistic recognition of the strategic status quo.[29] In fact, the one lesson that both sides drew from the 1971 crisis was that Pakistan did not have the capability to launch another military challenge to the status quo.

Oddly, the talks did not result in either Pakistani recognition of Bangladesh or an agreement for the return of the Pakistani prisoners of war. The prisoners were finally repatriated in 1973, and Bhutto's government officially recognized Bangladesh at an Islamic summit held in Lahore in February 1974.

Conclusions

Patterns of Behavior

There are no signs of improving conflict management in the four Indo-Pakistani crises. Each successive crisis escalated to a more violent conclusion than the one that preceded it. The regular forces of India and Pakistan avoided direct hostilities in the First Kashmir Crisis. In the Rann of Kutch Crisis the fighting remained limited in its intensity and geographical domain, with both sides accepting the British-mediated cease-fire before the hostilities escalated to war. The Second Kashmir Crisis escalated to war between India and Pakistan, with Indian forces extending the war beyond Kashmir into Pakistan proper, but this conflict too was terminated by third-party mediation. The Bangladesh Crisis produced a full-scale war that ended with India's decisive defeat of Pakistan.

Each of the first three crises began with a challenge from Pakistan. The lead in escalating the crisis switched back and forth during the First Kashmir Crisis, whereas Pakistan led in escalating the hostility throughout most the Rann of Kutch and Second Kashmir crises. The first three Indo-Pakistani crises were classic cases of a revisionist state (Pakistan)

---

28. A full discussion of the Simla Accord negotiations and the accord itself appears in Bokhari and Thornton 1988.

29. Bhutto, who publicly promised a thousand years of war with India in a September 22, 1965, speech to the United Nations Security Council, now admitted to Gandhi that he realized that Pakistan could never win a war with India (see Akbar 1991:179–80).

challenging the status quo against a larger adversary (India) that responded to the challenger's hostile behavior in a tit-for-tat manner. That impression is reinforced by the statistical measures of escalation in table 5.1 and the measures of reciprocity in table 5.2.

The reciprocity scores in table 5.2 indicate a pronounced difference between the first three crises and the Bangladesh Crisis. In the first three crises the degree of reciprocity is quite high, reflecting their tit-for-tat character. The Bangladesh Crisis is another matter. The high distance score (26.29) in table 5.2 indicates the extent to which India led in hostility, with Pakistan responding in kind but at a considerably lower magnitude.

It is possible to offer a straightforward realpolitik explanation for the observed behavior patterns based on four crisis structures. Both sides viewed the state of Kashmir as a vital security interest. Following the Indian military intervention in response to the 1947 invasion by the Pathen tribesmen, India gradually incorporated Kashmir into the Indian federation. Pakistan's government found itself faced with an increasingly intolerable status quo. To make matters worse for Pakistan, India enjoyed a considerable advantage in military manpower. When Pakistan challenged India in the Rann of Kutch in 1965, India prudently accepted a cease-fire because the fighting ground favored Pakistan and the strategic stakes were not worth the costs of a larger war. Pakistan mistook its success in the Rann of Kutch hostilities as proof of its military superiority; consequently, it accepted a high risk of war by attempting to create a crisis in Kashmir through its thinly disguised military incursion in the summer of 1965. This time the stakes warranted a major Indian military commitment, and the hostilities escalated to a war that ended only through the outside pressure of the major powers. The civil war between West and East Pakistan in 1971 offered India an opportunity to aid in the dismemberment of its principal adversary by supporting the Bangladeshi independence movement, initially through political support and covert military aid to the Mukti Bahini and ultimately through military intervention. Thus, from a realpolitik perspective, the behavior of the two sides over the first three crises can be explained by each side's calculation of the interests at stake and costs and risks of different courses of action.

Influence Strategies and Diplomacy

A realpolitik interpretation of the Indo-Pakistani crises gains further credence when the influence strategies of the two sides are considered. Table 5.3 lists the predominant influence strategy employed by each side in each of the four crises along with the crisis outcome.

With just one exception, each of the parties employed Bullying or

Cautious Bullying strategies in all four crises. The exception is the use of a Reciprocating strategy by Pakistan in its bargaining with India during the Bangladesh Crisis, although Pakistan did employ a Bullying influence strategy in its dealings with the Awami League in East Pakistan.

The overall pattern in table 5.3 shows Pakistan moving to more aggressive Bullying strategies at the start of the Rann of Kutch Crisis and during the Second Kashmir Crisis, as Pakistani confidence in its military capabilities grew, and then moving back to a Reciprocating strategy in the Bangladesh Crisis, when Yahya Khan's government recognized that it was militarily overmatched by India. India, conversely, moved to a Bullying strategy in the Second Kashmir Crisis and then took an even more aggressive approach in the Bangladesh Crisis (see figure 5.4). Adjustments in the degree of aggressiveness in the strategies of the two sides reflect their perceptions of their relative war-fighting capabilities; their increasing reliance on military means of influence reflects a pessimistic appraisal of their ability to achieve their goals through peaceful means. Table 5.4 depicts the proportion of each crisis that was devoted to direct talks between the two sides along with efforts to enlist the diplomatic support of one or the other superpower.

The figures in table 5.4 are the number of days the parties met in face-to-face talks to discuss the resolution of the crisis and the percentage of

TABLE 5.3.   India-Pakistan: Influence Strategies and Outcomes

Crisis	India	Pakistan	Outcome
First Kashmir	Cautious Bullying	Cautious Bullying	Indian Victory[a]
Rann of Kutch	Cautious Bullying	Bullying/ Reciprocating	Hostilities/ Pakistani Victory
Second Kashmir	Bullying	Bullying	War/Stalemate
Bangladesh	Bullying	Reciprocating	War/Indian Victory

[a]Officially a compromise, the outcome left India in control of most of Kashmir.

TABLE 5.4.   Negotiation and Mediation: Indo-Pakistani Crises

	Days (%)				
Crisis	India-Pakistan	India-USSR	Pakistan-U.S.	India-U.S.	Pakistan-USSR
First Kashmir	24 (5.5)	0	0	0	0
Rann[a]	17 (10.8)	0	0	0	0
Second Kashmir[b]	0	1 (.06)	1 (.06)	1 (.06)	0
Bangladesh	0	16 (.57)	15 (.54)	5 (.18)	1 (.04)

[a]Talks began in June, under the auspices of British mediation.
[b]The Soviet mediation, which began after the onset of war, is not included.

total days in the crisis that those talks represented. There are two intriguing patterns in table 5.4. One is the dramatic drop-off in direct Indo-Pakistani negotiations after the first two crises; the other is the effort to use one
of the two superpowers to intervene diplomatically in the Bangladesh Crisis. The statistics reflect the behavior of two parties that stopped attempting to resolve their crises through direct negotiations and relied increasingly on military coercion and the diplomatic intervention of outside
powers to keep the military hostilities within bounds.

That interpretation is generally supported by the analysis in the preceding case studies. Bilateral negotiations between India and Pakistan in
the first two crises went nowhere until a cease-fire was arranged through
outside mediation, by the United Nations in the First Kashmir Crisis and
by Great Britain in the Rann of Kutch Crisis. The two sides abandoned
any attempts at direct negotiations during the Second Kashmir Crisis.
Pakistan initiated the crisis with a military challenge, and India responded
militarily by expanding the theater of battle into West Pakistan. Pakistan's
willingness to accept the risk of war with its larger adversary in the Second
Kashmir Crisis was based on the country's expectation that superpower
intervention would lead to an early cease-fire.

The Bangladesh Crisis differs from the other three Indo-Pakistani
crises in that Pakistan, recognizing its precarious military position,
attempted to employ diplomatic means to avoid a war with India; nevertheless, those diplomatic efforts were directed through third parties, most
notably the United States, rather than through direct talks with Indian
representatives.

During the intervals between the four crises, Pakistan attempted to
internationalize the issue by calling for outside mediation. The attempt to
internationalize the issue is a common tactic chosen by weaker parties in
interstate crises, particularly when the party calling for the diplomatic
intervention believes that it has the stronger moral or legal argument—in
this case, Pakistan's call for Kashmiri self-determination through a
plebiscite. The intervention of the outside power can offset the diplomatic
advantage of the stronger, satisfied power.

It is clear from this summary as well as from the case studies that
India and Pakistan both viewed their relationship from a strictly competitive perspective. That attitude led each country to abandon attempts to
find a negotiated solution to their differences in favor of strengthening
their relative military capabilities. Although each side behaved in a manner consistent with its perceived interests, the strictly competitive bargaining was dysfunctional insofar as the peaceful management of interstate
crises is concerned. When the crises are viewed from a realpolitik perspec-

tive, it can be argued that Pakistan succeeded in effectively using its military power to achieve a diplomatic gain in the Rann of Kutch Crisis, and India's interventions in both the First Kashmir Crisis and the Bangladesh Crisis served its immediate security interests. It also can be argued that Pakistan's failure to achieve its objective in the Second Kashmir Crisis resulted from an inaccurate calculation of its comparative military capabilities. But a realpolitik analysis does not explain why India and Pakistan never broke away from the zero-sum perception of their relationship that continues to poison their relations to this day. That question leads to the third of our research questions: What, if anything, did the parties learn from their crisis experiences?

Learning

If ever there was a rivalry in which hostility begot greater hostility, it is the Indo-Pakistani rivalry. Beginning with the communal violence that accompanied the partition of the Indian subcontinent and continuing through the hostilities in the First Kashmir war, the Rann of Kutch Crisis, and the Second Kashmir war to the outbreak of the Bangladesh war, mutual distrust and animosity were reinforced with each successive crisis. Each side remained wedded to its belief that the other side was implacably hostile. That the central issue in the ongoing dispute—the status of Kashmir—represented a vital security interest to each side added to each side's zero-sum perspective.

The lessons drawn from one crisis led to misperceptions of intentions and miscalculations of comparative military power in the next crisis. When the Pathen tribesmen entered Kashmir, India assumed that the action was part of a plan by Pakistan to seize Kashmir by force; when India intervened on the side of the Singh government, the Pakistani leadership interpreted the action as the first step in an Indian attempt to reunite the subcontinent under Hindu rule. The experience of the First Kashmir Crisis and the Indian leadership's interpretation of the Rann of Kutch hostilities as a Pakistani test of its military forces led India to misinterpret Pakistani intentions in the Second Kashmir Crisis. When Pakistan sent irregular forces into Kashmir in the summer of 1965 in an effort to create sufficient domestic unrest to force negotiations to obtain a plebiscite, India interpreted that action as the first phase of a military campaign to seize Kashmir by force.

On the other hand, modest military successes encouraged both sides to overestimate their comparative military capabilities. India became complacent in the face of its modest success in the First Kashmir war and because of its manpower advantage. The Indian attitude resembled that of Israel after its military victory and occupation of the Sinai following the 1967 war. With India's occupation of most of Kashmir and its presumed military superiority, its government saw no need to find common ground with Pakistan over Kashmir.

Ayub Khan and his advisers' belief that India's Hindu troops could not match the fighting spirit of Pakistan's Muslim army skewed the perception of Pakistan's comparative military strength. The perception was reinforced by the Pakistani army's successes on the favorable terrain on which it engaged Indian forces in the Rann of Kutch Crisis. Together these perceptions encouraged Pakistan's high-risk strategy in the Second Kashmir Crisis.

Ayub Khan's risk acceptance in the Second Kashmir Crisis was also influenced by a lesson drawn from the diplomatic intervention of the major powers in the first two Indo-Pakistani crises. He expected that if the situation within Kashmir could be destabilized to the point of a crisis, the major powers would intervene to force negotiations. Ayub wanted, as an adviser put it, to "defreeze the Kashmir problem, weaken Indian resolve and bring her to the conference table" (Gauhar 1996:216). India, however, repeated the same strategy that it had used in a similar situation in the First Kashmir Crisis and immediately sent its troops into Kashmir to block any further action by Pakistan. But this time the Pakistani government responded by attacking a key post in Indian-occupied Kashmir.

After the Second Kashmir war, both parties took a more sober view of the situation, but neither initiated attempts to find diplomatic means of resolving the differences. Instead, the two countries competed in courting the superpowers' military aid and political support and in building up military strength for the next confrontation. Each side sought outside diplomatic support in the Bangladesh Crisis, but their relations with each other were based strictly on power politics.

Overestimating the hostile intentions of the adversary while underestimating its comparative military capabilities is the worst possible combination of misjudgments insofar as the peaceful resolution of a militarized crisis is concerned. It also may be a relatively common problem between adversaries intent on demonstrating their superior resolve to each other. In their pioneering study of the crisis leading to World War I, Holsti, North, and Brody (1968) found the same perceptual problem occurring in the governments of Austria and Germany as the 1914 crisis escalated. In the Indo-Pakistani case, this problem pervaded the two countries' perceptions of each other throughout the recurring crises between 1947 and 1971.

In sum, if the objectives of crisis management are to resolve disputes peacefully without escalating the intensity of hostility and the risk of war, the lessons that India and Pakistan drew from their crisis experiences were decidedly dysfunctional. And the decisive 1971 Indian victory did not bring an end to the rivalry. Within a short period of time, both sides began programs to develop nuclear weapons.

The Superpowers

Superpower participation in the Indo-Pakistani rivalry grew out of the U.S.-Soviet Cold War competition, and the military assistance provided to India and Pakistan added to the tension and distrust between the rival states. The United States initially sought a military alliance with Pakistan to strengthen the U.S. position vis-à-vis the two communist giants in the region, the Soviet Union and China. But that alliance, along with the military assistance that Pakistan received from the United States, encouraged the Pakistani military initiatives in the two 1965 crises. The American-Pakistani alliance also persuaded India, a strong proponent of nonalignment, to become a military client of the Soviet Union. When Pakistan developed friendlier relations with China, the United States began supplying aid to India as well. Pakistan then moved to improve its relations with the Soviet Union. Eventually, both superpowers were supplying military aid to both India and Pakistan. When the Indo-Pakistani crises escalated to war in 1965 and 1971, the military aid supplied by the superpowers contributed to the severity of the hostilities.

The United States and the Soviet Union shared coincidental interests in avoiding the escalation of the recurring crises to wars that could lead either to a superpower confrontation or to the military intervention of China. By 1965 both the United States and the USSR also were attempting to court both India and Pakistan, and neither the Americans nor the Soviets wanted to be forced to choose sides in an expanding Indo-Pakistani war. When each of the first three crises escalated to hostilities, the two superpowers and Great Britain collaborated to bring about cease-fires before the hostilities expanded to major wars. Unfortunately, as noted earlier, these efforts had the ironic effect of encouraging greater risk-taking by Pakistan in the two 1965 crises. A Soviet promise of support in the summer of 1971 encouraged India to resort to the use of force in the Bangladesh Crisis. Confidence in intervention by the major powers, either on their own or through the United Nations Security Council, reduced the sense of urgency as the crises escalated. That confidence also encouraged India and Pakistan to appeal to the Security Council or to one or both of the superpowers rather than to pursue bilateral negotiations.

The Ongoing Rivalry

More than a quarter of a century after the Bangladesh war, the future of Kashmir remains unresolved. The independence movement in Kashmir gained international prominence in December 1989 with the kidnapping of the daughter of the Indian home-affairs minister. By the middle of 1990, violent clashes between separatist groups and Indian paramilitary units were occurring almost daily. From 1990 to 1998 the separatist movement in Kashmir mounted an ongoing campaign of strikes, protests, kidnappings, assassinations, and other acts of terrorism. The Indian government responded almost in kind. In moves that are reminiscent of its actions to hide its support of the Mukti Bahini guerrillas in 1971, India expelled all foreign journalists from Kashmir in late January 1990 and announced in September of that year that it would not allow any international human-rights groups into the region.

Any Pakistani hopes for the accession of Kashmir to Pakistan died with its defeat in the Bangladesh war. After several efforts to achieve a negotiated settlement with India collapsed, Pakistan turned to open support of the Kashmiri independence movement. Pakistani Prime Minister Benazir Bhutto announced on January 28, 1990, that there could be no compromise with India over self-determination for Kashmir. Two days later the Indian government accused Pakistan of inciting the terrorist violence. By mid-April 1990, Indian and Pakistani forces had clashed in a series of engagements along the Kashmiri border. Diplomacy soon followed the pattern of previous Indo-Pakistani disputes over Kashmir. Bhutto toured foreign capitals in May 1990 in an attempt to gain support for Kashmiri independence. As Bhutto appealed for diplomatic intervention from the outside, the Indian government, as in the past, insisted that the crisis could only be resolved bilaterally between India and Pakistan.

Neither side, however, was interested in seeing the dispute escalate to hostilities, particularly now that both countries possessed nuclear weapons. The newly elected prime ministers of the two states, Chandra Shekhar in India and Nawaz Sharif in Pakistan, met late in 1990 and agreed to reduce the number of troops along the Kashmir border but made no further progress. Pakistan continued to demand Kashmiri self-determination; India continued to claim that Kashmir was an integral part of India.

Starting in 1991, the attention of Western governments was drawn to the Kashmir dispute by the separatists, who began a campaign of kidnapping and often murdering Western tourists. There also were a growing number of reports of human-rights violations by Indian troops in Kashmir. When a Hindu mob destroyed the Babri Masjid mosque in December 1992, the already strained relationship between India and Pakistan worsened. By May 1993 the Indian government turned over security in the Kashmir valley to the army.

India moved to a more conciliatory approach with the separatists in late 1994. The government announced in September that it was prepared to grant greater internal autonomy to Kashmir to end the separatist rebellion. The statement was followed by the release of four separatist leaders. But the Indian-separatist conflict escalated again in May 1995 following the burning of the shrine of Charar-e-Sharif in a firefight between separatists and Indian troops. The Indian government responded by extending "direct rule"—that is, martial law—in the state of Jammu and Kashmir for another six months. By the spring of 1996, Kashmiri separatists were conducting terrorist activities within India proper. On May 21 a car bomb in New Delhi killed 19 people and wounded another 50. By 1998 the struggle between the separatists and the Indian forces had claimed between 30,000 and 50,000 lives (Burns 1998b).

On June 5, 1996, the new Indian prime minister, Dev Gowda, announced a "policy blueprint" stating that peace could be brought to Kashmir by granting Kashmiri citizens maximum autonomy while retaining Kashmir's status as a province of India. Pakistan, meanwhile, returned to the diplomatic strategy that it pursued in previous disputes by urging outside mediation by the United States. And, as in the previous disputes, India continued to insist on bilateral talks. Bilateral talks began in New Delhi on March 28, 1997, and broke off three days later. When talks resumed on April 9, Indian and Pakistani troops were engaged in clashes across the Kashmiri border; they continued for six days. The prime ministers of the two states met again in May and agreed to release each other's nationals from prison and to set up a hot line between the two governments.

Tensions between the two countries flared in early 1998, when a Hindu nationalist government was voted into power in India. The new prime minister, Atal Vajpayee, had once advocated using military means to gain control of the Pakistani portion of Kashmir and had campaigned in favor of upgrading India's nuclear forces. In early April, Pakistan test fired an intermediate-range ballistic missile that could reach deep into Indian territory. Then on May 11, India set off three underground nuclear explosions. Although neither India nor Pakistan had signed the 1996 Comprehensive Nuclear Test Ban Treaty, the tests broke a worldwide moratorium. Two days later, India set off two more underground explosions. Tensions increased along the Kashmir cease-fire line, where the not-uncommon sporadic artillery fire across the boundary intensified. Despite strong diplomatic efforts by major powers, including the United States, to head off a nuclear arms race on the subcontinent, Pakistan followed suit on May 28 with five underground nuclear weapons tests of its own. The United States and international lending agencies applied economic sanctions to both countries.

Pakistani Prime Minister Sharif linked the Indian testing and Pakistani response to the long-standing issue of Kashmir, but India's leaders claimed that the principal reasons for upgrading its nuclear arsenal were the potential threat from China, an established nuclear power, and India's desire to achieve the diplomatic status of a major nuclear power. The Indian government also rejected new Pakistani demands for foreign mediation to resolve the Kashmir dispute, although Prime Minister Vajpayee said that he would welcome bilateral talks. Military leaders on both sides interestingly stated that the nuclear capabilities of the rival states now made another war over Kashmir "unthinkable" (Burns 1998a:1).

The tensions between the two sides eased during the summer of 1998, and when the United Nations General Assembly session began in late September, the prime ministers of the two states announced their intentions to sign the Comprehensive Test Ban Treaty within the next year in return for an end to the economic sanctions. The two states also announced that they had agreed to establish a hot line to insure better communication and to reduce the sporadic shelling across the Kashmir cease-fire line, and they stated that they would return to discussions regarding the status of Kashmir in the following weeks. Neither side, however, gave any indication that its basic position on Kashmir had changed. Tensions flared again in the late spring of 1999 when India conducted bombing raids against Kashmir's separatists along the border between the Indian and Pakistani sectors of Kashmir.

In many respects, little has changed in the behavior of the two rival states. The pattern includes tensions within Kashmir, Pakistani support of the separatists, India's use of military "direct rule" to maintain order, Pakistan's continuing efforts to internationalize the dispute, India's rejection of any outside mediation, and border clashes. There is, however, a significant difference. Over the past decade, both sides have been willing—even eager—to maintain open communication and ongoing negotiations to manage the rivalry if not resolve it. Both sides have made it clear that they do not want another war over Kashmir, and they appear willing to work together to prevent it. If nothing else, the two sides appear to have learned something about the costs and consequences of war and the need for ongoing communication to prevent its recurrence.

CHAPTER 6

Behavior, Learning, and Realpolitik

The underlying theme to this study has been that patterns of behavior and learning run through the recurring crises within each rivalry and across the three rivalries and that those patterns stem from realpolitik beliefs shared by policymakers. That theme will be highlighted in this chapter as it draws together the study's findings to answer the five questions posed in chapter 1.

The discussion that follows is divided into three sections. The first section focuses on crisis behavior per se, with particular attention to the control of escalation and the role played by the superpowers in each of the other two rivalries. Each rivalry is reviewed briefly before drawing some conclusions regarding crisis behavior and the management of crises across the three rivalries. The second section focuses on learning: when learning occurred, when it was most likely to be applied, and what types of lessons were learned. The third section turns to the central question of the study: How did the lessons drawn by policymakers from their crisis experiences affect their management of subsequent crises? It concludes that the crisis diplomacy in all three rivalries was based on realpolitik beliefs and that key policymakers in the rival states were predisposed to draw lessons from their crisis experiences that were consistent with those beliefs. When policymakers learned from their crisis experiences, the learning most often encouraged behavior that reinforced the hostility between the rival states and fueled the escalation of subsequent crises.

Patterns of Behavior

Patterns within Rivalries

The first two questions posed in chapter 1 asked whether there were significant changes in behavior from one crisis to the next within each of the rivalries and, if so, whether those changes led to more or less effective crisis management.

The answer to the first question is mixed. Although significant changes in behavior occurred within each of the three rivalries, the rival states also tended to repeat the same influence strategies from one crisis to the next. The answer to the second question turns on the definition of effective crisis management. If it is understood as the rival states' ability to resolve their crises peacefully with minimal hostility, only the Soviet-American rivalry offers any evidence of improved crisis management, and that evidence is mixed.

If the effectiveness of a state's diplomacy is defined according to the achievement of its objectives at an acceptable cost, the answer becomes more problematic because in three crises in the Egyptian-Israeli rivalry and two instances in the Indo-Pakistani rivalry, it raises the issue of whether it is appropriate to equate a successful war with effective crisis management. No less an advocate of realpolitik than Hans Morgenthau (1978:529) argued that "a diplomacy that ends in war has failed in its primary objective: the promotion of the national interest by peaceful means." Before answering the questions, however, it may be useful to review the crisis behavior in each of the three rivalries.

The Soviet-American Crises
At first glance, there appears to have been a steady progression to more effective crisis management in the four Soviet-American crises. War was avoided in all four crises, and each crisis was significantly shorter than its predecessor.

It would be a tidy pattern were it not for the fact that the third Soviet-American crisis, the Cuban Missile Crisis, ranks second on the composite escalation measure and next to last in the intensity of negotiation. As table 6.1 illustrates, the rate of escalation in the Cuban Missile Crisis is, in fact, the highest of any of the crises in the three rivalries. The Cuban Missile Crisis came the closest of any of the superpower crises to spiraling out of control, with the actions of both sides confounded by misperceptions and emotional reactions.

Two intriguing patterns emerge from the bargaining in the Soviet-American crises. First, each of the first three crises included a Soviet attempt to alter the strategic status quo through a military fait accompli: Stalin's blockade of West Berlin in 1948–49; Khrushchev's construction of the Berlin Wall in 1961, and Khrushchev's placement of offensive missiles in Cuba in 1962. Second, within each of the first three Soviet-American crises, efforts to reach a negotiated settlement did not commence until the crisis was deadlocked—that is, after each side had demonstrated its resolve through verbal threats and displays of force.

The Alert Crisis, which was the last Soviet-American crisis, was notable not only for its short duration and low escalation of hostility but also for the intensity of negotiation and the absence of inflammatory rhetoric and public threats. Based on the observed behavior patterns alone, if the rapid escalation of the Cuban Missile Crisis represented a step backward in the management of the superpower crises, the Alert Crisis was a step forward.

The Egyptian-Israeli Crises

Not only did all of the Middle East crises end in war, but, with the exception of the Six Day War crisis, they did so at a low level of escalation. As table 6.1 illustrates, the other three Egyptian-Israeli crises rank near the bottom in a ranking of the composite escalation scores for the 12 crises in the study.

It is not hard to find an explanation for the pattern. All three crises crossed the threshold of war as the result of an attack planned by one of the participants before the crisis began to escalate. The exception is the 1967 crisis, which exhibits the fifth-highest composite escalation score among the crises in the three rivalries and the third-highest rate of escalation, after the Cuban Missile and Bangladesh Crises (table 6.1). The only Egyptian-Israeli crisis in which neither of the two sides planned on war from the start, the 1967 crisis rapidly escalated in the final three weeks before Israel launched its preemptive attack.

If effective crisis management is understood to be the ability of two states to resolve their disputes peacefully with a low level of escalation, Egypt and Israel failed miserably. If crisis management is judged accord-

TABLE 6.1. Crisis Escalation Rankings across Rivalries

Crisis	Composite Rank	Magnitude Score (Rank)	Intensity Score (Rank)	Rate Score (Rank)
Berlin Blockade, 1948–49	1	380.50 (1)	268.51 (1)	3.53 (8)
Bangladesh, 1971	2	318.00 (2)	101.29 (3)	7.99 (2)
Cuban Missile, 1962	3	192.50 (4)	87.57 (4)	11.77 (1)
First Kashmir, 1947–48	4	307.00 (3)	180.00 (2)	4.60 (4)
Six Day, 1967	5	190.00 (5)	15.10 (11)	6.27 (3)
Berlin Wall, 1961	6	137.50 (7)	66.94 (5)	3.76 (7)
Second Kashmir, 1965	7	139.50 (6)	21.83 (10)	3.87 (6)
Rann of Kutch, 1965	8	106.50 (8)	47.74 (6)	2.31 (10)
Palestine, 1947–48	9	91.50 (9)	24.85 (9)	2.86 (9)
Suez, 1956	10	65.00 (11)	11.41 (12)	3.94 (5)
October War, 1973	11	87.00 (10)	32.28 (7)	2.09 (11)
Alert, 1973	12	45.00 (12)	31.83 (8)	0.60 (12)
Mean		171.67	74.11	4.47
Std. Deviation		104.71	74.60	2.87

ing to the ability of an individual participant to achieve its objectives, the judgment is more complicated. In three of the crises, the party launching a surprise attack on the other achieved its strategic or diplomatic objectives. Israel achieved strategic successes with its surprise attacks in 1956 and 1967, and Egypt achieved a diplomatic success with its surprise attack in 1973. As a result, the issue reemerges of whether one can ever equate a war with effective crisis management.

Israel's 1956 surprise attack had nothing to do with the management of the Suez Crisis; Israel simply seized the opportunity for military collaboration with Britain and France. Israel resorted to war in 1967 because its deterrent diplomacy had failed. Thus, neither of Israel's military initiatives could be described as effective crisis management.

A stronger case can be made for Sadat's limited-war strategy in 1973. The militarized crisis resulted partly from Sadat's military maneuvers in connection with his "cry wolf" strategy. Egypt's actions during the crisis were designed to prepare the ground for the effective use of force. The use of force, in turn, was part of a larger diplomatic strategy, which included intensive efforts to obtain American and Soviet guarantees of a cease-fire that would provide the conditions for a negotiated return of the Sinai. Egypt was not successful from a strictly military perspective, but Sadat's strategy achieved its main objectives—to restore Egyptian pride and to convince Israel that it was militarily vulnerable.

The Indo-Pakistani Crises

It would be hard to find a rivalry that better fits the adage that hostility begets greater hostility than the competition between India and Pakistan. Each successive crisis reinforced the mutual distrust and animosity spawned by partition and the communal violence that accompanied it. Far from showing signs of improved crisis management, each successive Indo-Pakistani crisis escalated to a more violent conclusion than its predecessor. India and Pakistan's regular forces avoided direct combat in the First Kashmir Crisis; brief hostilities occurred within a limited area during the Rann of Kutch Crisis; the Second Kashmir Crisis escalated to a war that produced 6,800 battle-connected deaths. The last Indo-Pakistani crisis, Bangladesh, had the highest escalation score of any of the four crises (table 5.1) and ended in a war that produced 11,000 battle deaths (Small and Singer 1982:93–94).

The lack of improved crisis management can be related to each party's attachment to escalating coercive Bullying strategies. With one exception, both parties used Bullying, or Cautions Bullying influence strategies in all four crises. The exception was the Reciprocating Pakistani strategy for dealing with India during the Bangladesh crisis. Even in that crisis, Pakistan used a Bullying strategy in dealing with its other adversary, the Bengali separatists (table 5.3). As the rivalry progressed and the mutual animosity and distrust grew, both sides relied increasingly on military strategies. Communication declined with each successive crisis, with no bilateral negotiations between India and Pakistan in either of the last two crises (table 5.4).

If effective crisis management is viewed as the ability of two sides to resolve their disputes without escalation to hostilities and war, the states' crisis behavior was decidedly dysfunctional. Judged from the perspective of the pursuit of the interests of the participant states, the record is only marginally better. Pakistan's challenges over Kashmir in 1947 and 1965 resulted in outcomes that only weakened the Pakistani diplomatic and strategic position. Pakistan effectively used a combination of limited military force and diplomacy to obtain minor territorial gains in the Rann of Kutch crisis, but the outcome encouraged its high-risk strategy over Kashmir, which led to a costly war with no gains.

It is possible, however, to make both moral and realpolitik arguments in support of India's military influence strategy in the Bangladesh crisis. India's use of force can be justified morally as humanitarian intervention in response to the atrocities committed by the West Pakistani forces in East Pakistan (see Walzer 1977:105–7). There is an argument for the necessity of Indian involvement based on the economic and social predicament that the refugees created. And there is the realpolitik argument that India significantly improved its security by reducing the size of its main rival. India used the Mukti Bahini rebel forces to weaken West Pakistan's military position, while Indira Gandhi's diplomacy achieved global acquiescence to India's use of force in the fall of 1971. In that respect, one can make a case similar to that for Sadat's limited war in 1973. Under the circumstances, India effectively managed the crisis.

Behavioral Patterns across Rivalries

A comparison of the crisis behavior across the three rivalries indicates that the realpolitik beliefs held in common by policymakers in the rival states frequently result in similar influence strategies and tactics by states facing similar circumstances. The greatest similarities appear in comparisons of the Egyptian-Israeli and Indo-Pakistani crises. None of those four states shared the superpowers' fear of war, and their strategies exhibit some shared patterns in which diplomacy is combined with the use of force.

The ability of the rival states to control the escalation of their recurring crises is an important measure of effective crisis management. It also represents one of the major issues regarding the efficacy of a realpolitik approach to crisis diplomacy—that is, whether the determination of each side to demonstrate its superior resolve is likely to cause the conflictual behavior to escalate out of control. The findings from the recurring crises in the three rivalries are mixed but suggest that the loss of control is less common than critics of realpolitik claim.

A comparison of the Soviet-American crises with those occurring in the other two rivalries indicates that states in enduring rivalries can tolerate a high level of escalation without crossing the threshold to military hostilities, provided that both sides have a strong aversion to war. Evidence of the loss of control appeared in only two of the twelve crises. The outbreak of hostilities more often resulted from a deliberate military strategy that was chosen before the crisis escalated to a high level. Each of these findings is discussed in greater detail in the remainder of this section.

The Egyptian-Israeli and Indo-Pakistani Rivalries

It is not surprising that there are more behavioral similarities between the Egyptian-Israeli and Indo-Pakistani rivalries than between either of those rivalries shared with that between the superpowers. To begin with, the Egyptian-Israeli and Indo-Pakistani rivalries share several important relational and structural attributes. Both were interstate rivalries between contiguous states, which grew out of the communal violence that preceded independence and partition, and which were focused on territorial issues of vital interest to both parties. In each of the rivalries, there also was an imbalance in military capabilities that favored the party defending the status quo. With the exception of the military advantage favoring the United States, which was the party defending the status quo in the Cuban Missile Crisis, the superpower rivalry shared none of those attributes. But perhaps the greatest difference between the superpower rivalry and the Egyptian-Israeli and Indo-Pakistani rivalries lay in the perceived costs and risks of war. Both United States and the Soviet Union viewed war as potentially catastrophic. No policymakers in any of the four states in the other two rivalries shared that view.

Besides the violent outcomes of their crises, the Egyptian-Israeli and Indo-Pakistani crises share behavioral patterns in their mutual attempts to exploit the superpower rivalry. As militarily weaker parties challenging the status quo, Egypt and Pakistan sought to redress the military balance through assistance from the Soviet Union and the United States, respectively. Their rivals each responded by turning to the other superpower. Israel sought and received military aid from the United States; India received military aid from the Soviet Union. The challenger in each of the rivalries also sought to strengthen its diplomatic position by internationalizing the conflict through appeals to the United Nations Security Council and to the superpowers in particular to bring pressure on the other party to negotiate a revision of the status quo. The tactic is not uncommon for a weaker power. The appeal to an international body on moral or legal grounds shifts the focus of the issue away from strictly realpolitik considerations while evening the balance in bargaining power.

Creating Crises to Force Negotiations

When diplomatic efforts alone were unsuccessful, both Egypt and Pakistan resorted to military force to create crises. The crises were intended to place pressure on the other side but also to push the dispute to the top of the agenda of the superpowers and the Security Council. Pakistan employed the tactic in the Rann of Kutch and Second Kashmir Crises; Egypt employed it in the 1973 Middle East crisis.[1] The success of the strategy depended on major-power intervention to keep the scope and intensity of hostilities limited, to mediate a cease-fire before the superior armed forces of the other side turned the tide of battle, and then to open negotiations over the territory at issue.

The strategy worked for Pakistan in Rann of Kutch crisis, but the hostilities in the Second Kashmir crisis escalated to war, with Indian attacks on Pakistan itself before a cease-fire was arranged. The cease-fire mediated by the superpowers in the 1973 war was obtained only after Israel had turned the tide of battle in its favor. During the Six Day War crisis, Egypt's Nasser also counted on superpower diplomatic intervention to restrain Israel or to at least avoid any loss of Egyptian territory if the 1967 crisis escalated to hostilities. But the United States did not restrain the Israelis, who ignored Soviet threats and launched a preemptive attack that led to a decisive victory before the superpowers could obtain a cease-fire.

The Mixed Role of the Superpowers

In sum, the superpowers played a mixed and sometimes contradictory role in the Egyptian-Israeli and Indo-Pakistani rivalries. The U.S.-Soviet competition for influence in both regions led the superpowers to provide modern military hardware and training to the rival states' armies, thereby encouraging the military challenges of Israel in 1956, Egypt in 1967 and 1973, Pakistan in the two 1965 crises, and India in 1971. As the crises escalated toward hostilities, the superpowers' diplomatic efforts to restrain the two sides were unsuccessful. U.S. efforts to restrain Israel in 1956 and 1967 and Soviet efforts to restrain Egypt in 1973 were unsuccessful in the Mid-

---

1. Pakistan hoped for American diplomatic intervention in both crises, but the United States stepped aside in favor of British mediation in the Rann of Kutch crisis and Soviet mediation in the Second Kashmir war.

dle East, as were American efforts to restrain India and Pakistan from going to war in 1971.

The superpowers achieved some success in obtaining cease-fires to limit hostilities in the Egyptian-Israeli and Indo-Pakistani crises, either through U.S. and Soviet efforts or through the Security Council. But the diplomatic intervention had the ironic effect of providing a false sense of security to the challenging party. That sense of security encouraged Egypt's high-risk military challenges in 1967 and 1973 and Pakistan's in the two 1965 crises.

The Control of Escalation

Another way of judging the ability of states to manage their crises is by examining their control of the escalation of hostility. It also affords a means of considering the consequences of the realpolitik beliefs held by national leaders. As noted in chapter 1, realpolitik assumes rational, calculating behavior on the part of the crisis participants, whereas realpolitik's critics focus on the pathological effects of escalating coercive bargaining.

Social scientists working from a psychological perspective offer two prominent hypotheses for why the control of escalation is more problematic than conflict strategists taking a realpolitik approach suggest. The first is the "conflict spiral" hypothesis, which posits that the actions and reactions of the two states set in motion a sequence of escalating hostility that is self-generating (North, Holsti, and Brody 1964; Jervis 1976).

The second, the "stress-induced-hostility" hypothesis, focuses on the effects of the stress generated by tension, fatigue, emotional reactions to the other party's coercive influence attempts, and the pressure of time (Holsti 1972, 1989). The first major empirical study of crisis behavior, which focused on the 1914 pre–World War I crisis, found that the cognitive and emotional effects of stress, particularly fear and anger, grew as the national leadership became more engaged in the crisis (Holsti, North, and Brody 1968). As a consequence, the key policymakers were likely to overestimate the other party's hostility and to respond with greater hostility.

Suedfeld and Tetlock (1977) found evidence that crisis-induced stress reduces the "integrative complexity" of policymakers—that is, their ability to integrate large amounts of information and make subtle judgments. Under the stress of an escalating crisis, policymakers are more likely to rely on their existing beliefs regarding the other side's intentions and motivation rather than exploring a wider range of explanations. It should be noted, however, that other researchers conducting comparative case studies (Brecher 1993; Oneal 1988; Lebow 1981) have found little evidence that crisis-induced stress affects the quality of judgments during militarized crises.

The following section considers the applicability of these hypotheses to the behavior of the states in the three rivalries. The discussion is divided into two parts to consider two distinct but highly escalatory behavioral patterns: the symmetrical pattern of escalating tit-for-tat exchanges of a Fight and the asymmetrical pattern of a Resistance crisis in which one party leads in the escalation throughout the crisis.

A Fight escalates rapidly and symmetrically with each side responding in kind but at a higher magnitude to the coercive tactics of the other. Two of the twelve crises in the study exhibit a pattern that is consistent with the type: the First Kashmir Crisis and, in its final phase, the Second Kashmir Crisis. Although the First Kashmir Crisis exhibits the intense escalation of a conflict spiral, war was avoided. The reasons were partly fortuitous—the restraining influence of the British military officers who still led the armed forces of both of the newly independent states. But there also was ongoing communication between the governments of India and Pakistan so that the rival states never became completely locked into the escalating coercive exchanges that one would expect to find in a classic conflict spiral. The Second Kashmir Crisis, conversely, quickly escalated to war following the infiltration into Kashmir by Pakistani troops disguised in civilian clothes. The incursion triggered the Indian intervention, to which Pakistan responded with an attack across the cease-fire line, thereby beginning the war.

There is evidence in both crises that both sides' leaders overestimated their opponents' hostile intentions, but there is no evidence that the stress of the crisis per se induced those perceptions. The two sides overestimated each other's hostility throughout the rivalry. Nor is there evidence that the stress generated by the escalation of either of the crises weakened the cognitive abilities of the policymakers in either of the two states.

Four crises exhibited the highly escalatory but asymmetric pattern of a Resistance model of crisis escalation. Those crises were the Berlin Blockade Crisis, Cuban Missile Crisis, Six Day War crisis, and Bangladesh Crisis.

The Berlin Blockade Crisis does not fit either the conflict spiral or the stress-induced-hostility hypothesis. Despite its high escalation, the blockade crisis leveled off rather than spiraling out of control, and there is no evidence of stress-induced hostility (see Shlaim 1983:410).

The intense escalation of hostility in the Bangladesh Crisis between India and Pakistan came in the late summer and fall of 1971, after India had decided to resort to the use of force. India's decision, however, was not significantly influenced by the escalation of the crisis between India and Pakistan per se. There is some evidence in the behavior of Pakistani president Yahya Khan to support the stress-induced-hostility hypothesis but no evidence to indicate that it led to the outbreak of war. As the crisis worsened, Yahya began to drink heavily, and, on occasion, he publicly expressed his frustration and anger with "that woman," India's Prime Minister Indira Gandhi (Shaplen 1972:55). But Khan continued to seek a means of avoiding war with India until late November, when Indian troops crossed the border into Pakistan. Furthermore, Khan's perception that India was preparing to use force was accurate. The remaining two cases—the Cuban Missile Crisis and the Six Day War—provide better candidates for the two escalation hypotheses.

The Cuban Missile Crisis came close to escalating out of control. Moreover, its rapid escalation was consistent with the conflict-spiral hypothesis in that the crisis was driven by both sides' determination to demonstrate their resolve, with each responding in kind to the other's coercive moves. Three factors appeared to have been most significant in avoiding war: (1) a shared fear of the consequences of war, (2) communication between the two states throughout the crisis, and (3) the willingness of the challenging party (the United States) to moderate its demands with concessions to the resisting party. The first of those three factors was the key element. The shared fear of war prompted the leaders of the two superpowers to pull back from the brink at the last moment.

Emotional arousal and misjudgments of the other party's intentions played a role in the missile crisis. At crucial points during the crisis, each side overestimated the other's hostile intentions. But what one might view as misperceptions—American speculation that Khrushchev's moves in Cuba were linked to future pressure on Berlin, erroneous Soviet intelligence reports of an imminent American invasion of Cuba on October 26, American speculation that the downing of a U-2 reconnaissance plane over Cuba on October 27 was a deliberate Soviet escalation of the crisis, and Soviet fear of an American invasion of Cuba following the U-2 downing—were attempts to interpret the meaning of ambiguous situations and events. Despite the two leaders' initial emotional reactions, there is no evidence that any of the misjudgments resulted from stress-induced cognitive rigidity.

The Six Day War crisis of 1967 is the only crisis in the study in which the spiraling escalation led to a war that both sides sought to avoid. The crisis escalation in the last four weeks before the war is consistent with the conflict-spiral hypothesis. Once Egyptian troops entered the Sinai, Egypt's actions consisted solely of escalating military moves and verbal threats, to which Israel responded in kind. When Nasser ordered Egyptian troops to occupy all of the Sinai and to mine the Strait of Tiran, he was aware that he was accepting a very high risk of triggering a war. But as a number of commentators have surmised, Nasser's actions were driven by the escalating crisis (Mor 1993; Nutting 1972; Yost 1968).

Despite Nasser's bellicose rhetoric, there is no evidence that the stress induced by the crisis caused him to overestimate Israeli hostility, but the escalation of the crisis may have led him to overestimate Egypt's comparative military capabilities. Nasser also underestimated the Israeli leadership's risk acceptance. Based on his experience in the Suez Crisis, Nasser believed that Israel would not risk a two-front war (Syria and Egypt) without the major powers' direct military support.

The Israeli government overestimated Nasser's aggressive intentions, but that judgment was not stress induced, and it does not qualify as a misperception. As in the Cuban Missile Crisis, the information was ambiguous, to say the least. Furthermore, when Egyptian troops moved into positions across the Sinai and then mined the Strait of Tiran, Israel's security was directly threatened. Nasser's intention to destroy Israel when the opportunity presented itself was real; his rhetoric proclaiming that war was imminent in the last weeks of May, not to mention the military preparations for war in Egypt and Syria, were sufficient grounds for any prudent government to prepare for war. Launching the first strike was the most effective means of winning the war with the minimum Israeli casualties.

Taken together, the preceding cases provide evidence that the outcomes of only two of the twelve crises were significantly influenced by the dynamics of the escalation process and only one instance (Egypt in 1967) when the outcome was influenced by stress-induced emotional arousal or cognitive limitations. More often, a tendency to expect the worst from the adversary appears to have grown out of the insecurity, hostility, and distrust generated by the rivalry.

Conclusion

There were significant behavioral differences between the Soviet-American crises and those in the Egypt-Israeli and Indo-Pakistani rivalries. The Soviet-American crises were marked by a mix of influence strategies, with Cautious Bullying by only one side. With one exception, the intensity of bilateral negotiations increased over the course of the rivalry, and the crises escalated to a high level without crossing the threshold to hostilities. Three of the Soviet-American crises rank in the top half of the twelve rivalries on the composite measure of escalation in table 6.1.[2] Crises in the other two rivalries were marked by the use of Bullying influence strategies

---

2. The high escalation scores for the first three Soviet-American crises are especially surprising given the operational rules for calculating the escalation scores. The Soviet-American crises had the highest proportion of days of negotiation and no military hostilities. Negotiations, which qualify as cooperative actions, lower the hostility scores for both parties, whereas ongoing military hostilities are heavily weighted to raise the hostility score for each party.

by both sides, the absence of bilateral negotiations, and the outbreak of hostilities at a relatively low level of escalation.

The seemingly contradictory findings suggest three propositions about crisis escalation and war. The first is that it is possible for national leaders to tolerate a high level of escalation without crossing the threshold to the use of military force provided that both states' key policymakers put a high priority on avoiding war, as was the case in the Soviet-American rivalry. The loss of control associated with the conflict-spiral and stress-induced-hostility hypotheses may be relatively uncommon. Second, the key threshold in the escalation of a crisis to war appears to be the outbreak of military hostilities, which is not surprising. The use of hostilities crosses a key qualitative boundary in the use of coercion, whereas the boundary between hostilities and war is a less obvious quantitative distinction.

The third conclusion is that the use of force more often resulted from a premeditated influence strategy than from spiraling escalation. In seven of the eight Egyptian-Israeli and Indo-Pakistani crises, the party challenging the status quo either launched a premeditated attack to achieve its objectives by force (Palestine, Suez, Bangladesh) or used a limited amount of military force in an attempt to create a crisis to force a negotiated revision of the status quo (First Kashmir war, Rann of Kutch, Second Kashmir war, and the 1973 Middle East war). The decision to use force was reached prior to the rapid escalation of the crisis in each of those instances.

The superpowers scrupulously avoided military hostilities because of their shared fear of war. The Soviet Union, however, did resort to military fait accompli (Berlin Blockade and Cuba) or ultimatums (Berlin Wall) to challenge the status quo in the first three Soviet-American crises. The high-risk tactics that the revisionist party used in all three rivalries illustrate the difficulty of achieving peaceful revisions of the status quo when each party views the relationship as a zero-sum competition.

These findings suggest that the states in the three rivalries approached crisis bargaining with greater consistency than might be suspected. The differences in the influence strategies and tactics in the Soviet-American crises and those in the other two rivalries can be largely attributed to their respective military capabilities and attitudes toward war. The strictly competitive strategies that were pursued in the eight Egyptian-Israeli and Indo-Pakistani crises did not change. If effective crisis management is understood to mean the resolution of crises without resort to the use of force, none of the influence strategies pursued in the Egyptian-Israeli and Indo-Pakistani crises led to improved crisis management.

The picture is a bit mixed in the Soviet-American rivalry. The Cuban Missile Crisis, which was the third of the four superpower crises, came the closest to ending in war. But the last superpower crisis, the Alert Crisis, is notable for both sides' awareness of the dangers of escalation, the intensity of communication, and the restraint shown in seeking peaceful resolution. However, the relationship between the superpowers had changed prior to the Alert Crisis, and the stakes were lower. Even then, superpower diplomacy was conducted within the bounds of realpolitik.

Learning

The final three questions posed in chapter 1 were directed to learning. Question 3 asked whether there is evidence of learning occurring within crises or of lessons being drawn from one crisis and applied in another. It is clear from the discussions in chapters 3–5 that the answer to that question is yes. Question 4 asked whether the states within rivalries and across the three rivalries drew similar lessons from their crisis experiences. The answer to that question is also yes. Policymakers' shared realpolitik beliefs, coupled with the highly competitive relationship created by the rivalries, predisposed policymakers in the six states to draw similar lessons from their crisis experiences. Question 5 asked whether the learning led to more effective crisis management. With one or two exceptions, the answer is no. The same factors that predisposed policymakers to draw similar lessons from their crisis experiences, along with misapplied analogies to individuals and past crises, led to learning that was dysfunctional in all but a few instances.

This section begins with a review of those instances in which policymakers purportedly learned from experience: from events during a crisis, from events occurring between crises, and from experience in or observations of previous crises. This section then considers when those lessons were applied in subsequent crises. As noted in chapter 1, there are many reasons why the lessons policymakers draw may not be put into action: political opposition within the policy-making body, competing domestic political considerations, a changed relationship with the rival state, and so forth. Those other factors include the changes (listed in chapter 1) within the state, in the relationship with the rival state, and in the regional or global environment.

A related question of interest concerns the types of lessons learned. Is there evidence of both diagnostic and causal learning—that is, changed views of the rival state and its intentions as well as of how to bargain with the rival state? Is there any evidence of complex as well as simple learning—that is, learning leading to changes in a state's understanding of the relationship with the rival state and the goals to be pursued as well as changes in tactics?

The chapter concludes with a discussion of learning and crisis management, including the relationship between learning and realpolitik. That discussion returns to the quantitative research (Leng 1983) that prompted this investigation and reconsiders that work's conclusions in light of this study's findings.

When Learning Occurred

Before attributing any changes in behavior to experiential learning, it is important to differentiate between policy changes that are simply adjustments to changed circumstances and substantive changes in beliefs. For example, India's declaration of "President's Rule" over Kashmir in December 1964 encouraged Pakistan's attempt to infiltrate troops into Kashmir in the summer of 1965. But the declaration did not change the Pakistani leadership's beliefs about India's intentions or how to bargain with India. The event simply added urgency to the Pakistani leaders' resolve to take more forceful action. The line between learning and adjustments to changed circumstances is often a fine one, particularly when accrediting events or situations to the reinforcement of existing beliefs.

Learning during a Crisis

Most within-crisis learning occurred during the Soviet-American crises, a finding that is not particularly surprising in light of the superpowers' mutual aversion to war, which did not exist in the other rivalries. The superpowers were intensely concerned with gauging the adversary's resolve, and most of the learning was related to interpretations of the other side's intentions. Khrushchev revised his view of Kennedy's resolve after Kennedy's public statement of his determination to defend Berlin; Kennedy revised his view of Khrushchev's risk acceptance after discovering Khrushchev's attempted fait accompli at the outset of the Cuban Missile Crisis; Brezhnev changed his view of American intentions during the Alert Crisis when Israel violated the cease-fire.

A different kind of learning occurred as the Cuban Missile Crisis rapidly escalated. Kennedy and Khrushchev became aware of the risk of the escalation running out of control and communicated their concerns to each other. It is more difficult in this case, however, to draw a line between learning and a mere adjustment to a changed situation. From their discussion at the Vienna summit, it is known that Kennedy and Khrushchev were aware of the risks associated with misperceived intentions and spiraling escalation before the Cuban Missile Crisis. Khrushchev dismissed Kennedy's concerns at the time, but the Soviet leader readjusted his thinking somewhat during the Berlin Wall Crisis, when he warned other Warsaw Pact leaders of the risk of pushing the American president into war. But until those risks became palpably clear as the Cuban Missile Crisis threatened to escalate out of control, the superpower leaders had been more concerned with signaling their resolve to avoid the risk that the other would underestimate their motivation than with communicating their desire to avoid war. Even though the escalation of the Cuban Missile Crisis was not an unknown phenomenon to the two leaders, its rapid acceleration changed perceptions of the degree of risk represented. Thus, the leaders' responses represented more than just an adjustment to the changed situation but also the application of a lesson learned during the crisis. As the crisis reached its peak, the two parties moved away from strictly competitive bargaining to a problem-solving approach (see also Lebow 1981:331).

One other instance of a changed perception that would qualify as within-crisis learning occurred in the 1967 Egyptian-Israeli crisis. Nasser's escalatory moves coupled with his bellicose rhetoric led Israeli leaders to change their views from their original perception that Nasser intended only a temporary show of force in the Sinai to the belief that he was preparing to attack.

Four of these five instances of within-crisis learning were cases of diagnostic learning. In each instance, one side's action caused the other side to perceive that it had underestimated the first side's risk acceptance or hostile intentions. Both Khrushchev during the Berlin Wall Crisis and Kennedy during the missile crisis were surprised by their adversary's risk acceptance, as were the Israelis by Nasser's move into all of the Sinai. Brezhnev was stunned by what he perceived to be Kissinger's hostile intentions during the Alert Crisis.

The learning by Kennedy and Khrushchev as the Cuban Missile Crisis escalated is the only case of within-crisis causal learning among the 12 crises. That the Cuban Missile Crisis is the only case in which the events in the crisis lead to causal learning prior to the outbreak of war reflects the different attitudes toward war held within the three rivalries.

Learning between Crises
The learning that occurred between crises was most often diagnostic—that is, it represented changed views of the rival state's intentions or capabilities. Khrushchev's conclusion from his 1965 Vienna summit with Kennedy offers a good example. Another example would be the Pakistani leadership's impression of India's war-fighting ability after India's poor performance against China in the 1962 Sino-Indian war. However, there were some instances of causal lessons as well. The Soviet Union was not a major participant in either the Suez or Bay of Pigs Crises, but what Khrushchev

interpreted as the successful outcome of his rocket rattling during the Suez Crisis and his threat to Kennedy during the Bay of Pigs operation encouraged the Soviet leader to issue an ultimatum on Berlin in 1961 (Zubok and Pleshakov 1996:242–43). Brezhnev's experience in dealing with Nixon and Kissinger during the SALT I negotiations encouraged the Soviet leader to expect to be able to collaborate with the United States in terminating the Middle East war in 1973. The Israeli government's experience with Egypt during the Rotem dispute of 1960 led the Israelis to conclude that Nasser's move into the Sinai in 1967 was another temporary show of force. When Sadat finally decided to use force to lay the groundwork for regaining the Sinai territory, he told his advisers that Israel's establishment of permanent settlements and fortifications convinced him that Israel would not budge without military coercion (el-Gamasy 1993:143).

More often, the highly competitive views that were formed during the first crisis in each rivalry—or even before the first crisis—were simply reinforced by the events that occurred between crises. Furthermore, it is difficult to separate some of these instances of learning from adjustments to changed relationships or circumstances. The spirit of détente that developed in the early 1970s, as well as the Soviet Union's newly achieved parity in strategic capabilities, changed the Soviet-American relationship in a way that encouraged greater collaboration and the avoidance of direct confrontations. While Sadat may have asserted that he learned about Israel's intentions with regard to the Sinai territory during the years before the 1973 crisis, he also was adjusting to the changed situation that followed the collapse of American and United Nations mediation efforts in 1971 and to his own failure to convince the United States to pressure Israel in 1972.

Lessons Drawn from One Crisis to Apply in Another
Chapter 1 described two potent influences on the types of lessons that individual policymakers are likely to draw from their experiences. The first influence is the policymakers' political beliefs, which predispose them to interpret political events and situations in certain ways. The second is the use of historical analogies. Policymakers tend to categorize situations by drawing analogies to past situations that they experienced, either directly or vicariously, so that historical analogies play an important role in learning.

Which historical analogy is chosen to fit a particular situation depends on the ease of recall and the policymaker's belief system. Ease of recall depends on the salience of the historical situation. A militarized crisis is likely to provide a salient historical analogy for anyone who was a participant or close observer. Three factors are likely to affect the probability that an analogy would be drawn to a previous crisis: the temporal proximity between the two crises, the similarity between the two situations, and the historical significance or traumatic quality of the crisis.

Other factors that are likely to be positively associated with the application of lessons from previous crises include a carryover of key policymakers from that crisis to the current crisis, lessons based on successful influence strategies and tactics in the previous crisis, and learning that reinforces existing beliefs. Some examples follow.

Temporal Proximity and Leadership Carryover
Temporal proximity and continuation of the same leadership between crises increases the likelihood that the lessons drawn by policymakers from the earlier crisis will be implemented in the current crisis. The Berlin Wall and Cuban Missile Crises and the Rann of Kutch and Second Kashmir Crises were the most temporally proximate of the crises in this study. They also were the only pairs of crises in which the same national leaders and key advisers on both sides participated in successive crises.

Both Khrushchev and Kennedy drew lessons from the Berlin Wall Crisis that were consistent with their behavior in the early phase of the Cuban Missile Crisis. The construction of the Berlin Wall probably suggested the bolder fait accompli that Khrushchev attempted a year later in Cuba. The fait accompli in Berlin worked because it had the advantage of surprise; it put the other side in the position of having to pursue a compellent strategy to reverse a new status quo, and it was backed by credible military deterrence. The same qualities would have been present in Cuba in 1962 had the United States had not prematurely discovered the offensive missile installations.

The most salient lesson that Kennedy drew from the Berlin Wall Crisis was the importance of demonstrating his resolve to discourage the Soviets from attempting to bully the Americans in a subsequent crisis (Schlesinger 1965:391). The lesson reinforced Kennedy's existing belief in the importance of negotiating from strength. Conversely, Khrushchev's verbal bullying over Berlin led Kennedy and his advisers to perceive the Soviet leader as something of a loose cannon with whom communications would have to be handled with great care (Blight and Welch 1989:34). The lesson was reinforced vicariously by Kennedy's reading of accounts of the pre–World War I crisis, (R. Kennedy 1969:62). Kennedy's determination to clearly demonstrate his resolve found its expression during the Cuban Missile Crisis in his October 22 "quarantine" speech and in the blockade.

The temporal proximity of the crises and leadership carryover led both Pakistan and India to draw lessons from the Rann of Kutch Crisis that were applied in the Second Kashmir Crisis. Pakistani President Ayub

Khan repeated his Rann of Kutch Crisis strategy of using limited military hostilities to create the Second Kashmir Crisis. The Pakistani army's success against Indian forces in the Rann also reinforced Ayub and his commanders' belief that India's Hindu troops lacked the fighting spirit of Pakistan's Muslim forces. That belief grew out of Ayub's stereotypical view of the Hindus as pacifists. Pakistan's military leaders drew a similar lesson from India's weak military performance in its 1962 border war with China. Ayub also concluded from the Rann experience that creating a crisis in Kashmir would encourage outside diplomatic intervention by the superpowers, acting either on their own or through the Security Council, to mediate the Kashmir dispute. Finally, if the crisis should escalate to war with India, the Rann experience had convinced Ayub and his commanders that the Pakistani army would hold its own.

On the other side of the rivalry, the outcome of the Rann of Kutch Crisis and the public criticism that accompanied it convinced the Indian government to choose a more aggressive strategy in the next confrontation with Pakistan. Indian leaders also had drawn their own lesson from the outside mediation and ultimate arbitration of the Rann of Kutch dispute. They would not make the same mistake with regard to Kashmir.

The only other instance in which the same leadership stayed in place from one crisis to the next was in Egypt, where Nasser remained in command between the Suez Crisis and the Six Day War. Although the crises occurred more than ten years apart, Nasser's risk taking in the Six Day War crisis can be linked to lessons that he drew from the Suez experience, specifically his expectation of diplomatic intervention by the superpowers. Based on his conversations with the Egyptian president during the 1967 crisis, Nutting (1972:410) described Nasser as "still living in 1956."

Similar Situations
The second crises over Berlin and Kashmir appeared to the United States and India respectively to be highly similar to the earlier Soviet and Pakistani challenges to the status quo. The experience of the Berlin Blockade reinforced the belief, which had begun to take shape among Truman and his advisers in 1947–48, that the only kind of diplomacy the Soviet leadership respected was that based on power politics. Kennedy's advisers who had participated in the blockade crisis carried over that lesson to the Berlin Wall Crisis. Their influence, however, was diluted by the beliefs of Kennedy's new appointees and by Kennedy himself, who were more optimistic regarding the possibility of reaching a negotiated settlement on Berlin.

If the lessons they drew from the Rann of Kutch Crisis were not sufficient to propel India and Pakistan into war in the Second Kashmir

Crisis, both sides also drew historical analogies to the First Kashmir Crisis. The Pakistani government remembered how in that crisis as well as in the Rann, the United Nations Security Council had intervened diplomatically to mediate an agreement. The Indian leadership drew its own analogy to the First Kashmir Crisis. When Pakistani irregulars infiltrated into Kashmir in 1965, the Indian government interpreted the action as the beginning of an invasion of Kashmir comparable to the 1947 invasion of the Pathen tribesmen. The interpretation was encouraged by Pakistan's initiation of hostilities in the Rann of Kutch dispute just a few months earlier. India returned to the strategy that it had employed successfully in blocking the advances of the Pathen tribesmen in the First Kashmir Crisis—that is, military intervention. During the First Kashmir Crisis, Pakistan's regular forces carefully avoided direct hostilities with the Indian troops. But as a result of the confidence its leadership gained from the Rann of Kutch hostilities, Pakistan did not do so in the Second Kashmir Crisis. Thus, both states acted on lessons drawn from their preceding crises, and those actions caused the crisis to escalate rapidly to war.

Previously Successful Strategies
It is reasonable to expect states to repeat influence strategies and tactics that worked well in preceding crises, and my earlier quantitative study of crisis behavior (Leng 1983) offered empirical support for that hypothesis. The current study contains a number of examples of states repeating influence strategies and tactics that succeeded in preceding crises. India's repetition in the Second Kashmir Crisis of the interventionary strategy that it used successfully in the First Kashmir Crisis is a case in point. Israel's use of a surprise first strike in the Suez Crisis was repeated in the Six Day War crisis. Khrushchev's use of a surprise fait accompli in the Berlin Wall Crisis was followed by his attempt to install offensive missiles in Cuba. Pakistan used a variant of the crisis-provoking strategy it employed in the Rann of Kutch Crisis in the Second Kashmir Crisis. In one instance, the successful user of the strategy was the rival state. When it attacked across the Suez Canal in 1973, the Egyptian government copied the surprise first-strike strategy that Israel employed in the 1956 and 1967 crises, albeit with Sadat's innovative "cry wolf" approach.

Success in one crisis can encourage a state to misapply lessons drawn from that success to a different situation in a subsequent crisis. Egypt learned from its experience in the Palestine War that it could not defeat Israel in a full-scale war, and that lesson was reinforced by Israel's Sinai campaign in 1956. But Nasser also drew an unwarranted lesson from Egypt's diplomatic success in the Suez war. Based on the superpowers' diplomatic intervention in 1956, Nasser believed that he could count on the superpowers either to restrain Israel from attacking Egypt or at least to prevent Israel from achieving any territorial gains should a war occur. Nasser's faith in superpower diplomatic intervention encouraged the high-risk bargaining strategy that he pursued in the Six Day War crisis. But other influences were at work as well, most notably Egypt's defense commitment to Syria, Soviet encouragement, domestic pressures to take more forceful action, Nasser's concern with his status in the Arab world, and the rapid escalation of events after the UNEF troops were withdrawn from the Sinai.

Other examples of successful strategies in one crisis leading to disasters in another include the Pakistani success in the Rann of Kutch Crisis, which led to an unsuccessful war in the Second Kashmir Crisis, and Khrushchev's attempted fait accompli in Cuba, which grew out of the successful installation of the Berlin Wall. In each instance, the misapplication of a lesson drawn from a success in one crisis led to an unwarranted high-risk strategy in a subsequent crisis.

Success can also lead to complacency and missed opportunities. The lessons that Israel drew from the Six Day War were strictly military. The IDF's quick and decisive victory, and the expanded borders that came with it, reinforced Israel's reliance on a strategy of deterrence and, when necessary, military force. The Holocaust remained the historical analogy of choice, and Sadat was equated with Nasser, who had been compared to Hitler. The Israeli leadership overlooked the new Egyptian president's more limited objectives. Consequently, the Israelis assumed that Sadat would commit Egypt to war only when he had the capability to decisively defeat Israel. Based on the 1967 war experience, they also assumed that Egypt would not attack until the Egyptian air force could compete with the IDF. The Israeli government overlooked Egypt's option of relying instead on surface-to-air missiles. The Israelis drew the wrong military lessons from the 1967 war, but the more serious error was their misreading of Sadat's political objectives. Israel's zero-sum view of the rivalry encouraged a rigid deterrent strategy of retaining the strategic territorial gains from the 1967 war to serve as a buffer zone. That approach may well have caused the Meir government to miss a diplomatic opportunity in 1971 to make the first steps toward peace with Egypt without suffering the costs of the 1973 war (see Maoz 1998). Israel's leadership carried the lessons of the Holocaust one crisis too far.

Historical Significance

The lessons drawn from particularly significant or traumatic events are more likely to be remembered. Throughout the quarter century following World War II, the unsuccessful attempt to appease Hitler at Munich was the favored historical analogy of hawkish American policymakers. The use of the analogy figured most prominently in the Berlin Blockade Crisis of 1948–49, when American policymakers vowed that they would not allow Berlin to become the "Munich of 1948" (Shlaim 1983:212). None of the American policymakers participated in the Munich crisis, but they all had experienced its consequences.

If the Munich crisis represented the most salient historical analogy for hawks in the American government, for Israeli leaders the experience of the Holocaust overshadowed all other historical analogies. The foreign-policy lesson that the Ben-Gurion government drew from the Holocaust was that the Jews stood alone in a hostile world where their survival depended on their military capabilities and their determination. That belief was reinforced by the events that followed the creation of Israel: the Palestine crisis and war, the fedayeen border raids in the period after the war, the Arab economic embargo, the closing of the Suez Canal to Israel and those trading with it, the blacklisting of firms doing business with Israel, and, not least, Nasser's apocalyptic rhetoric.

Among the crises in the study, the strongest candidate for providing a salient historical analogy would be the Cuban Missile Crisis. This crisis's dramatic escalation, with its high risk of nuclear war, led to a heightened awareness of the risks of crisis escalation that carried over to the superpower diplomacy that led to the 1963 Hot Line agreement. But one cannot draw a direct line from the Cuban Missile Crisis to the improved superpower relations of the early 1970s. Détente can be attributed more directly to the Soviet achievement of strategic parity with the United States, the interest of both sides in reducing the costs of the nuclear arms race, the triangular relationship created by the Sino-Soviet split, and the American desire to reduce the Soviet Union's support of the North Vietnamese in the Vietnam War. There are more direct links between the Cuban Missile Crisis experience in 1962 and the 1972 BPA and the 1973 APNW. Détente made it possible to complete the agreements, but their content was based on lessons drawn from the Cuban Missile Crisis.

Brezhnev's expectation that superpower collaboration would bring an end to the 1973 Middle East war added to his fury when he thought that Kissinger had deliberately encouraged the Israeli violation of the cease-fire. Kissinger's response to Brezhnev's threat of unilateral action was moderate, and his public explanation of the American action on October 25 makes implied comparisons to the Cuban Missile Crisis escalation as something to be avoided. The Soviets' decision to seek a political solution to the crisis rather than respond in a tit-for-tat manner to the American threat reflected their awareness of the risks of escalation. The Soviets were less concerned with the Americans carrying out the threat than with the escalation leading to a military confrontation that both sides wished to avoid.

Some of the restraint shown in the Alert Crisis can be explained by the spirit of détente, the mutual respect of the leaders that preceded the crisis, and the absence of a direct clash of vital interests in the crisis. But Kissinger's remarks on October 25 as well as the Soviet decision to seek a political settlement rather than respond in a tit-for-tat manner to the American alert represented a mutual awareness of the risks of escalation (Israelian 1995:178–83).

A second candidate for providing a salient historical analogy would be the Six Day War for its impact on Egypt's goals as well as Sadat's strategy in the 1973 crisis and war. The trauma of the decisive defeat and the loss of territory to Israel convinced the Egyptian government to abandon its goal of recovering all of Palestine through a decisive defeat of Israel in favor of finding a means of regaining the Sinai territory.

Learning and Belief Systems

Particularly traumatic or historically significant events, such as the Munich Crisis, the Holocaust, and the Cuban Missile Crisis, can lead to lessons that become permanent parts of a policymaker's belief system. The causal arrow, however, can point both ways. Policymakers are more likely to select and draw lessons from those historical analogies that are consistent with their existing beliefs. During the Cuban Missile Crisis, for example, hawkish Air Force Chief of Staff Curtis LeMay argued for an American invasion of Cuba by drawing analogies to both the failure of the negotiated settlement at Munich in 1939 and the successful use of a military show of force by the United States in Lebanon in 1958, while the more dovish George Ball drew a negative analogy between an invasion of Cuba and the Japanese surprise attack on Pearl Harbor in World War II (May and Zelikow 1997:178–79, 121, 143).

Drawing a causal link between the lessons drawn from one crisis to behavior in another can be problematic, especially when the lessons reinforce existing beliefs. Is the observed phenomenon learning, or is it the use of a convenient example to support existing beliefs? The answer depends on the origin of the lesson and its specificity. Was the lesson drawn from the crisis experience per se? And, if so, did it prescribe a specific strategy that is observed in the next crisis? In all three of the rivalries, the first crisis experience exacerbated the distrust and hostility that existed between the two parties prior to the crisis and reinforced each state's competitive view of the relationship with the other party. That in itself does not constitute learning as it is understood in this study. However, it also does not rule out learning in which the lessons are consistent with those views.

Consider the case of Israel's Ben-Gurion. His decidedly realpolitik beliefs regarding Israel's relations with its neighbors grew out of the Holocaust and were reinforced by the Zionist struggle to create a Jewish state. The views that he expressed after the Palestine War, specifically that Israel stood alone in the world and could rely only on its own strength, were consistent with his precrisis beliefs. But it was the Palestine War, when Israel had to stand alone against the armies of its Arab neighbors, that convinced Ben-Gurion that Israel would have to rely on a strategy of military deterrence until its demonstrated power reconciled the Arab states to Israel's permanent place in the Middle East. Ben-Gurion was predisposed by his beliefs to draw the lesson that he chose from the Palestine War, but the Palestine crisis and war led to Israel's essentially military strategy, which would be reinforced by continued Arab attempts at coercion and displayed in action in the Suez Crisis and the Six Day War crisis. In fact, with the partial exception of the Cuban Missile Crisis, policymakers in the rival states drew lessons from their first three crisis experiences that were consistent with their realpolitik beliefs. The next section examines just what types of lessons they were.

Types of Lessons Learned

The fourth question posed at the outset of the study asks whether policymakers are likely to draw the same lessons from their disparate crisis experiences. There is, in fact, some consistency in the tendency of the states to draw lessons that lead to strategies employing similar coercive tactics across the three rivalries. The discussion begins with the diagnostic lessons drawn by the participants and then turns to causal lessons learned and then applied in subsequent crises.

Diagnostic Lessons

The choice of an influence strategy depends on the policymakers' perceptions of the other party's intentions and motivation or resolve. Those judgments, in turn, are affected by what each policymaker has learned from observing the behavior of the other party, particularly in other crises. One of the remarkable findings in this study is how often lessons drawn from one crisis experience lead to misjudgments in another: Israel's misreading of Nasser's intentions in 1967 and Sadat's in 1973, Khrushchev's misjudgment of Kennedy's resolve in the Berlin Wall Crisis, or Ayub Khan's underestimation of India's resolve and war-fighting abilities in 1965.

A plausible explanation for this phenomenon is that policymakers are predisposed to select those experiences that are most consistent with their belief systems and to interpret the behavior of other states according to those beliefs. The Israeli worldview formed by the Holocaust led the country's leaders to view Nasser as another Hitler and Sadat as another Nasser. Ayub Khan and his military advisers held a stereotypical image of Hindus as pacifists that was reinforced by India's poor military showing against China and in the Rann of Kutch hostilities. One reason why policymakers' political beliefs exert such a strong influence over learning is because information regarding the other party's intentions and resolve is likely to be incomplete and ambiguous.

The problem may be exacerbated by "attributional distortion." Actions by the other party that are consistent with one's beliefs are attributed to the other party's personal traits; actions that are inconsistent with one's beliefs are attributed to the pressures of the situation (Hayden and Mischel 1976). For example, Israeli leaders interpreted Nasser's actions during the crisis leading to the Six Day War as behavior consistent with their image of his aggressive character rather than as the result of pressure to act assertively to maintain his political prestige within Egypt and among other Arab leaders. When the Pakistani army achieved some military success against Indian forces in the Rann of Kutch, Ayub Khan and his advisers attributed the events to the superior fighting qualities of Pakistan's Muslim troops rather than to the battlefield conditions that favored the Pakistanis. Conversely, Khrushchev had concluded from Kennedy's behavior during the Bay of Pigs Crisis and at the Vienna summit that the inexperienced American president could be bullied. When Kennedy took an unexpectedly strong stand in defense of Berlin during the 1961 crisis, Khrushchev turned to a situational interpretation: Kennedy was reacting to pressure from hawkish elements in the military.

When policymakers in the rival states drew the wrong diagnostic lessons from experience, they most often erred on the side of overestimating their adversary's hostility. The inclination reflected the realpolitik beliefs of the key policymakers and the contentious issues at the center of the three rivalries. But the tendency also appears to have been exacerbated by the "psychological residue" left behind after each militarized crisis (Rubin, Pruitt, and Kim 1994: chap. 7). The hostile atmosphere created by coercive bargaining does not evaporate when the crisis is over, especially when the crisis escalated to hostilities or war and the central issue in contention remains unresolved.

The exception to this pattern occurred in the Soviet-American rivalry. After the Cuban Missile Crisis, the superpowers recognized that they each viewed war as potentially catastrophic and that they each were aware of the other's fear of war. The mutual awareness developed over the course of the rivalry, but the missile crisis, with its frightening escalation and both leaders' open expressions of their fears, removed any remaining doubts and ultimately led to the BPA and APNW.

Causal Lessons

Diagnostic learning is intertwined with the causal lessons that policymakers draw from experience. Lessons regarding the intentions and resolve of the rival state have direct implications for how to deal with that state.

With one exception, the causal learning had a decidedly realpolitik quality. In fact, with the partial exception of the Cuban Missile Crisis, the causal lessons that the rival states drew from their crisis experiences all involved the use of coercive, or deterrent, influence strategies. Three stand out: (1) the resort to force through a surprise attack, (2) the use of a fait accompli to alter the situation in the challenger's favor, and (3) the creation of a crisis or hostilities to force a negotiated revision of the status quo.

After its successful attack across the Sinai in 1956, Israel recognized the advantages of a surprise first strike. It applied the same strategy when it launched its preemptive attack on Egypt and Syria to begin the 1967 Six Day War. Egypt learned from Israel's success in that war and prepared its own surprise attack in 1973.

The fait accompli was Soviet leaders' strategy of choice. Stalin used a fait accompli in the form of a blockade to alter the situation in Berlin in an attempt to coerce the Western powers into abandoning their plans to introduce a separate currency in the western sector. Khrushchev turned to a fait accompli in the form of the wall in the course of the 1961 Berlin crisis. There is no direct evidence that Khrushchev's 1961 fait accompli was influenced by Stalin's, but the practical success of the wall encouraged the Soviet leader to attempt his more audacious fait accompli in Cuba a year later.

Stalin and Khrushchev deliberately created crises over Berlin in attempts to challenge the Western occupation of West Berlin. But most intriguing are the crises deliberately created or escalated by states challenging the status quo in the other two rivalries. In each of those instances, a militarily weaker party accepted a high risk of war by deliberately creating or escalating a crisis, with the expectation that outside powers would intervene to contain the hostilities and mediate a negotiated revision of the status quo.

Consider Pakistan's actions in the second and third Indo-Pakistani crises. The Rann of Kutch crisis, which was initiated by Pakistan, was a testing ground for the newly modernized Pakistani army. But the incident also provided a second example, in addition to the First Kashmir Crisis, of how outside intervention by the major powers could force a negotiated revision of the status quo. British mediation over the Rann provided a model for Pakistan's attempt later that summer to create a crisis to force negotiations over Kashmir, preferably through U.S. diplomatic intervention. The strategy did not succeed, largely because India had drawn its own realpolitik lessons from the Rann experience. One of those lessons was that India would not repeat the Rann precedent of agreeing to outside mediation or arbitration of the status of Kashmir. Another was that if hostilities broke out, India would not limit its military activity to the immediate vicinity of the crisis, as it had done in the Rann of Kutch Crisis.

Nasser did not create the Six Day War crisis, but his willingness to accept a high risk of war with Israel when he escalated the crisis was related to his confidence in the superpowers' ability and willingness to restrain Israel. This confidence grew out of Nasser's experience in the Suez war, when the superpowers forced Israel to withdraw from the Sinai. Obtaining superpower intervention to achieve a cease-fire and set the stage for negotiations over the return of the Sinai also was a central component of Sadat's strategy in the 1973 war. As Nasser's former deputy, Sadat was well aware of the superpower efforts to achieve early cease-fires in the 1956 and 1967 crises and of their mutual interest in avoiding the escalation of a Middle East war to a superpower confrontation.

Controlling Escalation

The conclusion to chapter 3 argued that the two superpowers drew both hawkish and dovish lessons from the Cuban Missile Crisis. The dovish lessons were related to the dangers of uncontrollable escalation and war. More specifically, those lessons were: (1) a strengthened recognition by both sides that each of them placed a high priority on avoiding war; (2) mutual awareness of the risks of crises escalating out of control; (3) the importance of ongoing communication to avoid misperceptions that could lead to uncontrollable escalation; and (4) the necessity of conducting the Soviet-American competition in a manner that would not lead to future crises.

These lessons are reflected in the Hot Line accord, the BPA, and the APNW, which were signed in the period between the two crises, and in the restraint shown by the two sides during the Alert Crisis. Unfortunately, the dovish lessons drawn from the Cuban Missile Crisis were the exception. None of the lessons drawn from any of the other 11 crises was directed toward the peaceful management and resolution of future crises.

Complex Learning

There are no instances in the three rivalries in which a state's crisis experience resulted in complex learning—that is, a change in a state's view of its relationship with the rival state or in the first state's goals. One might argue that the Soviet leadership's changed view of its relationship with the

United States, which occurred between the Cuban Missile and Alert Crises, was indirectly related to its experience in the Cuban Missile Crisis. But the Soviet expectation of a more collaborative relationship can be more directly attributed to détente and the working relationships that Brezhnev and Gromyko established with Nixon and Kissinger. Furthermore, the Soviets returned to a more competitive view of their relationship with the United States following the breakdown of the cease-fire during the Alert Crisis and in its aftermath.

Egypt changed its goals vis-à-vis Israel after the Six Day War, but the change was a consequence of the territorial losses that accompanied the war; they were not related to the management of the crisis that preceded the war. The crisis experience led to a shift in Egyptian tactics, most notably the design for a surprise first strike, but that was simple, not complex, learning.

Learning and Crisis Management

If one judges the management of a militarized crisis according to the capacity of the two sides to resolve the crisis peacefully with a low level of escalation, then only the learning that occurred in the Cuban Missile Crisis can be said to have led to more effective crisis management in a subsequent crisis. The other instance in the study in which there is a peaceful termination of the crisis with a lower level of escalation than the crisis that preceded it occurs in the Berlin Wall Crisis, but the changes in crisis behavior cannot be linked to learning from the Berlin Blockade experience. All of the Egyptian-Israeli crises ended in war. Each of the Indo-Pakistani crises was more violent than its predecessor.

The picture becomes cloudier if effective crisis management is judged according to a state's success in achieving its objectives at an acceptable cost. The lessons most commonly drawn by the states in the three rivalries prescribed more coercive bargaining in subsequent crises. There are seven cases in the study in which there is a demonstrable connection between the lessons drawn from a state's experience in one crisis and the adoption of a more coercive bargaining strategy in the next crisis. In five of the seven cases, the next crisis ended in war. The exceptions are the U.S. and Soviet strategies in the Cuban Missile Crisis.

In the other five cases, only one of the wars led to a low-cost military victory, Israel's surprise attack in the Six Day War. Nasser's high-risk strategy in the same crisis resulted in a costly military defeat. The other wars ended in stalemates. As a result of lessons drawn from the Rann of

Kutch Crisis, India and Pakistan both adopted more coercive strategies in the Second Kashmir Crisis, which escalated into a costly war that ended in a stalemate.

The exception may be Egypt's strategy combining limited war with diplomacy in the 1973 crisis and war. Egypt did not achieve a military victory, but Sadat achieved his political objectives. The "cry wolf" strategy prepared the groundwork for Egypt's early military successes, and Sadat's careful assurances to each of the superpowers regarding his limited objectives opened the door for successful U.S. and Soviet diplomatic intervention. Sadat's diplomatic strategy grew out of his experience as a close observer of the 1956 and 1967 crises. It was the only case in the three rivalries in which lessons drawn from preceding crises appear to have led to a coercive strategy that might qualify as effective crisis management.

On balance, the six rival states learned little from their first three crisis experiences, and the learning that did occur was most often dysfunctional. That finding raises the question of why such is the case. Why did it take a quarter of a century before policymakers in the rival states were able to manage their relationships without becoming engaged in recurring militarized crises and, in the Egyptian-Israeli and Indo-Pakistani rivalries, wars?

Why the Wrong Lessons Were Learned

The forces operating on the rival states' leaders that encouraged them to draw dysfunctional lessons can be placed into three categories: self-reinforcing hostility, the misapplication of historical analogies, and policymakers' realpolitik beliefs.

Self-Reinforcing Hostility

The crises occurred within three very intense rivalries with highly contentious issues at stake. The recurring crises and the coercive diplomacy that the rival states employed during those crises exacerbated the hostility that existed at the beginning of the rivalries. With the possible exception of the aftermath of the Cuban Missile Crisis, each successive crisis left behind a residue that added to the distrust and hostility between the rival states. Most often, crisis experiences increased the influence of hawkish policymakers, and encouraged efforts to increase the state's military preparedness (see also Lebow 1981:315–16).

The mutual hostility also led to a breakdown of communications that occurred after the first crises in the Egyptian-Israeli and Indo-Pakistani rivalries. The pattern of "autistic hostility" had the effect of perpetuating the distrust and animosity that led to the original interruption of communication (Rubin, Pruitt, and Kim 1994:107–8). When the opportunity arose to achieve a negotiated settlement between Israel and Egypt in 1971, Israeli distrust of Egyptian intentions had become too great for the Meir government to accept a trade of land for peace.

Misapplied Analogies

As demonstrated earlier, the analogies that Israel drew first between Nasser and Hitler and then between Sadat and Nasser led to misinterpretations of the intentions of the Egyptian leaders in the 1967 and 1973 Middle East crises. The more common error, however, was to overdraw analogies from one situation to another. Khrushchev's misreading of Kennedy's resolve was related to lessons that the Soviet leader drew from Kennedy's behavior during the Bay of Pigs Crisis and at the Vienna summit; Nasser overdrew analogies to Suez during the 1967 crisis; Israel overdrew analogies to Egyptian intentions in 1967 when it judged Sadat's actions during the 1973 crisis; Ayub Khan overdrew military and diplomatic analogies between the Rann of Kutch and Second Kashmir Crises.

These errors were exacerbated by attributional distortion in several instances. Khrushchev's attribution of Kennedy's behavior during the Berlin Wall Crisis to the young president's inexperience and Ayub Khan's attribution of India's military restraint during the Rann of Kutch Crisis to Indian pacifism neglected important situational factors because the personal attributions fit existing beliefs.

The rival states' leaders tended to overestimate the role of their own influence strategies, as opposed to situational factors, in determining crisis outcomes. The analogies also were most likely to be overdrawn when an influence strategy succeeded in a preceding crisis. Jervis (1976:278–79) has described it as the "nothing fails like success" phenomenon. Khrushchev's attempted fait accompli in the Cuban Missile Crisis and Ayub Khan's deliberate creation of a crisis in Kashmir in 1965 were the most obvious examples of the misapplication of a previously successful strategy in a subsequent crisis. The states in the study were just as likely to discard strategies that were not successful. Unfortunately, the changes most often were to more coercive influence strategies.

Realpolitik Beliefs

Policymakers in the rival states were predisposed to move to more coercive strategies partly as a result of the animosity and distrust generated by the rivalry but also because of their shared realpolitik beliefs. The relationship between those beliefs and learning warrants a fuller discussion. To obtain some additional evidence to facilitate the discussion, it is useful to return to the model of realpolitik learning that prompted this study.

Realpolitik and Experiential Learning

The REL Model

My earlier quantitative study of crisis behavior (Leng 1983) suggested that when policymakers learned from experience, the learning occurred within the bounds of a realpolitik belief system. Because realpolitik views the relationship between rival states as strictly competitive, the crisis becomes a test of comparative resolve, and crisis bargaining becomes a competition to determine which side will accept a higher risk of war to achieve its objectives.

The hypotheses in the realpolitik experiential learning (REL) model make three predictions. First, when a state's policymakers are satisfied with the outcome of the previous crisis (diplomatic victory or satisfactory compromise), they will repeat the same influence strategy in the current crisis. The hypothesis assumes that experiential learning will encourage the policymakers to repeat strategies that were successful in similar situations. Second, if the state's policymakers are unsatisfied with the outcome of the previous crisis (diplomatic defeat or unsatisfactory compromise) they will move to a more coercive influence strategy—for example, from Reciprocating to Bullying—in the next crisis. The second hypothesis assumes that the policymakers' realpolitik beliefs will predispose the leaders to interpret the unsuccessful outcome in the preceding crisis as a consequence of the state's failure to demonstrate sufficient resolve. Third, if the crisis ended in war and the state was the party defending against the attack, the state will move to a more coercive influence strategy in the next crisis to discourage another attempt at bullying. If the preceding crisis ended in war but the state was the party that launched the attack, then it will switch to a less coercive influence strategy in the next crisis to signal that the state is not preparing for another attack.

The earlier study was based solely on quantitative measures of crisis behavior drawn from the BCOW data. Therefore, it was not possible to determine whether policymakers drew realpolitik lessons from their crisis experiences or whether other factors caused behavioral changes consistent with realpolitik. The case studies in chapters 3–5 of this work demonstrate that the policymakers in the three rivalries almost invariably drew lessons from their crisis experiences that were consistent with realpolitik. With that added information and the addition of crises that were not included in the earlier study, it is worth considering how well the REL model fares in predicting the rival states' behavior.[3]

---

3. The earlier study (Leng 1983) included recurring crises from the three rivalries in this study along with three other rivalries; however, there are three crises in this study that were not included in the earlier study: the 1973 Alert Crisis, the 1973 October War, and the 1965 Rann of Kutch Crisis. The first two cases add another prediction to the Soviet-American and Egyptian-Israeli rivalries; including the Rann of Kutch in the Indo-Pakistani rivalry has the added effect of changing the order of the cases and, consequently, the predicted behavior.

The hypotheses can be tested against the crises in this study's three rivalries by comparing the influence strategies applied by each state in successive crises within its rivalry. The U.S. influence strategy in the Berlin Blockade Crisis, for example, is compared with the strategy in the Berlin Wall Crisis. The United States used Reciprocating influence strategies in both crises. The outcome of the Berlin Blockade Crisis, a diplomatic victory, was viewed as satisfactory. Therefore, the American behavior was consistent with the first REL hypothesis: repeat the same influence strategy when the outcome of the preceding crisis was satisfactory. A special case arises when a state used a Bullying influence strategy in a preceding crisis and policymakers perceived the outcome to be unsatisfactory. The second REL hypothesis predicts that the state will use a more coercive influence strategy in the next crisis. Since a Bullying strategy is already the most coercive of the types of influence strategies included in the study, it is impossible to move to a more coercive influence strategy per se. Therefore, it is necessary in those cases to compare the composite escalation scores for the state in the two crises to determine whether there is a significant increase in its coercive behavior.

Table 6.2 presents comparisons of the predicted and actual influence strategies in the second, third, and fourth crises in each rivalry. The entries in the predicted influence strategy and actual influence strategy columns refer to the coerciveness of the influence strategy. Plus and minus signs are used to indicate changes to more or less coercive influence strategies. "Same" indicates the predicted (or actual) use of the same influence strategy in both crises. The last column in table 6.2 indicates whether the state's behavior is consistent with the appropriate REL hypothesis.

Differences between the Rivalries
The REL model does remarkably well in predicting changes to more or less coercive influence strategies in the Egyptian-Israeli and Indo-Pakistani crises. All six strategy changes are correctly predicted in the Egyptian-Israeli crises, and five of six changes are correctly predicted in the Indo-Pakistani crises. The model does not fare well, however, in predicting the strategies in the Soviet-American crises. Only three of the six strategies are predicted correctly. In the other three Soviet-American cases, the state in question adopted a less coercive influence strategy than the model predicted.

The difference between the superpower rivalry and the other two rivalries lay in the states' attitudes toward war. Key policymakers in both superpowers felt that their states could suffer very high, even catastrophic, losses in the event of war; therefore, these leaders went out of their way to avoid war in all four crises. Whether the threat of nuclear war or the potential of a conventional war of the severity of World War II restrained the superpowers is an open question.[4] The behavior of the two sides during the Berlin Blockade Crisis, when only the United States had nuclear weapons, supports the latter argument. But the fear that gripped both Khrushchev and Kennedy during the rapid escalation of the Cuban Missile Crisis was based to a large extent on the specter of nuclear war.

The states in the other two rivalries held markedly different attitudes toward war. Egypt, which along with its Arab neighbors attacked Israel in 1948, did not consider itself vulnerable to the consequences of war until after the 1967 Six Day War. By that time, Israel was the party that considered itself invulnerable. Only after the 1973 war did both sides fear the consequences of war. As a result of intensive efforts to modernize and strengthen its armed forces between 1947 and 1965, Pakistan considered war a reasonable option against a foe with three times its manpower until

TABLE 6.2.   Realpolitik Learning Predictions and Observed Crisis Behavior

Crisis	State	Previous Crisis Outcome	Predicted Influence Strategy	Actual Influence Strategy	Agree with REL?
Berlin Wall	U.S.	Diplomatic Victory	Same	Same	Yes
	USSR	Diplomatic Defeat	+ Coercive	Same	No[a]
Cuban Missile	U.S.	Stalemate	+ Coercive	+ Coercive	Yes
	USSR	Stalemate	+ Coercive	+ Coercive	Yes
Alert Crisis	U.S.	Diplomatic Victory	Same	– Coercive	No
	USSR	Diplomatic Defeat	+ Coercive	Same	No
Suez	Egypt	War/Attack	– Coercive	– Coercive	Yes
	Israel	War/Defend	+ Coercive	+ Coercive[b]	Yes[a]
Six-Day War	Egypt	War/Defend	+ Coercive	+Coercive	Yes
	Israel	War/Attack	– Coercive	– Coercive	Yes
October War	Egypt	War/Defend	+ Coercive	Same	Yes[a]
	Israel	War/Attack	– Coercive	– Coercive	Yes
Rann of Kutch	India	Diplomatic Victory	Same	Same	Yes
	Pakistan	Diplomatic Defeat	+ Coercive	+ Coercive	Yes
2nd Kashmir	India	Diplomatic Defeat	+ Coercive	+ Coercive	Yes
	Pakistan	Diplomatic Victory	Same	+ Coercive	No
Bangladesh	India	War/Defend	+ Coercive	Same	Yes[a]
	Pakistan	War/Attack	– Coercive	– Coercive	Yes

[a]Crises in which the predicted influence strategy was more coercive but in which the most coercive influence strategy (Bullying), which was used in the preceding crisis, is repeated, so that a comparison of escalation scores determines agreement with the predicted change.

[b]Israel's escalation score during the Suez Crisis does not increase significantly, but because Israel was planning a surprise attack, the influence strategy is coded as more coercive.

<hr/>

4. For statements of the two perspectives, see Gilpin 1981:218 and Mueller 1989: 114–15, respectively.

Pakistan was decisively defeated in 1971. Ironically, one of the reasons that the challengers were so willing to risk the consequences of war in the Egyptian-Israeli and Indo-Pakistani rivalries is because they believed that the superpowers would intervene before the fighting reached the level of a general war. The irony lies in their belief that the superpowers would intervene because they feared being drawn into a conflict that could lead to a confrontation with each other.

Despite the different attitudes toward war, the crisis bargaining in all three rivalries occurred within the bounds of realpolitik. The bargaining in the Soviet-American crises was simply a more prudential realpolitik. The frightening escalation of the Cuban Missile Crisis led Kennedy and Khrushchev, in the final days of the crisis, to come very close to moving away from a strictly competitive approach to crisis management and toward problem solving. But when Robert Kennedy presented President Kennedy's "carrot-and-stick" ultimatum to Dobrynin for transmission to Khrushchev on the evening of October 27, the United States still was engaging in coercive diplomacy. The superpowers began the Alert Crisis with each mixing competition for influence with collaboration to achieve a cease-fire. But when the cease-fire broke down, the superpower bargaining again became strictly competitive, although both sides prudentially avoided further escalation of the crisis.

In sum, the lessons that key policymakers in each state drew from their recurring crises were all within the bounds of realpolitik: negotiate from strength; demonstrate greater resolve; change the situation through a surprise fait accompli; create a crisis to encourage outside intervention to force negotiations; attack first to achieve a military advantage. Even the few instances of learning that led to greater restraint were based on a prudential application of realpolitik. The Americans and Soviets found common ground in slowing their arms race and avoiding a direct confrontation, but the essentially competitive nature of the relationship did not change, as the 1973 Middle East crisis demonstrated.

The diplomatic policies of the superpowers vis-à-vis the other two rivalries also were consistent with the prudential side of realpolitik. Despite United Nations efforts to resolve the outstanding issues in the Egyptian-Israeli and Indo-Pakistani rivalries, the superpowers devoted most of their efforts between the crises to arming their respective clients. The superpower concern with avoiding a direct confrontation did lead to collaborative efforts to achieve cease-fires when the Egyptian-Israeli and Indo-Pakistani crises escalated to war, but the collaboration took place within the context of an ongoing competition for influence in the Middle East and South Asia.

Conclusion

The failure of the six rival states to learn to manage their crises in a more peaceful manner or to find common ground that would serve the interests of both sides can be attributed to two mutually reinforcing influences: the intensity of the rivalries and the realpolitik belief systems of key policy-makers in all six states.

The intensity of the rivalries made any search for common ground difficult. There were vital territorial interests at stake for both sides in the Egyptian-Israeli and Indo-Pakistani rivalries, and the superpower rivalry grew out of an all-encompassing strategic and ideological competition. The rivalries themselves and the crises that they generated added to the animosity and distrust between the rival states. But to argue that those factors ruled out any integrative solutions confuses the limited vision of national leaders with objective limitations.

The vision of rival states' leaders was limited by their realpolitik beliefs. Those beliefs led the leaders to perceive the crises in strictly competitive terms rather than as resolvable problems in their relationships with rival states. The policymakers' realpolitik beliefs and coercive bargaining strategies were mutually reinforcing. When policymakers learned from their crisis experiences, the lessons led to influence strategies that increased the level of conflict in future crises. States that found themselves challenging the status quo deliberately created crises through fait accompli or attempts to destabilize the situation. Status quo parties learned to react more forcefully to counter such attempts.

The traditional means of resolving interstate conflicts are through mediation and negotiation. There is a positive association between the intensity of negotiation and lower escalation in the superpower crises, but direct negotiations did not play a significant role in the Egyptian-Israeli and Indo-Pakistani rivalries. With the exception of meetings at the end of the Palestine War, there were no direct negotiations during the Egyptian-Israeli rivalry, and there was less and less direct communication as the Indo-Pakistani rivalry evolved.

Attempts at mediation by outside powers did not fare much better. There were no states with sufficient power to intervene diplomatically in the superpower crises. In the Egyptian-Israeli and Indo-Pakistani crises, the major powers had some success in obtaining cease-fires after crises had escalated to hostilities or war, but the United States and Soviet Union provided the arms to fight those wars and sent mixed messages during the pre-war crises. Moreover, the superpowers' interventions to contain hostilities had the perverse effect of encouraging challenging parties to take greater risks in subsequent crises. Policymakers in Pakistan and Egypt assumed that they could use more coercive influence strategies in future crises because they could rely on outside intervention to contain the level of hostilities. Their realpolitik beliefs predisposed them to view even efforts at conflict resolution in terms of competitive advantage.

If realpolitik is the problem, what is the solution? Can rival states learn to manage their disputes effectively without changing their realpolitik beliefs? Is it possible for rivals to learn to change their relationship by moving beyond realpolitik? The three rivalries in this study do not offer much encouragement for either possibility. Most of the lessons that they provide are cautionary. There are, however, two possibilities worth considering. The first possibility is based on a prudential realpolitik; the second possibility requires statesmen with vision that transcends the bounds of realpolitik.

The Limits of Prudential Realpolitik

The realist prescription for maintaining peace within a strictly competitive relationship is based on balancing power with power. But the weaker party often deliberately created crises or even began hostilities in the Egyptian-Israeli and Indo-Pakistani crises. The risk acceptance of the challenging states went well beyond what would be expected from a cool calculation of comparative military capabilities. Conversely, the United States and the Soviet Union avoided war in all four of their militarized crises, even though they were at strategic parity only during the Alert Crisis. The Egyptian-Israeli and Indo-Pakistani crises illustrate that motivation may override balance-of-power considerations in an intense rivalry. The Soviet-American crises demonstrate that two states with an intensely competitive relationship can tolerate a high level of crisis escalation and still avoid war. The United States and Soviet Union avoided war in four crises because they realized that they shared a fear of the consequences of another world war as well as a nuclear cataclysm.

The Cuban Missile Crisis demonstrated, however, that attempts to manipulate the greater tolerance for coercion that comes with a mutual fear of war's consequences can lead to spiraling escalation. The palpable awareness of that danger during the Cuban Missile Crisis led to the Soviet-American agreements on crisis management in the 1960s and early 1970s and to the more prudential approach to crisis bargaining in the Alert Crisis.

If one were to list the conditions necessary for the prudential management of crises within the bounds of realpolitik, they would be: (1) a shared aversion to the costs of war; (2) mutual recognition that the aversion is shared by both sides (to eliminate preemption); (3) recognition by each side that its rival is aware that it recognizes the rival's aversion to war (to eliminate preemption out of fear of preemption by the other party); and (4) a mutual awareness of the dangers of tit-for-tat coercive exchanges leading to uncontrollable escalation. The United States and Soviet Union were well aware of the first two conditions before the Cuban Missile Crisis. The communication that occurred during that crisis and the trauma of the escalation of the crisis increased U.S. and Soviet awareness of points 3 and 4. Those were the critical lessons from the crisis.

Unfortunately, the superpower experience is not easily applied to other rivalries, particularly those between minor powers. First, the model does not apply in those cases where states see war as preferable to continuing to accept the status quo. Such was the case in six of the eight Egyptian-Israeli and Indo-Pakistani crises. Second, there is the high cost of getting to the point where war is viewed as unacceptable. Not any war will do, as the recurring wars in the Egyptian-Israeli and Indo-Pakistani rivalries demonstrated. A trauma of the scale of World War II may be necessary. Finally, without the third and fourth conditions there is the very real danger of one side preempting in a rapidly escalating crisis to achieve the advantage of striking first. The strategic importance of striking first, after all, was one of the main lessons rival states drew from the 1956 and 1967 Egyptian-Israeli crises.

Beyond Realpolitik

What of the possibility of rival states moving beyond the bounds of realpolitik to break away from a strictly competitive view of their relationship? There are two examples from the three rivalries that provide some grounds for optimism. The first assumes greater relevance today because of the long-term trend toward regional and global interdependence. The second example illustrates how national leaders with unusual courage might make the transition from competition to cooperation.

During the height of the 1973 Alert Crisis, the United States responded to the Soviet threat of unilateral intervention in the Middle East war with a counterthreat. In addition to declaring that the United States would not tolerate the intervention, Kissinger declared that such action "would end all we have striven so hard to achieve" (Kissinger 1982:591). He was referring to the mutual benefits of détente. During the discussion within the Soviet politburo following the American alert, Brezhnev rejected a tit-for-tat response on the grounds that it could endanger the principal Soviet objective, which was to "develop our relations with the United States" (Israelian 1995:183).

Soviet-American relations soured after the Alert Crisis, but the efforts to which Kissinger and Brezhnev referred were based on both sides' awareness of the political and economic benefits from cooperation. It is hard to imagine a similar argument being added to a threat in the earlier Soviet-American crises as well as in the Egyptian-Israeli and Indo-Pakistani crises. The Soviet-American relationship had changed sufficiently by 1973 that maintaining the benefits of cooperation had become an important consideration.

In the quarter century following the Alert Crisis, policymakers around the world have become increasingly conscious of global and regional interdependence in achieving the economic, environmental, and social well-being of their citizens. Cooperation is mixed with competition in the global marketplace. Security issues no longer dominate most states' foreign-policy agendas. States engaged in recurring crises and wars run the risk of becoming marginalized from the rest of the international community. It may be that realpolitik is becoming anachronistic.

Nevertheless, realpolitik has been the dominant approach to dealing with interstate conflict for so long that it will not be easy for the leaders of states in intense rivalries to extend their courage and imagination beyond its boundaries. To do so requires a willingness to take risks for peace and the imagination to understand what is necessary to meet the rival states' security concerns. There is one example that stands out in the three rivalries in this study—Egyptian President Anwar Sadat's dramatic 1977 initiative to break the Arab vow of "no negotiation, no recognition, no peace" by offering to meet with the Israelis, in Jerusalem, to discuss conditions for peace. Sadat unilaterally presented Israel with the recognition that it had sought since its founding. His perception of the requirements of a peace that would return the Sinai to Egypt extended beyond the boundaries of realpolitik. Sadat's vision and the risk that he took for peace constitute a lone exception. Moreover, this breakthrough came only after Israel and Egypt had fought four wars, and Sadat ultimately paid for his move with his life. Nevertheless, this action demonstrated what might have been possible earlier, in all three rivalries, if the leaders of the rival states had been able to break the bonds of realpolitik.

Epilogue: 25 Years Later

A recent aggregate-data study by Diehl and Hensel (1998) indicates that the level of hostility in interstate rivalries is likely to begin to decline after four or five militarized disputes. The rivalries in this study appear to follow that pattern, but when one considers the kind of learning that occurred, the educational costs were high. The Cold War ended with the dismantling of the Berlin Wall in 1989, but although détente did not survive the Alert

Crisis and the rivalry between the United States and the Soviet Union continued to ebb and flow, there had been no militarized crises between the superpowers in the 16 years between 1973 and 1989. Unlike the preceding Soviet-American crises, there was a sense in both countries that the Alert Crisis resulted from an overreaction by both sides. The Cuban Missile Crisis had left both superpowers with a new appreciation of the risks of a future confrontation. If the collaboration that Brezhnev had expected in the era of détente was not possible, both sides were now well aware of their mutual desire to avoid war. The competition for political influence continued in the Third World. But except for those nations that suffered from the consequences of American and Soviet arms transfers, the relationship became more consistent with what the Soviets had called peaceful coexistence—that is, political and economic competition without the threat of war, or realpolitik moderated by prudence.

The Soviet-American rivalry became more restrained as a consequence of the demonstrated risks of uncontrollable escalation, but the Egyptian-Israeli and Indo-Pakistani rivalries were moderated by the consequences of war itself, albeit for different reasons. Just as Egypt recognized its vulnerability to the potential costs of war after the 1967 war, Israel became aware of its own vulnerability after its experience in the 1973 war. Nevertheless, another four years passed before Sadat's dramatic offer to meet with the Israelis in Jerusalem. This breakthrough, followed by extensive American mediation efforts, led to the Camp David Accords of 1978 and to the 1979 Egyptian-Israeli peace treaty.

India and Pakistan have been the least successful in resolving their differences, but the 1971 war and the dismemberment of Pakistan that was its consequence demonstrated that Pakistan could not compete with India in a general war. There have been no wars since 1971 primarily because Pakistan has lacked the military capability to challenge its status quo rival. The rivalry, however, continues to simmer. Both sides are now armed with nuclear weapons. The official and public reactions to the nuclear tests conducted by both sides in the spring of 1998 suggested a relationship not unlike the Soviet-American rivalry in that the costs and risks of war are viewed by both sides as prohibitive. Whether that recognition ultimately will lead to a settlement of outstanding differences, particularly with regard to Kashmir, remains an open question. Meanwhile, the Indo-Pakistani relationship remains within the bounds of realpolitik.

Appendix

Sample of Militarized Crises, 1816–1980

Crisis	Side A	Side B	(Y/M/D–Y/M/D)
1. Pastry War	France	Mexico	1838/3/2–1839/3/9
2. Crimean War	Russia France England	Turkey	1853/4/19–1854/3/31
3. Second Schleswig-Holstein War	Prussia Austria-Hungary	Denmark	1863/3/30–1864/2/1
4. Russo-Turkish War	Russia	Turkey	1876/5/13–1877/4/12
5. British-Russian Crisis	Britain	Russia	1877/5/6–1878/5/30
6. British-Portuguese Crisis	Britain	Portugal	1889/8/19–1890/1/12
7. Spanish-American War	Spain	United States	1898/2/15–1898/4/21
8. Fashoda Crisis	Britain	France	1898/7/10–1898/12/4
9. First Moroccan Crisis	France	Germany	1905/3/31–1906/3/31
10. Second Central American War	Honduras El Salvador	Nicaragua	1906/12/1–1907/3/2
11. Bosnian Crisis	Austria-Hungary Germany	Serbia Russia Turkey	1908/10/6–1909/3/31
12. Second Moroccan Crisis	France Britain	Germany	1911/5/21–1911/11/4
13. First Balkan War	Serbia Bulgaria Greece	Turkey	1912/3/13–1913/10/18
14. Second Balkan War	Bulgaria	Rumania Greece Serbia	1913/2/20–1913/6/30
15. Pre–World War I	Austria-Hungary Germany	Serbia Russia France Britain	1914/6/28–1914/8/4
16. Teschen Crisis	Czechoslovakia	Poland	1918/12/10–1920/7/28
17. Chaco Dispute	Bolivia	Paraguay	1927/2/25–1930/5/1
18. Chaco War	Bolivia	Paraguay	1931/6/15–1932/6/15
19. Manchurian War	Japan	China	1931/6/27–1931/12/19
20. Italo-Ethiopian War	Ethiopia	Italy	1934/11/22–1935/10/3
21. Rhineland Crisis	France	Germany	1936/3/7–1936/10/31

(*continued*)

Crisis	Side A	Side B	(Y/M/D–Y/M/D)
	Belgium		
	Britain		
22. Anschluss Crisis	Austria	Germany	1938/2/12–1938/3/12
23. Munich Crisis	Czechoslovakia	Germany	1938/2/20–1938/9/30
	Britain		
	France		
24. Polish-Lithuanian Crisis	Lithuania	Poland	1938/3/12–1938/3/31
25. Danzig Crisis	Germany	Poland	1938/10/24–1939/9/1
(Pre–WWII)		Britain	
26. Italo-French Crisis	Italy	France	1938/11/30–1939/9/3
	Germany		
27. Trieste Crisis	Italy	Yugoslavia	1953/7/16–1954/10/5
28. Honduran Border	Honduras	Nicaragua	1957/2/2–1957/7/21
Dispute			
29. Sino-Indian	China	India	1958/10/18–1960/4/19
Border Dispute			
30. Bizerte Dispute	France	Tunisia	1961/7/8–1961/9/29
31. Cyprus Crisis	Greece	Turkey	1963/11/30–1964/9/15
	Gr. Cyp.	Tr. Cyp.	
32. Cod War	Britain	Iceland	1975/7/15–1976/6/1
33. Beagle Channel Dispute	Argentina	Chile	1977/4/19–1979/1/8
34. Sino-Vietnam War	China	Vietnam	1977/11/25–1979/2/17

Sample of Militarized Crises, Escalation Ranks and Scores

Crisis	Escalation Rank	Escalation Score	Rate Rank	Intensity Rank	Magnitude Rank
Pastry	16	0.83	26	13	19
Crimean	11	1.14	21	11	10
Schleswig-Holstein	14	10.77	5	25	12
Russo-Turkish	22	1.30	20	17	27
British-Russian	17	0.88	24	14	23
British-Portuguese	28	3.23	13	29	25
Spanish-American	3	25.06	2	5	4
Fashoda	7	10.18	8	12	7
First Moroccan	32	0.03	29	32	34
Central American	15	10.27	7	24	16
Bosnia	8	1.34	18	3	9
Second Moroccan	29	1.04	22	27	29
First Balkan	13	12.07	4	21	11
Second Balkan	12	1.69	16	8	14
Pre–World War I	1	69.90	1	7	2
Teschen	23	0.42	28	16	28
Chaco Dispute	30	–0.06	31	33	21
Chaco War	19	1.38	17	15	23
Manchurian	21	4.60	12	23	22
Italo-Ethiopian	2	12.27	3	1	1
Rhineland	10	0.88	24	6	13
Anschluss	25	6.90	10	28	26
Munich	5	10.76	6	4	6
Polish-Lithuanian	34	–23.75	34	30	31
Italo-French	27	1.00	23	19	33
Danzig (Pre–WWII)	9	5.20	11	10	8
Trieste	26	–0.69	32	26	17
Honduran Border	31	–0.04	30	31	30
Sino-Indian	18	0.60	27	18	15
Bizerte	33	–3.56	33	34	32
Cyprus	4	10.00	9	2	3
Cod War	20	1.77	15	20	20
Beagle Channel	6	2.11	14	9	5
Sino-Vietnam	24	1.33	19	22	18
Sample Mean		5.32			
Sample Standard Deviation		13.39			
Sample Median		1.36			

Sample Reciprocity Ranks and Scores

Crisis	Rank	Score	Direction	Distance
Pastry	17	–0.21	5.06	33.30
Crimean	30	1.36	8.54	44.31
Schleswig-Holstein	18	–0.18	7.20	6.43
Russo-Turkish	27	0.59	5.06	45.06
British-Russian	25	0.29	2.13	56.18
British-Portuguese	7	–1.18	3.41	2.13
Spanish-American	31	1.42	10.27	34.19
Fashoda	28	0.81	7.27	36.35
First Moroccan	4	–1.23	2.14	9.55
Central-American	11	–1.10	3.18	6.27
Bosnian	29	0.96	11.35	12.67
Second Moroccan	3	–1.33	3.04	0.15
First Balkan	6	–1.19	3.50	1.33
Second Balkan	13	–0.96	3.94	5.18
Pre–World War I	33	4.49	25.20	24.70
Teschen	8	–1.18	1.09	18.36
Chaco Dispute	2	–1.54	0.72	9.95
Chaco War	22	0.11	2.47	48.40
Manchurian	20	–0.16	7.27	6.70
Italo-Ethiopian	34	5.44	9.00	166.20
Rhineland	5	–1.22	2.82	5.21
Anschluss	24	0.27	9.10	7.09
Munich	32	2.20	9.08	66.36
Polish-Lithuanian	15	–0.71	5.00	5.67
Italo-French	23	0.17	3.88	40.34
Pre–World War II	14	–0.88	4.44	4.27
Trieste	9	–1.13	3.83	0.85
Honduran Border	1	–1.55	1.80	1.96
Sino-Indian	10	–1.11	2.40	11.25
Bizerte	26	0.35	6.79	25.54
Cyprus	21	–0.09	8.07	3.25
Cod War	12	–1.04	3.38	6.72
Beagle Channel	19	–0.18	3.46	32.52
Sino-Vietnam	16	–0.71	2.47	23.26
Mean Reciprocity		–0.01	5.54	23.58
Standard Deviation		1.55	4.41	30.61
Median		–0.20	3.91	10.60

A Note on Sources

The quantitative data for this study were drawn from the Behavioral Correlates of War (BCOW) data set, which was generated from accounts in the press, primarily but not exclusively the *New York Times,* and from diplomatic histories, government documents, and participant memoirs. The BCOW data for the 12 crises were generated prior to the qualitative research, but when that research uncovered additional actions by the rival states, those actions were coded and added to the BCOW data set.

The number of crises considered precluded extensive archival research on each of the crises; however, an effort was made to consider a wide range of secondary sources, memoirs, and collections of documents. The annotated list that follows supplements the bibliography by providing a brief account of sources that I found most useful in conducting the qualitative analyses of each of the 12 crises.

Soviet-American Rivalry

The documentary materials and extant case studies for the Soviet-American crises are the most complete of those in the three rivalries. A major boon to this study has been the recent opening of the Soviet archives and the translation of key documents into English, largely as a result of the Woodrow Wilson Center's Cold War International History Project (CWIHP).

Berlin Blockade Crisis
The standard American account of the Berlin Blockade Crisis is Davison (1958). Adomeit's (1982) more recent account provides a better perspective of the Soviet position, and Shlaim (1983) presents a more complete account of American policymaking during the crisis. Zubok and Pleshakov (1996) have used recently opened Soviet archival material to provide a fuller account of Soviet thinking. Pechatnov (1995) provides useful background on Soviet attitudes toward the United States in the period preceding the crisis. My account of Truman's thinking draws on Truman's (1956) memoirs and McCullough's (1992) biography of the president.

Berlin Wall Crisis
Beschloss (1991) offers a balanced account of Soviet-American diplomacy that covers the period of the Berlin Wall and Cuban Missile Crises. Two earlier case studies of the Berlin Wall Crisis by Schick (1971) and Slusser (1978) stand up quite well in the face of additional material from the Soviet archives. Zubok's (1993) use of that material provides an excellent supplement to Khrushchev's (1970) account of the Soviet perspective on the crisis. Schlesinger (1965) provides some useful insights on Kennedy's thinking. Adomeit (1982) adds useful information on communication between the two sides during the course of the crisis as well as an overall analysis of the crisis diplomacy.

Cuban Missile Crisis
One could fill a public library with recent material on the Cuban Missile Crisis. The transcript of the ExComm meetings has been published in May and Zelikow (1997). The CWIHP Bulletin has published the reports filed by Soviet representatives, including Gromyko and Dobrynin, who met with Kennedy or his advisers during the crisis. Blight and Welch (1989) have presented a thorough account of the recollections of crisis participants on both sides and have added their own

reflections on the crisis. The issue of learning from the crisis is treated by Blight (1990) and by Jarosz and Nye (1993). Excellent accounts of Soviet decision making that use recently released documents appear in Zubok and Pleshakov (1996). Their analysis balances the more self-serving accounts of Khrushchev (1970, 1974) and Dobrynin (1995a).

Middle East Alert Crisis

Three excellent detailed accounts of the Alert Crisis that offer the added advantage of balancing each other's perspectives are the memoirs of Kissinger (1982) and Israelian (1995) and Lebow and Stein's (1994) detailed account. Lebow and Stein make extensive use of interviews with American and Soviet participants in the crisis and draw conclusions that are quite critical of the policies of both sides, particularly the United States. Kissinger (1982) provides the ultimate insider's perspective on American policy-making. Nixon's (1978) memoirs offer another useful perspective on American-Soviet relations at the time. An insider's perspective on the Soviet side is provided by Israelian (1995), a career foreign-service officer who was assigned to prepare memoranda for the politburo and to take notes at its meetings during the Yom Kippur War and Alert Crisis.

Egyptian-Israeli Rivalry

Sachar (1981) provides a good overview of the Egyptian-Israeli rivalry that includes narrative accounts of all four crises.

Palestine Crisis

The most useful sources for Arab decision making in 1947–48 were Pappé (1992) for all the Arab states and Heikal (1988) for Egypt. Heikal, whose numerous writings were useful for each of the first three crises, edited the influential Egyptian newspaper *Al Ahram* and was a foreign-policy insider. Avi-Hai (1974) and Zweig (1991) provide two good accounts of Ben-Gurion's thinking. Eban's (1972) memoirs offer another useful Israeli perspective. Rabinovich (1991) describes the early efforts to achieve a negotiated settlement.

Suez Crisis

Thomas (1966) gives a good overview of the crisis. Hewedy (1989) provides an excellent account of the crisis from the Egyptian perspective. Nasser's personal perspective on the crisis can be gleaned from his interview in Calvocoressi (1967) and Nutting's (1972) biography. Nutting was British minister of state in Cairo and a confidant of Nasser. The Israeli perspective is described in Bar-On (1994) and Avi-Hai (1974). Morris (1993) provides a blow-by-blow account of the origins of the war from an Israeli perspective.

Six Day War Crisis

Laqueur (1968) offers a balanced narrative account of the unfolding crisis. El-Gamasy (1993) provides an insider's account of the Egyptian strategy. Nutting (1972) offers interesting insights on Nasser's views. Excellent accounts of Israeli decision making appear in Brecher and Geist (1980) and Mor (1993). A complication of various sources of information on Israeli policy appears in Dishon (1971). Eshkol's (1969) papers also are useful. U.S. Deputy United Nations Representative Yost (1968) presented a contemporary analysis of the escalation to war that anticipated the conflict-spiral model.

October War Crisis
Korn (1992) offers a solid overview of the crisis. El-Gamasy (1993) and Heikal (1975) offer the best accounts of Egyptian policy. Sadat's (1977) autobiography provides some insight into his thinking, as does Kissinger's (1982) account. Brecher and Raz (1977) and Brecher and Geist (1980) provide convincing analyses of Israeli policy-making. Kissinger (1982) and Lebow and Stein (1994) are particularly useful in providing details on the Egyptian and Israeli relationships with the superpowers. Shlaim's (1976) report on the findings of the Agranat Commission offers additional insights in Israeli perceptions of Egyptian intentions.

Indo-Pakistani Rivalry

First Kashmir Crisis
Blinkenberg (1972) and Korbel (1966) stand out for presenting thorough and impartial accounts of the first Indo-Pakistani crisis. Korbel was a member of the United Nations Commission on India and Pakistan that mediated the 1949 ceasefire. Burke (1973) provides a reliable account of Pakistani foreign policy, not only toward India but also with the superpowers and China, throughout the rivalry period. These three works also were useful sources for the Rann of Kutch and Second Kashmir Crises. Choudhury (1968) presents an unabashedly pro-Pakistani perspective. Das Gupta's (1968) analysis is pro-Indian but more balanced than that of Choudhury. Hasan's (1966) collection of official correspondence between India and Pakistan is a useful source for both Kashmir crises.

Rann of Kutch and Second Kashmir Crises
The most objective full account of the two crises is in Lamb (1966), although Blinkenberg (1972) and Burke (1973) also are useful. Gauhar was Ayub Khan's minister of information and confidant; Gauhar (1996) is an indispensable source for the perceptions and policies of Ayub and his advisers, including the degree of Pakistan's involvement in the origins of the Second Kashmir Crisis. Feldman (1972) provides a balanced overview of Pakistani relations with India during this period. Jha (1972) offers a useful account of Indian policy-making.

Bangladesh
The best single account of the Bangladesh crisis is Sisson and Rose (1990), which is thorough and balanced. Blinkenberg (1972) and Burke (1973) also are useful. Khan (1973) and Jha (1972) are useful albeit somewhat biased sources for Pakistani and Indian perceptions and intentions, respectively. Kissinger's (1982) memoirs add useful detail on American interactions with both sides during the course of the crisis. Wirsing (1994) provides an excellent account of events since 1971.

References

Acheson, D. G. 1969. *Present at Creation: My Years in the State Department.* New York: Norton.

Adomeit, H. 1982. *Soviet Risk-Taking and Crisis Behavior.* London: Allen and Unwin.

Akbar, M. J. 1991. *Kashmir: Behind the Vale.* New Delhi: Viking.

Archer, J., and F. Huntingford. 1994. "Game Theory Models and Escalation of Animal Fights." In *The Dynamics of Aggression: Biological and Social Processes in Dyads and Groups,* ed. M. Potegal. Hillsdale, NJ: Lawrence Erlbaum.

Avi-Hai, A. 1974. *Ben-Gurion, State Builder: Principles and Pragmatism, 1948-1963.* New York: Halsted Press.

Axelrod, R. 1984. *The Evolution of Cooperation.* New York: Basic Books.

Azar, E. E. 1972. "Conflict Escalation and Conflict Reduction in an International Crisis: Suez, 1956." *Journal of Conflict Resolution* 16:183-202.

Bandura, A. 1971. *Social Learning Theory.* New York: General Learning.

Bandura, A. 1973. *Aggression: A Social Learning Analysis.* Englewood Cliffs, NJ: Prentice-Hall.

Barnds, W. J. 1972. *India, Pakistan, and the Great Powers.* New York: Praeger.

Bar-On, M. 1994. *The Gates of Gaza: Israel's Road to Suez and Back, 1955-1957.* New York: St. Martin's Press.

Baron, R. A. 1977. *Human Aggression.* New York: Plenum.

Bell, C. 1971. *The Conventions of Crisis: A Study in Diplomatic Management.* London: Oxford University Press.

Bem, D. J. 1972. "Self-Perception Theory." In *Advances in Experimental Social Psychology,* ed. L. Berkowitz. New York: Academic Press.

Berkowitz, L. 1993. *Aggression: Its Causes, Consequences, and Control.* New York: McGraw-Hill.

Berkowitz, L. 1994. "On the Escalation of Aggression." In *The Dynamics of Aggression: Biological and Social Processes in Dyads and Groups,* ed. M. Potegal and J. F. Knutson. Hillsdale, NJ: Lawrence Erlbaum.

Beschloss, M. R. 1991. *The Crisis Years: Kennedy and Khrushchev, 1960-1963.* New York: HarperCollins.

Black, I., and B. Morris. 1991. *Israel's Secret Wars: A History of Israel's Intelligence Sources.* New York: Grove Press.

Blainey, G. 1977. *The Causes of War.* New York: Free Press.

Blight, J. G. 1990. *The Shattered Crystal Ball: Fear and Learning in the Cuban Missile Crisis.* Savage, MD: Rowman and Littlefield.

Blight, J. G., J. S. Nye, and D. A. Welch. 1987. "The Cuban Missile Crisis Revisited." *Foreign Affairs* 66:170–89.

Blight, J. G., and D. A. Welch. 1989. *On the Brink.* New York: Hill and Wang.

Blinkenberg, L. 1972. *India-Pakistan: The History of Unsolved Conflicts.* Copenhagen: Dansk Udenrigspolitisk Instituts.

Bokhari, I. H., and T. P. Thornton. 1988. *The 1972 Simla Agreement: An Asymmetrical Negotiation.* Pew Program Case Study 420. Pittsburgh: University of Pittsburgh Graduate School of Public and International Affairs.

Brecher, M. 1953. *The Struggle for Kashmir.* New York: Oxford University Press.

Brecher, M. 1975. *Decisions in Israel's Foreign Policy.* New Haven: Yale University Press.

Brecher, M. 1993. *Crises in World Politics: Theory and Reality.* New York: Pergamon.

Brecher, M., and B. Geist. 1980. *Decisions in Crisis: Israel, 1967 and 1973.* Berkeley: University of California Press.

Brecher, M., and P. James. 1986. *Crisis and Change in World Politics.* Boulder, CO: Westview.

Brecher, M., and M. Raz. 1977. "Images and Behavior: Israel's Yom Kippur War Crisis, 1973." *International Journal* 32:476–500.

Brecher, M., and J. Wilkenfeld. 1997. *A Study of Crisis.* Ann Arbor: University of Michigan Press.

Bremer, S. A. 1992. "Dangerous Dyads: Interstate War, 1816–1965." *Journal of Conflict Resolution* 36:309–41.

Breslauer, G. W. 1979. "Soviet Policy in the Middle East, 1967–1972: Unalterable Policy or Collaborative Competition." In *Managing U.S.-Soviet Rivalry: Problems of Crisis Prevention,* ed. A. L. George. Boulder, CO: Westview.

Breslauer, G. W., and P. E. Tetlock, eds. 1991. *Learning in U.S. and Soviet Foreign Policy.* Boulder, CO: Westview.

Brines, Russell. 1968. *The Indo-Pakistani Conflict.* London: Oxford University Press.

Burke, S. M. 1973. *Pakistan's Foreign Policy: An Historical Analysis.* London: Oxford University Press.

Burns, John. 1998a. "On Kashmir's Dividing Line, Nuclear Fears Enforce Calm." *New York Times,* June 14.

Burns, John. 1998b. "Some Disputes Get Settled. Then There's Kashmir." *New York Times,* August 9, sec. 4, p. 4.

Calvocoressi, P. 1967. *Suez Ten Years After.* Clinton, MA: Colonial Press.

Chang, L., and P. Kornbluh. 1992. *The Cuban Missile Crisis: A National Security Archive Documents Reader.* New York: New Press.

Cheema, P. I. 1997. "Arms Procurement in Pakistan: Balancing the Need for Quality, Self-Reliance, and Diversity of Supply." In *Military Capacity and the Risk of War,* ed. Eric Arnett. New York: Oxford University Press.

Choudhury, G. W. 1968. *Pakistan's Relations with India, 1947–1966.* New York: Praeger.

Clay, L. D. 1950. *Decision in Germany.* Garden City, NY: Doubleday.

Das Gupta, J. B. 1968. *Jammu and Kashmir.* The Hague: Martinus Nijhoff.

Davison, W. P. 1958. *The Berlin Blockade: A Study in Cold War Politics.* Princeton: Princeton University Press.

Dayan, M. 1966. *Diary of the Sinai Campaign.* Jerusalem: Steimatzky's.

Dayan, M. 1976. *Moshe Dayan: Story of My Life.* New York: Morrow.

Diehl, P. F., and P. R. Hensel. 1998. "Punctuated Equilibrium or Evolution?: A Research Note on Model of Rivalry Development." Paper presented at the annual meeting of the Peace Science Society, October 16–18, New Brunswick, NJ.

Dishon, D., ed. 1971. *Middle East Record.* Vol. 3, *1967.* Jerusalem: Israel Universities Press.

Djilas, M. 1962. *Conversations with Stalin.* Trans. Michael B. Petrovich. New York: Harcourt Brace and World.

Dobrynin, A. F. 1995a. *In Confidence: Moscow's Ambassador to America's Six Cold War Presidents, 1962–1986.* New York: Random House.

Dobrynin, A. F. 1995b. "Telegram from Soviet Ambassador to the USA Dobrynin to the USSR MFA, 24 October 1962." *Cold War International History Project Bulletin 5.* Washington, DC: Woodrow Wilson Center.

Dobrynin, A. F. 1996–97. "Cable from Soviet Ambassador to the USA. A. Dobrynin to Soviet Foreign Ministry, 25 October 1962." *Cold War International History Project Bulletin 8–9.* Washington, DC: Woodrow Wilson Center.

Donaldson, R. 1974. *Soviet Policy toward India: Ideology and Strategy.* Cambridge: Harvard University Press.

Dupuy, T. N. 1978. *Elusive Victory: The Arab Israeli Wars, 1947–1974.* New York: Harper and Row.

Eban, A. 1972. *My Country: The Story of Modern Israel.* New York: Random House.

Eban, A. 1977. *An Autobiography.* New York: Random House.

Eban, A. 1992. *Personal Witness: Israel through My Eyes.* New York: Putnam.

Eisenhower, D. D. 1965. *The White House Years.* Vol. 2. Garden City, NY: Doubleday.

El-Gamasy, M. A. G. 1993. *The October War: Memoirs of Field Marshal El-Gamasy of Egypt.* Cairo: American University in Cairo Press.

Elon, A. 1996. "Israel and the End of Zionism." *New York Review* vol. 43, no. 20 (December 19):22–29.

Eshkol, L. 1969. *The State Papers of Levi Eshkol.* Ed. H. M. Christman. New York: Funk and Wagnalls.

Farnham, B., ed. 1994. *Avoiding Losses/Taking Risks: Prospect Theory and International Conflict.* Ann Arbor: University of Michigan Press.

Feldman, H. 1972. *From Crisis to Crisis: Pakistan, 1962–1969.* London: Oxford University Press.

Feron, J. 1967. "Israelis Ponder Blow at Syrians." *New York Times,* May 13, p. 1.

Festinger, L. 1957. *A Theory of Cognitive Dissonance.* Stanford, CA: Stanford University Press.

Fish, M. S. 1991. "The Berlin Blockade Crisis of 1948–49." In *Avoiding War: Problems in Crisis Management,* ed. A. L. George. Boulder, CO: Westview.

Fursenko, A., and T. Naftali. 1995. "Using KGB Documents: The Scali-Fursenko Channel in the Cuban Missile Crisis." *Cold War International History Project Bulletin 5.* Washington, DC: Woodrow Wilson Center.

Gaddis, J. L. 1972. *The United States and the Origins of the Cold War, 1941–1947.* New York: Columbia University Press.

Gauhar, A. 1996. *Ayub Khan: Pakistan's First Military Ruler.* Karachi: Oxford University Press.

Geller, D. 1990. "Nuclear Weapons, Deterrence, and Crisis Escalation." *Journal of Conflict Resolution* 34:291–310.

Geller, D. 1993. "Power Differentials in Rival Dyads." *International Studies Quarterly* 37:173–93.

George, A. L. 1969. "The Operational Code." *International Studies Quarterly* 13:190–222.

George, A. L. 1979. "Case Studies and Theory Development: The Method of Structured, Focused Comparison." In *Diplomacy: New Approaches to History, Theory, and Policy,* ed. P. Lauren. New York: Free Press.

George, A. L. 1991a. *Avoiding War: Problems of Crisis Management.* Boulder, CO: Westview.

George, A. L. 1991b. *Forceful Persuasion.* Washington, DC: U.S. Institute of Peace.

Gerner, D. J. 1991. *One Land, Two Peoples: The Conflict over Palestine.* Boulder, CO: Westview.

Gilpin, R. 1981. *War and Change in World Politics.* Cambridge: Cambridge University Press.

Goertz, G., and P. Diehl. 1993. "Enduring Rivalries: Theoretical Constructs and Empirical Patterns." *International Studies Quarterly* 37:147–71.

Goertz, G., and P. Diehl. 1995. "Taking the Enduring out of Enduring Rivalries: The Rivalry Approach to War and Peace." *International Interactions* 21:291–308.

Goertz, G., and P. Diehl. 1998. "The 'Volcano Model' and Other Patterns in the Evolution of Enduring Rivalries." In *The Dynamics of Enduring Rivalries,* ed. P. F. Diehl. Urbana: University of Illinois Press.

Golan, G. 1990. *Soviet Policies in the Middle East: From World War II to Gorbachev.* Cambridge: Cambridge University Press.

Griffith, W. E. 1967. *Sino-Soviet Relations, 1964–1965.* Cambridge: MIT Press.

Gromyko, A. 1995. "Telegram from Soviet Foreign Minister Gromyko to the CC CPSU, 20 October 1962." *Cold War International History Project Bulletin 5.* Washington, DC: Woodrow Wilson Center.

Gromyko, A. 1996–97. "Cable from Soviet Foreign Minister Gromyko on 18 October 1962 Meeting with President Kennedy, 20 October 1962." *Cold War International History Project Bulletin 5.* Washington, DC: Woodrow Wilson Center.

Gupta, H. R. 1969. *The Kutch Affair.* Delhi: U. C. Kapur.

Gupta, S. 1966. *Kashmir: A Study in India-Pakistan Relations.* New Delhi: Asia Publishing.

Hasan, K. S. 1966. *The Kashmir Question.* Karachi: Pakistan Institute of International Affairs.

Hayden, T., and W. Mischel. 1976. "Maintaining Trait Consistency in the Resolution of Behavioral Inconsistency: The Wolf in Sheep's Clothing." *Journal of Personality* 44:109–32.

Heikal, M. H. 1975. *The Road to Ramadan.* New York: Quadrangle.

Heikal, M. H. 1978. *Sphinx and Commissar.* London: Collins.

Heikal, M. H. 1988. "Reflections on a Nation in Crisis." *Journal of Palestinian Studies* 18:112–20.

Hensel, P. R. 1994. "An Evolutionary Approach to the Study of Interstate Rivalry." Paper presented at the annual meeting of the American Political Science Association, New York.

Hershberg, J. G. 1996–97. "New Evidence on the Cuban Missile Crisis: More Documents from the Russian Archives." *Cold War International History Project Bulletin 8–9.* Washington, DC: Woodrow Wilson Center.

Hewedy, A. 1989. "Nasser and the Crisis of 1956." In *Suez 1956: The Crisis and Its Consequences,* ed. R. Louis and R. Owen. Oxford: Clarendon Press.

Holmberg, B. 1997. "The Window No One Jumped Through: A Study in Changes in the Military Balance and Escalation of Protracted Conflicts: The Case of India and Pakistan." Paper presented at the annual meeting of the Peace Science Society, November 21–23, Indianapolis.

Holsti, O. 1972. *Crises, Escalation, and War.* Montreal: McGill University Press.

Holsti, O. 1979. "Theories of Crisis Decision Making." In *Diplomacy: New Approaches to History, Theory, and Policy,* ed. P. G. Lauren. New York: Free Press.

Holsti, O. 1989. "Crisis Decision Making." *Behavior, Society, and Nuclear War,* vol. 1, ed. P. E. Tetlack et al. New York: Oxford University Press.

Holsti, O., R. North, and R. Brody. 1968. "Perception and Action in the 1914 Crisis." In *Quantitative International Politics,* ed. J. D. Singer. New York: Free Press.

Hunt, M. H. 1996. *Crises in U.S. Foreign Policy.* New Haven: Yale University Press.

India, Government. 1947–48. *White Paper on Jammu and Kashmir.* New Delhi: Publication Division.

India, Government. 1965. *Pakistan's New Attempt to Grab Kashmir.* New Delhi: Publication Division.

Israel Department of Information. 1960. *Israel's Struggle for Peace.* New York: Marstin.

Israel, Ministry of Foreign Affairs. 1972. *Menace: the Events that Led Up to the Six Day War and their Lessons.* Jerusalem: Ministry of Foreign Affairs.

Israelian, V. 1995. *Inside the Kremlin during the Yom Kippur War.* University Park: Pennsylvania State University Press.

Jarosz, W. W., and J. Nye. 1993. "The Shadow of the Past: Learning from History in National Security Decision Making." In *Behavior, Society, and International Conflict*, ed. P. E. Tetlock, et al. New York: Oxford University Press.

Jervis, R. 1976. *Perception and Misperception in International Politics*. Princeton: Princeton University Press.

Jha, D. C. 1972. *Indo-Pakistan Relations*. Patna: Bharati Bhawan

Jha, P. S. 1996. *Kashmir, 1947: Rival Versions of History*. New Delhi: Oxford University Press.

Johnson, L. B. 1971. *The Vantage Point: Perspectives of the Presidency, 1963–1969*. New York: Holt, Rinehart, and Winston.

Kahn, H. 1965. *On Escalation: Metaphors and Scenarios*. New York: Praeger.

Kahneman, D., and A. Tversky. 1979. "Prospect Theory: An Analysis of Decision Under Risk." *Econometrica* 47:263–91.

Kahneman, D., and A. Tversky. 1982. "Availability: A Heuristic for Judging Frequency and Probability." In *Judgment under Uncertainty: Heuristics and Biases*, ed. D. Kahneman, P. Slovic, and A. Tversky. Cambridge: Cambridge University Press.

Kaul, Lt.-Gen. B. M. 1971. *Confrontation with Pakistan*. New York: Barnes and Noble.

Kennan, G. F. 1947. "The Sources of Soviet Conduct." *Foreign Affairs* 25:575–82.

Kennedy, J. F. 1961. "Text of Speech by Kennedy and Transcript of His News Conference in Paris." *New York Times*, June 3.

Kennedy, R. F. 1969. *Thirteen Days: a Memoir of the Cuban Missile Crisis*. New York: W.W. Norton.

Khan, F. M. 1973. *Pakistan's Crisis in Leadership*. Islamabad: National Books Foundation.

Khong, Y. F. 1992. *Analogies at War: Korea, Munich, Dien Bien Phu, and the Vietnam Decision of 1965*. Princeton: Princeton University Press.

Khrushchev, N. S. 1959. *For Peaceful Competition and Cooperation*. New York: Arts and Sciences Press.

Khrushchev, N. S. 1970. *Khrushchev Remembers*. Vol. 1. Boston: Little, Brown.

Khrushchev, N. S. 1974. *Khrushchev Remembers: The Last Testament*. Boston: Little, Brown.

Khrushchev, N. S. 1982. "Khrushchev's Report of January 6, 1961." In *Soviet Risk-Taking and Crisis Behavior*, by Hannes Adomeit. London: Allen and Unwin.

Kissinger, H. A. 1979. *White House Years*. Boston: Little, Brown.

Kissinger, H. A. 1982. *Years of Upheaval*. Boston: Little, Brown.

Kissinger, H. A. 1994. *Diplomacy*. New York: Simon and Schuster.

Korbel, J. 1966. *Danger in Kashmir*. Princeton: Princeton University Press.

Korn, D. A. 1992. *Stalemate: The War of Attrition and Great Power Diplomacy in the Middle East, 1967–1970*. San Francisco: Westview Press.

Lamb, A. 1966. *The Kashmir Problem: A Historical Survey*. New York: Praeger.

Laqueur, W. 1968. *The Road to War, 1967*. London: Weidenfeld and Nicolson.

Larson, D. W. 1985. *Origins of Containment: A Psychological Explanation*. Princeton: Princeton University Press.

Lebow, R. N. 1981. *Between War and Peace.* Baltimore: Johns Hopkins University Press.

Lebow, R. N., and J. G. Stein. 1994. *We All Lost the Cold War.* Princeton: Princeton University Press.

Leng, R. J. 1983. "When Will They Ever Learn: Coercive Bargaining in Recurrent Crises." *Journal of Conflict Resolution* 27:379–419.

Leng, R. J. 1987. "Structure and Action in Militarized Disputes," In *New Directions in the Study of Foreign Policy,* eds. C. F. Hermann, C. W. Kegley, Jr., and J. N. Rosenau. Boston: Allen & Unwin.

Leng, R. J. 1993. *Interstate Crisis Behavior, 1816–1980: Realism versus Reciprocity.* Cambridge: Cambridge University Press.

Leng, R. J., and J. D. Singer. 1988. "Militarized Interstate Crises: The BCOW Typology and Its Applications." *International Studies Quarterly* 32:155–173.

Leng, R. J., and H. Wheeler. 1979. "Influence Strategies, Success, and War." *Journal of Conflict Resolution* 23:655–84.

Levy, J. S. 1994a. "Learning and Foreign Policy: Sweeping a Conceptual Minefield." *International Organization* 48:279–312.

Levy, J. S. 1994b. "Learning from Experience in U.S. and Soviet Foreign Policy." In *From Rivalry to Cooperation: Russian and American Perspectives on the Post–Cold War Era,* ed. J. A. Vasquez and P. V. Gladkov. New York: HarperCollins.

Lippmann, W. 1961. *The Coming Tests with Russia.* Boston: Little, Brown.

Louis, R., and R. Owen, eds. 1989. *Suez 1956: The Crisis and Its Consequences.* Oxford: Clarendon Press.

Lucas, N. 1975. *The Modern History of Israel.* New York: Praeger.

Mahajan, M. C. 1963. *Looking Back.* London: Asia Publishing House.

Maoz, Z. 1990. *National Choices and International Processes.* Cambridge: Cambridge University Press.

Maoz, Z. 1998. "Waging War, Waging Peace: Decision Making, Bargaining, and the Politics of the Arab-Israeli Conflict, 1970–78." Unpublished ms. Tel Aviv: Jaffee Center for Strategic Studies.

May, E. R. 1973. *"Lessons" of the Past.* New York: Oxford University Press.

May, E. R., and P. D. Zelikow, eds. 1997. *The Kennedy Tapes: Inside the White House during the Cuban Missile Crisis.* Cambridge: Harvard University Press.

McClelland, C. A. 1961. "The Acute International Crisis." *World Politics* 41:182–204.

McCullough, D. M. 1992. *Truman.* New York: Simon and Schuster.

McMahon, R. J. 1994. *The Cold War on the Periphery: The United States, India, and Pakistan.* New York: Columbia University Press.

Medvedev, R. 1985. *All Stalin's Men.* New York: Doubleday.

Meir, G. 1973. *A Land of Our Own: An Oral Autobiography.* New York: Putnam.

Meir, G. 1975. *My Life.* New York: Putnam.

Moore, J. N., ed. 1974. *The Arab-Israeli Conflict.* Vol. 3, *Documents.* Princeton: Princeton University Press.

Mor, B. D. 1993. *Decision and Interaction in Crisis: A Model of International Crisis Behavior.* Westport, CT: Praeger.

Morgenthau, H. J. 1946. *Scientific Man versus Power Politics.* Chicago: University of Chicago Press.

Morgenthau, H. J. 1978. *Politics among Nations.* 5th rev. ed. New York: Knopf.

Morris, B. 1993. *Israel's Border Wars, 1949–1956.* Oxford: Clarendon Press.

Mueller, J. 1989. *Retreat from Doomsday: The Obsolescence of Major War.* New York: Basic Books.

Nandy, A. 1997. "Too Painful for Words." *Times of India,* July 20.

Nasser, G. A. 1955. *Egypt's Liberation: The Philosophy of the Revolution.* Washington, DC: Public Affairs Press.

Neff, D. 1981. *Warriors at Suez.* New York: Simon and Schuster.

Neff, D. 1984. *Warriors for Jerusalem.* New York: Linden Press.

Neustadt, R. E. 1970. *Alliance Politics.* New York: Columbia University Press.

New York Times. 1961. "President Kennedy's Press Conference." June 3.

New York Times. 1966. "Text of Indian-Pakistani Declaration on Tashkent." January 11, p. 15.

Nisbett, R., and L. Ross. 1980. *Human Inference: Strategies and Shortcomings of Social Judgment.* Englewood Cliffs, NJ: Prentice-Hall.

Nixon, R. M. 1971. "President Nixon's News Conference of August 4." *U.S. Department of State Bulletin* 65 (August 23).

Nixon, R. M. 1978. *RN: The Memoirs of Richard Nixon.* New York: Grosset and Dunlap.

North, R., O. Holsti, and R. Brody. 1964. "Some Empirical Data on the Conflict Spiral." *Peace Research Society International Papers* 1:1–14.

Nutting, A. 1972. *Nasser.* New York: Dutton.

Nye, J. 1989. "Nuclear Learning and U.S.-Soviet Security Regimes." *International Organization* 41:371–402.

Oneal, J. R. 1988. "The Rationality of Decision Making during International Crises." *Polity* 20:598–622.

Ostermann, C. F. 1994. *The United States, the East German Uprising of 1953, and the Limits of Rollback.* Cold War International History Project Working Paper 1. Washington, DC: Woodrow Wilson Center.

Ovendale, R. 1984. *The Origins of the Arab-Israeli Wars.* Harlow Essex, Eng.: Longman.

Pakistan, Government. 1971. *White Paper on the Crisis in East Pakistan.* Karachi: Government of Pakistan.

Pappé, I. 1992. *The Making of the Arab-Israeli Conflict, 1947–51.* New York: Tauris.

Parker, R. B. 1993. *The Politics of Miscalculation in the Middle East.* Bloomington: Indiana University Press.

Pechatnov, V. O. 1995. *The Big Three after World War II: New Documents on Soviet Thinking about Postwar Relations with the United States and Great Britain.* Cold War International History Project Working Paper 13. Washington, DC: Woodrow Wilson Center.

Peres, S. 1995. *Battling for Peace: A Memoir.* New York: Random House.

Public Papers of the Presidents of the United States: Richard Nixon, 1970. 1972. Washington, DC: U.S. Government Printing Office.

Pyarelal, S. 1958. *Mahatma Gandhi: The Last Phase.* Ahmedabad: Navajivan Publishing.

Rabin, Y. 1979. *The Rabin Memoirs.* Boston: Little, Brown.

Rabinovich, I. 1991. *The Road Not Taken: Early Arab-Israeli Negotiations.* New York: Oxford University Press.

Rapoport, A. 1960. *Fights, Games, and Debates.* Ann Arbor: University of Michigan Press.

Reiter, D. 1996. *Crucible of Beliefs: Learning, Alliances, and World Wars.* Ithaca: Cornell University Press.

Rubin, J. Z., D. G. Pruitt, and S. H. Kim. 1994. *Social Conflict: Escalation, Stalemate, and Settlement.* 2d ed. New York: McGraw-Hill.

Rusk, D. 1990. *As I Saw It.* New York: Norton.

Rusk, D., R. McNamara, G. W. Ball, R. Gilpatric, T. Sorensen, and M. Bundy. 1982. "The Lessons of the Cuban Missile Crisis." *Time,* September 27.

Sachar, H. M. 1952. *Israel: The Establishment of a State.* Westport, CT: Hyperion.

Sachar, H. M. 1976. *A History of Israel: From the Rise of Zionism to Our Time.* New York: Knopf.

Sachar, H. M. 1981. *Egypt and Israel.* New York: Richard Marek.

Sadat, A. 1977. *In Search of Identity: An Autobiography.* New York: Harper and Row.

Schelling, T. C. 1960. *Strategy of Conflict.* London: Oxford University Press.

Schelling, T. C. 1966. *Arms and Influence.* New Haven: Yale University Press.

Schick, J. M. 1971. *The Berlin Crisis, 1958–1962.* Philadelphia: University of Pennsylvania Press.

Schlesinger, A. M., Jr. 1965. *A Thousand Days.* Boston: Houghton Mifflin.

Schofield, V. 1996. *Kashmir in the Crossfire.* London: Tauris.

Shaplen, R. 1972. "The Birth of Bangladesh." *New Yorker,* February 12.

Shlaim, A. 1976. "Failures in National Intelligence Estimates: The Case of the Yom Kippur War." *World Politics* 28:348–80.

Shlaim, A. 1983. *The United States and the Berlin Blockade, 1948–49.* Berkeley: University of California Press.

Shulman, M. D. 1963. *Stalin's Foreign Policy Reappraised.* Cambridge: Harvard University Press.

Singer, J. D., S. Bremer, and J. Stuckey. 1972. "Capability Distribution, Uncertainty, and Major Power War, 1820–1965." In *Peace, War, and Numbers,* ed. B. M. Russett. Beverly Hills, CA: Sage.

Singh, K. 1982. *Heir Apparent: An Autobiography.* Delhi: Oxford University Press.

Sisson, R., and L. E. Rose. 1990. *War and Secession: Pakistan, India, and the Creation of Bangladesh.* Berkeley: University of California Press.

Slusser, R. M. 1973. *The Berlin Crisis of 1961.* Baltimore: Johns Hopkins University Press.

Small, M., and J. D. Singer. 1982. *Resort to Arms: International and Civil War, 1816–1980.* Beverly Hills: Sage.

Smith, J. E., ed. 1974. *The Papers of General Lucius D. Clay: Germany, 1945–49.* Bloomington: Indiana University Press.

Smith, W. B. 1950. *My Three Years in Moscow.* Philadelphia: Lippincott.

Snyder, G., and P. Diesing. 1977. *Conflict among Nations.* Princeton: Princeton University Press.

Sobel, L. A., ed. 1974. *Israel and the Arabs: The October 1973 War.* New York: Facts on File.

Sorensen, T. C. 1997. "The Leader Who Led." *New York Times,* October 18.

Stein, A. 1969. *India and the Soviet Union: The Nehru Era.* Chicago: University of Chicago Press.

Stein, J. G. 1991. "The Arab-Israeli War of 1967: Inadvertent War through Miscalculated Escalation." In *Avoiding War: Problems of Crisis Management,* ed. A. L. George. Boulder, CO: Westview.

Suedfeld, P., and P. E. Tetlock. 1977. "Integrative Complexity of Communications in International Crises." *Journal of Conflict Resolution* 21:169–86.

Sulzberger, C. L. 1972. "Mrs. Meir Asserts Israel Is Ready to Resume Talks." *New York Times,* January 30, p. 1.

Taubman, W. 1982. *Stalin's American Policy: From Detente to Cold War.* New York: Norton.

Tetlock, P. E. 1991. "In Search of an Elusive Concept." In *Learning in U.S. and Soviet Foreign Policy,* ed. G. W. Breslauer and P. E. Tetlock. Boulder, CO: Westview.

Thomas, H. 1966. *Suez.* New York: Harper and Row.

Truman, H. S. 1956. *Memoirs.* Vol. 2, *Years of Trial and Hope, 1946–1953.* Garden City, NY: Doubleday.

Truman, M. 1973. *Harry S. Truman.* New York: Morrow.

Tuchman, B. W. 1962. *The Guns of August.* New York: Macmillan.

Tversky, A., and D. Kahneman. 1986. "Rational Choice and the Framing of Decisions." *Journal of Business* 59:251–78.

Ulam, A. B. 1983. *Dangerous Relations: The Soviet Union in World Politics, 1970–1982.* New York: Oxford University Press.

United Nations Security Council. 1948. *Official Records: Supplement for November 1948.* New York: United Nations Publications.

United Nations Security Council. 1950. *Official Records: Meeting 464.* New York: United Nations Publications.

U.S. Department of State. 1962. "Statement by President Kennedy on Cuba, September 13, 1962." *Bulletin* 47:481–82.

U.S. Office of the Federal Register. 1962. *John F. Kennedy: Containing the Public Messages, Speeches and Statements of the President, January 20 to December 31, 1961.* Washington, DC: U.S. Government Printing Office.

Vasquez, J. A. 1996. "Distinguishing Rivals That Go to War from Those That Do Not: A Quantitative Comparative Case Study of the Two Paths to War." *International Studies Quarterly* 40:531–58.

Walton, R. E., and R. B. McKersie. *A Behavioral Theory of Labor Negotiations: An Analysis of a Social Interaction System.* New York: McGraw-Hill.

Waltz, K. N. 1954. *Man, the State, and War.* New York: Columbia University Press.

Waltz, K. N. 1979. *Theory of International Politics.* Reading, MA: Addison-Wesley.

Walzer, M. 1977. *Just and Unjust Wars: A Moral Argument with Historical Illustrations.* New York: Basic Books.

Wayman, F. W. 1984. "Bipolarity and War: The Role of Capability Concentration and Alliance Patterns among Major Powers, 1816–1965." *Journal of Peace Research* 21:61–78.

Wheelock, K. 1960. *Nasser's New Egypt: A Critical Analysis.* New York: Praeger.

Whetten, L. L. 1974. *The Canal War: Four-Power Conflict in the Middle East.* Cambridge: MIT Press.

Wirsing, R. G. 1994. *India, Pakistan, and the Kashmir Dispute: On Regional Conflict and Its Resolution.* New York: St. Martin's.

Yaniv, A. 1987. *Deterrence without the Bomb: The Politics of Israeli Strategy.* Lexington, MA: Lexington Books.

Yost, C. 1968. "The Arab-Israeli War: How It Began." *Foreign Affairs* 46:304–20.

Zartman, I. W. 1986. "Ripening Conflict, Ripe Moment, Formula, and Mediation." In *Perspectives on Negotiation: Four Case Studies and Interpretations,* ed. D. B. Bendahmane and J. W. McDonald Jr. Washington, DC: U.S. Department of State, Foreign Service Institute.

Zubok, V. M. 1993. *Khrushchev and the Berlin Crisis, 1958–1962.* Cold War International History Project Working Paper 6. Washington, DC: Woodrow Wilson Center.

Zubok, V. M., and C. Pleshakov. 1996. *Inside the Kremlin's Cold War: From Stalin to Khrushchev.* Cambridge: Harvard University Press.

Zweig, R. W., ed. 1991. *David Ben-Gurion: Politics and Leadership in Israel.* London: Cass.

Index